Lecture Notes of the Institute for Computer Sciences, Social Informatics and Telecommunications Engineering 151

More information about this series at http://www.springer.com/series/8197

Raffaele Giaffreda · Dagmar Cagáňová
Yong Li · Roberto Riggio
Agnès Voisard (Eds.)

Internet of Things

IoT Infrastructures

First International Summit, IoT360 2014
Rome, Italy, October 27–28, 2014
Revised Selected Papers, Part II

 Springer

Editors
Raffaele Giaffreda
CREATE-NET
Trento
Italy

Roberto Riggio
CREATE-NET
Trento
Italy

Dagmar Cagáňová
Slovak University of Technology
Bratislava
Slovakia

Agnès Voisard
Freie Universität Berlin
Berlin
Germany

Yong Li
Tsinghua University
Beijing
China

ISSN 1867-8211   ISSN 1867-822X (electronic)
Lecture Notes of the Institute for Computer Sciences, Social Informatics
and Telecommunications Engineering
ISBN 978-3-319-19742-5   ISBN 978-3-319-19743-2 (eBook)
DOI 10.1007/978-3-319-19743-2

Library of Congress Control Number: 2015940418

Springer Cham Heidelberg New York Dordrecht London

Springer International Publishing AG Switzerland is part of Springer Science+Business Media
(www.springer.com)

IOT360 2014 - IoT Infrastructures

Preface

This publication collects the proceedings of three conferences dedicated to infrastructure-based solutions that will support the deployment of Internet of Things (IoT) services and applications in the future. The 30 revised full papers in this volume were carefully reviewed and selected from a total of 51 submissions. The conferences also featured 16 special contributions from recognized experts in the field.

The first one, the International Conference on Mobility and Smart Cities 2014, was to provide a platform for the cross-fertilization of ideas and to present cutting-edge innovation and technologies for sustainable solutions to the mobility and smart cities agenda. The focus of the conference reflected the EU thematic priorities for research and innovation to improve the quality of life of citizens and make cities more sustainable with less impact on the environment.

The second conference, SDWN, focused on software-defined techniques for supporting more flexible use of wireless and wireless sensor networks. As we approach the 5G space, it is envisaged that the merge between software-defined techniques and the IoT will indeed bring new value in the networking infrastructure to support the challenges of accommodating exponentially growing M2M traffic.

Finally the proceedings of the last conference, SaSeIoT, provide an outlook on the safety and security in the IoT domain, highlighting both opportunities and risks. The risks stem from the integration of numerous distributed devices that belong to a plethora of (sometimes unknown) owners, have limited computational power, and are located in unsecured environments without any access controls. The opportunities come from the ability to add resilience to our IoT systems, detecting threats to public safety and security at an earlier stage so that the impact of such threats can be mitigated more easily, and by providing additional support during disaster management and recovery.

April 2015   Raffaele Giaffreda

International Conference on Mobility and Smart Cities, Mobility IoT 2014
Rome – October 27–28, 2014

Preface

In this dedicated mobility and smart cities section of the publication, it is our pleasure to introduce to you a wide selection of cutting-edge and insightful research papers that were presented at the First International Conference on Mobility and Smart Cities 2014.

The 2014 conference was an IoT co-located event that took place in Rome, Italy, during October 27–29, 2014, forming one of the main conferences in the IoT360 Summit. The conference was organized by the Faculty of Materials Science and Technology (MTF STU) in Trnava, Institute of Industrial Engineering and Management in collaboration with the European Alliance for Innovation in Slovakia, and its partner, the European Alliance for Innovation, in Trento, Italy.

As co-chairs of the conference and members of the Organizing Committee, it was with great satisfaction that we had the opportunity to welcome and meet individuals from around the world, all of whom share a common interest in the area of mobility and smart cities. In particular, we would like to thank the presenters who showcased their latest research and also the audience members who added to active discussions and debate regarding the recent developments and the outlook for the future of the field.

The goal of the International Conference on Mobility and Smart Cities 2014 was to provide a platform for the cross-fertilization of ideas and to present cutting-edge innovation and technologies for sustainable solutions to the mobility and smart cities agenda. The focus of the conference reflected the EU thematic priorities for research and innovation to improve the quality of life of citizens and make cities more sustainable with less impact on the environment. The conference presented participants with a unique opportunity to engage with different stakeholders from across Europe and around the world. In doing so, the conference offered an ideal platform to empower the triple helix of university research, industry, and government, while also providing innovative opportunities focusing on the growth and development of mobility and smart cities.

A total of 32 research papers are featured in this publication, with contributions by researchers from across Europe and around the world. The publication includes articles written and presented by authors from 17 countries, including China, Croatia, the Czech Republic, Germany, Greece, Italy, Japan, Norway, Poland, Portugal, Romania, Singapore, Slovakia, South Africa, South Korea, Sweden, and the UK.

Among the papers featured in the publication are those written by the conference keynote speakers, Prof. MSc. Milan Dado, PhD., the Dean of the Faculty of Electronics, TU Zilina, Slovakia, and a coordinator of the project ERA Chair H2020, who discusses the "Challenges and Unwanted Features of the Smarter Cities Development" and Prof. George Teodorescu PhD, from the International Institute for Integral Innovation, Köln, Germany, who discusses the topic of "Parking Zero."

As co-chairs of the conference, we were particularly impressed by the wide range of innovative research solutions presented during the conference. The conference was divided into six sessions covering the areas of smart mobility and security, social innovation and infrastructural research, smart cities, the SUPERHUB Project, urban mobility and e-mobility, innovation in transport methods and services, and creative cities. As a result, the papers included, in our opinion, accurately reflect the diversity of content and rapidly developing nature of the mobility and smart cities agenda. The research not only illustrates the current state of the art in the field but it also helps to contribute to defining the future thematic areas of debate.

In conclusion, we would like to once again express our sincere thanks to all the authors and audience members who attended the conference in Rome, Italy, and also the authors who contributed to the creation of this mobility and smart cities publication.

Dagmar Cagáňová
Jana Šujanová
Paul Woolliscroft

International Conference on Software-Defined and Virtualized Future Wireless Networks
SDWN 2014
Rome – October 28, 2014

Preface

We are very pleased to introduce the papers that were presented at the First International Conference on Software-Defined and Virtualized Future Wireless Networks (SDWN) 2014. While the past few decades have witnessed a rapid growth in mobile and wireless networks, numerous problems and challenges become increasingly serious, such as heterogeneous wireless networks, spectrum scarcity, smooth evolving and fast deployment, technologies innovations, QoS and QoE support, etc. Traditional mobile and wireless network technologies can hardly overcome these challenges. Against this background, Software-Defined and Virtualized Future Wireless Network is a new conference that aims to explore the new design space, the new challenges and solutions, as well as new applications and services of software-defined virtualized future mobile and wireless networks. The goal of this workshop is to solicit original and inspiring research contributions from technology experts, designers, researchers, and architects in academia and industry. Bringing together practitioners and researchers to share knowledge, experiences, and best practices.

The event is endorsed by the European Alliance for Innovation, a leading community-based organization devoted to the advancement of innovation in the field of ICT and was co-located with the IoT360 Summit. At the same time, participation in this event gave attendees the unique opportunity to be exposed to all technical scientific aspects of IoT-related topic areas at co-located conferences, as well as be able to have full access to the IoT marketplace and business aspects in practice at the IoT360 Summit. This was the first such workshop in Italy, and we were extremely pleased and proud that it attracted such a large number of submissions. We are hopeful that its outstanding technical content contributed by leading international researchers in the field will ensure its continued success for the future.

The main themes addressed by the paper presented at this conference are:

- New end-to-end mobile and wireless network architecture based on SDWN, cloud computing, and virtualization technologies
- Cloud computing and network virtualization technologies for RAN, backhaul, and core networks
- Software defining and abstracting strategies for network function and air interface technologies in future wireless networks
- Convergence of heterogeneous wireless networks in SDWN
- Network devices programmability and customizability

- QoS/E and traffic-awareness in SDWN
- Date center technologies for future wireless networks
- Fast deployment and smooth network evolving
- Future wireless network management
- Dynamic resource allocation in future wireless networks
- Immersive collaborative future wireless media
- Network evaluations and testbeds
- New applications and use cases

For this workshop, all accepted papers were published by Springer and made available through SpringerLink Digital Library, one of the world's largest scientific libraries. Several best papers were included in the MONET special issue on Software-Defined and Virtualized Future Wireless Networks. We had two invited talks and several invited papers. All these features contributed a successful workshop. We express our sincere thanks to the invited speakers, authors, session chairs, Technical Program Committee members, and additional reviewers who made this conference a success.

Yong Li
Roberto Riggio
V. Vasilakos Athanasios

First International Conference Safety and Security in Internet of Things
SaSeIot 2014
Rome, Italy, October 28, 2014

Preface

If we look at the Internet of Things (IoT) from a safety and security perspective, we can see both opportunities and risks.

The risks stem from the integration of numerous distributed devices that belong to a plethora of (sometimes unknown) owners, have limited computational power, and are located in unsecured environments without any access controls. All these properties make the "things" in the IoT vulnerable. Therefore, concepts and solutions are needed to detect and contain malicious or corrupted things, to secure communication between things, and to ensure compliance of the IoT infrastructure with legal requirements, in particular on the protection and management of personal data.

The first set of papers presented here address these issues by discussing self-identification mechanisms of IoT devices, secure peer-to-peer services using NFC, and security aspects of the collaborative data acquisition on which many IoT services rely.

However, the IoT can also create substantial benefits in terms of citizens' safety: by providing local communication infrastructures that make our societies more resilient, by detecting threats to public safety and security at an earlier stage so that the impact of such threats can be mitigated more easily, and by providing additional support during disaster management and recovery. These positive aspects of the IoT are also reflected in the proceedings with papers on crowd sourcing applications for emergency response, on the use of the IoT for earthquake management, and on the importance of the IoT for network resilience.

Finally, privacy and technology acceptance issues are addressed by a contribution on the use of things for home security applications in gated communities.

We would like to thank all authors, reviewers, and organizers for their support and hope that these proceedings will provide input for fruitful discussions and for future research related to safety and security in the IoT.

Michael Klafft
Ulrich Meissen
Agnès Voisard

International Conference on Mobility and Smart Cities, Mobility IoT 2014
Rome – October 27–28, 2014

Organization

Steering Committee Chairs

Imrich Chlamtac
Dagmar Cagáňová

Organizing Committee Members

Dagmar Cagáňová
Jana Šujanová
Anna Saniuk
Giorgia Nisi
Paul Woolliscroft
Tibor Zvonár
Marek Vyskoč
Iveta Petrovičová
Lubomir Hlavatý

Technical Program Chairs

Milan Dado
Michal Balog
Oscar Mayora
Daniela Špirková
Dagmar Cagáňová
Miloš Čambál
Jana Šujanová
Neven Vrček
Daynier Rolando Delgado Sobrino
Paul Woolliscroft
Soňa Ferenčíková
Anna Saniuk
Cristian-Gyözö Haba
Dorin Dumitru Lucache
Eduardo Tome

Elena Šúbertová
Florinda Matos
Katarina Stachová
František Horňák
George Teodorescu
Anna Saniuk
Cristian-Gyözö Haba
Ingrid Součková
Krzysztof Witkowski
Marta Cristina Suciu
Peter Bindzár
Sebastian Saniuk
Nikolay Madzahrov
Tibor Zvonár

Local Chair

Raffaele Giaffreda

Website Chair

Marek Vyskoč

International Conference on Software-Defined and Virtualized Future Wireless Networks
SDWN 2014
Rome – October 28, 2014

Organization

General Chair

Yong Li   Tsinghua University, China

General Co-chair

Roberto Riggio   Create-Net, Italy

Steering Committee Chair

Imrich Chlamtac   Create-Net, Italy

Steering Committee Members

Xin Wu   Big Switch, USA
Xin Zhang   Google, USA
Athanasios, V. Vasilakos   University of Western Macedonia, Greece

Technical Program Chair

Roberto Riggio   Create-Net, Italy

Technical Program Members

Liang Zhou   Najing University, China
Min Chen   HUST, China
Chin-Feng Lai   National Cheng Kung University, Taiwan
Honggang Wang   UMASS, USA
Giancarlo Fortino   University of Calabria, Italy
Xin Zhang   Google, USA

First International Conference Safety and Security in Internet of Things
SaSeIot 2014
Rome, Italy, October 28, 2014

Organization

Steering Committee Chair

Imrich Chlamtac   Create-Net, Trento, Italy

General Chair

Agnès Voisard   Databases and Information Systems, Freie Universität Berlin, Berlin, Germany

Technical Program Chair

Ulrich Meissen   Head of the Competence Center Electronic Safety and Security Systems for the Public and Industries (ESPRI) at the Fraunhofer Institute for Open Communication Systems FOKUS, Berlin, Germany

Technical Program Co-chair

Jan Henrik Ziesing   Head of Innovation Cluster Next Generation ID - Electronic Government and Applications Competence Center at the Fraunhofer Institute for Open Communication Systems FOKUS, Berlin, Germany

Publishing Chair

Michael Klafft   Competence Center Electronic Safety and Security Systems for the Public and Industries (ESPRI) at the Fraunhofer Institute for Open Communication Systems FOKUS, Berlin, Germany

Conference Coordinator

Holger Schloesser   Strategic Communication, Public Innovation
                             Management, Fraunhofer Institute for Open
                             Communication Systems FOKUS, Berlin, Germany

Technical Program Chair

Ulrich Meissen   Head of the Competence Center Electronic Safety and
                             Security Systems for the Public and Industries
                             (ESPRI) at the Fraunhofer Institute for Open
                             Communication Systems FOKUS, Berlin, Germany

Technical Program Co-chair

Jan Henrik Ziesing   Head of Innovation Cluster Next Generation ID -
                             Electronic Government and Applications
                             Competence Center at the Fraunhofer Institute for
                             Open Communication Systems *FOKUS*, Berlin,
                             Germany

Publishing Chair

Michael Klafft   Competence Center Electronic Safety and Security
                             Systems for the Public and Industries (ESPRI) at the
                             Fraunhofer Institute for Open Communication
                             Systems FOKUS, Berlin, Germany

Technical Program Members

Emmanuel Baccelli   Scientific Researcher at Inria, Paris, France - Guest
                             Professor at Freie Universität, Berlin, Germany
Joachim Wächter   Head of Centre for GeoInformation Technology -
                             CeGIT at GFZ German Research Centre for
                             Geosciences, Helmholtz Centre Potsdam, Germany
Dieter Pfoser   George Mason University, USA
Dimitrios Skoutas   Institute for the Management of Information Systems
                             (IMIS), "Athena" Innovation Center, Athens,
                             Greece

Contents – Part II

SaSeIoT 2014

Contents – Part I

PERGAMES 2014

IoTaaS 2014

Mobility IoT 2014

Challenges and Unwanted Features
of the Smarter Cities Development

Milan Dado$^{(\boxtimes)}$, Aleš Janota, and Juraj Spalek

University of Žilina, Univerzitná 8215/1, 010 26 Žilina, Slovakia
{milan.dado,ales.janota,juraj.spalek}@fel.uniza.sk

Abstract. This keynote paper establishes the framework for three introductory sessions at the Mobility and Smart Cities conference held in Roma 27–28 October 2014. In the light of the latest knowledge and scientific projects findings the authors present actual R&D trends in the field of smart solutions for sustainable mobility based on ICT. New ideas, cutting-edge innovations and technologies for mobility agenda are needed together with multidisciplinary perspective and holistic approach applied. However, the positive expectations of sustainable mobility growth might also have some negative effects on the life and behaviour of citizens and institutions. The paper indicates both positive and negative aspects of the smart city developments to open the floor for cross-fertilization of critical and incentive ideas.

Keywords: Smart city · Mobility · Infrastructure · Security · Sustainability

1 Introduction

This contribution has been prepared as the keynote paper whose principal intention is to flag up the core message of the conference and to set the mood and tone for it. The main term being in the centre of the attention is the "Smart City" concept. Although it can refer to futuristic concepts such as fridges that order groceries from the local supermarket when their stocks run low, we can already see examples of smart city systems in the Gulf in countries such as Qatar, Kuwait, Saudi Arabia and the UAE. Therefore, when defining the content of this term we could identify with the definition applied in documents of the EC DG CONNECT [1, 2]: "Smart cities should be regarded as systems of people interacting with and using flows of energy, materials, services and financing to catalyse sustainable economic development, resilience, and high quality of life; these flows and interactions become smart through making strategic use of information and communication infrastructure and services in a process of transparent urban planning and management that is responsive to the social and economic needs of society". The concept of the "smart city" emerged during the last decade as a fusion of ideas about how Information and Communication Technologies (ICTs) might improve the functioning of cities, enhancing their efficiency, improving their competitiveness, contributing to sustainable development and high quality of life and providing new ways in which problems of poverty, social deprivation, and poor environment might be addressed [3, 4]. The essence of the idea has revolved around the need to coordinate and integrate technologies that have previously been developed

R. Giaffreda et al. (Eds.): IoT360 2014, Part II, LNICST 151, pp. 3–8, 2015.
DOI: 10.1007/978-3-319-19743-2_1

separately from one another but have clear synergies in their operation and need to be coupled so that many new opportunities which will improve the quality of life can be realized. Thus the ICT is merged with traditional infrastructures, coordinated and integrated using new digital technologies. Cities are becoming smart not only in terms of the way we can automate routine functions serving individual persons, buildings, traffic systems but in ways that enable us to monitor, understand, analyse and plan the city to improve the efficiency, equity and quality of life for its citizens in real time... [5]. Currently the central role of ICT lies at the core of the concept, but the term "smart city" goes beyond the idea of ICT-driven cities, embracing also the investment in human, social, and environmental capital.

The topic of Smart Cities has been on the table for more than a decade, discussed at different forums. Inevitably the interest in the agenda permanently grows - this conference is one of many events on the way towards integrated, interdisciplinary and holistic understanding of the whole concept.

It is not surprising that Smart Cities have become an Agenda of the European Innovation Partnership on Smart Cities and Communities (EIP-SCC) which brings together cities, industry and citizens to improve urban life through more sustainable integrated solutions. This includes applied innovation, better planning, a more participatory approach, higher energy efficiency, better transport solutions, intelligent use of ICTs, etc. The Partnership aims to overcome bottlenecks impeding the changeover to smart cities, to co-fund demonstration projects and to help coordinate existing city initiatives and projects, by pooling its resources together. This initiative has a budget of €365 Million and includes energy, transport and ICT sector with the launch of the Partnership in July 2012 [7]. The Action Clusters Kick-Off Conference was held on 9th October 2014 in Brussels where key objectives and role of Action Clusters under the Partnership were presented.

2   Challenges and Unwanted Features

The concept of Smart City brings a lot of challenges when seen from various perspectives of different stakeholders with different interests and expectations. They should be seen in the context and solved within the given EU framework: the level of urbanization in EU is above 75 %, to rise to 80 % by 2020, with cities consuming over 70 % of energy and emitting as much of greenhouse gases in EU. To achieve EU 20-20-20 climate and energy goals there is need to act now [1]:

- 20 % reduction of CO_2 compared to 1990.
- 20 % share of renewable energy in total energy mix.
- 20 % improvement in energy efficiency.

To create the markets the EU has adopted the approach mostly based on:

- Tackling common challenges and bottlenecks.
- Developing innovative and replicable solutions.
- Bundling demand from cities and regions.
- Attracting and involving business and banks.

The common aim is to transform a number of European cities by exchanging of Best Practices, learning from each other and funding through H2020 for selected demonstration projects. The following areas have been given the highest priority [1]:

- Urban sustainable mobility (multi-modal transport planning, alternative energy carriers, smart logistics, etc.).
- Districts and built environment (integration of renewables, positive energy districts, deep retrofitting, etc.).
- Integrated infrastructures (cross-sectorial infrastructures integration, joint planning and business models, common standards, …).

Development and implementation of partial goals gives a lot of challenges together with potential obstacles and unwanted features. Official documents summarize existing challenges - a reader may go through them easily. Therefore at this point let us leave the official frame of EU documents, goals, projects and/or initiatives and try to consider at least some of them, explaining their subjective understanding by the authors.

Common Language: The success of smart cities solutions highly depends on understandability and the common language used by all involved parties - stakeholders. For the sake of illustration let us mention particular example of situation which occurred within EIP-SCC Action Cluster Kick-off Conference on 9th October 2014 in Brussels. When presenting the City Platform action cluster, the given Criteria, Key questions etc. were typically based on ICT language (Open APIs, Open SDK, Open authentication, Interoperability of OSs …). Logically this became a point of criticism raised from the presented mayors. Their practice requires completely different language based on solutions of everyday problems of citizens and their needs. Not many of them are ICT-educated and fully understand potential of technical solutions for development of urban areas.

Focus on Citizens: To make any successful application – two subjects are very important: citizens and their needs. Any change must come bottom-up, i.e. be based on (smart) citizens' needs. The problem is what these needs are? Are they really known? How to collect them? How to scale their importance? Are there any "common problems" typical for every city/town that bring some "common needs"? What about specific needs resulting from local specificities – what do they depend on? Building a change without knowing the needs is risky since it may cause wide public unacceptance and thus losing invested money and opportunities to grow. It is not a good strategy to bring a technical solution fulfil some needs (e.g. because a "suitable provider" is at disposal) and consequently to search for potential recipients. Vice versa approach must be ensured.

Involvement of Local Government: Politicians on the local level (and usually not only on that) may be often close minded if talking about the projects exceeding time of their election period. The sore point is then how to really involve mayors into such projects especially if some long-term financing/co-financing is needed to reach goals behind duration of their mandates. Municipalities should know the actual (and predict the future) needs of their citizens. However, at present we are often observers of collecting data without any output.

Focus on the Right Target Group: Another legitimate question is who is the proper audience for the Smart City and Mobility agenda? Some of the previously mentioned events (e.g. Smart Living City – Dubai 2014) could raise a presumption that we are mostly talking about projects focused on either existing cities or on Greenfield initiatives, building the cities from the ground up and investing billions of dollars. The European statistics gives a little bit different dimension to our considerations: 65 % of EU population can be found living in the cities with population about ca 60.000 inhabitants. Those cities seem to be ideal candidates and recipients of the EU initiatives on Smart Cities and Mobility.

Concentration on Abstract or Technical Level First?: Actually predominant view is that technical solutions are in principle well available and thus one should concentrate on the abstract level first and postpone discussions about technical aspects to later stages to avoid technocracy approach, overshadowing the real needs and added values for each group of stakeholders (mayors, citizens, energy suppliers, traffic operators, etc.). In any project it must be clear from the very beginning who is a partner to whom and what the roles of all stakeholders are. That requires an abstract and high-level approach first.

A Kind of Needed Research Generally: Implementing the smart cities is more on integration and sharing of existing sources and solutions than on a specially focused new research. Obviously, validity of this statement is not categorical – new scientific findings are coming and being implemented all the time. The progress is needed, motivated by achieving new solutions ensuring energy savings, less negative impacts on environment, or helping focused group of citizens (e.g. disabled, elderly, children etc.). New interrelations and social behaviour will also bring the need to search for new data models. Talking about Smart Cities is often about executing sustainable activities in a more integrated way.

Replicability and Open Solutions: What is actually most needed are open data and open solutions (knowledge) how to do something that could be replicated and shared. The question is what is common and transferrable since every city/town is unique, having its historical heritage, fragmentation to various city islands, etc. The risk is that cities pursue the wrong concepts that may need huge amounts of money. They often don't realise availability of quick-win solutions that suit the city. Replicable solution can be available after finding what is common in the existing problem (needs) and in open data. The process may be fastened by standardisation and harmonization. One of the introductory steps to be taken is creation of the list what is and what should be standardized (ETSI, CEN, ISO, etc.). Both technical (application platforms) and non-technical standards (best practices) are valuable. As inspiring examples the BSI standards PA180 and PA181 could be mentioned – the former related to the Smart Cities vocabulary, the latter establishing a Smart City network [8]. The application domain is so large-scale and complex that coincidence and interrelation of multiple standards must be expected. However, the consequences of complexity may be analogical to standardisation of the ITS domain: lack of the standards in the proper time (remember non-interoperable electronic toll collection devices spread across Europe), and a high number of existing standards which makes difficult or even impossible to effective work with those standards, related to the given task. The latter indicated problem could be effectively solved by applying the ontological approach. From technical point of view open data and open standards indicate a trend of building one European cloud solution.

Scalability and Measurability: According to Haydee Sheombar from IBM [10] a part of a Smart City vision is indeed people driven, and does not require technology. However, in order to solve a specific problem, things must be measurable and incentives must be transparent. A new paradigm of smart city solutions evokes a question of scalability and measurability, i.e. how to measure performance of the achieved "smart systems". The most common approach relies on the use of Key Performance Indicators (KPIs) that define a set of values against which to measure. They enable evaluation of the success of an organization or of a particular activity in which it engages, or defined in terms of making progress toward strategic goals. There is a need to understand well what is important, various techniques to assess the present state of the business, and the key activities, are associated with the selection of performance indicators. New ISO 37120:2014 gives cities a common performance yardstick. It provides a set of clearly defined city performance indicators and a standard approach to measure each.

Legislation Frame: Increasingly we can see sensors embedded in our environments that monitor and interpret our behaviour. Sensors, including cameras and microphones, position, proximity, and wearable physiological sensors, gather knowledge about our activities, interpret them in real-time, and anticipate future activities and behaviour. Actuators allow making changes to the environment, its physical appearance and its interaction and display facilities, including augmented and virtual reality display and interaction possibilities. The problem that will highly probably occur and possibly block replication of achieved sustainable solutions may rice from the actually existing legislation. As a typical example the problem of "privacy" might be indicated - privacy as the ability of an individual or group to seclude themselves. The boundaries and content of what is considered private differ among cultures and individuals, but share common themes. At the moment there are many across Europe, concerning the ways of how and where to allow collection of personal data, what are concepts of appropriate use, storage and protection of personal information. Thus the domain of privacy partially overlaps security.

Social Dimension: The worst thing to happen in the future is to prefer a different kind of profit (financial, personal...) of involved parties to social dimension. Reality of this threat can be seen even nowadays – one could find examples of activities where money profit prevails over humanity. The new solution may not disqualify, handicap or eliminate any selected group of citizens (disabled, elderly, children, etc.). For example the neighbourhood public open space is recognised as particularly important for older people in terms of its potential role in providing opportunities for physical activity, social contact and contact with nature. Opportunities of what could be involved in relation to social dimension of human life are practically unlimited. Being able to control a physical environment and the way its inhabitants can interact with it designers of smart (urban) environments can even create humorous situations or provide the environment with the possibility to create humorous situations or to create potentially humorous situations that can be exploited by their human inhabitants [9]. What is more, the city is a unique location for play: its vibrancy, diverse material environments and intense social interactions provide a great basis for the creativity and challenges of playing. The goals and challenges could then be as follows: to achieve real impact on citizen's lives, to promote social cohesion in urban area, to provide support to local projects and partnerships and promote networks from local base, to reconcile the vision of decision-makers with the ideas and visions of citizens and make decision makers learn from the people they are deciding for.

3   Conclusions

The paper has been written with the motivation to frame the program of 3 sessions on the 1st day of the conference. The paragraph 1 and the introductory part of paragraph 2 summarize state-of-art based on publicly available official sources and research results. The rest of structured parts of the paragraph 2 contains discussion on selected problems (challenges together with threats) and reflects subjective meanings of the authors. As such it has a potential to generate discussions and information exchange.

Acknowledgments. The paper has been elaborated with support of the Slovak scientific grant agency VEGA, grant No. 1/0453/12 "Study of interactions of a motor vehicle, traffic flow and road" and with support of the project: University Science Park of the University of Zilina (ITMS: 26220220184) supported by the Research & Development Operational Program funded by the European Regional Development Fund.

References

1. Griera, M.: An EU view on smart cities (presentation). In: COST Conference on the Cities of Tomorrow. The Challenges of Horizon 2020, Torino, Italy (2014). http://www.cost.eu/download/47217
2. European Innovation Partnership on Smart Cities and Communities - Strategic Implementation Plan. http://ec.europa.eu/eip/smartcities/files/sip_final_en.pdf
3. CityNet (2014). http://ec.europa.eu/environment/europeangreencapital/news/events/citinet-2014/
4. Harrison, C., et al.: Foundations for smarter cities. IBM J. Res. Dev. **54**(4), 1–16 (2010)
5. Batty, M. et al.: Smart cities of the future. Working papers series, paper 188 (2012)
6. Market Place of the EIP on Smart Cities and Communities > Events. http://eu-smartcities.eu/calendar/month/2014–11
7. Smart Cities and Communities. http://ec.europa.eu/eip/smartcities/about-partnership/what-is-it/index_en.htm
8. Smart Cities: Background Paper. https://www.gov.uk/government/publications/smart-cities-background-paper
9. Nijholt, A.: Cities with a sense of humour. http://www.dcrc.org.uk/making-the-city-playable-abstracts/cities-with-a-sense-of-humour
10. Smart Cities in Europe. http://www.smartcitiesineurope.com/2011/11/the-role-of-ict/

Multicultural Collaborative Team Working as a Driver for Innovation in the Slovak Automotive Sector

Paul Woolliscroft[(✉)], Dagmar Cagáňová, Miloš Čambál,
and Jana Makraiová

Faculty of Materials Science and Technology in Trnava,
Institute of Industrial Engineering and Management, The Slovak University
of Technology in Bratislava, Paulínska 16, 917 24 Trnava, Slovakia
{paul.woolliscroft, dagmar.caganova, milos.cambal,
jana.makraiova}@stuba.sk

Abstract. The accelerated trend towards globalisation, facilitated by the expansion of the European Union in the Slovak context has led to a rapid influx of foreign direct investment into the country. In particular, numerous automotive manufacturers have relocated to Slovakia in order to capitalise upon a lower cost base and the advanced infrastructure. Despite achieving lowering manufacturing costs, the overarching requirement for automotive manufacturers remains the need to innovate in order to create enhanced product value. One key driver of innovation in the automotive sector is to foster collaboration with members throughout the complex supply chain thus enhancing innovation at every stage. This process however requires close cooperation both vertically and horizontally and therefore clear practices and processes are necessary to ensure facilitation of inter-organisational and multicultural collaboration. The focus of this paper is to study the impact of multicultural collaboration and to propose a framework for enhanced working practices.

Keywords: Multicultural knowledge management · Collaborative working · Innovation · Slovakia · Automotive

1 Introduction

The automotive sector in the Slovak Republic represents one of the most important industrial sectors for inflows of FDI during the past 20 years. This influx is predominately due to the relocation of numerous automotive manufacturers and suppliers seeking to gain competitive advantage. Furthermore, manufacturers are increasingly identifying innovative techniques in order to gain increased competitive advantage.

One area of innovation, illustrated by the rapid influx of foreign investment in Slovakia is the requirement to understand and manage cultural knowledge and to work collaboratively throughout a multicultural supply chain. Several authors in the field of Knowledge Management (KM) emphasis that the innovation paradigm is now moving beyond the search for "Competitive Advantage" to a new world order described as "Collaborative Advantage" [1]. Collaborative advantage emphasises the need for

© Institute for Computer Sciences, Social Informatics and Telecommunications Engineering 2015
R. Giaffreda et al. (Eds.): IoT360 2014, Part II, LNICST 151, pp. 9–15, 2015.
DOI: 10.1007/978-3-319-19743-2_2

collaborative working practices which enable organisations to work together in order to combine their key skills and attributes. Collaborative advantage presents a unique opportunity for industrial enterprises in Slovakia however a prerequisite is firstly the need to develop a clear understanding of the impact of culture internally on a national and organisational level and externally on a collaborative team level.

Within this research paper the authors will firstly explore the existing innovation landscape within the Slovak automotive sector and determine the importance of collaborative innovation. The research findings focus on results from a research study conducted amongst 169 Slovak industrial enterprises and a case study analysis of the *West Slovakia Automotive Cluster Innovation Network*. The findings support the proposed application of a new model which provides a framework for the facilitation of collaborative innovation practices within the Slovak automotive industry.

2   Culture as a Knowledge Driver for Facilitating Collaborative Innovation

Several authors have developed models to classify national and organisational cultural knowledge such as those proposed by Hofstede [2, 3] and Trompenaars [4]. A valuable framework in the context of this study is the framework proposed by Nonaka and Takeuchi [5] which conceptualises the process of knowledge transition through the proposed "Spiral of Knowledge Creation" (SECI model) and explains knowledge creation in innovating companies. The model (shown in Fig. 2) is comprised of four modes of knowledge conversion:

1. Tacit knowledge to tacit knowledge transfer (Socialisation)
2. Tacit knowledge to explicit knowledge conversion and transfer (Externalisation)
3. Explicit knowledge to explicit knowledge transfer (Combination)
4. Explicit knowledge to tacit knowledge transfer and conversion (Internalisation)

The model depicts the process as four phases with knowledge transcending through each stage. For tacit knowledge to transfer to explicit knowledge, firstly the process of "socialisation" must take place whereby tacit knowledge it shared between individuals. The second phase is the process of "externalisation", whereby tacit knowledge is translated into forms which can be understood by others. The following two stages are "combination", whereby explicit knowledge is analysed and interpreted to a deeper extent and lastly, "Internalisation" whereby explicit knowledge is explained in clear tacit terms.

Within this research the impact of both national and organisational culture dimensions proposed by Hofstede [2] will be included as part of a holistic framework in order to illustrate the impact of the dimensions upon collaborative team working.

The interaction between national and organisational culture is summarised by Pauleen [6] (Fig. 1) who illustrates that the impact of culture is closely aligning with organisational knowledge. The model illustrates that organisational knowledge emanates from a combination of national culture influences, which subsequently feeds into the organisational culture and then forms part of the knowledge sharing behaviour of

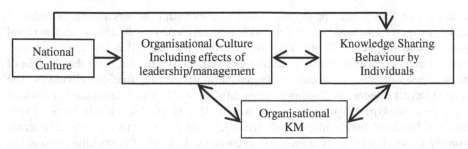

Fig. 1. National culture, organisational culture and knowledge management [6]

individuals. The organisational culture and knowledge sharing behaviour subsequently combine to create organisational knowledge management.

In order to capture the knowledge of a culture within an organisation, it is essential to facilitate the transition of tacit knowledge into explicit knowledge. Therefore both the SECI framework developed by Nonaka and Takeuchi [5] and the framework proposed by Pauleen [6] provide valuable tools to develop a deeper understanding of the capture and the transfer of cultural knowledge.

3 Research Methodology

The research methodology adopted utilises two different approaches, firstly to contextualise the significance of the research and secondly to assess the impact of culture upon the collaborative innovation process within the Slovak automotive industry. The first method used was an online-administered quantitative survey. The objective was to gain a deeper understanding of multicultural working practices in Slovakia. 169 responses were collected from managers across a wide range of industrial enterprises. This was followed by a case study analysis of the *West Slovakia Automotive Cluster Innovation Network,* comprised of 5 depth interviews with individuals in the organisation. The objective of the analysis was to categorise collaborative team working activities within the spiral of knowledge creation [5].

The questionnaire was administered across a wide selection of Slovak industrial enterprises. The largest single group, 37 responses (25.3 %) was from, "Engineering" enterprises and the second largest group, 28 responses (19.2 %) was from the automotive industry. This correlates with the extent to which automotive enterprises are represented within for the Slovak economy.

4 Research Findings

The questionnaire research findings report that from the 169 responses, 65.97 % of the respondents work for an enterprise which has a subsidiary or head office abroad. This illustrates the significant impact of culture within Slovak enterprises and the necessity for managers to cooperate with other cultures in their own organisation. The findings indicate that Slovak enterprises must adopt multicultural understanding in order to collaborate and cooperate effectively with internal departments abroad and external partners and suppliers. The findings also conclude that there is a low level of multi-cultural diversity within Slovak industrial enterprises. The results show that 44.6 % of respondents work in a "monoculture" organisation without any foreign individuals. The second largest category is "low multiculturality" (1 %–10 % of foreign workers) which represents the type of organisation in which 43.2 % of respondents work. These findings highlight that whilst Slovak managers are required to collaborate interna-tionally to develop innovative practices, a comparable level of multiculturalism is not evident within their daily practices. As a result, management may often lack the multicultural competencies and understanding to operative effectively within multi-cultural collaborative teams.

The research findings also show that English is the most commonly spoken official foreign language in Slovak enterprises, with 50 % of respondents working in English speaking enterprises. This is followed by German, which is an official language within organisations of 17.6 % respondents. From the overall sample, respondents indicated that 13 official languages were used within Slovak enterprises. These findings illustrate that whilst the workforce in many cases is not diverse there is predominately a requirement to communicate with foreign customers or colleagues in a head office abroad.

5   Case Study Analysis: *West Slovakia Automotive Cluster Innovation Network*

The second stage of the research was to analyse the *West Slovakia Automotive Cluster Innovation Network* to determine and classify the activities which promote collabo-rative team working. Following a series of depth interviews with individuals in the organisation, the key activities were classified based upon which aspect of the SECI model (Fig. 2) they most closely relate to.

It is evident from the classification utilising the SECI model that the practices adopted by the *West Slovakia Automotive Cluster Innovation* network assist with facilitating the externalisation of tacit knowledge through the creation of an active dialogue between supply chain members. The second stage is the combination phase, whereby explicit knowledge transfer is facilitated through the creation of the supplier database and clear procedures for knowledge sharing. The third stage of knowledge creation reflects the internalisation process whereby investment is made in training and R&D to ensure that all individuals undergo training to develop the tacit skills for effective team working. The fourth stage is the socialisation phase whereby individuals utilise their newly acquired tacit skills to share knowledge and work effectively together. This can take the form of effective team working with an open dialogue and the ability to work together collectively and share investment relating to infrastructure, marketing and recruitment. To achieve effective team working it is necessary for knowledge to transcend through all four stages [5] ensuring that individuals possess the skills to collaborate effectively.

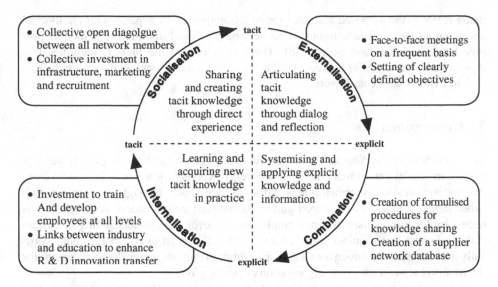

Fig. 2. Application of the SECI model for the *West Slovakia Automotive Cluster Innovation Network.* Author elaboration based on [5]

6 Proposed Framework and Requirements for Future Research

It is evident from the research findings that collaborative working is critical to success of organisations in order to gain competitive advantage. To provide a methodology for facilitating collaborative team working the authors propose a framework (Fig. 3) summarising the team working process based on existing literature.

The first phase of the model is comprised of Hofstede's [2] cultural dimensions. To emphasise national and organisational culture simultaneously, Hofstede's national culture dimensions and organisational culture dimensions are utilised. The second

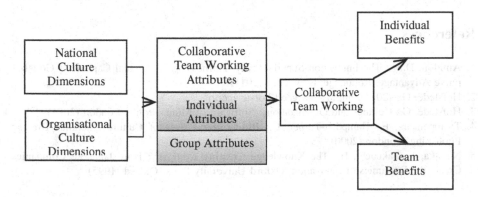

Fig. 3. Directional hypotheses model for collaborative working. author own work based on [2, 7, 8]

phase refers to the proposed attributes for collaborative teams, separated into individual and team attributes. The attributes were determined based upon existing models proposed by Lewis [7] and Skyrme [8]. The final phase of the process identifies that mutual benefits must exist for successful collaborative team working, which are divided into individual and team factors.

7 Conclusions

In the context of the Slovak automotive industry the research findings indicate that Slovak industrial enterprises employ few foreign workers, however it is evident from the findings that many organisations work multiculturally through cooperation with subsidiaries or head offices abroad and cross-national collaboration. As a result it is necessary for Slovak managers and employees to develop an understanding of culture and the impact upon multicultural team working. The need to collaborate both vertically and horizontally throughout the supply chain greatly increases the requirement for intercultural team working as organisations operate globally.

It is evident from the *West Slovakia Automotive Cluster Innovation Network* case study that a clear strategy was necessary to ensure knowledge was shared effectively. Without the implementation of such processes, the ability to collaborate across the multicultural diverse supply chain would present limited opportunities for innovation. It can be concluded that both national culture and organisational culture should be viewed as drivers of collaborative team work because they specifically define the characteristics, values, attributes, skills and competence of each individual team member. The next stage of the research is to conduct a quantitative survey of collaborative team members within the Slovak automotive industry in order to determine which attributes impact upon the collaborative innovation process.

Acknowledgements. This paper was written as part of the VEGA project No. 1/0787/12 "The Identification of Sustainable Performance Key Parameters in Industrial Enterprises within Multicultural Environment", at the Slovak University of Technology in Bratislava, Faculty of Materials Science and Technology in Trnava, Institute of Industrial Engineering and Management.

References

1. Amidon, D.M.: The Innovation Superhighway: Harnessing Intellectual Capital for Collaborative Advantage. Routledge, New York (2011)
2. Hofstede, G.: (2013). http://www.geert-hofstede.com
3. Hofstede, G.: Cultures and Organizations: Software of Mind. Profile, London (2003)
4. Trompenaars, F., Hampden-Turner, C.: Riding the Waves of Culture. Nicholas Brealey Publishing, London (2000)
5. Nonaka, I., Takeuchi, H.: The Knowledge Creating Company: How Japanese Companies Create the Dynamics of Innovation. Oxford University Press, Oxford (1995)

6. Pauleen, D.J.: Cross-Cultural Perspectives on Knowledge Management. Green Publishing Group, Westport (2007)
7. Lewis, R.D.: When Teams Collide: Managing the International Team Successfully. Brealey Publishing, London (2012)
8. Sykrme, D.J.: Knowledge Networking: Creating the Collaborative Enterprise. Butterworth-Heinemann, Oxford (1999)

Evaluation of More Economical Collection and Removal of Old Vehicles

Ingrid Součková[✉] and Marián Králik

Institute of Manufacturing Systems, Environmental Technology
and Quality Management, Slovak University of Technology,
Námestie Slobody 17, 812 31 Bratislava, Slovak Republic
{ingrid.souckova,marian.kralik}@stuba.sk

Abstract. The duty of every person is to maintain such a world as we know it today. To fulfill this obligation, each of us should strive to ensure that together we are able to evaluate different types of waste, and thus again "transform" them into something useful. One of the types of everyday waste which people should deal with is the constantly increasing volume of waste created by old cars. Because of this, we have decided to focus on the following issue in order to point out the fact that if we process waste at substantially lower costs, we can maintain the current ecology. The administrative decisions we will try to build on current information legislation, technology processing or directly from the processor to waste. We will evaluate the collection points and authorized recyclers of old cars. This work was supported by project VEGA 1/1056/12.

Keywords: Reverse logistics · Decisions · Old car · Environment · Waste

1 Introduction

In the present time it should be the duty of every person to conserve nature and in fact the whole world in the state we find it in today – and not to damage, devastate and destroy it. Although this topic is drawing ever more attention, in many production and non-production enterprises and in households this issue is still being neglected or underestimated. In manufacturing companies return (reverse) logistics and recycling should deal with these problems. Despite the fact that reverse logistics was formulated back in the 1990 s, the attention being paid to it is insufficient, or interpreted in different ways. In the literature too there exist two streams: American authors perceive exclusively goods which are returned from stores in the form of unsold products or returns, while German authors who have carried out detailed analyses of the possibilities of recycling industrial and communal waste, have another view on reverse logistics. This relates principally to growing ecological demands and not just that from pressure groups, but also to proposed legislation in this area. In the present period, reverse logistics has come to be oriented not only on returned goods but also on the possibilities for adopting legislation in the form of manufacturing products which are made from recyclable materials. As has been mentioned previously, this should be a priority for each of us. We should be trying to achieve valuations of different types of waste, in other words to 'remake' them into something useful. One of these types of waste which

R. Giaffreda et al. (Eds.): IoT360 2014, Part II, LNICST 151, pp. 16–20, 2015.
DOI: 10.1007/978-3-319-19743-2_3

people should closely examine is discarded vehicles, whose volume is continually on the upturn. Through this theme, we will try to point to the fact that if we can process waste at lower costs, we can manage to maintain contemporary ecological levels. In making decisions, managers should start from existing information on legislation, processing technologies, and this right at the creators of such waste. In the following text we will evaluate collection points and authorized old car dealers.

2 Parameters and Methods of Evaluating Distribution Chains

Contemporary collection center have their places in distribution channels. Their task is pivotal in the storing of used automobiles. We will evaluate one firm which administers 28 collection centers, and will look at it on the basis of the following selected three parameters. This will help us gain an overall picture of its successfulness. The parameters are as follows:

- *Number of vehicles purchased per* year – this is a positive parameter, which tells us about the maximum capacity of the distribution channel. It is essentially a summary evaluation number which characterizes how many used vehicles are taken into the collection center per year.
- *Distance to a collection center* – this is a negative parameter, since an increase in the number of kilometers from a processing center reduces the financial 'benefit,' since it is necessary to transport a car from a further distance. This parameter naturally increases costs since the shipping of a discarded vehicle includes expenses such as tolls, petrol costs and the time a driver spends delivering the vehicle.
- *Number of pick-ups* – in this parameter, one pick-up represents one necessary stop by the haulage truck to 'collect' an old car. With an increased number of purchased vehicles, the number of pick-ups also directly increases proportionally.

2.1 Graph Method

In the following Fig. 1 we perform a comparison of centers in the three parameters listed above. It is necessary to mention however that the height of the columns do not correspond mutually among each other for each collection center, but only in the given category with other collection centers (according to color).

From this it can be seen that although some collection centers have roughly as far a distance as the others, the number of automobiles purchased can be essentially different. From the graph it can be seen which centers are most successful in terms of vehicles purchased per year.

On the contrary, in relation to the distance from the collection center it is evident which centers are not positive. But this graph method does not provide specific quantifiable results, and so we consider it only as provisional. Its advantage however is that it allows a very clear graphic comparison and is sufficient for 'basic decision-making'.

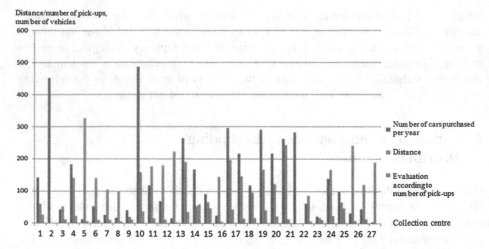

Fig. 1. Comparison of collection centers according to the parameters [3]

2.2 Point Method

Another means or method to express the relationship, evaluating the individual centers by points according to a coefficient of costing, is described below.

We can define the coefficient of costing as a coefficient expressing how many discarded vehicles were stored at collection centers per given year per shipment. It is clear that if this number is low, the given center did not manage to collect a sufficient number of old cars and so the haulage trucks after pick-ups, travel half-empty or insufficiently loaded. We calculate this coefficient according to a formula drawn up by us:

$$k_n = \frac{P_{OVx}}{P_{ZVx}} \tag{1}$$

With the individual parameters having the following meaning:

P_{OVx} – number of vehicles purchased per given year 'x' (for the specific collection center)

P_{ZVx} – number of pick-ups per given year 'x' (for the specific collection center).

This means therefore that this coefficient expresses numerically how many old automobiles are hauled away on average by a haulage truck per load. It is understandable that if the value of this coefficient is for example '1', it would mean that the truck leaves the collection center after leaving one old vehicle. The higher the coefficient, the more is the center attractive from the viewpoint of lower expenses per pick-up.

In Fig. 2 can be seen, the color differentiated values which indicate how many vehicles per individual center were picked up per trip. We can consider the red values as negative numbers since the haulage trucks carrying wrecks returned to the collection centers insufficiently loaded.

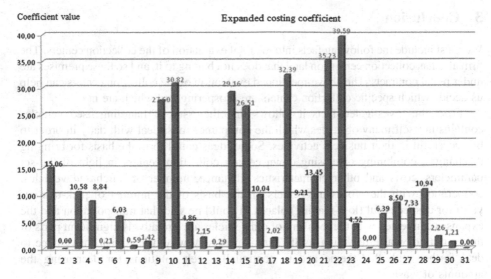

Fig. 2. Expanded costing coefficient

2.3   Quantification Method

A third approach to evaluation is the method on the basis of quantifiable parameters expressed by the formula:

$$k_{n2} = \frac{(P_{OVx-1} + P_{OVx}) * k_n}{S} \qquad (2)$$

Meaning of the individual parameters:

P_{OVx-1} – number of vehicles purchased in the preceding year for the given year x (for a specific collection center)

P_{OVx} - number of vehicles purchased for the given year x (for a specific collection center)

S – distance to the collection center from the place of processing.

Through this third evaluation we are attempting to express an evaluation of the centers only for the last two years. At present, the existing collection centers have been in operation for the last two years, so the statistical selection of the given formula will have the most accurate values of the considered phenomenon precisely in these two years. Their existence in the period prior to the past two years need not be relevant. This evaluation can be considered as the most important, since the future prediction of the successfulness of the centers is of main interest to us, and this is preferably derived from the most up-to-date data. As with the preceding indicators, a higher final value is characteristic of greater success. The resulting values - data do not describe the specific properties of the collection center, but only a 'point' evaluation of a given collection center. However, such information is always of interest to us.

3   Conclusion

We must include the following facts into the total evaluation of the collection centers. The firm also has collection centers on land that does not belong to it, and so these premises are under rental contracts. The above-mentioned evaluation of the collection centers can help us decide which specific collection centers are prospering and which are not.

From the investigated facts it follows that the issue of handling used vehicles contains in itself many obstacles which the companies must deal with daily in order to be successful in their business activities. Some ideas could form the basis for bringing in changes, combining or closing down certain collection centers in light of the set parameters, costs and other characteristics (distance, number of purchased vehicles, cooperation with the processing centers on the basis of the number of pick-ups per year) for unsuccessful (loss-making) places. It could be said that transportation and the expenses connected with the recovery of old vehicles are a relatively significant parts of the activity of waste recycling itself. That is precisely why it has great importance to deal further with this theme and to continually seek solutions for decreasing the amounts of waste.

Acknowledgement. *This work was supported by project VEGA 1/1056/12.*

References

1. Badida, M., Kol, A: Recyklácia a recyklačné technológie II. Košice: Edícia študijnej literatúry (2011). ISBN 978-80-553-0792-3
2. Sosedová, I.,- Šlesinger, J.: Účinky pôsobiace na náklad v prepravnom reťazci, roč.5, č.2, s. 9 (2010) ISSN 1336–7676
3. Mäsiar, L.: Dopravné náklady a logistika spojené so zhodnocovaním odpadov zo starých vozidiel. Diplomová práca. SjF STU Bratislava (2013) SjF-17394–62435
4. Magdolenová, J.: Empirické metódy rozhodovania v manažmente. [Online]. Žilina. Dostupné na: https://dspace.upce.cz:8443/bitstream/10195/32318/1/CL662.pdf [cit.16. May. 2014]

Rating Attractiveness of Sectoral Environment-Performance Indicators

Zuzana Tekulová[✉] and Marián Králik

Institute of Manufacturing Systems, Environmental Technology
and Quality Management, Slovak University of Technology,
Námestie Slobody 17, 81243 Bratislava, Slovak Republic
{zuzana.tekulova,marian.kralik}@stuba.sk

Abstract. The paper is focused on managerial tool - benchmarking, explains its basic mission as the process of comparing one's business processes and performance metrics to industry bests or best practices from other industries. Dimensions typically measured are quality, time and cost. In the process of best practice benchmarking, management identifies the best firms in their industry, or in another industry where similar processes exist, and compares the results and processes of those studied to one's own results and processes. In this way, they learn how well the targets perform and, more importantly, the business processes that explain why these firms are successful. Article defines assess performance indicators of production processes in relation to attractiveness industry, their meaning and mission. The practical part is focused on the evaluation of selected indicators of sectoral environment in manufacturing in subclassifications of object manufacturing activities called Manufacture of other machine. This work was supported by project VEGA 1/1056/12.

Keywords: Business · Rating attractiveness of sectoral environment · Benchmarking · Performance indicators of production processes

1 Introduction

In today's dynamic business world companies has a very difficult position. Market calls for maximum performance, optimal adaptation, as well as prospective prospects. Company's performance is becoming a very hot topic today. If companies want to achieve top position and maintain a competitive advantage, they need to set such control system that can ensure controlled use of their resources towards achieving the vision.

In the opening of business is one of the basic strategic decisions the decision of business sphere - in selected sectors of business. About business in Slovakia has been written many considerations, but as is the practice, which industry is successful - or less, and possibly which industry is worth to join with the intention of business plan? These considerations are supported by calculation of indicators attractiveness of industry mainly to highlight the profitability and overall profitability either deposited funds and other assets. Of course when deciding about joining the business play a role other attributes as the opportunity - or the ability to have the know-how and be competitive in this industry.

© Institute for Computer Sciences, Social Informatics and Telecommunications Engineering 2015
R. Giaffreda et al. (Eds.): IoT360 2014, Part II, LNICST 151, pp. 21–26, 2015.
DOI: 10.1007/978-3-319-19743-2_4

The predisposition to business sectors closely related to the mobility and concentration of business in areas with developed infrastructure. This creates the potential pressure on the area of development, mostly concentrated with relation to one place in the developed city. Urban transport plays a key role in the creation of maintainable European cities. The key to improvement is coordinated and targeted planning, say European experts in the field of mobility. It is important that cities create long-term objectives of their transport systems.

2 Benchmarking Performance Indicators of Production Processes

Competitiveness is the core of the success or failure of a business. Competition is one of the key indicators of performance. As reported by H. Sedláčková, "competition has gained global nature, competitive rivalry has higher intensity." Reference [4] In view of the constantly changing business environment conditions a new concept of competition also requires new approaches.

To ensure the quality of all business processes is necessary to apply a range of appropriate methods and tools. Some methods are applicable to the identification and transformation of customer requirements, other to the quality of newly developed products, a large range of methods are formed by methods for securing and managing implementation processes and so on. In general, each process in the company may use a variety of methods, tools and techniques of quality. Quality methods widely used existing methods and tools used in other management disciplines. To ensure the continuous analysis of the sectoral environment in the competitive environment, it is appropriate to use the method of quality – benchmarking.

Benchmarking is one of the analytic-synthetic methods of quality management. The concept of benchmarking is derived from the English word benchmark which in translation means levelling brand to which the measurements relate. Usually the term is used in geodesy. In the literature we can meet with multiple definitions of benchmarking, which we approaching it from different perspectives. The basic principle of benchmarking aptly characterizes the definition: „Benchmarking is a systematic and continuous process of comparison and measurement products, services, processes and methods of organizations with those who have been recognized as suitable for this measurement (Model competitors) in order to define targets to improve its own activities.

Based on the above definitions, we can say that benchmarking is a continuous process, which emphasizes the need to integrate the observed results and findings. Basis Value of benchmarking is that it is the evaluation comparison which aims at enhancement. Evaluation is the backbone of competitive benchmarking, which must include:

- knowledge of the quality level of the object,
- solution to improve the quality of the object.

In our case it is not a common benchmarking of the performance of one organization with others in the industry. This method was used in evaluating of the attractiveness of a sector by use benchmarking of the performance of manufacturing processes represented by existing businesses subjects. Overall, we were interested in the nature of the manufacturing sector due to their overall share of the added value. As can be seen from the table, the most appropriate sector of economic activity from this perspective appears Manufacturing sector, the indicators are specified in detail in engineering production - production area of other machines.

Regional gross value added by economic activities [5]

Mill EUR, at current prices

Year	Gross value added in total	On which in:		Construction	Trade, transport, accom., food serv.	Information, communication	Financial, insurance activities	Real estate activities	Profession., techn. activ., administr.	Public admin., education, health
		Industry in total	Manufacturing							
2007	55387	16592	12802	4 682	12220	2291	1953	3317	3666	6862
2008	60638	17462	13602	6 070	13599	2447	2000	3635	4300	7311
2009	57075	14005	10174	5 654	12570	2721	2195	3761	4342	8089
2010	59916	15991	12561	5 418	13109	2728	2130	3919	4551	8482
2011	62396	16979	13435	5 576	13301	2804	2409	4202	4569	8351

It follows that benchmarking is a tool for improving internal processes and is an active part of quality management.

As can be seen from the table above, the choice of indicators is broad, it is logical that in practice, the used indicators are a combination of universal and special characteristics. To select the most appropriate indicators must be met not condition of their abundance, but the quality and relevance ability of indicators. Literature recommends the following procedure:

1. Precisely define the process or product which performance properties would we monitor and measure.
2. Brainstorming applied for the selection of performance measuring indicators.
3. Selection of the most appropriate indicators (maximum information value ability about the performance, without increasing amount of work on their application).
4. Proposal of mathematical relations for the calculation of indicators and their interdependencies.
5. Determining the sources of information inputs.

For comparison, we have defined processes that characterize the performance of the sector, particularly earnings, revenue, size of capital, the total amount of assets. In selecting these attributes we watched availability of resources that are generally available from the accounts and the obligation to publish the results in individual subjects. For practical evaluation of selected environmental indicators of sectoral industrial production through benchmarking methods we selected indicators of production processes, the evaluation of which we used accounts for 2011 and selected 543 subjects whose main or predominant activity is focused on retaliation Manufacture of other machine. From 543 selected entities we acquire information from the financial statements. We evaluated the profit and loss account and balance sheet accounts cover a period of 2011. Results were obtained from the web site or directly from the company's rating.

Overall we valorize 543 of the subject from total of 13.090 subjects in the manufacturing sector, which is 3.3% of the total. Unfortunately the results for individual SK NACE and thus sector of Manufacture of other parts of mechanical engineering is not included in the statistics. We therefore based on analysis publications Middle financial indicators in Slovakia in 2011 where for this sector recorded 570 subjects together, so our selection sample represents 95%, which is relevant sample for the interpretation of compared benchmarking.

Results indicators were compared with the values for the total manufacturing sector, disclosed in Middle values of the financial indicators of economic activities in Slovakia in 2011 as representative industry. Purpose was drawn to the specifics of mechanical engineering, and especially in its overall attractiveness or using market interest and business opportunities throughout whole manufacturing.

Between selected indicators were included mainly profitability indicators that characterize the recovery of capital invested in the business, respectively the effectiveness of the company. To assess the company's capital expressed usable profit after tax is a together Variable return on equity. To express the overall efficiency of the overall capital regardless of the source measured pre-tax profits is a Variable return on assets. Assess the effectiveness of the transformation process unladen other influenceable factors represents indicator operational profitability of sales - as a measure of operating income in euro sales. Ability to form higher value production of their performance against the purchased inputs forms indicator Share of value added in sales. To express the overall effectiveness of the company expressed as a measure of earnings before taxes, interest expense and depreciation sheltered proceeds indicator expresses the Share of EBITDA in sales.

Selected indicators were compared with the average for the manufacturing sector. Calculated indicators say on the performance of sectoral environment. Calculated results are expressed in the following table:

Indicator	Average indicator industry of Manufacture of other machine	Average indicator industry of manufacturing [6]
Return on equity	6,28	1,69
Return on assets	3,12	0,55
Operating return on sales	3,20	1,57
Share of value added in sales	26,99	20,46
EBITDA share in sales	9,56	4,58

Source: own calculations, [6]

Indicator Return on equity talks about the return on the own resources invested into the business in the conversion of net profit. On average the result is 6.28% which is 4.59% higher than the profitability throughout industrial production. In comparison with other possible alternative business - eg. use of funds for such investment ag. deposits to term deposits or purchase of securities, we can characterize the result as satisfactory given the current interest rate yield in fixing five years ranging from 2.5% to 3%. This implies the result in favour of the business where the percentage recovery is on average 3% higher than the non-business activities. The average value of return on equity for the business is a total of 0.16%, among the most profitable industry belongs the rated industry.

Return on assets indicator tells the evaluation of the general assets contributed to the company, regardless of its origin or source of coverage. From this perspective represents recovery of funds invested in the business, as well as evaluating the overall economic activity of the company. Compared to the average for the sector is the result of 2.57% higher. Also in this sense we can say that the overall attractiveness of the sector of mechanical engineering: Manufacture of other machine is attractive from the perspective of business.

Operating return on sales indicator shows the profitability of the main business of the company, therefore how much effect company can produce 1 € sales, the evaluation result is an average indicator of industry Manufacture of other machinery operating profit of € 0.32 per euro of revenue, compared with average indicator in manufacturing by 50% higher. Height 32% of the profit per one euro in sales compared with the previous analysis is supported argument attraction to business in that sector.

Indicator of added value share in sales is the ability of company to establish a value on purchased inputs precisely this figure is a significant indicator of GDP in developing and determining the significance of countries in the creation of value. This figure thus says how much added effect is created by the euro from sales, the calculation of the indicator is 26.99%. This figure is among the highest in all production areas and suggests an attractive environment. The aim is to promote the interest of the state GDP growth and thus the sector where the added value of most forms. This indicator talks about the future of the industry in favour of his support.

Indicator Share of EBITDA in sales as a measure of profit before tax, interest and depreciation cost in euro of sales, talks about the effectiveness of profit, but also the ability to cover the payment ability of the company and the costs resulting from depreciation. This indicator is compared to the average indicator in manufacturing increased by 50% and also talks about paying ability to meet interest and amortization of fixed costs. Calculated indicator considering the average values of individual sectors is satisfactory and argues in favour of the company in the reporting sector.

3 Conclusion

How is it then with the attractiveness of engineering production, output may be referred to the analyzed indicators characterize the attractiveness of the environment? In defining the attractiveness of the environment come from other factors, mainly from the growth potential of the sector, industry prospects, stability and variability of competitive forces, uncertainty or risk of future development of the sector. The given data are strong explanatory power of earnings and profitability, which when considering entering into a business has an important role.

When assessing the attractiveness of the environment are routines and methods, however, the emphasis on the use of modern approaches to the management of the company across all management structures as a condition for a well-functioning companies and asset that gives the assumptions for the future of continuous ongoing development and improvement of all management and executive activities of the company. Among the most effective methods (although in the current business practice in Slovakia implemented a few) seems to be the method of benchmarking. Provides models towards excellence. Its role is to set goals so that the organization could start improving a realistic picture of improvement and to understand the changes that are necessary for improving not only on internal evaluations, but also in the context of societal conditions in which it carries out business.

Acknowledgement. This work was supported by project VEGA 1/1056/12.

References

1. Nenadál, J., Vykydal, D., Halfarová, P.: Benchmarking - Mýty a skutečnost, Praha: Management Press 2011.265 strán, ISBN 978-80-7261-224-6
2. Nenadál, J., Noskievičová, D., Petříková, R., Plura, J., Tošenovský, J.: Moderní systémy řízení jakosti. Praha: Management Press 2002. 282 strán. ISBN 80-7261-071-6
3. Mateides, A., Kol, A.: Manažérstvo kvality.Bratislava, Ing. Mračko, 2006, 751 strán, ISBN 80-8057-656-4
4. Sedláčková, H.: Strategická analýza, 1. vydanie, Praha: C. H. Beck (2000)
5. Statistical Office of the Slovak Republic: REGIONAL STATISTICAL YEARBOOK of Slovakia 2013, Statistical Office of the Slovak Republic, p. 522 (2013). ISBN 978-80-8121-301-4
6. Slovak Credit Bureau, Stredné hodnoty finančných ukazovateľov ekonomických činnosti v Slovenskej republike za rok 2011, Bratislava 2012, ISBN 978-80-971109-0-1

Collective Creativity: Utilizing the Potentials of Multimodal Environments

Predrag K. Nikolic(✉)

Faculty of Digital Production, EDUCONS University,
Vojvode Putnika 87, 21208 Sremska Kamenica, Serbia
Predrag.nikolic@educons.edu.rs

Abstract. Advances in technology have expanded the methods by which users interact with computer-based systems beyond the screen and into physical space. To design these types of innovative interfaces, new design techniques and practices will be needed to understand how users perceive and interact with such multimodal environments. One area where we can look for such novel approaches is the field of interactive media art and design. An interactive art installation called Art Machine: MindCatcher was built to allow users to create audio-visual sentences (artifacts) by moving through a field of sensors that generate circles and sounds that varied depending upon the amount of time spent on the sensor. This research experiment has intention to contribute to the field of collective creativity and participatory design by representing a test-of-concept regarding the viability of interactive media art and design as a method that contributes to the repertoire of techniques and practices for engaging participants in design activities.

Keywords: Collective creativity · Multimodal environments · Activity Theory · Human-centered design

1 Introduction

Technology now allows us to create many different types of user interfaces to technology, and to computer-based systems in particular. Interfaces are no longer constrained by the use of a keyboard, mouse, or even a touch screen. It is now possible to use human movement and gestures as a means of providing commands and interacting with technology.

Many of the techniques that have been successfully used to facilitate user participation in the design of systems and interfaces such as storyboards, mock-ups, and game boards [1], are not directly applicable to the design of interfaces which use gestures, body movement, location, and other physical characteristics observable by the system itself as input.

It is proposed that interactive art installations can be created with the intention of providing users and designers a fun and functional three-dimensional space in which they to explore a wide variety of physical, visual, and audio stimuli and responses, subject to constraints which can be manipulated in many different ways. Through data collection, including observation, of the interactions between user and the

© Institute for Computer Sciences, Social Informatics and Telecommunications Engineering 2015
R. Giaffreda et al. (Eds.): IoT360 2014, Part II, LNICST 151, pp. 27–37, 2015.
DOI: 10.1007/978-3-319-19743-2_5

technological interface as well as between users as co-creators, designers can gain understanding of the impact of constraints on human involvement, interactive experience, incentives which can enrich users' creativity, and cognition, and contribute to sustainable interactive and interface design practices.

This paper will present a brief background section, a description of a specific art installation that could be used in such a way, a discussion of the data collected from the installation, and suggestions for where to go from here.

2   Background

The concept of interactive art, the art which allows viewers to become participants in the co-creation of the art (artefact) itself, has been implemented in many different ways. Frank Oppenheimer, the late director of the Exploratorium in San Francisco, was one of the pioneers who anticipated the necessity of interactive methods of presentation. In 1969 the development of computer-controlled Interactive Art started with American mathematician Myron Krueger and colleagues in GlowFlow, a visual and auditory reactive environment triggered by pressure sensors which start choreography of light and sound. The concepts for designing the interface and the interaction have continued to develop and become more diverse [2]. While interactive art installations may be motivated by different intentions, such as moderating perception by allowing the viewer access to a virtual world by using a handheld virtual eye (Handsight by Agnes Hegedus) or purposely confusing the visitor with the nature and cause of the images generated (Silicon Remembers Carbon by Rokeby), many are supported by computer systems that use feedback from the participants' actions to change the behaviour of the system creating the art. In most cases the participant has to perceive the system rules or constraints as a result of his or her interactions with the installation. Therefore users could quite passively interact without learning, or could actively experiment with the reactions of the installation to determine and then use the underlying constraints to obtain a desired outcome.

We propose that interactive art installations can be used to expand the techniques of participatory design in such a way that its supports collective creativity directed by a conceptual framework. Using interactive art as a tool for understanding user interactions with technology allows us to use a language whose components are not only both visual and verbal [3] but also experiential in the sense that the participant can see and hear (and potentially feel) the response of the art installation to his or her actions. Collaborative creation such as that addresses the aesthetic and emotional sides of the experience, by allowing users to "escape the limitations of existing structures of meaning and expectation within a given practice" as with the Fictional Inquiry technique used by [4], and to experiment with new ways of communicating with technology.

Iversen and Dindler [4] describe the concept of *aesthetic* as "a profoundly meaningful transformation that provides a refreshed attitude towards the practices of everyday life, and as a change in our modes of perceiving and acting in the world". We support this view which opens possibilities of various aesthetical interventions and applications of transcendence in Collective Creativity. The use of imaginative artifacts may result in better, more creative, collaboration between participants in the process and eventually to more innovative design by providing a means of exploring those desires (deeply-felt preferences regarding the interface) that cannot be articulated on a purely conscious level [5].

Activity Theory has been used as a theoretical foundation in design evaluation and human-computer problem analysis, which serves as a useful framework for understanding MindCatcher in the broader participative design context. In Activity Theory the unit of analysis is motivated activity directed toward a goal [6]. In the case of MindCatcher this activity is the movement through the installation, pressing on certain spots. The activity is mediated by the structure of the MindCatcher installation – the artefact – and constrained by the rules built into the installation. Other theory framework components that can be studied using MindCatcher are the environment, the characteristics of the participants (history and culture), and differences in motivations and the complexity of the interaction.

Activity Theory emphasizes the distinction between internal and external activities. The interactive art installation MindCatcher tries to capture internal processes such as perceptions and emotions and express them through external activities represented by participants' behavioral changes. The theory also highlights the importance of tool development for further mediation between internal and external human activities [7]. This opens the experimental space to artistic forms and aesthetically composed environments. This is where artistic concepts could contribute to the design process especially in the sphere of innovative human-centered interactive and interface design. Further, this should lead to deeper investigation of how people perceive and engage in the world. Having that in mind, we could say that individual and collaborative experience vastly depends on respect of people's choices and lifestyles, personal beliefs and values. Pervasive technologies and the future vision of ubiquitous computing, foresees novel scenarios of highly interactive environments in which communication is taking place between users and devices, between devices and devices, and between users and other users. Such responsive environments enable automation, interactivity, ubiquity [8] while meeting user expectations and allowing interaction at almost a subconscious level [9]. For more than a decade researchers have been working on sustainable concepts for integration of real and virtual space. Followed by technology improvements, cross-reality ideas and technologies started widely to appear in various projects, ranging from interactive art installations to industry and commercial based systems.

In order to explore world around us we use all our senses. Numerous studies have suggested that the greater the number of sensory modalities stimulated at any time, the richer our experiences will be [10–12]. As a consequence, increasing number of modalities of sensory input, presented in a virtual environment, can help increase people's sense of presence and also increase their memory for objects placed within the virtual environment [13–15]. The way we interact with such an environment is through an interface placed between us, and the non-physical, often abstract, world we experience. What we try to investigate is where and how such a human-centred design can be utilized in practice, and what can be the outcomes of such collaborative and communication-oriented multimodal environments. We used aesthetically-based experiment design in a form of interactive installation as a platform for user participation in research, as we assumed that such enriched perceptive surrounding could provide us with more comprehensive data regarding user emotional reactions, feeling and behaviours to contribute to better future sustainable interactive environments design.

3   The MindCatcher Experiment

In the interactive installation Art Machine: Mind Catcher the goal was to investigate how an interface based on body-movement interaction and sound-visual response could affect visitors' perception during interaction, and how it could deliver a rich and varied multisensory experience. The intention was to explore how this human-computer interaction could make people feel comfortable to collaborate, express their feelings and emotions, on which is based every sustainable environmental but also product or service design.

The installation uses sensory data to output a 3D real-time, open-GL-based rendering of a graphical-based universe. It can be seen on the wall projection situated in front of the user. Those data are collected through participants' interaction with floor interface and are based on offered audio-visual vocabulary which consists of three colours (red, blue, yellow), three tones (C, G, E), three sized circles, and a touch sensitive space for creative dialogue between artwork as a paradigm of complexity system in a phase of creation and participants as co-creators.

The purpose of using different media and technologies is to increase the perceptual manipulation of the participants in order to achieve a higher degree of persuasive experience [16]. The Art Machine: Mind Catcher installation invites visitors to step on the interactive floor interface and visualize their multisensory experience by pressing floor switches. Every switch has its colour and its tone which corresponds to created output and could be modulated depending on pressure duration. This interface allows users to create audio-visual patterns (composed of circles of varying colors and size that corresponded to different tones) based on simple rules. At a deeper level, to provoke emotions and communication in the perceived space we used imaginative abstract artifacts which we named *audio-visual sentences*. The sentences are a paradigm for meaningful communication that can be built and made visible with abstract signs we call *letters*. Based on that we can build our creative vocabulary on any sign, color or form and proclaim it as the letters we are using to build sentences and express ourselves.

In contemporary design methodology it is crucial to allow participants to create. By observing the creative process, users' behavior and analyzing the creative artifact itself, designers are in a position to fulfill user expectations and meet their needs. In the MindCatcher installation, the creative activity occurs when participants interact with the installation to produce the audio-visual sentences that are the creative outcomes.

The interface itself is placed on the floor of the installation. It is a circular arrangement of pressure-sensitive circles of red, blue, and yellow, with one white circle in the middle to serve as the "start" indicator. This interface and the area where the pattern would display are shown in Fig. 1.

After starting the session the participants move around and press the colored circles. The way audio-visual sentences are generated such as in a form, direction or movement

Fig. 1. The MindCatcher installation

depends on rules defined by the author (designer). Having that in mind we were able to affect users' collaboration, involvement, cognition and trigger their emotions based on observed user behavior and thought they shared with interviewers after the sessions. Based on that the installation evolved through three versions named Essentiality, Universality and the last one I, Universe. The last version of the installation will not be part of the research presented in this paper.

In the first version Essentiality, once the first circle is pressed the rest of the circles generated in the audio-visual display go in the same direction as the participant moved to press the first one (left, right, up, down, etc.) In order to change the direction of the "branch", the participant must make a pause. (Physical inactivity is perceived to involve mental contemplation.) As a result the created artifact can increase in richness by showing more complex patterns. Examples of these patterns are shown in Fig. 2.

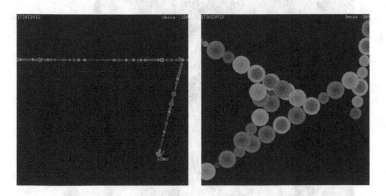

Fig. 2. Simple (left) and more complex (right) patterns produced by MindCatcher participants

Finally, the finished individual creation is joined to the collective audio-visual art piece on a daily and global level. This is illustrated in Fig. 3. Collaboration between users were not in a physical space, it was spread over audio-visual user-generated virtual space projected on the wall and transferred also into web space, where everybody could follow the evolution of their collaborative artifact patterns, over the project's website.

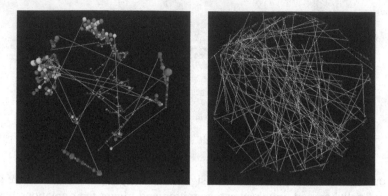

Fig. 3. Daily (left) and global (right) collective patterns.

In the second version Universality collaboration between users in a physical space became very important creative factor and as such deeply affected rules upon which the installation responded on participants' actions, behavior and interpersonal collaborations. The maximum number of participants hosted by the installation was six, as shown in Fig. 4.

Fig. 4. Direct collaboration on the floor interface

The artifacts they created were different then in the first version of the installation, as reflection of a new generative rule applied to leverage users' collaboration and involvement, provoking different meaning and feelings as incentives to participants' involvement and creative contributions. Example of the sessions is shown in Fig. 5.

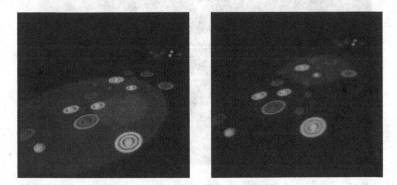

Fig. 5. The audio-visual artifacts generated by one or more participants at the same time.

4 Findings

First version of the installation Art Machine: MindCatcher was exposed in the Museum of Applied Art in Belgrade, Serbia, from 7 to 21 September 2011. A total of 140 interactions were recorded. Every participant was recorded with a video camera and observed directly by the researchers. Metrics collected about each interactive session included the time spent in the installation, the number of repeated visits, gender, date of birth, number of each color, as well as the number of each tone used. In addition, the pattern of behavior on the floor interface was captured. Errors made by the participants were also recorded. Errors would include actions such as pressing the central white circle after the session has started even though it was clear that doing so would not affect the colorful creation, pressing the colored circles without stepping on the white circle to begin, or pressing the switches which are selectively disabled during the duration of the installation even though the participants were told which switches were disabled.

Second version of the installation Art Machine: Mind Catcher has been exposed at the Educational Museum in Belgrade. During the period of 12 days 112 sessions were recorded, with a presence of various numbers of participants in the installation floor interface, with different interpersonal relationships. Example of mother and daughter who interacted together on the floor interface is shown in Fig. 6.

Based on personal observations three mayor types of the user behavior were similar for both versions of the installation:

Type 1: Participants focused only on interaction with the floor interface - they used it as a musical instrument or a stage for their performance. This user type ignored the audio-visual artifact they were producing during the session.

Fig. 6. Mother and daughter in the collective creative session, interacting together on the floor interface.

Type 2: Participants focused only on audio-visual artifact they were producing (by interacting with the floor interface) during the session and how to control raising visual complexity. They used floor interface as some kind of a painting tool. For them, sound generated through interaction with the installation was of a secondary or of none importance. They concentrated on finding out how to synchronize their body movements with the visual creation they were producing.

Type 3: Participants focused on all aspects of available creative and sensory experiences they were immersing, starting from the physical interaction with the floor interface through 2D visual creation and finally observing joint of it to the 3D artificial structure co-created with other users.

Besides these characteristics attached to certain groups of users, what was common for all participants, there were transfers from the phase of surprise and uncertainty in the beginning, through phases of cognitive thinking, intuition problem solving and conclusions and ending with joy, excitement and satisfaction as they became fully embodied with the installation space and certain about how to fulfill their task.

In this experiment it was important to explore how the new installation rules, defined in the Art Machine: Mind Catcher *Universality* together with the opening of a new interactive space for physical collaboration, reflect on collective creativity and the audio-visual sentences, produced by the participants. Based on interviews taken from the users, the first installation version *Essentiality* did not achieve expected collaboration due to participants' lack of understanding regarding:

- the individual contribution to group sessions;
- the group contribution to individual sessions;
- the correlation between generated creative artefacts;
- the possibility to control created collective artefact.

In the second version named *Universality*, by allowing direct physical interaction and simplification of the audio-visual respond on collective users' behavior we delivered more meaningful collaboration between participants. As a result, the percentage of repeated visits and continuing the sessions increased dramatically, from 3.7 % to 27 %. The youngest group of visitors (age 6–10) showed huge interest to repeat their interactive sessions, usually one after another, but sometimes even within a period of several days. Second group of the most active users showed interest to share experience and collaborate with different people, so they were returning to interact with the installation. By changing the way creative artifact are generated they became a more quantitative parameter despite qualitative and quantitative role they had in the first installation data analyses. The relevant data we used to measure user engagement and embodiment was the number of produced audio-visual dots and the created artefact size and complexity.

The mentioned simplifications of the installation functional and conceptual system helped us also to validate with more clarity the immersion, interaction and information intensity with only one interaction complexity evaluation parameter. We derived it from personal observations, answers collected through a questionnaire and measurements of the following metrics:

- number of visits;
- time spent in the installation;
- number of generated audio-visual dots (Fig. 7);
- size of the created audio-visual structure/artefact.

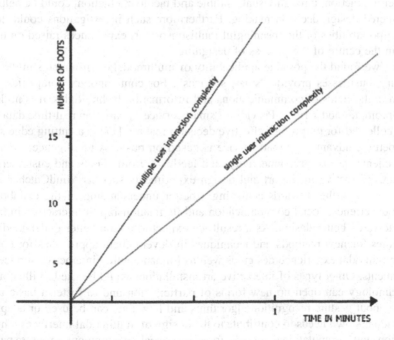

Fig. 7. Graphic of the Art Machine: MindCatcher v2.0 users' involvement and embodiment throughout time.

With the defined metrics and parameters we were also able to evaluate achieved collaboration between participants in a sense of mutual understanding of the tool they use to generate the artifacts and physical and virtual synchronization of the interaction in order to archive desired interactive experience and potential creative results.

5   Conclusions and Future Directions

The results collected from two separate installations: the Art Machine: MindCatcher *Essentiality* and its second version *Universality*, could lead us to the new collective creativity practices in developing designers tools toward innovations in interactive and user experience design.

MindCatcher experiment demonstrated that it is possible to use an interactive computer-based art system to better understand perception, affected emotions and behavior. The level of involvement directly affects the level of creativity generated by the environment. Results can be analyzed not only by using statistical data but also by examining the created artifacts as illustrating the perceptional and emotional states experienced. Hence, based on the final user-generated forms and meanings we believe it is possible to derive certain conclusions on usability and new approaches to interface development particularly in the case of collaborative, creative or educational tools. MindCatcher combines aesthetics with metrics, and visual language with human experience and habits.

Based on our experiment we believe that adoption and introduction of human-computer interaction, through visual, audible and tactile interaction, could be helpful in user-centered design decision making. Furthermore such investigations could help in applying possibilities of the meaningful multisensory art experiences raised on human values in the centre of the process of designing.

Thus, we found the possible applicability of multimodal environments in the sense of helping businesses provide "smart services". For contemporary companies, especially from the fields of communications and information technologies, it is no longer to offer prompt, good service. Providing "smart services", based on real-time data about clients, collected for purpose of effective decision making [17] is a cutting edge source of competitive advantage. Smart service is based on business intelligence, on awareness of clients' needs, on connectivity, and feedback from clients and customers.

Future interactive media art and design experiments such as MindCatcher installations can go further towards achieving a better understanding of the collaborative creative experience, social communication and its relationship to interaction in human actions towards better design. As a result we expect to gain a better understanding of possibilities for new methods and techniques in development approaches for collaborative-multimodal experience design as well as human-centred interactive services and environments. Other types of interactive art installations could be used to illustrate the way technology can open up new forms of participation and to foster a basic understanding about gesture recognition algorithms and how they can be used or adapted to an individual's own needs to contribute to the design of multimodal interfaces, physical interaction and computational models for audiovisual environments, thus expanding the field of collaborative creativity and participatory design into new territories.

References

1. Sanders, E.B.-N., Brandt, E., Binder, T.A.: Framework for organizing the tools and techniques of participatory design. In: Proceedings of the PDC 2010, pp. 195–198 (2010)
2. Dinkla, S.: The history of the interface in interactive art. In: The Fifth International Symposium on Electronic Art Symposium ISEA 1994, Helsinki (1994)
3. Sanders, E.B.-N.: Generative tools for coDesigning. In: Scrivener, S.A.R., Ball, L.J., Woodcock, A. (eds.) Collaborative Design, pp. 3–12. Springer, London (2000)
4. Iversen, O.S., Dindler, C.: Pursuing aesthetic inquiry in participatory design. In: Proceedings of the PDC 2008, pp. 138–145 (2008)
5. Nelson, H., Stolterman, E.: The Design Way – Intentional Change in an Unpredictable World. Foundations and Fundamentals of Design Competence. Educational Technology Publications, New Jersey (2003)
6. Engeström, Y.: Learning, Working and Imagining: Twelve Studies in Activity Theory. Orienta-Konsultit Oy, Helsinki (1990)
7. Nardi, B. (ed.): Context and Consciousness: Activity Theory and Human-Computer Interaction. MIT Press, Cambridge (1996)
8. Muller, J., Alt, F., Michelis, D. (eds.): Pervasive Advertising, pp. 1–30. Springer, London (2011)
9. Weiser, M., Brown, J.S.: The coming age of calm technology. In: Denning, P.J., Metcalfe, R.M. (eds.) Beyond Calculation: The Next Fifty Years of Computing, Copernicus (1998)
10. Bahrick, L.E., Lickliter, R.: Intersensory redundancy guides attentional selectivity and perceptual learning in infancy. Dev. Psychol. **36**, 190–201 (2000)
11. Spence, C.: The ICI Report on the Secret of the Senses. The Communication Group, London (2002)
12. Stein, B.E., Meredith, M.A.: The Merging of the Senses. MIT Press, Cambridge (1993)
13. Dinh, H.Q., Walker, N., Song, C., Kobayashi, A., Hodges, L. F.: Evaluating the importance of Multi-sensory input on memory and the sense of presence in virtual environments. In: IEEE Virtual Reality Conference, Houston, TX (1999)
14. Hoffman, H.G., Hollander, A., Schroder, K., Rousseau, S., Furness, T.I.: Physically touching and tasting virtual objects enhances the realism of virtual experiences. J. Virtual Real. **3**, 226–234 (1998)
15. Washburn, D.A., Jones, L.M., Vijaya Satya, R., Bowers, C.A., Cortes, A.: Olfactory use in virtual environment training. Model Simul. Mag. **2**, 19–25 (2003)
16. Stenslie, S.: Virtual Touch. Ph.D. dissertation. Oslo School of Architecture and Design, p. 223 (2010)
17. Allmendinger, G., Lombreglia, R.: Four Stages for the Age of the Smart Services (2012) http://courses.ischool.berkeley.edu/i290 1/f08/readings/StrategiesSmartServices.pdf. Accessed 14 January 2013

Strategic Management in SMEs in Selected European Countries

Pavel Zufan$^{(\boxtimes)}$ and Tomas Pysny

Faculty of Business and Economics, Mendel University in Brno, Zemedelska 1,
613 00 Brno, Czech Republic
pavel.zufan@gmail.com, tomas.pysny@mendelu.cz

Abstract. The paper focuses on situation of strategic management principles implementation within the SMEs in Czech Republic, Slovakia, Sweden, and Finland. Data come from a quota sampling research done in May-July 2014 among 1004 SMEs in the above-listed countries. Focusing on the key aspects of strategic management (setting objectives, their internal communication, coordination, and performance monitoring) authors found that the level of use of principal strategic management tools is relatively high–80 % of SMEs do set goals in the main business areas, 74 % communicates majority of plans with employees, 84 % pay significant attention to coordination, and 84 % systematically monitors performance. Results in the particular countries were very similar; major difference appeared in the case of Slovakia and Finland in the area of internal communication, where the chi-square test resulted in the lowest value – but, still, the value of 0.9941 shows almost complete compliance.

Keywords: Setting objectives · Communication · Coordination · Performance monitoring · Level of difference · Czech, Slovak, Swedish, and Finnish SMEs

1 Introduction

Small and medium size enterprises (SMEs) represent the backbone of the economies of all EU countries amounting for 90 % of all registered companies, creating more than 65 % of jobs in the private sector, and over 54 % of the overall value added [1]. Their sustainable development, competitiveness, and growth are therefore on of the EU's economic priorities [2]. Research, though, indicates, that SMEs do have certain weaknesses, which negatively impact their long-term competitiveness – more specifically, their managers and/or owners do not manage their firms strategically [3–5]. One of the key reasons for this is that the SMEs owners and/or managers lack the necessary knowledge.

International research suggests, that implemented strategic management systems in SMEs lead to their better financial [6], and overall performance [7–9], and to their faster growth [10].

These findings have lead the author to participate in a project consortium and submit a project addressing these issues within the Leonardo da Vinci scheme (the project was accepted, and is being solved in the period of December 2012 to February 2015, No. CZ/12/LLP-LdV/TOI/134004. This paper uses a part of the results achieved,

© Institute for Computer Sciences, Social Informatics and Telecommunications Engineering 2015
R. Giaffreda et al. (Eds.): IoT360 2014, Part II, LNICST 151, pp. 38–42, 2015.
DOI: 10.1007/978-3-319-19743-2_6

and aims on identifying the real status of strategic management implementation in Czech Republic, Slovakia, Sweden, and Finland based on the research done on a representative group of companies by STEM/MARK agency.

2 Objectives and Methods

Objective of the paper is to evaluate the overall situation of strategic management implementation in SMEs in Czech Republic (Cz), Slovakia (Sk), Sweden (Sw), and Finland (Fi), and to identify the existence of possible differences among SMEs in the above-listed countries.

The research was done in a form of CATI,[1] based on quota sampling with the sample sizes shown in Table 1. Micro-entreprises (less than 10 employees) were excluded from the research.

Table 1. Sample sizes in the selected countries

Country	Number of SMEs with 10-249 employees	Sample size
Czech Republic	34 048	311
Slovak Republic	13 707	200
Sweden	29 044	277
Finland	15 005	216

Source: Eurostat, and STEM/MARK

Research questionnaire consisted of 25 main questions focusing on identification of the level of implementation of principal tools of strategic management (e.g. setting objectives, their communication within the organization, performance monitoring etc.). Respondents answered on five-point scale (definitely yes – definitely no). Due to the limited extent of the paper, authors selected four areas to be paid attention to, aiming on reaching the objective of the paper – these include:

- Setting objectives;
- Communication of objectives within the organization;
- Coordination of particular activities;
- Performance monitoring.

These areas are analyzed in terms of semantic differential in the whole set of answers, and differences among the four countries are examined (using chi-square test).

3 Results and Discussion

One of the key features showing the very basic condition for strategic management implementation can be seen in setting objectives, which also represented the first question asked. Overall results are presented in Fig. 1. It is apparent, that 80 % of the

---

[1] Computer-Aided Telephone Interview.

respondents use objective setting as an obvious component of business management. Within such a result, it is not surprising, that the differences among the particular countries are insignificant – chi-square test showed almost no differences comparing the particular countries (ranging from 0.9965 in case of Sk-Fi to 0.9999 for Fi-Sw). Best result of this indicator was reached in Finland (84 % of companies setting objectives in all or most of the areas), lowest percentage was noted in case of Slovakia (76 %).

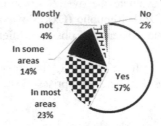

Fig. 1. We manage our business by specifying goals related to turnover, profit etc.

Another important aspect of strategic management implementation is internal communication within the company – whether the people actually know the business plans they should contribute to within their fulfilment. As shown in Fig. 2, the situation is not so unambiguous, here, as far as only 29 % of respondents fully confirmed the communication with employees in this respect. On the other hand, at least majority of the business plans is communicated in 74 % of the cases, which still shows relatively high level of communication about the business plans. Major differences were found between Sk and Fi (chi-square test result was 0.9941), but in all other cases the differences were very low (the lowest between Fi and Sw, with the chi-square of 0.9999, again). Best result of this indicator was reached in Slovakia (80 % of respondents reported communication in at least majority of the areas/employees), lowest percentage was noted in case of Finland (68 %).

Another examined aspect was internal coordination of particular activities. In this respect, full coordination was reported by 44 % of SMEs in total, and coordination of at least majority of activities by 84 % of SMES. In this area, major difference was identified between the situation of SMEs in Slovakia and Finland, again, where the chi-square test resulted in the value of 0.9979. Other comparisons, showed similar values as in previous cases, no difference being noted between Cz and Sw, and Sk and Sw (chi-square of 1.00). Best result of this indicator was reached in Slovakia (88 % of companies reported coordination of at least majority of the activities), lowest percentage was noted in case of Finland (77 %).

Last examined area within this paper is the performance monitoring, where, again, the results are very positive with 84 % of companies reported systematic monitoring of at least majority of the areas. Major difference was noted between Sk and Fi, again, where the chi-square test reached the value of 0.9953, full compliance being found in the case of Fi and Sw. Best result of this indicator was reached in Slovakia, again (93 % of companies monitoring all or majority of performance indicators), lowest percentage was noted in case of Finland and Sweden (79 %).

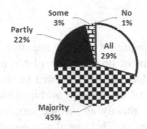

Fig. 2. Our employees know our business plans and their role in their fulfilment

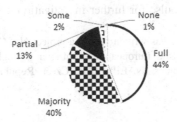

Fig. 3. Particular activities (procurement, production, marketing etc.) clearly contribute to reaching overall goals

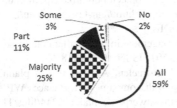

Fig. 4. We systematically monitor development of the key performance indicators

Thus, "major" difference was identified between Slovakia and Finland in the area of internal communication, where the chi-square test resulted in the lowest value – but, still, the value of 0.9941 shows almost complete compliance, which is a rather surprising result for the authors.

Lowest variability of the answers was found in the area of performance monitoring in Slovakia, where the standard deviation reached the value of 0.76 (lowest overall variability was reached in the setting objectives area – standard deviation of 0.99). Highest variability, on the other hand, was reached in the case of Slovakia in the area of setting objectives (1.01), highest overall variability being identified in the area of internal coordination (0.82).

Major limitation of the research done, represents its basis on the subjective perception of SME representatives, which might not always reflect the reality of business activities. Therefore it is too soon to make comparisons, at the moment. Authors aim on continuing with analyzing the acquired data and connect them with economic data on the companies, as far as majority of them provided also their identification details.

4   Conclusion

There is no doubt that SMEs require a specific attention in terms of general support, and specifically support in terms of providing available theoretical tools applicable in business practice. These tools have to be presented in an understandable form, which has also been the major focus of the project, within which this paper has been elaborated. Results of the project – mainly an on-line scoring and eLearning portal – are available on www.strategy4smes.cz. This portal also enables authors a continuous data collection and a good potential for further deepening of the research done.

Even though no major differences have been identified, so far, this finding also represents an interesting impulse for further investigation.

Acknowledgments. The paper was written within a project No. CZ/12/LLP-LdV/TOI/134004 financed from the support of the European Commission through the National Agency for European Educational Programmes (NAEP) of the Czech Republic, Leonardo da Vinci Call "Innovation Transfer 2012".

References

1. Eurostat. http://epp.eurostat.ec.europa.eu/portal/page/portal/eurostat/home/
2. Small Business Act for Europe. http://eur-lex.europa.eu/LexUriServ/LexUriServ.do?uri=COM:2008:0394:FIN:EN:PDF
3. Beaver, G.: Strategy and management in the smaller enterprise. Strateg. Chang. **11**(4), 175–181 (2002). doi:10.1002/jsc.591. ISSN 1086-1718
4. Jorissen, A., Laveren, E., Vanstraelen, A.: The use of planning and control practices in SME's and the relationship with company performance. WP No. 2002039 (2002) https://www.uantwerpen.be/images/uantwerpen/container1244/files/TEW%20-%20Onderzoek/Working%20Papers/RPS/2002/RPS-2002-039.pdf
5. Mazzarol, T.: Strategic management of small firms: a proposed framework for entrepreneurial ventures. In: 17th Annual SEAANZ Conference (2004)
6. Schwenk, C.R., Shrader, C.B.: Effects of formal strategic planning on financial performance in small firms: a meta analysis. Entrepreneurship Theory Pract. **17**, 53–64 (1993)
7. Perry, T.: Totožnost je príma kšeft (Identity is a perfect bargain). Doplněk, Brno (2001)
8. Rue, L.W., Ibrahim, N.A.: Boards of directors of family-owned businesses: the relationship between members' involvement and company performance. Fam. Bus. Annu. **1**(1), 14–21 (1995)
9. Smith, K.G., Gannon, M.J., Grimm, C., Mitchell, T.R.: Decision making behavior in smaller entrepreneurial and larger professionally managed firms. J. Bus. Ventur. **3**(3), 223–232 (1988)
10. Upton, N., Teal, E.J., Felan, J.T.: Strategic and business planning practices of fast growth family firms. J. Small Bus. Manage. **39**(1), 60–72 (2001)

Cities Auditing Model

Florinda Matos[✉]

IC Lab Research Centre, Intellectual Capital Accreditation Association - ICAA,
Praceta Manuel Pereira, Lote 88, 8º Esq., 2005-162 Santarém, Portugal
florinda.matos@icaa.pt

Abstract. In the last decade, the world economy has undergone numerous transformations and knowledge management, based on the management of intangible assets, became a factor of differentiation and competitiveness. Lisbon Strategy [1] and "Leipzig Charter [2] on Sustainable European Cities" both recognize that cities are "centers of knowledge and sources of growth and innovation". Developing intelligent and innovative solutions, using responsible and sustainable resources, many cities are implementing strategies for transforming themselves into a "knowledge city", but the results still have little significance, particularly because it is necessary to identify and manage the intangible assets, recognized as intellectual capital. This paper proposes an approach to audit this knowledge using the same concept of intellectual capital that is applied to companies. According to our research, auditing the intellectual capital of companies, countries or cities can be done with the same model, just changing the metrics.

Keywords: Cities · Management · Intellectual capital

1 Introduction

According the UN's "State of the World's Cities Report 2012" [3] by the middle of this century, it is expected that out of every 10 people on the planet, seven will be living in urban areas. Therefore, we need to modify the concept of city and this Report advocates for a new type of city – the city of the 21st century – that is a 'good', people centered city, one that is capable of integrating the tangible and intangible aspects of prosperity in the process of eliminating the inefficient, unsustainable forms and functionalities of the city of the previous century.

The rise of the knowledge society, where the principal asset is the intangible knowledge, has originated significant changes in cities. Some cities have been working on strategies of city branding. For example, by reducing greenhouse gas emissions by 50 % within 2030, Oslo wants to be recognized as the "green city"; by increasing its potential of knowledge, Barcelona wants to be recognized as the "city of knowledge"; by improving the design, development and perception of the capital, Vienna wants to be recognized as "the leading smart city"; by considering the gastronomy of excellence, the entertainment and the places to discover, Lisbon wants to be recognized as the "most cool city".

There are also several studies that attempt to measure the development of the cities, relating it to the investment and management in intellectual capital, but few of them

© Institute for Computer Sciences, Social Informatics and Telecommunications Engineering 2015
R. Giaffreda et al. (Eds.): IoT360 2014, Part II, LNICST 151, pp. 43–51, 2015.
DOI: 10.1007/978-3-319-19743-2_7

have sufficient objectivity and credibility to serve as strategic guidance of the construction of an ideal city or even a city branding.

Based on the literature review and preliminary studies that compare the metrics for evaluating the intellectual capital of companies with the intellectual capital of the countries, this paper presents a theoretical model supporting the audit of the management of intellectual capital of cities.

2 Representative Models and Principles Underlying the Theory

In the current context there is a large consensus on the importance of intangible assets as a source of economic competitiveness of firms, cities, regions and countries.

Although the term "intellectual capital" has its origins in a publication of Galbraith [4], we find the beginning of the movement of intellectual capital management in three distinct origins: the first, in the works of Itami [5], who studied the effects of invisible assets in the management of Japanese companies; the second, in the work of several economists (e.g. Penrose, Rumelt, and others) and finally, the third, in the work of Karl-Erik Sveiby, in Sweden, whose works gave prominence to intellectual capital.

The author gave a new vision of intellectual capital considering the intangible assets as the main strategic issue that should be used by the organizations.

Sveiby [6] developed a measurement methodology, "The Intangible Asset Monitor", by dividing the intangible assets into three groups: individual competence, internal structure and external structure. To assess the intellectual capital, this methodology is based on quantitative and qualitative indicators. "The Intangible Asset Monitor" is used by several companies around the world and offers an overview of intellectual capital. After Sveiby [6], several authors proposed models and methodologies for assessing the intellectual capital of organizations.

The further development of these models was found with authors such as Edvinsson and Malone [7]. Edvinsson and Malone [7] proposed a model, "Skandia Navigator", which divides intellectual capital into two categories: human capital and structural capital. Thus, according to this vision, intellectual capital is the sum of structural capital and human capital, being this the basic capacity for the creation of high quality value.

The macroeconomic researches on intellectual capital are more recent. These researches have emerged in the early 2000s. Researchers and some governments (particularly the Danish and the Dutch) realized that it was important to know and measure the intellectual capital of countries, regions or cities.

Academic studies, comparative analyses and macroeconomic rankings have been conducted, almost always based on the model presented by Edvinsson and Malone [7] for companies.

If we analyze the intellectual capital models applied to cities or smaller urban units (e.g. villages), we found that the literature is very similar to the literature of companies and countries, almost always considering the same concepts.

Usually, we consider two approaches: the first one, based on the measurement of intellectual capital of companies as proposed by Edvinsson and Malone [7]; the second one, based on the macro-level of countries.

There are some approaches to the subject of intellectual capital applied to cities, in particular: Carrillo [8] studied the knowledge cities, identifying three types of capital (human capital, meta-capital and instrumental capital).

Viedma [9] proposed a methodology (CICBS - Cities' Intellectual Capital Benchmarking System) to measure the intellectual capital of cities, consisting of two models: a model formed by the vision, resources, skills and indicators, based on "Skandia Navigator", and another that identifies the micro-clusters of the city.

Bossi et al. [10] adapted to the cities the methodology of intellectual capital in the public sector.

To Schiuma et al. [11], city's competitiveness depends on its innovation capacity. Authors divided city's knowledge capital into the four categories: human, relational, structural and social.

To Cabrita and Cabrita [12], the most important factors influencing cities intellectual capital are the operations of creative industries. They divided the creative industries resources into four categories: human, institutional, organizational, physical and social.

Ergazakis and Metaxiotis [13] presented the "KnowCis 2.0 methodology", a methodology proposed for the formulation of a Knowledge Cities strategy.

Alfaro, López and Nevado [14] presented the MEICC, a theoretical model to measure and evaluate the cities intellectual capital.

There are other studies that have ranked the cities, for example, the study by PricewaterhouseCoopers [15] and the studies and Mercer's Location Evaluation and Quality of Living Reports [16]. These studies have rakings of cities based on some recognized indicators of intellectual capital.

The majority of this methodologies are theoretical and so, they had little impact in the strategy of cities.

3   Cities Auditing ICM Methodology

3.1   Formulation of Hypothesis

Considering the exploration of the theory we have just held and other studies we have conducted using *Biplots* (vide Matos et al. 2014 [17]) where we try to compare the common aspects between the measurement of intellectual capital of countries and companies, we put the hypothesis:

H1 - Intellectual Capital, regardless of the object for which it is defined (countries, regions, cities or firms) is always measured based on the same components.

Aiming to verify this theoretical hypothesis, we analyzed the different methodological proposals for measuring intellectual capital of cities and concluded that it does not exist a framework accepted by the scientific community to evaluate the intellectual capital of the cities, but there is consensus about the main components.

Therefore, we can say that the main authors are unanimous in considering as components of intellectual capital: human capital, structural capital and market capital with the integration of other forms of capital (e.g. social capital).

3.2   Development of the Model

Matos and Lopes [18] proposed a dynamic model – ICM - to audit intellectual capital in the business context.

Considering that the context of cities could be similar to the context of companies, we did the adaptation of ICM to the cities and we created the Cities Auditing ICM.

According to our methodology, this model considers that the intellectual capital is a combination of Human capital, Organizational capital, Processes capital and Market capital, articulated by Networking capital and Technological capital (Fig. 1).

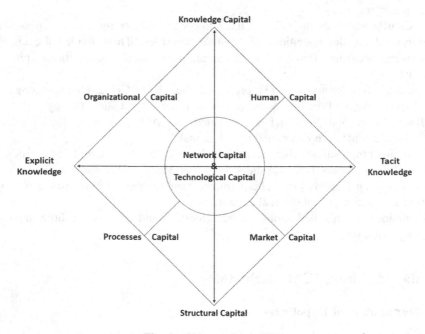

Fig. 1. Cities auditing ICM.

3.2.1   Human Capital

Human capital represents one of the most important sources of value because it is the support of the creativity and the innovation of the city, as well as the basis of renewal of the city.

Cities with aging populations have much difficulty in renewing and developing competitive performances.

Human capital can be increased and enhanced through the investment in education and training or, for example, when we take actions that promote entrepreneurship and innovation or improve the culture of citizens.

One of the main responsibilities of city governments is the investment in human capital so that it is valued and can meet the needs of the business world, so it is important that governors know how to map the knowledge of the city.

For example, if a city wants to attract investors for the development of creative industries, it has to know first if it has people with the skills needed for these industries or if it has the ability to attract people with those skills.

Cities need to attract creative talent to live and work in the city but, as in companies, this talent has to be retained and managed. Therefore, governors of cities have to create conditions so that the city is desirable, attracting and retaining the best talents.

3.2.2 Organizational Capital

Organizational capital allows the sharing of tacit knowledge from individuals and converts it into explicit knowledge or formalized in the form of specifications, process descriptions, rules, regulations, among others. When this tacit knowledge of individuals is shared with the collective, it earns a higher value and is able to become structural capital.

The effect of leadership is visible and becomes more evident in this indicator. Cities require leaders capable of managing and coordinate the different leaderships.

The organizational capital includes the political, social and economic systems and how they are articulated (e.g. the extent to which investment policies are articulated with the qualification of the population, the extent to which programs of research and development respond to the needs of businesses in the city, the extent to which public funds are properly targeted to the needs of the city).

Organizational capital can also include what some authors call "cultural capital" and "democratic capital". Cultural capital includes the values of society and the forms of cultural expression. The democratic capital includes how citizens are encouraged to participate in society and how the leaders rule the cities, promoting transparency and dialogue with citizens.

3.2.3 Processes Capital

Processes capital refers to the organizational memory that is the essence of the competitive process.

This type of knowledge covers, among other dimensions, the organizational routines or the organizational memory of the city. Organizational memory of the city represents the register of a city, represented by a set of documents and artefacts. Represents too, the detailed history of the city.

Cities have their own history, which is documented through computerized files or paper files resulting from routines that are being assimilated and standardized in procedures manuals.

Access to this information is facilitated through information management, held with the support of technologies.

This processes capital is very important because it allows the creation of more structural capital, necessary to develop the city's reputation and to attract more investors or more residents.

Processes capital helps the city to develop, improve and maximize its organizational capital.

The quality of the infrastructures of the city and the respective quality of life (e.g. cleaning, environment, social support) depends, therefore, on how the structural capital is developed and incorporated in the city's organizational processes.

In processes capital we can also find the stocks of knowledge stored in databases and how this knowledge is available to serve as a support to decision making in the management processes of the city.

The processes capital is essential for the construction of standards that command the operating rules of the city and help to generate trust, based on the predictability of processes.

The existence of electronic governance systems and the citizens' access to internet are examples of this type of capital.

In processes capital we can find too the financial reserves of the city and how the financial capital is transformed into tangible assets such as buildings, transports, roads, schools, utilities, hardware, etc.

The processes capital is essential for the differentiation of cities and the creation of city branding.

3.2.4   Market Capital

Market capital refers to how the city renews and adapts its human and organizational capital to the demands of the market, producing goods and services that can sustain its competitiveness and meet the challenges of the economy, society and environment.

For example, when the city of Oslo wants to reduce carbon emissions, what kind of innovations have to be incorporated in the city management and how it can become a brand for the city?

The correct use of knowledge management is crucial in interacting with the market and to build a stable market. There is a continued investment in innovation and development in order to meet needs previously scheduled.

Thus, this capital includes all the knowledge that the city has in the market, including indicators to know the size of the target market and potential market, clients' preferences, the purchasing decision factors and reputation or image of the city.

The analysis of the movements of this should enable indicators to predict the direction in which the city should follow their strategies for economic growth and investment attraction.

Innovation, research and development in the city is essential to keep the renewal of the capital, which is essential to competitiveness.

In this topic, we consider too the social innovation and the relation of not-profit organizations working in this area.

3.2.5   Networking and Technological Capital

Networking capital comprises both formal and informal social networks, including the interaction among citizens, city, regional, national and global environment.

Using networks, to share personal and local knowledge, the cities transform tacit knowledge into explicit knowledge, essential to the creation of wealth.

In the networking capital, we include social capital, which is essential to understand the development of a city.

The technological capital is essential to support the services and infrastructures. This capital is responsible for the interaction between the other types of capital.

3.3 Operationalization of the Model

This theoretical model will be supported by a set of intangible indicators of the intellectual capital of the cities. The list of these indicators is not definitive and static. The system should permit the installation of new data sources and the integration of these new sources in the current system configuration - without having to reprogram the entire system.

The model will allow the creation of intellectual capital indicators indices of the cities.

These indices will be based on statistical indicators of each city. These indicators should follow the research base of official data bases (e.g. national statistics and Eurostat) and will allow to create maps of positioning of each component of intellectual capital (e.g. human capital potential of a city or market capital potential of the same city).

It will be possible to build comparative maps of cities (by region, by country or even by a global region, such as the European Union) or even ratings. These maps can guide the investment and strategic planning in public policies. From these maps, we can also create more sustainable strategies for city branding

In Fig. 2, we can verify a proposal of the cities auditing ICM, considering the ideal city (thick line) and the experimental city - the city of Santarém (one of the district capitals of Portugal with 61505 inhabitants and 560.2 km^2).

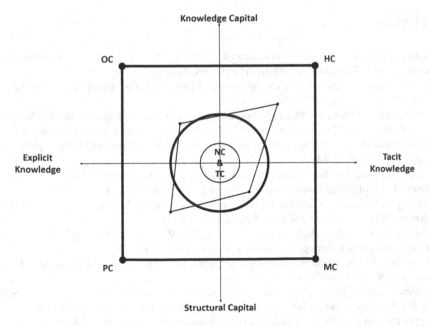

Fig. 2. Cities Auditing ICM applied to Santarém, Portugal.

An analysis of the configuration of the management of intellectual capital in this city shows that there is a good potential of human capital (about 60 %), some balance between organizational capital and processes capital (approximately 40 %–50 %), but quite imbalance in capital market (about 30 %), demonstrating a great difficulty of the city to attract investments and talents to generate innovation and renew their intellectual capital.

The network capital and technological capital also have low parameters (approximately 40 %).

The specification and a detailed description of the indicators underlying the model would allow us to draw strategic guidelines for the management of the city.

4 Conclusion

The hypothesis is confirmed: Intellectual Capital, regardless of the object for which it is defined (countries, regions, cities or firms) is always measured based on the same components.

It is possible to create a model of intellectual capital to the cities based on numerous studies that already exist at the micro-level and macro-level.

Underlying these components, we always find the enhancement of human resources, the organization of the different resources, systematization and processes control, business relations, research and development, renewal of knowledge, etc.

If cities know how to recognize and value the management of these resources, they can become more prosperous and sustainable.

References

1. European Council: Presidency conclusions (2000) http://www.consilium.europa.eu/uedocs/cms_data/docs/pressdata/en/ec/00100-r1.en0.htm. Accessed 5 July 2014
2. EUMinisters: Leipzig Charter on Sustainable European Cities. European Union, Leipzig (2007)
3. United Nations Human Settlements Programme (UN-HABITAT): State of the World's cities report 2012/2013: Prosperity of cities, United Nations (2012). http://mirror.unhabitat.org/pmss/Publications.aspx?pageview=popularDownloads&page=bookFullListingPopular. Accessed 10 July 2014
4. Galbraith, J.K.: The New Industrial State. Penguin, Harmondsworth (1969)
5. Itami, H.: Mobilizing Invisible Assets. Harvard University Press, Boston (1980)
6. Sveiby, K.E.: The New Organizational Wealth: Managing and Measuring Knowledge-Based Assets. Berrett-Koehler Publishers, San Francisco (1997)
7. Edvinsson, L., Malone, M.S.: Intellectual Capital: Realizing your Company's True Value by Finding its Hidden Brainpower. HarperBusiness, New York (1997)
8. Carrillo, F.J.: Capital cities: a taxanomy of capital accounts for knowledge cities. J. Knowl. Manage. 8(5), 28–46 (2004)
9. Viedma, J.M.: CICBS: Cities Intellectual Capital Benchmarking System. A methodology and a framework for measuring and managing intellectual capital of cities. A practical application in the city of Mataró. J. Knowl. Manage. Res. Pract. 2(1), 13–23 (2003)

10. Bossi, A., Fuertes, Y., Serrano, C.: Reflexiones en torno a la aplicación del capital intelectual en el sector público. Revista Española de Financiación y Contabilidad **34**(124), 211–245 (2005)
11. Schiuma, G., Lerro, A., Carlucci, D.: The knoware tree and the regional intellectual capital index: an assessment within Italy. J. Intellect. Capital **9**(2), 283–300 (2008)
12. Cabrita, M R, Cabrita, C.: The role of creative industries in stimulating intellectual capital in cities and regions. In: Proceedings of European Conference on Intellectual Capital, Lisbon, Portugal, 29-30 March 2010
13. Ergazakis, K., Metaxiotis, K.: Formulating integrated knowledge city development strategies: the KnowCis 2.0 methodology. Knowl. Manage. Res. Pract. **9**, 172–184 (2011)
14. Alfaro, J.L., López, V.R., Nevado, D.: A theoretical intellectual capital model applied to cities. Amfiteatru Econ. **15**(34), 455–468 (2013)
15. PricewaterhouseCoopers: Cities of opportunity (2012). http://www.pwc.com/us/en/cities-of-opportunity/index.jhtml. Accessed 1 July 2014
16. Mercer Human Resource: Consulting location evaluation and quality of living reports (2014). http://www.imercer.com/products/quality-of-living.aspx. Accessed 22 July 2014
17. Matos, F., Vairinhos, V., Cabrita, M.R.: The intellectual capital of the countries: a new perspective using biplots. In: Proceedings of the European Conference on Intellectual Capital, Slovak University of Technology (STU), Trnava, Slovak Republic, 10–11 April 2014
18. Matos, F., Lopes, A.: Intellectual capital management – SMEs accreditation methodology. In: Proceedings of the European Conference on Intellectual Capital, INHolland University of Applied Sciences, Haarlem, Netherlands, 28–29 April 2009

Smart Housing in Sustainable Development

Daniela Spirkova[1(✉)] and Dagmar Cagáňová[2]

[1] Institute of Management, Slovak University of Technology in Bratislava,
Bratislava, Slovakia
daniela.spirkova@stuba.sk
[2] Faculty of Materials Science and Technology in Trnava,
Slovak University of Technology in Bratislava, Bratislava, Slovakia
dagmar.caganova@stuba.sk

Abstract. Reducing the energy consumption is one of the pillars of sustainable development. In European scale is consumed nearly 40 % of power on operation of buildings because we spend 90 % of our time inside the buildings. Reducing energy consumption of buildings can be considered as the basis for innovative solutions for housing construction and rehabilitation of housing stock in the future which also generates significant user experience - ensuring a healthy indoor environment with an optimal design of the building. Paper presents an interesting solution of energy saving rooftop extensions - SOLTAG concept, which is the result of collaboration of experts from several countries including Slovakia.

Keywords: rooftop extension · sustainable housing · modular housing

1 Introduction

The latest initiative of the European Commission in the field of environment is to reduce CO_2 emissions, which buildings release. The newly released Directives already in some European countries contributed to energy savings of 25 to 30 % higher than previously required. Until the year 2015, the EU's energy consumption also gradually decrease. But it also means that housing will need to address issues of major importance. Statistics show that over the past decades, global energy consumption has been growing by approx. 2 % annually [1]. For the period by 2030, the reference scenario of the International Energy Agency projects a marginally slower growth in global energy consumption by 1.7 % annually. At the same time for the period, the projection expects 1.7 % annual growth in atmospheric CO_2 emissions [1]. Per capita consumption of electricity varies in different countries.

The average electricity consumption in the household sector of the energy market in Slovakia is 2.5 MWh per year and the average electricity price is approx. 140 EUR/MWh (excl. VAT). As presented above, the highest average electricity consumption in the household sector of the energy market is in Cyprus and Slovenia, with an average of 4.2 MWh and 4.0 MWh per household and year. The price of electricity (without distribution charges and VAT) is the highest in Malta and Cyprus, approx. 219 EUR/MWh and 145 EUR/MWh, respectively [2].

The new millennium is marked by new technologies and still more people's demands for comfort and quality of living are rising. Every day of an human being is

© Institute for Computer Sciences, Social Informatics and Telecommunications Engineering 2015
R. Giaffreda et al. (Eds.): IoT360 2014, Part II, LNICST 151, pp. 52–59, 2015.
DOI: 10.1007/978-3-319-19743-2_8

extremely valuable and to use it fully, it is necessary to accelerate and simplify the performance of routine activities by deployment of central management systems such as lighting, heating and air conditioning, which provide more efficient operation and reduce energy consumption and optimization, which means SMART Technologies Simply said, intelligent and smart features provide more functionalities in our houses.

Even greater savings could be achieved, however, the implementation of intelligent networks of sensors which would bring together smart homes with smart cities which current research focuses on. Subjects which are being tested are processors, sensors, and network connectivity built into articles of daily activities which may perform in the future management the role of technology in building and contributing to optimal utilization of urban resources. Except of introduction (implementation) of intelligent home control systems, it is also necessary to take into account the "green living" (environmentally friendly) and "modular housing".

Modular housing is focused on the actual needs of people and also on the possible future development of their living situations with regard to safety, optimum availability of kindergartens, schools, health facilities, offices as well as the public transport station. The modular design is based 90 % on the quality of industrially pre-prepared elements. Its advantage is that the material and facade appearance can be customized, the same types of windows and doors can be used which helps achieving a high-quality combination of old and new. The modular system can be combined also with a conventional design.

The response to demands of energy-efficiency and in terms of CO_2 -neutral housing of the future has become the SOLTAG project, which is the result of cooperation between urban planners, architects, experts on energy and daylight, research institutes, university departments, housing associations and manufacturing companies from housing sector which are dealing with energy efficiency of buildings. This system is designed as a solution for adaptation of roof - a flat (module), which can be built up on existing residential buildings with flat roofs, without the need of connecting it to the current energy system of the building. Principles of the project can also be used in new buildings [3].

2 SOLTAG Project – Modern and Sustainable Way of Housing

Approximately 60 % of investments in the construction sector of Europe are in the fields of conversion, revitalization, restoration and rehabilitation. Most projects try to involve important current topics, such as sustainability, material saving, increasing the supply of housing and enlarging the building itself.

Building the housing units on the roof of existing buildings can meet the criteria of modern era for housing reconstruction. It enables to extend the housing space in the building, modernize the facilities, and adapt the housing units to the modern requirements, and to the segmentation of the housing demand. The construction of the new housing units does not require the additional space, so it is sustainable from the view of land saving. The new housing units do not need the new foundations, and thus a large quantity of saved materials and the amount of diminished construction waste. Related flow of materials is reduced. Rooftop extension also enables solving the problem of the flat roofs that are not very suitable for the climate with frequent precipitation and icy winters. The leaking roofs then have to be repaired frequently. Sloping roofs on the contrary have the longer lifespan, can add the additional architectural value to refurbished building and the space under the sloping roofs is than effectively used for attics [4].

The really high effects from the rooftop extensions can be achieved when sustainability measures, renovation of all building and energy efficiency measures are combined together with the housing market analysis. Situation in housing market can be the source of the new opportunities. For instance there may be the demand for the penthouses, high quality, non-standard elegant houses that may cover more than one floor, and may have the garden on the roof as well. The roofs of the houses are suitable for the construction of such housing units, especially if there are nice views from the rooftops on surrounding areas which are highly valued by many families. Refurbished buildings, together with the revitalization of the surrounding areas have important positive externalities for the area. As a result of it, the local market value of the housing units grows and more positive tenant mix can be achieved, although in some examples the effects of the gentrification may be expected. Surely enough, the bank which provides the mortgage credits for the clients in rooftop extensions should benefit from the rising value of the real estate that reduce their mortgage risk. Comprehensive refurbishment also provides the opportunity to make the existing housing stocks more enjoyable by for instance with enlarging the balconies or rearranging the facade. Adding the additional housing units may help also to solve some of the problems of family life cycle. Older families may need less space for living, because they already had raised children, however they do not want to move out from their habitual neighborhood. Therefore if they obtain the possibility to move to the new smaller housing units, on the rooftop, they may be quite satisfied. Although many high-rise buildings need renovation, they are often situated in the attractive areas of the town, for instance close to the centre, or in relatively quiet environment. After their refurbishment, their value can substantially increase.

The new housing units on the top of the buildings may become the interesting source of revenue for the owners. From such revenues, the costs of the older refurbished part of the building can be partly offset. This moment is especially important for the social houses, but also for the condominiums. For instance in the Eastern European countries people often lack the necessary resources to pay the full costs of the building renovation. Revenues from selling the rooftop extension may become the additional source of financing such reconstruction, so the financial burden is reduced.

The important initiative in the area of the refurbishment of the panel housing is SURE-Fit (Sustainable Roof Extension Retrofit) project funded by the European Commission in the framework of Intelligent Energy program. The project is oriented on the rooftop extension retrofit for high-rise social housing in Europe. Participants in the projects are Netherlands, France, Germany, Italy, Slovakia, Czech Republic, Poland, Sweden and Denmark. The main goals of the project are defined as:

1. Consolidate the existing cutting edge technologies and best practices of roof top extension retrofit for high-rise social housing and develop process models and custom-made guidelines for broader implementing the innovative solution in Europe.

2. Disseminate the knowledge and promoting the application of the integration of small-scale RES (renewable energy systems) installations, particularly PV panels, into the rooftop extension retrofit for high-rise social housing in Europe.

The rooftop extension as defined in the project may help to cope with several problems of the high-rise buildings. First of all it is the funding of their comprehensive refurbishment. Selling the additional housing units on the rooftop enables to create the additional financial sources that can be used for the refurbishment of the whole multiple-family houses, making the financial burden for the existing owners lower. The use of innovative technologies, such as better insulation materials, photovoltaic (PV) modules etc. enables to produce the energy neutral housing units on the top of existing houses.

The important moment of the retrofit scheme is intelligent flexible design (IFD) of the new housing units. Approach of IFD buildings includes:

- a smart, systemized approach of producing and delivering affordable and comfortable roof top extensions,
- a reduction of waste production (re-use of existing building structures, possible re-use of demountable and modular IFD components),
- less maintenance which is required over the building's lifetime.

The refurbished building may stimulate urban area improvement as a joint effort between the local authority, housing associations, market parties, and the citizens [5].

The current trend of reducing the energy consumption of buildings is an ideal solution for low energy concept. Technology of those houses, however, requires stricter requirements for theoretical preparation of the project - proper selection of building components and particularly the observance of technological processes and quality of construction.

The complex project in the use of prefabricated systems (see Figs. 1, 2 and 3) is the SOLTAG concept. This system uses energy roof, which integrates sunlight with photovoltaic cells. The basis of the system was to achieve a balance between heat gain, insulation capacity and air exchange. Thus designed house can be described as "energy production plant", which in addition to savings has also pleasing and healthy indoor environment.

Sample house of this type was able to realize in 2005 by an expert within Demohouse project research in Denmark. SOLTAG is an example of the future sustainable housing. It responds to the strict European Union legislation in the field of reducing CO_2 emissions and also reduce overall energy consumption in the construction. The house is designed as a pair of prefabricated modules that forms the rooftop extension of the apartment buildings built in the 60−70 years.

The concept of roof extensions SOLTAG was included in the international project ANNEX 60 - Building restoration with the use of prefabricated systems. The aim of this project is to evaluate the advantages and possibilities of prefabrication in the reconstruction of existing residential buildings, to improve quality and accelerate the implementation of measures which result is the achievement of low-energy standard. According to experts, the project builds on trends in the approach to reduce energy consumption of buildings in Western Europe, where high hopes are put just into

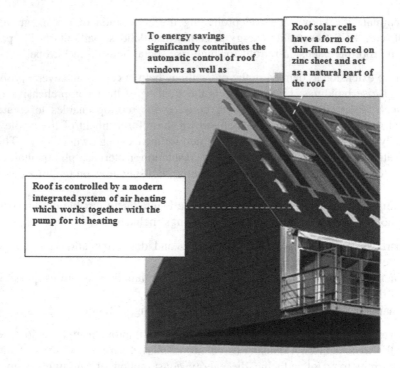

Fig. 1. Energy roof superstructure of SOLTAG concept [3]

Fig. 2. SOLTAG project - prefabricated system [3]

prefabricated systems, reducing the energy intensity of older buildings and the construction level of the maximum extension of the physical and moral life of the building.

3 Potential of Rooftop Extensions in Europe

The SURE-Fit team tried to estimate the maximum theoretical potential of the rooftop extensions in Europe. The methodological approach has been following. On the basis of the national statistics, the number of low-rise building (the buildings with maximum

Fig. 3. Rooftop extension (SOLTAG system) in the City Copenhagen, Denmark [6]

of eight floors) was found. From this number, the selected buildings were from years from 1960 to 1980. According to the opinion of the expert team, it does not make sense to build the rooftop extension on older buildings because their lifespan will be too short or they may be protected as the historical buildings. Roof topping on the buildings built after 1980 could be less efficient, because these buildings will need comprehensive refurbishment later, and they are also more energy efficient. Later the experts defined on how many low-rise buildings (built from 1960−80) the rooftop extensions could be mounted [6]. The resulting appraisal of number of buildings suitable for rooftop extensions depended on the character of housing ownership in the different countries and the expert opinions. The resulting estimation of the potential is shown in the following Table 1. A total number of 7,369,763 dwellings belongs to the theoretical potential of the rooftop extensions in Europe.

Table 1. Potential of rooftop extensions in Europe [7]

	Total # Dwellings	Multi-family	Low-rise	Built '60-'80	Max. potential
WEST EUROPE					
Austria	3,261,368	1,699,173	1,359,338	429,551	211,554
Belgium	4,097,125	1,028,378	984,158	245,165	87,397
France	28,668,114	12,413,293	7,855,063	2,694,287	987,456
Germany	38,709,853	20,864,611	1,9612,734	9,620,217	600,000
Luxembourg	171,870	50,014	41,912	11,830	6,719
Netherlands	6,634,647	2,063,375	1,925,129	965,928	391,201
NORDIC					
Denmark	2,540,543	985,731	883,215	282,756	35,000
Finland	2,548,043	1,467,673	1144785	585257	32,7744
Sweden	4,312,018	2,237,937	1,790,350	662,429	314,654
SOUTH EUROPE					
Greece	5,467,049	2,219,622	1,775,697	783,083	214,565
Italy	27,300,961	20,311,915	1,5701,110	6566029	807153
Portugal	5,044,526	1,140,063	1,115,438	420,007	111,932
Spain	20,954,701	9,953,483	6,907,717	3,666,944	1,245,844

(Continued)

Table 1. (*Continued*)

	Total # Dwellings	Multi-family	Low-rise	Built '60-'80	Max. potential
GREAT BRITAIN & IRELAND					
Ireland	1,281,840	110,238	8,8191	22,753	10,683
Great Britain	21,130,360	3,951,377	3,856,544	1,218,263	732,176
CENTRAL EUROPE					
Czech Republic	3,826,042	2,161,714	1,431,055	65,8493	60,000
Hungary	4,313,887	1,449,466	1,113,190	535,094	145,813
Poland	12,535,678	7,910,013	4,833,018	1,798,800	741,106
Slovakia	1,667,631	858,830	536,769	281310	104,085
Slovenia	777,758	220,883	193,494	109281	35,626
NORTH EAST EUROPE					
Estonia	617,440	421,094	336,875	168775	43,881
Latvia	958,085	679,283	543,426	219,544	74,645
Lithuania	1,292,554	791,043	632,834	202,507	55,487
TOTAL	**19,8583,96**	**95,049,225**	**74,778,852**	**32,191,958**	**7,369,763**
		48 %	**38 %**		**4 %**

4   Conclusion

Reducing the energy consumption of buildings, reducing CO_2 emissions and increasing the share of renewable energy sources in the construction and reconstruction is a hot topic which nearly all the countries of Europe and the world deals with now. Most of these problems are connected to housing renovation and equipment in a way that the technical solution significantly improved their thermal characteristics as well as the effectiveness and efficiency of technical equipment. SOLTAG project is addressing a modern and sustainable way of living, which uses the latest knowledge and technology to reduce energy consumption of buildings. Described concept is an example of using the prefabrication system in the reconstruction of existing residential buildings, which has great advantages in faster and more efficiently improving the quality of the reconstruction work during the implementation. Offers the possibility to optimize the prefabricated panels with improved thermal insulating integrated in the latest technology and last but not least, with lower production costs thanks to repeatability and variability of solutions.

Acknowledgments. This paper is supported by grant VEGA no. 1/1013/12 "Economic aspects of energy savings in buildings".

References

1. World Energy Scenarios. Composing energy futures to 2050. World Energy Council, United Kingdom (2014)
2. Janicek, F., et al.: Renewable Energy Sources 1. Faculty of Electrical Engineering and Information Technology, Slovak University of Technology, Bratislava (2009)
3. SOLTAG – Energy housing. Velux materials (2009)

4. World Economic Forum. The Global Competitiveness Report 2010–2011. http://www3. weforum.org/docs/WEF_GlobalCompetitivenessReport_2010-11.pdf
5. Szekeres, K.: Experimental housing the new way of sustainable building constructions. Real Estate and Housing. Vol. 2. (2009)
6. Spirkova, D., Ivanicka, K., Zubkova, M.: Economic aspects of sustainable development of built environment in Europe. MCDP International UG, Germany (2013)
7. Potential Study. Study of the potential for rooftop extension retrofit of energy efficiency in social housing. Part I/II pp. 32– 34 (2007)

Parking Zero

George Teodorescu[(⊠)]

International Institute for Integral Innovation, Danubius Academic Consortium,
Am Wingert 38, 50999 Cologne, Germany
george_teodorescu@yahoo.de
www.integralinnovation.org

Abstract. The impact of innovation might end up in an unexpected fall out of problems, which need an even more creative outcome for getting solved.

The automotive car seemed to fulfill the dream of personal mobility, but generated two human generations later, by tremendous acceptance worldwide, many of the thorny problems and even conflicts, which we have to deal with today.

The absurd paradox is the urban immobility, the result of the stand by cars on the drive ways and parking lots, which shrink aggressively the available surface and hinder the traffic.

We are addressing the topic and the potential ways to addressing it, with a vision.

1 Reasons

Every major innovation is a great promise to fulfill an expectation and many are able to fulfill the desire at least for a time. Some of them are so successfully, that by their dissemination new problems rise, which are growing bigger than the initial one, the innovation has been supposed to solve.

A cascade of subsequent innovations follows, addressing down the stream the problems, created by previous solutions.

This fractal pattern is nowhere else more evident than along the major coordinate of life, which is the mobility.

Mobility is inherent to the life, as it answers the existential need for browsing options and reaching targets. Mobility is about the reach, the encompassed distance.

Along the time and across the civilizations, the human mobility was determined either by the own fitness or by biological or material carriers. These carriers came with an additional volume, which was left behind or in stand by after reaching the target.

Howsoever these external platforms have been: either other humans or animals, either palanquins or rickshaws, either carriages or motorized cars, they always required a special surface for the stand by time, "the parking place".

The situation grew dramatically with the multiuser and heavy duty motor vehicles, which grew from 980 millions in 2009 to 1015 millions in 2010 and since then shows a growth rate of more than 35 millions vehicles an year.

In order to figure out one billion cars, just remember, that a parking lot needs a fairly large space, around 25 m^2, this is just 40,000 cars /km^2. One billion cars needs

© Institute for Computer Sciences, Social Informatics and Telecommunications Engineering 2015
R. Giaffreda et al. (Eds.): IoT360 2014, Part II, LNICST 151, pp. 60–63, 2015.
DOI: 10.1007/978-3-319-19743-2_9

hence a neat 25,000 km^2, roughly the surface of Belgium and is growing by 1,000 km^2 every year. This loss of living surface is worse than earth warming and the consequent growth of the planetary ocean level.

More scaring is the stationary image of this huge surface for most of the time, as a car is used in average just 200 h an year.

We have reached the stage of URBAN IMMOBILITY.

All these figures show, the need a radical, new approach.

We need disruptive concepts, enhancing the usual human reach, without letting any "vehicle" behind, realizing a reminder-less mobility.

They are some options, which have been already addressed:

– **Fitness** (slides)
   This enables one's natural walking capacity and maintains his endurance, but doesn't extend the reach.
– **Enhancing the walking skills** (slides)
   Understanding the human potential and dynamic of walking and optimizing the walking procedure.
      The Olympic "Walking" competition induced a process of optimizing the walking procedure, which might be efficient, but is acceptable on running track only.
– **Plyometrics** (slides)
   The jump and the equipment enhanced jump are great sport challenges, but no procedures for urban mobility, even if sometimes happens.
– **Exoskeleton aided walking** (slides)
   There is an intensive research and a lot experimental output, mainly for rescue and military purposes. Exoskeletons and leg bound equipment enhances many times the endurance even under heavy loads.
      It might promise relieve for elderly and other motoric impaired people.
      The cyborg character of this equipment must be overcome, in order to reach a more general acceptance in the future.
– **Wearable** (slides)
   Even if in the same conceptual segment like the exoskeletons, the "wearable one's" impact is just the interface between the street and human.
      Started in early XX century as "skates", the wearable's diversified as typology, some of them getting motorized, but managed to leave behind the sport and play grounds, getting a large presence in the urban environment. They enhance manifold the reach and even the speed and show a major Urban Mobility potential, accompanying the owner everywhere and not affecting in stand by the street or side walk.
– **Portable** (slides)
   They are venerable as well and show a spectacular development either as boards, power boards or foldable and portable wheeled platforms.
      The acceptance is even higher than of the wearable ones. When in use remind the urban bicycle or scooter.
      Lightweight, compact and expensive the portables are stored indoors and don't crowd the public urban space.

– **Mobile sidewalks** (slides)

Result of a creative mental process of inversion, the mobile sidewalks seemed to be a curiosity of the end of XIX century exhibitions.

However they managed to develop recently to human conveyors endorsing the mobility indoors, for short tracks in airports and malls.

The mechanical drive is limiting the application field.

There is a serious potential to develop the street and sidewalk to a dynamic vector from the passive surface of today.

A special approach is the "Mobile Road" concept, which has been realized as a Moving Sidewalk and as a Shared Vehicle system.

They are concepts of autonomous vehicles, like Google's SDC, Self Driving Car, which are increasing the operating time by sharing vehicle system. They are still volume presences in stand by and planked surfaces on the street.

Their success will recreate the actual problem within a short time.

– **Shrinking the stand by vehicle** (slides)

The foldable object, from the tent to the yurt, is the attribute of the traveller, of the ephemeral, of the mobility per se.

The conceptual proximity should have invited to reflect about the collapsible, implosive, foldable vehicle and it did.

Sharing the mobile platform, which becomes a dynamic vector of the street, leaves still a stationary, parked platform behind, but increases her frequency of use.

Shrinking Vehicle is a better option of shared use with minimal footprint in parking position. We have dedicated a special attention to this approach in the project "Bus-Bank".

Many urban areas have rails for streetcars or the peripheral rail system. The problem is the stations, which are bottlenecks, supposed to be reached and the trains, which have their own schedule and the inconveniences of mass transportation.

But the rails have the major advantage of a smooth ride on a metal track, which can transport information and energy.

These features would help overcome the energy storage disadvantage inherent to electrical cars and open a new dimension to the urban mobility.

In our solution we are considering the "minimal footprint in parking" criteria, reducing occupied surface in stand by foldable capacity and sharing the use. (Animation)

– **Dematerialization**

The ideal vehicle is having a presence just in use, fading away after that, in order to return into materiality, when is needed.

Fernando Cortés gave this example as he burnt down his ships, after reaching the American shore. He meant "no way back", but gave an example of "just for a ride" expandable mobility platform.

However we would like this way, Einstein says perhaps, sir Isaac Newton says "nothing is for free = entropy".

- **Virtual Presence** (slides)
    We have started wondering, how the car, promising ultimate personal mobility led soon to urban i-mobility for all.
    As usually, there is another conceptual space, where a radical approach is coming from, virtual reality.

There is a significant progress in holographic representation and cave technology, allowing realistic 3D visual presence. These telecommunication tools are beyond the experimental stage and promise some relieve to the schedule and traffic problems related to the business meetings.
    This horizon of Immobile Ubiquity shall not be the ultimate urban mobility bliss.
    PARKING ZERO, "the parking lot in the trunk" is still a challenge to the human creativity and I want to invite you all, to accept this challenge, inviting you to a PARKING ZERO contest of concepts.
    Meanwhile the available world is shrinking by 1000 sq/km an year for parking.
    It is time for action!
    Our Danubius Academic Consortium invites the students from Europe, to address successfully the topic of mobility without leftovers.
    We would win for the life 25,000 km^2 plus 1,000 km^2 every year. This is a lot, a great award.
    Join us!

2 Conclusion

The emerging horizon of Immobile Ubiquity shall not be the ultimate urban mobility bliss. It is up to our creative power. Let's overcome the expected by unusual, disruptive new concepts.

Informatization of Rail Freight Transport by Applying RF Identification Technology

Michal Balog[1(✉)], Pavol Semanco[1], and Zofia Simeková[2]

[1] Faculty of Manufacturing Technologies with a Seat in Presov,
Technical University of Kosice, Bayerova 1, 08001 Presov, Slovakia
{michal.balog,pavol.semanco}@tuke.sk
[2] Faculty of Mining, Ecology, Process Control and Geotechnology,
Technical University of Kosice, Letna 9, 04200 Kosice, Slovakia
zofia.simekova@tuke.sk

Abstract. The purpose of the paper is to outline advantages and obstacles of RFID application in informatization of the rail freight transport. Development and improvement in the field of information technologies and automatization are the pillars towards increase of operations and transaction effectiveness in rail freight transport. This research analyzes and describes range of RFID technology application in rail freight transport. Subsequently, we designed the experiment to test a functionality of the RFID system. In order to ensure the reliable results, we used railroad model that reflects infrastructure of the actual railroad together with station interlocking system, line signaling and level crossing systems managed via unified active control place. For experimentation purpose Taguchi design of experiment was applied to analyze the variation of the essential controllable factors. However, it has to be kept in mind that final effect of the experiment depends on a level of physical resemblance between inputs and reality.

Keywords: Cargo · Transport · RFID · Experiment · Taguchi · Telematics

1 Introduction

One of the systems that successfully develops and fits into the concept of transport telematics is automated identification working on the basis of radiofrequency identification technology. From the current open literature and other sources it is evident that RFID technology has a wide-range of application in almost every field of our life. Figure 1 depicts current usage of RFID technology in transport. Considering the fact that it is expected from the rail transport to be driving force in transport of materials of heavy and power industry, the problem of traceability improvement of materials transported by railroad is actual and on place. Use of RFID in the rail transport (only 17 %) shows the extensive possibilities to enhance innovative research into traceability improvement in rail freight transport.

The intention of the paper is to identify and describe major application areas where RFID technology is used in the rail transport. The second part of the paper is dedicated to experiment where we test the functionality of the RFID system. [2].

© Institute for Computer Sciences, Social Informatics and Telecommunications Engineering 2015
R. Giaffreda et al. (Eds.): IoT360 2014, Part II, LNICST 151, pp. 64–69, 2015.
DOI: 10.1007/978-3-319-19743-2_10

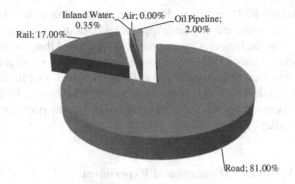

Fig. 1. Use of RF identification technology in transport in the world [3]

2 Background and Motivation

Focusing on rail transport we depicted the main application areas of RFID technology in rail freight transport. We identified five main domains: traceability of the cargo, positioning of the train unit in cooperation with GPS and within the train unit, automated data collection of the shipment, smart wagons.

The RFID tag is attached on specific place where the functionalities of the tag and whole RFID system are established. Consequently, traceability and automated data collection by employing RFID tags can be used in terms of rail freight transport for train unit, individual wagons, cargo care, or particular product. In tracking and tracing of the shipment in rail freight transport GPS space-based navigation system is widely used in rail freight transport that it can localize RFID tag with GPS module mounted on the transport unit.

The motivation of the paper is the fact that wagons identification is nowadays still done manually by workers on entering to the station. These workers have to do a visual inspection of the train unit and railroad consignment notes. After this procedure another staff member input data into information system. Applying RFID technology the ID of train unit and wagons would be automatically loaded into information systems through RFID gate that would be located on entering the station.

In summary automatic RF identification for the rail transport offers many advantages i.e. accurate evidence of the wagons, automatic maintenance and quality control, increased safety for operator and maintenance staff etc. These and others advantages are based on studies of good practices of successfully implemented RFID technology into rail industry.

For the experimental purposes we used the training simulator with the railroad model set where we analyzed the reading performance of the RFID tag attached on the transport unit.

3 Analysis of the Reading Performance of RFID System

In the experiment we tested the reading performance of the RFID system for railroad model set to find out the factors that affect the reading performance of the RFID significantly. In our RFID system configuration the RFID tag is mounted on the moving object and the RFID reader with antenna are stationary. We decided to apply design of experiments using the Taguchi Approach [1]. In the experiment, we took into consideration all possible factors. Consequently, we included three controllable factors and two noise factors. This RFID system configuration works in ultra high frequency (UHF) spectrum specifically within the 860 to 960 MHz band. The Impinj RFID reader and the software (multireader 6.4) were used. UHF RFID-tag AD 223 is weather resistant, and for special purposes it can be encapsulated in the package with thermally and chemically resistant silver coating.

3.1 Design of Parameter Diagram and Experiment

While designing and establishing a static P-diagram (Fig. 2), we identified possible noise factors. Considering these factors and other relevant circumstances, we finally selected and set two uncontrollable factors: the cargo on the wagon and existence of electromagnetic interferences nearby. In the experiment we also assumed three controllable factors to be adjusted by the users. The final parameter diagram is depicted in Fig. 4 below.

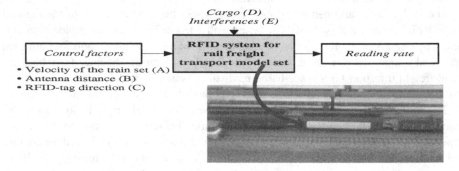

Fig. 2. Static P-diagram

In the study we selected L9 orthogonal array for the controllable factors (parameters) with three levels of parameter settings, and L4 orthogonal array was chosen for two noise factors, where each factor is given by two levels. The selected controllable and noise factors are given in Table 1. For this RFID test, the reading rate was chosen as quality characteristic. We also analyzed the impact of RFID-tag orientation on the wagon and distance from the reader on output reading rate.

For controllable factors we used The L9 orthogonal array with three columns and nine rows, which is in total of 36 trials. Where each selected parameter was assigned to a column and nine controllable parameter combinations were tested.

The advantage of the Taguchi approach for design of experiments is that only nine experiment trials are required to explore the entire parameter space using L9. The experimental layout of controllable parameters using L9 orthogonal array is shown in Table 2. For noise factors we used The L4 orthogonal array with two columns and four

Table 1. Factors and levels

Parameter designation	Parameter	Range [unit]	Level 1	Level 2	Level 3
A	Velocity of train unit	40–126 [kmph]	40	80	126
B	Distance of Antenna	0,5–3 [m]	0.5	1	3
C	Direction of RFID tag	–	Long Edge	Upper	Short Edge
D	Interferences	0,1	none	with interferences	–
E	Cargo	0,1	empty	with cargo	–

rows, which resulted in four samples for each experiment run (Table 3). Our study focuses on maximization of the signal to noise ratio that means the less quality loss of reading rate. The SN equation is expressed by Eq. 1.

$$SN = -10\log_{10}\left(1/n \sum_{i=1}^{n} 1/y_i^2\right) \tag{1}$$

Table 2. Combinations of controllable parameters

Expt. No.	Velocity of train unit [kmph]	Distance of Antenna [m]	Direction of RFID tag
	A	B	C
1	40	0.5	Long Edge
2	40	1	Upper
3	40	3	Short Edge
4	80	0.5	Upper
5	80	1	Short Edge
6	80	3	Long Edge
7	126	0.5	Short Edge
8	126	1	Long Edge
9	126	3	Upper

Table 3. Combinations of uncontrollable parameters

Noise factor /Sample No.	1	2	3	4
Interferences D	none	none	with interferences	with interferences
Cargo E	empty	with cargo	empty	with cargo

3.2   Results

Each control factor of given experiment is adjustable and has three levels. In the experiment, we observed SN ratio, which is the most important measurement of variation in the RFID quality characteristic (reading rate). The summarized data with reading rate translated into SN ratio is listed in Table 4.

Table 4. Experiment results with S/N ratio

Expt. run	Factors		DxE	Sample 1	Sample 2	Sample 3	Sample 4	Mean	S.D.	S/N
	A	B	C							
1	1	1	1	18.80	18.80	15.70	15.70	17.25	1.790	24.63
2	1	2	2	19.60	19.60	18.50	18.50	19.05	0.635	25.59
3	1	3	3	21.30	21.30	19.10	19.10	20.2	1.270	26.07
4	2	1	2	15.20	15.20	10.00	10.00	12.6	3.002	21.45
5	2	2	3	16.50	16.50	14.50	14.50	15.5	1.155	23.75
6	2	3	1	20.30	20.30	18.20	18.20	19.25	1.212	25.65
7	3	1	3	17.10	17.10	14.60	14.60	15.85	1.443	23.92
8	3	2	1	20.60	20.60	18.20	18.00	19.35	1.446	25.68
9	3	3	2	17.80	17.80	16.30	16.30	17.05	0.866	24.61

The overall mean reading rate is 17.34. From the practical point of view it is needed only one RFID tag read. The overall mean S/N ratio is 24.58 dB. To find an optimal combination of parameters setting, we extracted S/N figures of each level of each control factor from the experiment results and expressed it in the form graph diagram shown in Fig. 3. Subsequently, we distinguished the optimum settings of control factors. The bold numbers in Fig. 3 represent optimal level combination for each control factor.

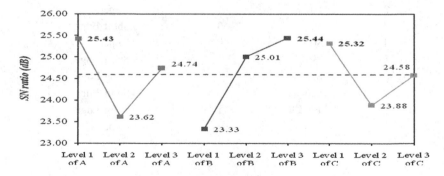

Fig. 3. SN effect plot for control factor

Subsequently, the interaction among control factors was analyzed. An interaction between control factors occurs when the effect of one control factor is dependent on another control factor. From the Fig. 4 it is evident that only one significantly interaction occurred between control factor A and C, particularly.

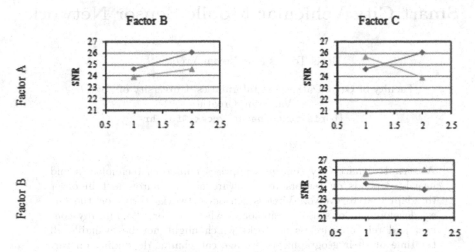

Fig. 4. SN effect plot for control factor

4 Conclusion

The subsequent conclusions were drawn from the presented study. The analysis of experiment results showed that the velocity of model of electric locomotive, distance of the antenna from RFID tag, and direction of the tag are these parameters that affect the reading performance of the system. Specifically, parameters A_1, B_3, and C_1 performed as the best combination in experiment. Subsequently, we verified the existing inter-action between velocity of the train set and the RFID-tag direction. The results are valid within the above range of the controllable parameters and for specified RFID system configuration. In the experiment RFID components were adapted to the conditions of railroad model.

Research reported in this paper was supported by EU Structural Funds within the project"Promotion & Enhancement of Center for Research on Transportation" ITMS code 26220220160.

"We support research activities in Slovakia / Project is co-financed by the EU"

References

1. Kern, C.: Radio-frequency-identification for security and media circulation in libraries. Electron. Libr. **22**(4), 317–324 (2004). 0264-0473
2. Lahiri, S.: RFID Sourcebook. IBM Press, New York (2005). ISBN -10: 0-13-185137
3. Banks, J., et al.: RFID Applied. John Wiley and Sons, New Jersey (2007). ISBN 978-0471-79365-6

Smart City Vehicular Mobile Sensor Network

Boris Tomaš and Neven Vrček[✉]

Faculty of Organization and Informatics, University of Zagreb,
Varaždin, Croatia
{boris.tomas,neven.vrcek}@foi.hr

Abstract. Smart City concept comprises numerous technologies and heavily depends on sensors to be aware of its environment in order to adapt and to evolve. Wireless sensors networks thrive on the latest development of sensor technologies where sensors dynamically connect and rely on wireless networks which might not be available all the time or their geographical coverage can change depending on various circumstances. Special challenge are mobile wireless sensors where data transmission can be significantly obstructed. Therefore in a Smart City environment sensor data can be gathered by using powerful sensors on mobile devices(smart-phones), static sensors or vehicular sensors that rely on heterogeneous and changing network infrastructure. This paper presents one possible approach to build such network infrastructure where vehicular networks, augmented with existing city's WiFi network, can be used to transmit (relay) and gather sensor data.

Keywords: Smart city · Sensor network · WiFi sensor

1 Introduction

One way to cope with challenges of modern urban environment (increasing population, pollution, energy consumption, etc.) and to introduce city to a next century is by making it smart. Smart cites leverage the benefits gained from using modern technologies to improve life of citizens and city integration into natural and eco-friendly environment. Governance of the city may benefit of modern technologies by properly responding to incidents, reallocating resources based on new environment conditions or any unnatural issues like accidents or disasters. Cities are highly integrated with traffic infrastructure meaning networks of roads and vehicles them-self. Therefore, along with standard infrastructure facilities such as water supply or electricity, smart city development is highly dependent on development of traffic infrastructure i.e. roads and streets because they are potential location of sensors and data transfer paths. Also, road infrastructure is used by modern vehicles that are becoming increasingly smart and heavily equipped with sensors and actuators. These, already existing, vehicular functionalities can be further enhanced by making vehicles capable of gathering more general sensor data and also become data transfer points of such heterogeneous mobile sensor network. Combining stationary and mobile sensors and network

© Institute for Computer Sciences, Social Informatics and Telecommunications Engineering 2015
R. Giaffreda et al. (Eds.): IoT360 2014, Part II, LNICST 151, pp. 70–77, 2015.
DOI: 10.1007/978-3-319-19743-2_11

technologies into agile, error prone, modern and powerful network can prove to be valuable data infrastructure of smart cities. However, such network faces it's own challenges in which some points are stationary and some are mobile and there is constant need to determine best possible path for data transfer. What we want to achieve is constant presence of sensors in all parts of the city and their inter-connection without heavy investment into stationary network infrastructure. To achieve this we should use heterogeneous approach that will utilize all possi-ble network access points and achieve dynamic interconnection of all possible smart devices and sensors. By such approach we can develop robust information nervous system capable of functioning in various circumstances.

2 Related Work

Next section reviews state of the art and some of the major research directions in modern vehicular sensor networks.

2.1 Smart Cities

In the future, cities will account for nearly 90 % of global population growth, 80 % of wealth creation, and 60 % of total energy consumption. Developing better strategies for the creation of new cities, is therefore, a global imperative [1]. Besides global world initiative, according to [2] EU has intensive strategy to increase Competitiveness and Innovation, promote development of Smart Cities and Future Internet. Important part of this strategy are smart cities. EU strategy related to smart cities is shown on Fig. 1 as a roadmap towards year 2020. EU Smart city strategy contains four main directions:

- Building
- Heating & Cooling
- Electricity
- Transport

A city is considered smart when investments in human and social capital align with development of traditional (transport) and modern (ICT) communication infrastructure to fuel sustainable economic growth and a high quality of life, with a wise management of natural resources, through participatory governance [4]. It is noticeable that beside utilizing technological development, making a city smart requires a lot of government agility and political will to change and adapt. Many initiatives and definitions of a Smart City recognize transportation as notable element that makes the backbone of Smart City infrastructure. Across Europe there are many attempts and examples of Smart Cities, Centre of Regional Science [5] has created the list of smart cities in Europe according to several criteria, top 10 cities on the list are:

1. Luxembourg (LU)
2. Aarhus (DK)

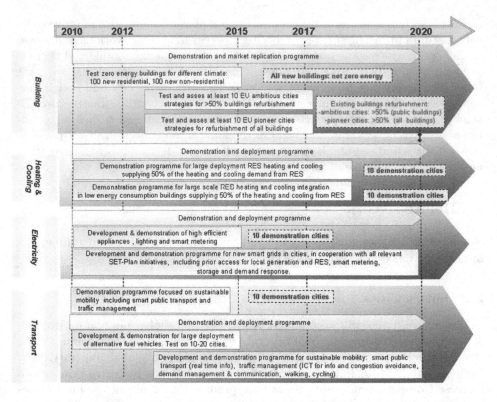

Fig. 1. EU Smart cities roadmap [3]

3. Turku (FI)
4. Aalborg (DK)
5. Odense (DK)
6. Tampere (FI)
7. Oulu (FI)
8. Eindhoven (NL)
9. Linz (AT)
10. Salzburg (AT)

Complete study considered 70 cities across Europe.

Future Cities Project. One, recent (2013) and notable project gathers a lot of attention and is supported by EU funds (2.5 million EUR). Purpose of this Future Cities Project[1] is to transform city of Porto into a living laboratory, currently more than 900 sensors have been installed around the city of Porto [6]. Project is coordinated by Competence Centre for the Cities of the Future at Faculty of Engineering of University of Porto. Along with several European universities, project partners are notable USA universities: MIT and Carnegie Mellon University, which makes this project worldwide.

---

[1] futurecities.up.pt.

2.2   Wireless Sensor Networks

A wireless sensor network is distributed network of independent sensors that monitor environmental conditions like: temperature, pollution, traffic, noise, air pressure,... Data gathered by one node is propagated throughout entire network, usually towards consuming nodes. Figure 2 shows sample wireless sensor network. According to [7] it is usual for a sensor nodes to communicate using wireless radio technology e.g. WiFi. However we must note that standard WiFi might not be always available and there must be alternative approach to transfer data. One of such alternatives is using vehicles as sensors and data transfer points at the same time. Vehicles are ideal because they move along entire city and can gather various data and provide strong alternative to standard network infrastructure. Vehicular ad-hoc networks (VANET) [8] provide new and integrated approach toward sensor networks. In urban environments it is convenient to have existing infrastructure restructured for a new use, thus: instead of making a new infrastructure and construction endeavors, authors suggest using vehicular networks for sensor communication.

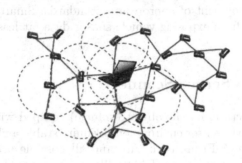

Fig. 2. Example of a wireless sensor network based on the Berkeley mote platform. The circles represent the transmission range of each node, which are connected by radio links (represented by edges) to all other nodes within range. [source: [7]]

2.3   Modern Vehicle as Sensor

Traffic networks in the city connect every essential entity (location) in the city. In essence traffic networks make the city. Using traffic, people and goods move inside and outside the city. Because of this mobility and omnipresence traffic networks and vehicles are perfect medium for deploying city-wide wireless sensor networks. With current advances in technology, improvements are made in vehicle infrastructure design: both sensors and actuators. Modern vehicle is highly equipped with sensors that improve driver experience and safety.
Some of modern vehicle sensors include:

– speed
– throttle

- acceleration
- fuel consumption
- OBD^2 data
- weight (passenger count)
- camera and optical recognition systems
- temperature and humidity sensor
- gyroscope*
- ambient light detector
- impact detector (airbag)
- GPS location,
- radar/lidar*
- ultrasound distance detector
- wifi*

Many of sensors* are currently being used and tested by Google Driverless Car[3] Issue with vehicular sensors is that they are not standardized and interconnected and most of them are private (used only by vehicle systems). Further step is vehicular interconectivity which depends on cooperation of vehicle manufacturers and development of appropriate standards. Smart Cities and smart traffic could benefit from exposing vehicle sensor data, at least for temperature measurements.

3   WiFi Urban Sensor Scanner

In described architecture, mobile object (vehicle) equiped with sensors, during movement in the urban sensor environment, require stable and constant internet access using existing WiFi infrastructure and all possible network alternatives [9]. Urban multi-sensor networks (UMN) like one described in [10] are implemented in the city environments that do have many WiFi hotspots deployed around the city area.

Static WiFi access points are positioned in the living spaces of city inhabitants and can form large scope WiFi network that can serve as information backbone of a Smart City. Along with static WiFi access points, there can be mobile access points like mobile hotspots or any other mobile device.

WiFi urban sensor scanner (WUSS) is usually an integrated solution that is made of:

- hardware: wifi network controller. like one used in smartphone devices and a GPS device.
- software: operating system like android, arduino, or raspberryPi

Purpose of (WUSS) would be to scan and monitor WiFi environment. WUSS can be implemented as an android application like one presented at SenseMyCity project[4]

---

^{2} On Board Diagnostic.

^{3} en.wikipedia.org/wiki/Google_driverless_car/.

^{4} http://cloud.futurecities.up.pt/sensemycity.

Simplest form of WUSC would be to map state of WiFi networks in the city along with GPS location from where sensor measurement was taken. Measurements can be made by users (citizens) using private smartphones or system can be implemented as dedicated hardware equipment that is positioned on board of public transportation vehicles. For a successful Wireless Sensor Network (WSN) operation, reliable data exchange platform would be necessary, WUSS can be used to identify and map appropriate WiFi access points that can be used for WSN to transmit and/or exchange sensor data. Research that is carried out at University of Zagreb, Faculty of Organization and Informatics uses trillateration algorithm using free space pathloss model to localize WiFi access point position [9]. Each moving object scans its surroundings for the existing WiFi networks. Procedure follows the case shown on Fig. 3 where for each scan circle the coverage area is calculated. Assume that A, B and C are GPS location of the moving object. Radius represents the distance to the probable WiFi location. Radius(r) is calculated using *free-space path loss* formula:

$$r = 10^{\frac{\ln(10)(T - R - K - 20\log(f))}{10n}} \tag{1}$$

where:

- R - receive power level, this value is being gathered using WiFi scanning equipment.
- T - transmit signal power strength is 17 dBm. According to IEEE 802.11b standard[5] the maximum power output level is 20 dBm and the minimum gives 13 dBm, this gives average of 17 dBm.
- K - path loss constant, value is -147.55,
- f - the WiFi frequency and is set to 2450 Mhz.
- n - the path loss exponent, it is set to 3 because we are measuring distances in the highly urban environment.
- r - is the distance (radius), the result in meters.

After the radius has been calculated circle around each moving object can be created. This circle represents "how well does an object hear an WiFi AP" not the location estimation of a WiFi AP. To determine the AP location it would be necessary to undertake the trilateration procedure. Figure 3 shows a case with 3 scan points from a moving object, each with its own radius. Trilateration procedures starts with selected starting circle: one with the strongest signal strength. After that, procedure calculates the intersection with all the other circles like this: for each circle, intersection is calculated between the circle and the current intersection area derived by previous round of intersection calculation. Each iteration makes intersection (polygon) smaller because it shrinks with every circle considered(intersected).

Radius of WiFi AP coverage estimation is calculated using the same pathloss formula (1) Input signal strength is the lowest signal strength of scan circle that contributed in the forming of final intersection.

---

[5] http://www.cisco.com/en/US/docs/optical/15000r7_0/15327/reference/guide/ 2770spcx.html.

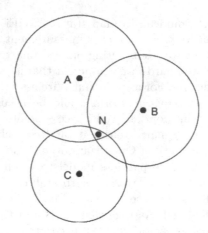

Fig. 3. Circle intersections with clustering [11]

4   Conclusion

Smart city can be observed as a living entity, it has all of vital functions like power supply, water, governance, inhabitants, traffic, etc. that can be augmented by information technologies and make the city smarter. By such approach we can make it self aware, not in a sense of artificial intelligence, but to be able to measure and record data about its current states. Traffic and vehicular networks provide mean to exchange dynamic data and information. By augmenting vehicular networks with sensor data, and network location technologies city becomes more self aware where each vehicle behaves as a mobile remote probe that gathers data. Wireless networks (if known) provide stable backbone for the data transmission. This paper addressed one challenge of smart cities - composition of heterogeneous sensor and network infrastructure by using vehicles as remote sensors, data transfer points and network location devices. Described combination of technologies enables integration of various networks and propagation of sensor data with higher reliability.

References

1. MIT City Science Initiative, City Science @ MIT (2012). http://cpowerhouse. media.mit.edu/Public/CityScienceBrochureOct2012.pdf
2. Paskaleva, K.A.: The smart city: a nexus for open innovation? Intell. Build. Int. **3**(3), 153–171 (2011)
3. Philosoph, M.: Smart Cities - Standardization, Israeli Standards Institution, Tel Aviv, Technical report (2014). http://energy.gov.il/Subjects/EnergyConservation/ Documents/SmartCity/MichalPhilosoph.pdf
4. Caragliu, A., Del Bo, C., Nijkamp, P.: Smart Cities in Europe, pp. 65–82 (2011). http://www.inta-aivn.org/images/cc/Urbanism/backgrounddocuments/01_03_ Nijkamp.pdf

5. Centre of Regional Science, Smart cities Ranking of European medium-sized cities, Vienna University of Technology, Vienna, Technical report (2007). http://www. smart-cities.eu/download/smart_cities_final_report.pdf
6. Pereira, V.: Porto City of the Future (2014). http://www.smartcityevent.com/ porto-city-future/
7. Barros, J.: Sensor networks: An overview, in Learning from Data Streams: Processing Techniques in Sensor Networks, pp. 9–24 (2007). http://www.cs.bme.hu/ nagyadat/Learning_from_data_streams.pdf#page=17
8. Zarmehri, M.N., Aguiar, A.: Data gathering for sensing applications in vehicular networks. In: 2011 IEEE Vehicular Networking Conference, pp. 139–156 (2011)
9. Tomaš, B.: WiFi roaming access point optimum assignment in urban multi-sensor networks. Research papers Faculty of Materials Science and Technology Slovak University of Technology in Trnava **21**, 109–115 (2013)
10. Rodrigues, J.G.P., Aguiar, A., Vieira, F., Barros, J., Cunha, J.P.S.: A mobile sensing architecture for massive urban scanning. In: IEEE Conference on Intelligent Transportation Systems, Proceedings, ITSC, pp. 1132–1137 (2011)
11. Kaminsky, A.: Trilateration. Comput. Aided Des. **13**(4), 8–11 (1981)

Modeling Transportation Preferences of Urban Residents: The Case of Poland

Katarzyna Cheba[1], Maja Kiba-Janiak[2], Sebastian Saniuk[3],
and Krzysztof Witkowski[3(✉)]

[1] West Pomeranian University of Technology in Szczecin, Szczecin, Poland
katarzyna.cheba@zut.edu.pl
[2] Wrocław University of Economics, Wrocław, Poland
maja.kiba-janiak@ue.wroc.pl
[3] University of Zielona Góra, Zielona Góra, Poland
{s.saniuk,k.witkowski}@wez.uz.zgora.pl

Abstract. The paper presents the application of selected methods of multi-variate statistical analysis including factor and conjoint analyses in terms of modeling transportation preferences of urban residents. The introduced methodologies can be useful tools for local authorities while designing solutions in order to improve the competitiveness of public transport to private transport. The results of the studies presented in the article are part of the research project implemented in 2010–2013 under a title. "Reference model of city logistics and the quality of life". For the study undertaken in this paper, three medium-sized cities, located in the western part of Poland, were selected.

Keywords: Transportation preferences · Factor analysis · Conjoint analysis

1 Introduction

Life in the city and the areas directly adjacent to cities is becoming more and more burdensome. The main reason for this situation, besides environmental pollution and security threats, is constantly increasing number of residents which cause difficulty with moving. The effect of dynamic urban development in urban and industrial agglomeration is often congestive transportation also called congestion. The problem of congestion is the subject of numerous studies [1–6].

The growing wealth of societies and consequently a greater access to passenger cars is responsible for the significant increase of the motorization index with a simultaneous fall in public transportation usage [7]. Forecasts of the European Commission indicate that passenger individual transportation will have increased by 51 % by 2050, while the public transportation will further deteriorate [8].

The impact of transport on the urban environment depends on many different factors. A special place among them takes the implementation of the transportation service, which is an important part of strategy for urban transport. The right choice of development strategy, especially public road transport can help to solve the problems of traffic organization. It is important in this case the proper identification of existing and future challenges that the transport system faces [9] and the formulation of

© Institute for Computer Sciences, Social Informatics and Telecommunications Engineering 2015
R. Giaffreda et al. (Eds.): IoT360 2014, Part II, LNICST 151, pp. 78–83, 2015.
DOI: 10.1007/978-3-319-19743-2_12

transport development programs that meet indicated tasks in changing environmental conditions [10].

The purpose of the study is an attempt to model transportation preferences of urban residents in one of medium-sized city in Poland. In this paper the selected methods of multivariate statistical analysis including factor and conjoint analyses were proposed. The study results can be a useful tool for local authorities in order to design solutions that improve the competitiveness of public transport to private transport. The results of the studies presented in the article are part of a project implemented in 2010–2013 titled "Reference model of urban logistics and the quality of life".

The structure of the paper is as follows. The second section presents the significance of the application of multidimensional statistical analysis in order to identify citizens' transportation preferences and behaviors. The next section introduces research results. The final part of the paper presents conclusion.

2 The Study of Transportation Preferences and Behavior of Urban Residents

Modeling of travelers' transportation behavior is a part of a more complex modeling process of a trip, which is conditioned, among others, by the density of urban networks and associated with the traffic noise or lengthening of the travel time, [11]. An important element of this process is to study the preferences of buyers, in this case travelers. Knowledge of the preferences and transportation behavior of the inhabitants is essential in the process of shaping transportation offer. Particularly important in this regard are studies on: the identification and prioritization of traffic demands and satisfaction with services and comprehensive assessment of the quality of transportation services. It is assumed that the fundamental postulates reported by residents to the urban transport sector are: punctuality, directness, frequency and availability, making up the level of passenger satisfaction with the services provided.

An important problem in the course of a lot of research is the correct interpretation of numerous, interlinked information. The solution to the problems with too much individual information can be e.g. a reduction in dimensionality and search for the interplay of many factors, e.g. on the basis of factor analysis.

Factor analysis is used to convert the mutually correlated system of variables into a new system of variables to be determined as common factors mutually uncorrelated, comparable with an output system [12–14].

Another method of measuring the preferences of buyers is conjoint analysis. The essence of conjoint analysis is to evaluate a set of profiles (real or hypothetical products and services) described with the selected attributes (explanatory variables) in order to obtain information about the overall preferences for the profiles (a set of values of the dependent variable) made by the respondents to the survey.

The complexity of the test procedure in the framework of conjoint analysis requires decision-making at every stage of research including among others determining the form of the model (depending on model variables, model preferences), the choice of how to collect data (solid profiles, pairwise comparisons, the presentation of pairs of attributes), the choice of the presentation profiles (physical product, the product model, a verbal description of figure), the scale of preferences (non-metric, metric) estimation method (metric: MONANOVA, PREFMAP, LINMAP, CCM, Metric: KMNK, MSAE, probabilistic: MNW, EM), assessing the credibility of the model (rating accuracy, reliability assessment), the interpretation of the results of measurements and the sample size determined mostly on the basis of earlier research (typical test is usually from 300 to 550 respondents) [15].

In the work the analysis of travelers' preferences was based on the research sample, which consisted of adult residents of three Polish cities of West Poland who were between 18 and 70 years of age. An attempt was selected from the population at random. The total sample size was set at 1,600 inhabitants.

3   The Results of Travelers' Transport Preferences

The respondents evaluated 12 different quality criteria concerning urban transport services, estimated from the available literature on the subject studies of this type. In the study of exploration the following dimensions of evaluation were considered: punctuality and frequency of the line, safety and travel conditions in vehicles, the conditions of waiting at bus stops, the availability of public transport, ticket prices and the immediacy of connections.

The research found that 12 of the original criteria for the quality of services can be reduced due to the application of factor analysis to two factors. The first derived factor mainly explains determinants associated with conditions of movement within the city offered in urban transport services. The variables described by this factor include the four most frequent transport demands: travel time, convenience - access to public transport, cost and safety.

The second factor is related to the additional (supplementary) areas of offered transport services, such as courtesy of drivers, access to information about the time of service delivery and readability of timetables. The system of variables forming the defined dimensions is shown in Table 1.

Table 1. The results of the factor analysis

Factor 1	Factor 2
punctuality of vehicles (x_1),	courtesy of drivers (x_9),
frequency of vehicles (x_2),	the overall quality of the information (at bus stops, in vehicles and on vehicles) (x_{10}),
travel safety (x_3),	readability and simplicity of memorizing timetables (x_{11}),
the conditions of traveling in vehicles (x_4),	the opportunity to comment on the functioning of public transport (x_{12}).
the conditions of waiting at bus stops (x_5),	
accessibility to public transport (x_6),	
ticket prices (x_7),	
directness of connections (x_8).	

During the study the significantly higher impact of variables was confirmed which was described by the first appointed agent to assess the quality of transport services, mainly including: ticket prices, travel time, service frequency and distance from a bus stop to the place of residing. For further research using conjoint analysis indicated variables (criteria) were used described by the first factor directly connected with the ongoing transport services. The validity of these variables was assessed by most respondents. The participants of the study felt that price, time, frequency, and further distance of a bus stop from home are the most important criteria for the quality of transport services.

Respondents were asked to evaluate a set of 12 profiles out of 36 possible variants generated by the method of orthogonal plan. Utility values that each respondent is associated with a given level of the variable set by means of a least-squares method with artificial explanatory variables. After estimating the relative partial utility the validity of each considered variable was specified.

The results obtained during the study confirmed the findings of other authors [16, 17]. In fact, all of the criteria related to the fundamental postulates of lading are significant while choosing the public transport as a means of movement within the city. The lowest percentage was obtained for criterion: time travel. Time travel for residents of medium-sized cities, with relatively close distances to overcome, is not a criterion as significantly influencing the preferences of the inhabitants as the other analyzed variables.

The highest preferences identified during the research (maximum score profile) relate to services provided by the urban public transport characterized primarily by low price, high frequency of the circulation, with close proximity to the bus stop from the place of residing (Fig. 1). In contrast, the travel time can be as long as in the case of travelling by car. Time travel for residents of medium-sized cities is not a decisive factor for the travelers' preferences related to the choice of public transport.

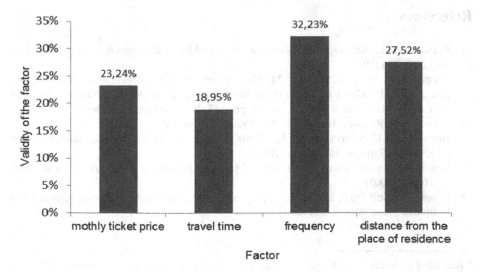

Fig. 1. The relative importance of the attributes

4 Conclusions

The problem of many cities, beside the surge in the number of cars,[1] it is also a significant increase in road freight transport, which puts a burden on municipal systems. Easy transportation within cities is also impeded due to housing development in suburban areas and placement outside concentrated urban housing large shopping centers. The solution to traffic problems of cities should be adequate to the implementation of transport policy allowing to increase the competitiveness of public transport and consequently reducing congestion, noise and pollution while increasing security. Public transport except that reduces traffic is more environmentally friendly than individual transport by car. Due to the constantly decreasing interest in this form of travel, it is important to take proper measures to encourage residents to use this kind of transport. It is also vital to monitor the quality of service offered by the public transport services.

The presented results of the modeling transportation preferences of urban residents with the application of the methods of multidimensional statistical analysis allowed to identify the comprehensive travelers' preferences. From a practical point of view, these studies are significant because of the possibility of simultaneous comparison of many individual preferences of travelers. It is also important opportunity to introduce the proposed methods to a comprehensive and more complex modeling of transport behavior.

The results of carried out studies clearly indicate that price, frequency and distance from the main stops are the key factors affecting the assessment of the quality of public transport in medium-sized cities. Travel time due to the rather short distances turned out to be a less important factor. It will be certainly more important aspect in the case of residents of large cities, more congested and less efficient in communication.

References

1. Brandeau, M.L., Samuel, S.C.: A center location problem with congestion. Ann. Oper. Res. **40**(1), 17–32 (1992)
2. Cooper, W.W., Deng, H., Seiford, L.M., Zhu, J.: Congestion. In: Cooper, W.W., Seiford, L.M., Zhu, J. (eds.) Handbook on Data Envelopment Analysis Internatiional Series in Operations Research & Management Science, vol. 71, pp. 177–201. Springer, Heidelberg (2004)
3. Kerner, B.S., Rehborn, H., Aleksic, M.: Forecasting of traffic congestion. In: Helbing, D., Herrmann, H.I., Schreckenberg, M., Wolf, D.E. (eds.) Traffic and Granular Flow'99, pp 339–344. Springer, Heidelberg (2000)
4. Welzl, M.: Network Congestion Control: Managing Internet Traffic. John Wiley & Sons, Chichester (2005)
5. Downs, A.: Still Stuck in Traffic: Coping with Peak-hour Traffic Congestion. Brookings Institution Press, Washington (2005)

---

[1] According to the Energy & Transport in Figs. 2006, European Commission Luxembourg, 2007, the number of private cars per 1,000 inhabitants increased from 15 in 1970 to 323 in 2007.

6. Richardson, H.W., Bae, C.-H.C.: Road Congestion Pricing in Europe: Implications for the United States. Edward Elgar Publishing, Cheltenham (2008)
7. Leea, R., Rivasplata, C.: Metropolitan transportation planning in the 1990s: comparisons and contrasts in New Zealand. Chile Calif. Transp. Policy **8**, 47–61 (2001)
8. European Commission. Commission Staff Working Document Accompanying the White Paper - Roadmap to a Single European Transport Area – Towards a competitive and resource efficient transport system, Brussels, 28.3.2011, SEC, 391 final, pp 12–14 (2012) http://eur-lex.europa.eu/LexUriServ/LexUriServ.do?uri=SEC:2011:0391:FIN:EN:PDF, 25.07.2014
9. Janecki, R., Krawiec, S., Sierpiński, G.: Public collective transport as a key element of a sustainable transport system in Górnośląsko-Zagłębiowska, Silesia Metropolis, UM Katowice, pp 105–132 (2010)
10. Masser, I., Sviden, O., Wegener, M.: Transport planning for equity and sustainability. Transp. Plann. Technol. **17**, 319–330 (1993)
11. Żochowska, R.: Modelling routing in dense urban networks, Scientific Papers of Silesian University of Technology, Series: TRANSPORTATION 71 (2011)
12. Green, P.E., Wind, Y.: New way to measure consumers' judgments. Harvard Bus. Rev. **53**, 107–117 (1975)
13. Green, P.E., Srinivasan, V.: Conjoint analysis in marketing: new developments with implications for research and practice. J. Mark. **54**, 3–19 (1990)
14. Hair, J.F., Anderson, R.E., Tatham, R.L., Black, W.C.: Multivariatae Data Analysis with Readings. Prentice-Hall, Englewood Cliffs (1995)
15. Walesiak, M., Bąk, A.: Conjoint analysis in marketing research. AE Wrocław, Wrocław (2000)
16. Scheiner, J.: Mobiliät in Deutschland 2002–2008, Bundesministerium für Verkehr, Bau und Stadtentwicklung (Hrsg.) (2009)
17. Cheba, K., Kiba-Janiak, M.: Conjoint analysis as a method of analysing consumer preferences on example of municipal transport market, Acta Universitatis Lodziensis, Folia OECONOMICA, pp 56–61 (2013)

Extracting Meaningful User Locations
from Temporally Annotated Geospatial Data

Alasdair Thomason[✉], Nathan Griffiths, and Matthew Leeke

University of Warwick, Coventry CV4 7AL, UK
{ali,nathan,matt}@dcs.warwick.ac.uk

Abstract. The pervasive nature of location-aware devices has enabled
the collection of geospatial data for the provision of personalised services.
Despite this, the extraction of meaningful user locations from temporally
annotated geospatial data remains an open problem. Meaningful location
extraction is typically considered to be a 2-step process, consisting of visit
extraction and clustering. This paper evaluates techniques for meaningful
location extraction, with an emphasis on visit extraction. In particular,
we propose an algorithm for the extraction of visits that does not impose
a minimum bound on visit duration and makes no assumption of evenly
spaced observation.

Keywords: Clustering · Extraction · Geospatial · Location · Visits

1 Introduction

To leverage location-aware devices for service enhancement, systems must be able
to interpret and reason about the movements of users. The extraction of meaningful locations from temporally annotated location data is central to achieving
this goal, permitting the labelling of locations, e.g., 'home', 'work' or 'supermarket', which increases the capacity of systems to reason about user locations. In
particular, meaningful location extraction is fundamental to location prediction,
since it establishes the grouping of disparate but related sensor readings.

As vital as meaningful location extraction is to location-based services, the
problem remains open. This paper proposes a novel algorithm for *visit extraction*,
which is the first stage of meaningful location extraction. The proposed algorithm
builds upon previous work and does not impose a minimum bound on visit
duration, or have an assumption of evenly spaced location observations. We
then evaluate the performance difference between the proposed algorithm in
meaningful location extraction and the STA visit extractor [2].

2 Related Work

Extracting locations from a geospatial dataset is often considered a clustering
problem. However, when the dataset from which meaningful locations are to be

© Institute for Computer Sciences, Social Informatics and Telecommunications Engineering 2015
R. Giaffreda et al. (Eds.): IoT360 2014, Part II, LNICST 151, pp. 84–90, 2015.
DOI: 10.1007/978-3-319-19743-2_13

extracted is temporally annotated, this additional information can be leveraged. *Visit extraction* is concerned with detecting periods of time during which a user remained at a single location, henceforth referred to as *visits*, and consequently summarising the dataset. Traditionally, a road travelled frequently by a user would contain many points, while a location visited only once would contain few points, leading to the possibility of it being overlooked. This summary reduces the computational cost of clustering, as the size of the dataset is reduced.

A discussion of existing approaches to visit extraction can be found in [2]. Such approaches include the use of thresholds to specify maximum visit size relative to either the first point discovered [5,10] or to the visit's centroid [3], but this is highly sensitive to noisy data. Other approaches have used knowledge of the properties of specific GPS devices [1], but such methods are not generic.

Addressing these issues, Bamis and Savvides presented their algorithm for the extraction of *Spatio-Temporal Activities (STAs)* [2]. Although aiming to determine activities that repeat in cycles, they first extract periods of time spent at a single location. The algorithm uses a filter and a buffer of points to detect a consistent change in location of the user, and hence, when the user ends an activity. In contrast to previous approaches, this method is far more resilient to noise. However, the algorithm assumes that points will arrive at even time intervals, and it requires that the buffer be full before a visit can exist, in turn requiring the user to know the minimum length of a visit a priori. The algorithm presented in this paper, *GVE*, does not have such requirements.

Techniques shown to be applicable to the clustering of extracted visits into meaningful locations include k-means [1,7] and DBSCAN [4,6,8,9]. DBSCAN is more popular for this domain as it does not require the number of locations to be known a priori, and is therefore the algorithm adopted in this paper.

3   Gradient-Based Visit Extractor

We propose a Gradient-based Visit Extractor (GVE, Algorithm 1) which extracts visits from temporally annotated geospatial datasets, addressing some of the drawbacks in the STA visit extractor proposed in [2]. GVE works linearly over the dataset by building visits until adding another point would cause the recent trend of motion to be consistently away from the visit already extracted. Although similar in idea to STA, GVE can consider visits without having a full buffer of points over which to analyse the trend of motion and allows for points collected at a varying rate.

The buffer over which the trend of motion of the user is considered has a maximum size of N_{points}, but the buffer does not need to be filled for a comparison to take place. Parameters, α and β, are used to define a threshold function on the size of the buffer. If the buffer contains a small number of points, adding an additional point that is further from p_1 than p_2 could be an indication that the user is moving away from the visit or it could be attributed to noise. This problem is combated by using a negative logarithmic function to ensure that the threshold for trend of motion is higher with fewer points in the buffer. Trend of motion is

---

Algorithm 1. Gradient-based Visit Extractor Algorithm

1: $N_{points}, \alpha, \beta \leftarrow$ input parameters
2: $visits \leftarrow [\ ]$ empty array, to be filled with visits
3: $visit \leftarrow [\ p_0\ ]$ array containing the first point in the dataset
4:
5: **function** Process($point$)
6:     **if** $MovingAway?(visit, point)$ **then**
7:         $visits.append(visit)$ **if** $visit.length > 1$
8:         $visit \leftarrow [\ point\ ]$
9:     **else**
10:         $visit.append(point)$
11:     **end if**
12: **end function**
13:
14: **function** MovingAway?($visit, point$)
15:     $buffer \leftarrow visit.last(N_{points} - 1) + point$
16:     **return** $Gradient(buffer, visit) > Threshold(buffer.length)$
17: **end function**

---

defined using a gradient, that includes both spatial and temporal components and therefore allows for the possibility of points of varying temporal distances. The *gradient* of the buffer is defined as:

$$Gradient(b) = \frac{l(b) \sum\limits_{p \in b}(t(p) \times d(p)) - \sum\limits_{p \in b} t(p) \sum\limits_{p \in b} d(p)}{l(b) \sum\limits_{p \in b} t(p)^2 - (\sum\limits_{p \in b} t(p))^2}$$

where $l(b)$ is the length of buffer b, $t(p)$ is the time since the first point of the buffer for point p in seconds, and $d(p)$ is the distance between point p and the centroid of the current visit, in metres. A gradient greater than the threshold indicates that the visit has ended:

$$Threshold(length) = -log\left(length * \frac{1}{\beta}\right) * \alpha$$

By combining these two equations, we are able to summarise the movement trend of the user relative to the visit, the *gradient*, and set a threshold for this gradient dependent upon the number of points that it was drawn over. This ensures resilience to noise by monitoring the movement trend over a set of points, but still allows for visits with few points.

4   Evaluation

Using data collected over several months from a smartphone application and a map of the University of Warwick campus, the parameters for the two algorithms were empirically determined such that the locations extracted were consistent with expectations. Results are presented for GVE (Fig. 1) and the STA

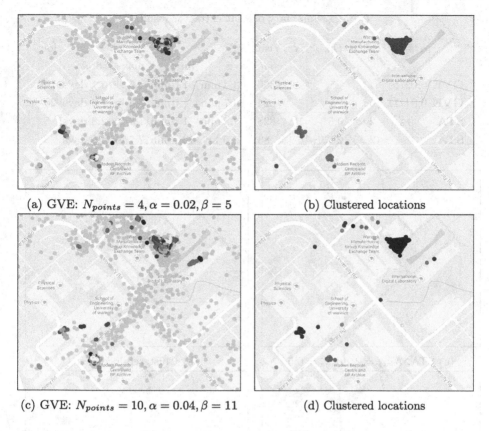

(a) GVE: $N_{points} = 4, \alpha = 0.02, \beta = 5$ (b) Clustered locations

(c) GVE: $N_{points} = 10, \alpha = 0.04, \beta = 11$ (d) Clustered locations

Fig. 1. Gradient-based Visit Extractor

visit extractor (Fig. 2), where the visits identified are clustered using DBSCAN. Results for each algorithm are presented for parameters optimised for accuracy of extracted location and coverage of visits. An immediate observation is that a similar set of primary locations is extracted in all cases, with smaller locations being extracted in only some cases. Specifically, GVE extracts several more locations than STA, since GVE is likely to extract visits of shorter duration. This is substantiated by results in Table 1 where the properties of the extracted visits and locations are detailed. It can be seen that GVE routinely extracts visits of shorter duration, extracting visits of 1 min. STA is capable of extracting similar length visits (1.6 min), but requires that the buffer size be reduced to its minimum of 2. With a larger buffer size (N_{buf} parameter), the minimum length visit extracted is 12.7 min. From the results, it can be seen that when STA is tuned to allow the extraction of short visits, the average and maximum visit lengths are reduced, whilst the total time covered by visits is also reduced.

The algorithm and parameters that produces the greatest temporal coverage is the second run of GVE (with buffer size, N_{points}, of 10). 7.3 days of visits are extracted from the dataset, significantly higher than any other run. This increase

Table 1. Summary of visit extractor results

	α	β	Buffer	D_{thres}	N_d	Visits					loc
						count	avg	min	max	total	
GVE	0.02	5	4			1360	3.4 min	1.0 min	1.5 hr	3.1 days	10
GVE	0.04	11	10			624	16.7 min	1.0 min	3.4 hr	7.3 days	20
STA			2	0.5	1	828	4.8 min	1.6 min	1.8 hr	2.8 days	5
STA			12	2	6	83	2.0 hr	12.7 min	7.7 hr	4.6 days	5

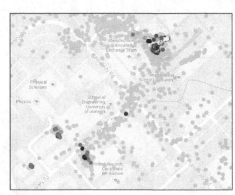
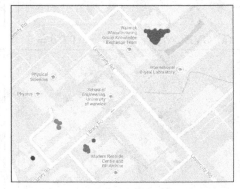

(a) STA: $N_{buf} = 2, d_{thres} = 0.5$ (b) Clustered locations

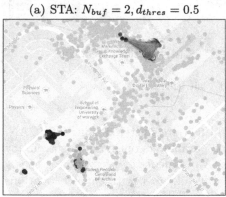
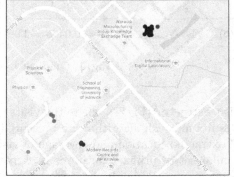

(c) STA: $N_{buf} = 12, d_{thres} = 2$ (d) Clustered locations

Fig. 2. Spatio-temporal activity extractor

in coverage produces a larger set of locations (as shown in Fig. 3d). Interestingly, however, the number of visits is reduced from the previous run of GVE. This finding indicates that visits which were being split into multiple parts using a smaller buffer size were detected as single visits when a larger buffer is used. Figure 1c shows the visits extracted as representative, with no visit clearly spanning multiple buildings, indicating that the accuracy of extraction has not been impacted.

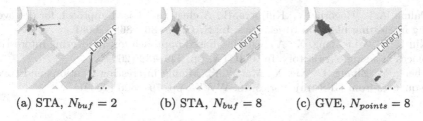

(a) STA, $N_{buf} = 2$ (b) STA, $N_{buf} = 8$ (c) GVE, $N_{points} = 8$

Fig. 3. GVE and STA Extractor on a visit with few points

An example of the difference between the two algorithms for visits of short duration can be seen in Fig. 3. In the data there exists one visit to the library (bottom right) and two visits to the biology concourse (top left). While it is possible for STA to extract the library visit, the buffer size must be set to 2 which comes at the cost of extracting erroneous biology concourse visits. Selecting parameters that optimise the extraction of visits to the biology concourse means that the algorithm is no longer capable of extracting the short visit to the library (Fig. 3b). Figure 3c shows the results of using GVE to extract the visits. In this case, GVE is capable of extracting all 3 visits correctly.

5   Conclusion

This paper explored the use of visit extraction to better extract meaningful locations from temporally-annotated geospatial datasets. Specifically, a novel algorithm, GVE, has been presented. The algorithm builds on existing work but removed the requirements for visits to have a minimum duration and the dataset to contain points at a constant rate. Further, the paper demonstrated the workings of the GVE algorithm and how it relates to STA for the purpose of extracting visits to aid in meaningful location extraction.

References

1. Ashbrook, D., Starner, T.: Learning significant locations and predicting user movement with GPS. In: ISWC, pp. 101–108 (2002)
2. Bamis, A., Savvides, A.: Lightweight extraction of frequent spatio-temporal activities from GPS traces. In: RTSS, pp. 281–291 (2010)
3. Kang, J.H., Welbourne, W., Stewart, B.: Extracting places from traces of locations. In: WMASH, pp. 110–118 (2004)
4. Lei, P., Shen, T., Peng, W., Su, I.: Exploring spatial-temporal trajectory model for location prediction. In: MDM, pp. 58–67 (2011)
5. Liu, S., Cao, H., Li, L., Zhou, M.: Predicting stay time of mobile users with contextual information. IEEE T-ASE **10**(4), 1026–1036 (2013)
6. Mamoulis, N., Cao, H., Kollios, G.: Mining, indexing, and querying historical spatiotemporal data. In: KDD, pp. 236–245 (2004)
7. Nguyen, L., Cheng, H.T., Wu, P., Buthpitiya, S.: Pnlum: system for prediction of next location for users with mobility. In: Mobile Data Challenge at Pervasive (2012)

8. Palma, A.T., Bogorny, V., Kuijpers, B.: A clustering-based approach for discovering interesting places in trajectories. In: SAC, pp. 863–868 (2008)
9. Xiu-Li, Z., Wei-Xiang, X.: A clustering-based approach for discovering interesting places in a single trajectory. In: ICICTA, pp. 429–432 (2009)
10. Zheng, Y., Zhang, L., Xie, X., Ma, W.Y.: Mining interesting locations and travel sequences from GPS trajectories. In: WWW, pp. 791–800 (2009)

Development of Autonomous Wheelchair for Indoor and Outdoor Traveling

Masashi Yokozuka(✉), Naohisa Hashimoto, Kohji Tomita, and Osamu Matsumoto

National Institute of Advanced Industrial Science and Technology (AIST), 1-1-1 Umezono, Tsukuba, Ibaraki 305–8568, Japan yokotsuka-masashi@aist.go.jp

Abstract. In order to assist elderly people and disabled people, this paper describes development of autonomous wheelchair to travel in indoor and outdoor environments for providing traveling ability to any where. For this aim, the autonomous wheelchairs should have traveling-capability without choosing indoor and outdoor environments. Position detection is a key technology for autonomous driving since people decides a traveling direction from a current position and a destination. GPS is a fundamental technology for position detection. However GPS is not available in indoor cases, and GPS is not always available in outdoor cases when tall buildings occlude satellites. In these cases autonomous wheelchair has to detect a self-position by other sensor systems. In this study we have adopted a localization system utilizing 3D maps and a 3D laser range finder. By the 3D localization system our wheelchair system can detect a self-position robustly if the wheelchair is surrounded by obstacles such as pedestrians. To avoid collision our wheelchair system uses short and long term planning. The short planning finds a safe motion-pattern from every conceivable pattern by the simulation on a map. The long term planning generates a feasible route to destination. If the route generated by the long-term planner collides to some obstacles our wheelchair avoids collision by the short term planning. By the localization system and the planning system our wheelchair could operate in public spaces.

Keywords: Autonomous vehicle · Wheelchair · SLAM

1 Introduction

We have developed an autonomous wheelchair system for assisting travel of elderly people and disabled people in order to help their daily living. This paper describes about our developed autonomous wheelchair systems.

Autonomous driving systems have spread out toward many applications that are airplanes, ships, trains, cars and small personal mobilities such as wheelchairs. Especially, autonomous driving cars and wheelchairs have difficulty compared with other vehicles because environments using these vehicles are complicated.

© Institute for Computer Sciences, Social Informatics and Telecommunications Engineering 2015
R. Giaffreda et al. (Eds.): IoT360 2014, Part II, LNICST 151, pp. 91–96, 2015.
DOI: 10.1007/978-3-319-19743-2_14

There are many obstacles such as cars, pedestrians, etc. in roadways and sidewalks. Autonomous driving cars and wheelchairs have to detect the obstacles to prevent collisions. Moreover, GPS can not always detect accurate position in the roadways and sidewalks because upper tall buildings reduce the precision of GPS for occluding satellites. Autonomous driving systems control the self-velocity by comparing target routes and current position. Inaccurate positioning triggers undesirable driving to autonomous vehicles. The vehicles should have other devices to detect accurate position when GPS is unavailable.

In comparison with autonomous driving cars, the wheelchairs have to travel on not only outdoor environments but also indoor environments. There are no clear rules for smooth traffic in the environments using the wheelchairs. The wheelchairs can freely travel on any routes. Similarly, the pedestrians freely walk in the environments. The autonomous driving wheelchairs have to decide a route for smooth traffic in response to motion of pedestrians. In roadways cars and pedestrians move under the traffic regulation. The traffic regulation restricts routes for cars and pedestrians. The cars can only move forward, and can not move backward on lanes. Basically, autonomous driving cars avoid collisions by speed control. Against the cars, the wheelchairs have to decide a route to avoid collisions.

Autonomous driving wheelchairs have other difficulty for positioning in comparison with autonomous driving cars. In roadways there are specific features for the traffic regulation, which are traffic signs, white lines, pedestrian crossings, etc. Autonomous driving cars can use the features as landmarks for positioning. Against the case of cars the specific features do not always exist in the environments using the wheelchairs. Autonomous driving wheelchairs have to detect self-position without using the specific landmarks when GPS is unavailable.

In this paper, we introduce our developed autonomous driving wheelchair [2] that can detect self-position without using specific landmarks and can decide a route in response to motion of pedestrians. Our autonomous wheelchair can travel in indoor-outdoor environments by the self-positioning and the route planning seamlessly.

2   System Architecture

Figure 1 is our developed autonomous wheelchair "MARCUS". Our wheelchair equips a 3D laser range finder (3D-LRF) unit for making maps, two wheel encoders for measuring self-velocity, and a 2D laser range finder (2D-LRF) for collision avoidance.

The 3D-LRF unit obtains 3D points by rotating a 2D-LRF, which is a LMS-151 manufactured by SICK. The rotation axes are a roll axis and a pitch axis. The range of rotation angle is from -22.5 degree to $+22.5$ degree for each axis. The measurement time of obtaining 3D points until rotating the range is 1.5 s Our wheelchair uses the 3D-LRF unit for making 3D maps, and does not use the unit for collision avoidance because the length of time for 3D scanning is long.

The 2D-LRF is a UTM-30LX manufactured by Hokuyo Automatic Co. LTD. The 2D-LRF is rigidly clamped to the wheelchair frame, and does not rotate.

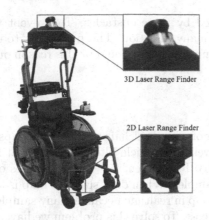

Fig. 1. Our developed autonomous wheelchair.

In comparison with the 3D-LRF unit this 2D-LRF can detect the obstacles rapidly. The scanning time is 25 ms. Our wheelchair uses this sensor to avoid collision for this rapid scanning.

The two wheel encoders measure self-velocity from wheel angular velocity of left and right wheels. Our wheelchair detects self-position by computing relative displacement from wheel encoders, and by correcting the displacement by matching 3D-scanning data and map data. The details of localization and mapping is written in the next section.

3   Localization and Mapping

For detecting self position in outdoor and indoor environments our wheelchair performs 3D scan-matching by using the 3D-LRF unit. This section describes the positioning method.

3.1   Localization

To detect a correct position after movement, we adopted a monte carlo localization (MCL) based algorithm [4]. MCL finds a correct position from position-samples that are generated randomly by using a dynamics model of wheelchair. If many samples are generated, the possibility to find a correct position becomes high. Evaluation of correctness of a position-sample is done by shape matching. If a position-sample is correct, a scanned shape by LRF matches to map-shape when the scanned shape is drawn from the sampled position. The evaluation is to calculate similarity between matched shapes.

Our wheelchair calculates the similarity by 3D shapes to gain robustness of localization. In the environments running wheelchairs there are not only static objects but many dynamic obstacles such as pedestrians, cars, etc. If using 2D-LRF only, scanning shapes of environments becomes difficult when the wheelchair is surrounded by these obstacles. To prevent this surrounded case our solution is to scan many direction. The possibility to scan mapped objects becomes high by scanning many direction. For this reason our wheelchair uses 3D scanning.

3.2 Mapping

The localization system of our wheelchair requires 3D maps. To obtain 3D maps we adopted Rao-Blackwellized particle filter (RBPF) that is extension of MCL. The basic concept of RBPF is to generate many samples of map, and to find a correct map from the samples. When data size of a map is large, RBPF becomes difficult to construct a map in realtime because many samples require huge memory and computational cost. To solve this problem we have proposed a improved RBPF method [1] that is sub-map dividing and re-alignment. In our method the number of map-samples is one. To find a correct map our method divides the map and realigns sub-maps by generating samples of alinement between sub-maps. By this re-aligning procedure our method can generate a correct 3D map although the memory size of 3D map is large because our method does not require generation of map-samples.

4 Collision Avoidance and Route Planning

Our wheelchair is driven by short term planning and long term planning to avoid unsafe self-driving [3]. The short term planning considers the wheelchair motion in a few seconds. This planning is corresponding to collision avoidance, and is a crucial issue against safety. The long term planning considers the route until arriving at a destination. This planning aims to generate a feasible route to arriving at a destination.

4.1 Collision Avoidance

For collision avoidance our wheelchair uses the dynamic window approach (DWA)[5]. DWA searches target wheel-velocity without collision from every conceivable pattern of wheel-velocity. In DWA vehicle-controllers utilize patterns of wheel-velocity that are possible by acceleration and deceleration in performance limitations of vehicles. DWA searches a pattern of wheel-velocity without collision by simulation. In the simulation DWA checks the collision on environment-maps generated by LRF. When a virtual vehicle continues a velocity-pattern within a specified time, and does not collide on the map, DWA adopts the non-colliding pattern.

4.2 Route Planning

For route planning in outdoor and indoor environments our wheelchair adopts A* algorithms on the 3D-map generated by our mapping method. A* algorithm finds a shortest path on the map by combination of motion patterns. Each motion patterns are simple. For example, the patterns are forward movement, backward movement, left and right turns. By the combination of motion patterns A* algorithm generates a shortest path and can generate a feasible route in response to dynamic obstacles.

Our wheelchair system has two motion planner that are the short and long term planner. If there is no collisions in the simulation, the system uses a result of long term planner. Conversely, If there is a collision in the simulation, the system uses a result of short term planner. Basically, our system takes precedence of the short term planner.

5 Experiments and Discussions

We have performed an experiment of 3D map building by using our RBPF algorithm described in the Sect. 3.2. Figure 2 shows the mapping result. The map size is 350m × 250m, and was constructed in realtime. From this experimental result our wheelchair can perform autonomous driving after construction of a map immediately.

This rapid map construction provides portability to our autonomous wheelchair because if a map is not constructed our wheelchair generates a map in realtime and can perform autonomous driving immediately. Our wheelchair can operate in any places because our system can generate maps immediately.

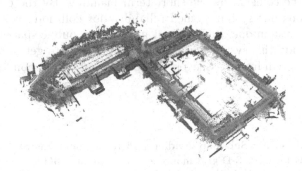

Fig. 2. A 3D map generated by our RBPF algorithm.

Figure 3 shows an experiment of autonomous driving in public space. Our wheelchair could operate without any incident in the public space by the short and long term planning. The short term planning provides high reliable collision avoidance because this planning finds out a safe motion-pattern from every conceivable pattern exhaustively. By combination of the short an long term planning

Fig. 3. Experiment in a public space.

if the route planning generate a path collided obstacles our wheelchair can avoid collision because our system takes precedence of the short term planner.

6   Conclusion

In this paper we have described a development of autonomous driving wheelchair. In order to travel indoor and outdoor environments we have developed a localization method and a mapping method on 3D maps. By using 3D map based localization our system can operate in indoor environments and in outdoor environments in which GPS does not function for occlusion of satellites. To realize reliable collision avoidance our wheelchair has short and long term planning. The short term planning finds a safe motion-pattern from every conceivable pattern by the simulation on a 3D map. The long term planning finds a feasible route to a destination. If the long term planning generate a route with collision our system avoids the collision by the short term planning. By the combination of planning methods our system gained reliability for collision avoidance. In the experiment our system operated without incidents in public spaces. As a future work we will study this system in various environments to get informations for improving the system from passengers and pedestrians about comfortability and safety.

References

1. Yokozuka, M., et al.: Sub-map dividing and realignment FastSLAM by blocking gibbs MCEM for large 3-D grid mapping. Adv. Robot. **26**(14), 3838–3844 (2012)
2. Yokozuka, M., et al.: Robotic wheelchair with autonomous traveling capability for transportation assistance in an urban environment. In: Proceedings of IEEE/RSJ International Conference on Intelligent Robots and Systems, pp. 3838–3844 (2012)
3. Yokozuka, M., et al.: A reasonable path planning via path energy minimization. J. Robot. Mechatron. **26**(2), 236–244 (2014)
4. Yokozuka, M., et al.: Auxiliary particle filter localization for intelligent wheelchair systems in urban environment. J. Robot. Mechatron. **22**(6), 758–765 (2010)
5. Fox, D., Burgard, W., Thrun, S.: The dynamic window approach to collision avoidance. IEEE Robot. Autom. Mag. **4**(1), 23–33 (1997)

Safety and Privacy Perceptions in Public Spaces: An Empirical Study on User Requirements for City Mobility

Julia van Heek[✉], Katrin Arning, and Martina Ziefle

Human-Computer Interaction Center, RWTH Aachen University,
Campus Boulevard 57, 52074 Aachen, Germany
{vanheek,arning,ziefle}@comm.rwth-aachen.de

Abstract. Mobility represents an essential prerequisite for the participation in social lives in urban environments. However, seamless mobility and traveling is based on dwellers' perception of a high personal safety at different urban locations. Safety can be supported by adequate surveillance technologies (e.g., cameras, but any surveillance undermines individual wishes for protection of privacy. In this empirical study, we explore users' perceptions on safety and privacy. Using an online survey, 99 users were requested to indicate their acceptance of different types of technologies that increase safety, differentiating perceived benefits and barriers. Also, we explored acceptance differences towards surveillance technologies during day- and nighttime at various locations (private and public). Finally, we determined the trade-off between the wish for increasing safety and the wish for privacy.

Keywords: Privacy · Safety · Mobility · User diversity · Technology acceptance · Tradeoff between privacy and security

1 Introduction

One of the major challenges of modern societies is to meet the complex demands of urbanization processes and to maintain livable, sustainable, and resilient cities. Up to 2030, more people will live in cities than in other regions and this development is forecasted to increase further. In line with these fundamental urbanization processes, consecutive challenges arise. Beyond climate change-related and environmental issues, nowadays' major keystones of urban planning are the broadly accepted implementation of technical infrastructures and (smart) mobility concepts [1]. Mobility represents an essential prerequisite for the participation in social and economic life. Mobility services must meet a wide range of travellers' needs, including easy accessibility, high comfort regarding safety and security, sustainability, and affordability. Mobility options must be flexible and intermodal, especially when considering different traveller profiles in both professional and private travel contexts [2, 3]. Facing the demographic change, urban mobility is essential for all dwellers, but specifically for seniors and persons living alone, in order to participate actively, autonomously, and independently in social living [4].

© Institute for Computer Sciences, Social Informatics and Telecommunications Engineering 2015
R. Giaffreda et al. (Eds.): IoT360 2014, Part II, LNICST 151, pp. 97–103, 2015.
DOI: 10.1007/978-3-319-19743-2_15

2 Security and Privacy – Prerequisites of Urban Mobility

For free and unrestricted mobility in urban areas, people need to feel safe. Crime threat in cities is a time-consuming challenge [5, 6]. The consequences of crime for urban safety and individual risk perception are well described and represent a serious barrier for many travellers [7]. While it is undisputed that safety and crime prevention are major goals for mobility and urban development, the realization of safety is controversially evaluated [8, 9]. Technically, surveillance technologies are at hand and might be helpful to increase urban safety [10, 11]. However, at least two arguments militate in favor of not exclusively relying on predominantly technology-centered planning of infrastructural mobility concepts. One argument relates to the contradictory nature of the wish for increasing safety by adequate technologies, on the one hand, and the understandable wish for protecting dwellers' and travellers privacy, on the other [12], which can only be understood if the trade-off between both basic motives is empirically addressed. Second, travellers' profiles are increasingly diverse, and age [13] and gender [14] of travellers might specifically impact the perceived tradeoff between safety and privacy in urban environments.

So far, only sparse knowledge is available about the specific acceptance patterns of dwellers towards the benefits and barriers of surveillance technologies that are assumed to increase safety perceptions. The goal of the present study is, thus, to understand the key drivers of surveillance technologies in urban environments, taking security and privacy as prominent factors into account.

3 Exploratory Study: Acceptance of Surveillance Technology

Data was collected in an online survey conducted in Germany. Completing the questionnaire took about 20 min. Questionnaire items were taken from a focus group study carried out prior to this study. In total, 99 participants (16–75 years) filled in the survey. Mean age was 37.8 (SD = 15.5), with 58.6 % females and 41.4 % males. Participants volunteered to take part and were not gratified for their efforts.

The questionnaire was arranged in five sections. The *first part* addressed demographic characteristics of the participants. In the *second part*, we asked for the individual perception of crime threat at different places by day and by night. For clarity reasons, locations were arranged into four categories (*private* (e.g., garden), *semiprivate* (e.g., own street), *semi-public* (e.g., shopping mall), and *public* (e.g., train station) locations). The question "To what extent do you feel threatened by crime during the day?" had to be evaluated for more than 20 different public and private locations (see Fig. 1). Threat perceptions had to be rated on a six-point Likert scale (1 = not at all; 6 strong threat perception). In addition, looking for possible differences of threat during day- and nighttime, participants had to evaluate on a five-point scale (-2 = much lower threat; -1 = lower threat; 0 = no difference; 1 = higher threat; and 2 = much higher threat) if they would feel a different crime threat at the same locations by night. The *third part* assessed the perceived security provided by technologies and other measures. Thus, different technologies (e.g., camera surveillance, ambient lighting, microphones) but also social measures (e.g., police presence, guard dog) had to be rated on a six-point Likert scale (1 = strongly disagree; 6 = strongly agree). The *fourth part* of the questionnaire asked about the acceptance of crime surveillance technologies at different locations, as well as the perceived benefits and barriers of crime surveillance (6-point Likert scale, 1 = strongly disagree; 6 = strongly agree). Benefits of crime surveillance were examined in seven items which referred to security aspects, e.g., prevention of crime, sense of security, the felt deterrent effect for potential criminals. Barriers referred to eight items relating to privacy aspects, e.g., protection of civil rights and personal freedom, storage of recorded data, inference of being under general suspicion. The *fifth and last part* focused on the trade-off between looking for security, on the one, and protecting individual privacy, on the other hand. Participants had to consider whether privacy or security is more important to them at different locations on a 10-point scale (1 = increase of security; 10 = protection of privacy).

4 Results

Data was analyzed descriptively and, with respect to the effects of gender and age, by (M)ANOVA procedures (significance level at 5 %).

4.1 Perceived Crime Threat

Daytime: The perceived crime threat by day can generally be seen as rather low (see Fig. 1; grey bars show the perceived crime threat by day (left axis); black line by night (right axis)). The majority of private locations is perceived as only lightly threatened, e.g., *own garden* (M = 1.3; SD = 0.6) or *own home* (M = 1.4; SD = 0.8). Semi-private locations are noticed as lightly threatened, e.g., *own street* (M = 1.8; SD = 1) or *hotel* (M = 1.8; SD = 0.9). Semi-public locations are observed as slightly threatened, e.g., *market* (M = 2.4; SD = 1.2) and *public transport* (M = 2.6; SD = 1.3). Public locations are perceived as more threatened, e.g., *parks* (M = 2.8; SD = 1.3), *train station* (M = 3; SD = 1.4) or *underground car park* (M = 3.3; SD = 1.6).

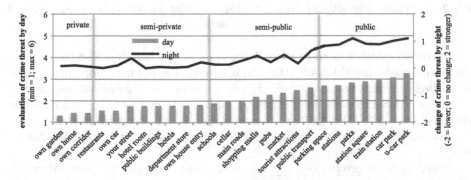

Fig. 1. Perceived crime threat by day and by night (min = 1, max = 6)

Night Time: The perceived threat at night did not vary strongly across the different locations. <u>Private</u> and <u>semi-private</u> locations are not perceived differently by day or by night, except for the *own street* (M = 0.3; SD = 0.8). Concerning *semi-public* locations a higher perceived crime threat was found, e.g., for *market* (M = 0.5; SD = 0.8) or *public transport* (M = 0.6; SD = 0.8) by night. Regarding <u>public locations</u>, nearly all locations are perceived as more threatened by night, e.g., *train station* (M = 0.9; SD = 0.9) as well as *parks* (M = 1.1; SD = 0.8).

4.2   Acceptance of Crime Surveillance

Generally, surveillance technologies that are *visible* (M = 4.6; SD = 1.5) are more accepted than *invisible* (M = 3.9;SD = 1.8) technologies (see Fig. 2). Increase in *ambient lighting* (M = 5.4; SD = 0.8) is most wanted, followed by *cameras* (M = 4.6; SD = 1.4). *Motion detectors* (M = 3.7; SD = 1.7) and *localization technologies* (M = 3.2;SD = 1.6) are considered neutral, whereas *microphones* are rather rejected (M = 2.9; SD = 1.5).

Other security measures (see Fig. 3), e.g., *to be in society with others* (M = 5.3; SD = 0.8), *more police presence* (M = 5.2; SD = 0.98), *private security services* (M = 4.2; SD = 1.6), or *staying only on a place during the day* (M = 4.1; SD = 1.5) received also high acceptance scores.

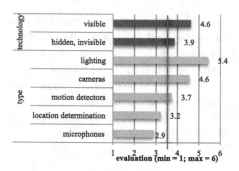

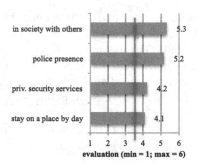

Fig. 2. Acceptance of surveillance technologies   **Fig. 3.** Other measures enhancing perceived crime threat

Perceived benefits of crime surveillance are rated similarly positive (see Fig. 4). *Investigation of crime* (M = 4.9;SD = 1.5) is perceived as the most important benefit. Regarding perceived barriers (see Fig. 5), *protection of sensitive personal information* (M = 4.8; SD = 1.6) is the most important aspect. *Inference of being under general suspicion* (M = 3.5; SD = 1.6), an assumed barrier, is quite accepted though.

The acceptance of crime surveillance technologies depends on the type of locations (see Fig. 6).

Surveillance of <u>private locations</u> is not accepted, e.g., the *bedroom* (M = 1.3; SD = 0.7), and also rejected at <u>semi-private locations</u>, e.g., at *church* (M = 2.5; SD = 1.6). Crime surveillance at <u>semi-public locations</u>, in contrast, is quite accepted,

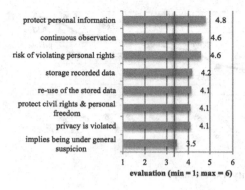

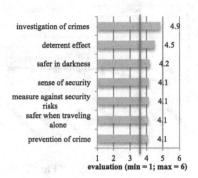

Fig. 4. Benefits of surveillance   **Fig. 5.** Barriers of surveillance

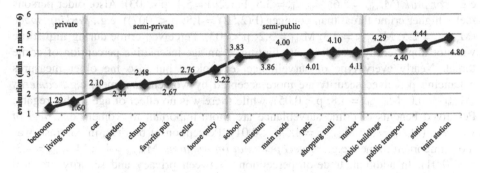

Fig. 6. Crime surveillance acceptance

e.g., at a *museum* (M = 3.4; SD = 1.7) as well as in *schools* (M = 3.8; SD = 1.7). At public locations, crime surveillance is most accepted, e.g., at *train stations* (M = 4.8; SD = 1.4).

4.3 Security Versus Privacy

Finally, the trade-off between looking for security and protecting one's own privacy is reported (see Fig. 7). Outcomes can be summarized quite simply. Whenever private locations, e.g., *living room* (M = 9; SD = 1.9), or semi-private locations, e.g., *church* (M = 7; SD = 3), are addressed, privacy is preferred over security. On the other hand, security is preferred over privacy at public locations, e.g., *train station* (M = 2.6; SD = 2.3) and at semi-public locations, e.g., *shopping mall* (M = 4.1; SD = 2.7).

4.4 User Diversity

As user diversity might be crucial for security perception and acceptance of surveillance technologies, we analyzed effects of age and gender on acceptance patterns. During **daytime**, women feel more threatened by crime than men ($F(1,26) = 2; p < .02$),

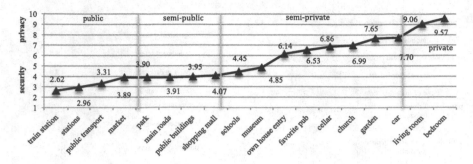

Fig. 7. Security vs. Privacy

e.g., *car park* ($M_{male} = 2.6$; $M_{female} = 3.5$; $F(1,26) = 5,1$; $p < .03$). Also, older persons feel a higher crime threat than younger ($F(2,52) = 1,8$; $p < .007$)), e.g., *parking space* ($M_{young} = 2.5$; $M_{middle} = 2.3$; $M_{old} = 3.2$; $p < .03$). Perceived crime during **nighttime** was not impacted by user diversity, hinting at an age-insensitive perception of crime threat. Nearly every type of surveillance technology but also the other measures enhancing perceived security are more accepted by women than men, e.g., *cameras* ($M_{male} = 4.0$; $M_{female} = 4.8$; $p < 0.05$), while there was no effect of age in this regard. Perceived benefits of crime surveillance are more important to women, e.g., *feel of security*: ($M_{male} = 3.6$; $M_{female} = 4.5$; $p < 0.01$). Perception of barriers, in contrast, was more important to men, e.g., *protect personal information* ($M_{male} = 4.9$; $M_{female} = 4.3$; $p < 0.01$). In addition, trade-off-perceptions between privacy and security are also gendered: while privacy is more important to men, security is much more important to women ($F(1,18) = 2.3$; $p < .006$).

5   Conclusion

This study revealed insights into acceptance patterns regarding the use of crime surveillance technologies in urban environments. In order to understand the specific needs of a diverse traveller population, we examined the tolerance towards such technologies at various public and private urban locations. Results show a differentiated picture. In private locations, the perceived crime threat was quite low, in contrast to public spaces. Surveillance technologies are accepted in those locations in which crime threat is present. Users then prefer safety over privacy. User diversity is a crucial factor in this context: Women attach a higher importance to safety in general, in contrast to men, while men prefer the protection of their privacy. Overall, the predominantly technology-centered planning of infrastructural mobility concepts, without integrating citizens into the decision-making processes, seems not sufficient to cover human attitudes and regarding safety and privacy concerns in the context of urban mobility.

References

1. Ziefle, M., Schneider, C., Vallee, D., Schnettler, A., Krempels K.-H., Jarke, M.: Urban Future outline (UFO). A roadmap on research for livable cities. ERCIM News (N. 98). http://ercim-news.ercim.eu/en98/keynote-smart-cities (2014)
2. Wilkowska, W., Farrokhikhiavi, R., Ziefle, M., Vallée, D.: Mobility requirements for the use of carpooling among different user groups. In: Ahram, T. et al. (eds.) 5th International Conference on Applied Human Factors & Ergonomics, pp. 401–413 (2014)
3. Arning, K., Ziefle, M., Muehlhans, H.: Join the ride! user requirements and interface design guidelines for a commuter carpooling platform. In: Marcus, A. (ed.) DUXU 2013, Part III. LNCS, vol. 8014, pp. 10–19. Springer, Heidelberg (2013)
4. Schaar, A.K., Ziefle, M.: Potential of e-Travel assistants to increase older adults' mobility. In: Leitner, G., Hitz, M., Holzinger, A. (eds.) USAB 2010. LNCS, vol. 6389, pp. 138–155. Springer, Heidelberg (2010)
5. Smith, M.J., Clarke, R.V.: Crime and public transport. Crime Justice 27, 169–233 (2000)
6. Marshall, R.D., Bryant, R.A., Amsel, L., Suh, E.J., Cook, J.M., Neria, Y.: The psychology of ongoing threat: relative risk appraisal, the September 11 attacks, and terrorism-related fears. Am. Psychol. 62(4), 304 (2007)
7. Quigley, J.M., Weinberg, D.H.: Intra-urban residential mobility: a review and synthesis. Int. Reg. Sci. Rev. 2(1), 41–66 (1977)
8. Isnard, A.: Can surveillance cameras be successful in preventing crime and controlling anti-social behaviours. In: The character, impact and prevention of crime in regional Australia Conference, Townsville. 2-3 October 2001
9. Wiecek, C., Saetnan, A.R.: Restrictive? Permissive? The Contradictory Framing of Video Surveillance in Norway and Denmark. Norwegian University of Science and Technology. Working paper 4. Trondheim (2002)
10. Chattopadhyayr, D., Dasgupta, R., Banerjee, R., Chakraborty, A.: Event driven video surveillance system using city cloud. In: First International Conference on Intelligent Infrastructure at the 47th Annual National Convention Computer Society of India (2013)
11. Song, M., Tao, D., Maybank, S.J.: Sparse Camera Network for Visual Surveillance – A Comprehensive Survey, Cornell University, http://arxiv.org/abs/1302.0446 (2013)
12. Himmel, S., Ziefle, M., Arning, K.: From living space to urban quarter: acceptance of ICT monitoring solutions in an ageing society. In: Kurosu, M. (ed.) HCII/HCI 2013, Part III. LNCS, vol. 8006, pp. 49–58. Springer, Heidelberg (2013)
13. Akers, R.L., Greca, A.J., Sellers, C., Cochran, J.: Fear of crime and victimization among the elderly in different types of communities. Criminology 25(3), 487–506 (1987)
14. Stanko, E.A.: Women, crime, and fear. Ann. Am. Acad. Polit. Soc. Sci. 539(1), 46–58 (1995)
15 Ziefle, M.,Wilkowska, W.: What makes people change their preferences in public transportation – opinions in different user groups. In: Giaffreda, R., Caganova, D., Li, Y., Riggio, R., Voisard, A. (eds.) IoT 2014, LNICST, vol. 151, pp. 137–143. Springer, Heidelberg (2015)

A Study on Context Information Collection for Personal Mobile Device Identification in BYOD and Smart Work Environment

Taeeun Kim$^{(\boxtimes)}$, MyoungSun Noh, Kyungho Chung, and Chaetae Im

IT Venture Tower, Jungdaero 135, Songpagu, Seoul, Korea
{tekim31,nmsnms,khc,chtim}@kisa.or.kr

Abstract. With the advent of BYOD (bring your own device) environment where personal mobile devices are used in work, companies began introducing NAC and MDM systems to prevent the leaks of, to access control and to efficiently manage confidential information. However, NAC and MDM access control policy is uniformly applied to users, and thus BYOD is not being actively introduced as of current where security threats exist as a result of frequent device loss and theft as well as low security level. Therefore, flexible policy setting and control method through personalized information collection are necessary. This study discusses the definition of context information and a method to collect the information to detect users' abnormal behaviors considering the diversity of devices used and connection environments for BYOD.

Keywords: BYOD · Security · Context information · Network management

1 Introduction

As the use of various mobile devices, such as smartphone and tablet PC, is increasing as a result of wireless communication technology advancement in recent times, the scope of mobile device use is expanding from simple personal communication to corporate work processing.

Accordingly, companies have introduced a working environment using mobile devices in order to improve their work productivity. They purchased and supplied devices in order to break away from closed working environment and, accordingly, to realize a working environment using mobile devices. However, it was not activated due to difficulties in device management and maintenance arising from device loss and changes as well as purchasing cost.

Recently, the concept of BYOD (bring your own device) is drawing attention as a new corporate working environment because of changes in working environment to use personally owned mobile devices [1]. BYOD environment is where individual employees work by accessing internal corporate data using their personal mobile devices, such as laptop computers, tablet PCs and smartphones. It is anticipated to produce work productivity improvement and cost reduction effects.

As convenience was improved as a result of the advent of BYOD, a new IT environment, the instances of personal devices accessing internal corporate

© Institute for Computer Sciences, Social Informatics and Telecommunications Engineering 2015
R. Giaffreda et al. (Eds.): IoT360 2014, Part II, LNICST 151, pp. 104–109, 2015.
DOI: 10.1007/978-3-319-19743-2_16

infrastructures increased and this led to such security issues as corporate data leaks. Personal devices are easily exposed to loss, theft and attacks as a result of their low security level and thus it has been investigated that accesses to and attacks on internal corporate infrastructures through personal devices are occurring frequently.

For BYOD security, NAC (network access control), a network access control security equipment, and MDM (mobile device management) for mobile device control are being proposed. However, these methods are subject to limitations. NAC controls users through authentication at the time of access to internal corporate infrastructures. However, it does not interfere with user behaviors after the authentication. In case of MDM, it is a method to install a corporate security program in personal devices, and thus to monitor and control the devices. It generates a sense of rejection among users, however, and thus does not conform to the direction pursued by BYOD.

Therefore, to respond to various situations that can occur in BYOD environment, methods for abnormal behavior detection and control through device and user identification are necessary.

In this paper proposed context information composition and collection method to create patterned information and detect abnormal behaviors based on user and device characteristics and diverse environmental elements. The proposed method is to organize captive portal for the existing corporate network access control, to administer user identification and context information collection/analysis through mirroring of traffic for service use and thus to pattern user behaviors. Using information created as such, abnormal behaviors are examined independently for individual users that display different patterns of use [5].

Technology trend for internal corporate infrastructure protection in BYOD and smart work environment and the method of context information collection are analyzed in Sect. 2 and the proposed method is described in Sect. 3. In Sect. 4, plans for applying the proposed method to BYOD environment and the direction of studies to be pursued in the future are discussed.

2 Related Work and Research

NAC security technology targeting BYOD environment controls network accesses by inspecting whether or not user's devices satisfy security policy standard before they access the network.

NAC blocks access to the network of infected PC in order to prevent the spreading of malicious code in corporate network. At present, wired and wireless integrated security functions, such as IP-based access control, authentication by mobile terminal, terminal security and integrity verification, are provided. However, as the main purpose of NAC is to control user authentication and access, it lacks the function to detect and respond to abnormal behaviors of users or devices after network access. In addition, it centers on the registered user authentication, and thus the functions for device authentication/management are insufficient [6, 7].

As such, BYOD environment is subject to a special security requirement to protect corporate data through isolation of users displaying abnormal behaviors in addition to the ensuring of work continuity and the use of various personal devices. Therefore, it is impossible to solve security issues in BYOD environment using NAC solution only.

MDM technology provides the functions for device registration/management, suspension of the use of lost devices and device tracking based on administrator authority in a remote location for powered-on mobile devices anytime, anywhere using OTA (over the air) [8].

There are also problems in MDM system-based access control, which provides a function to directly control personal devices in BYOD environment. MDM is an application in itself. Therefore, it is difficult to control and monitor accesses made by other applications. In addition, it is impossible to analyze behaviors in relation to network data of mobile devices. Most of all, users feel reluctant about MDM agent installation in their personal devices out of fear for violation of their privacy, and thus the system distribution and diffusion are difficult to achieve. At the same time, it is subject to an increase in the cost for continuous version management on various terminal devices.

3   Proposed Method

The proposed method is for context information that can be collected for abnormal behavior detection in BYOD and smart work environment and it outlines the structure and operating method of a system to collect the context information.

The overall system structure is as shown in Fig. 1. Context information is collected based on the user's captive portal connection and network traffic information, and thus the user's profile is created. The patterned information created as such is used in deciding users' abnormal behaviors. Users and devices detected of abnormalities are controlled real-time.

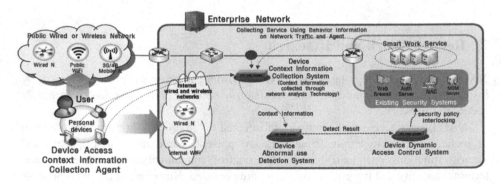

Fig. 1. Security system in BYOD and smart work environment

3.1   Context Information Collection System Structure and Operation

In BYOD environment, a technology to collect context information based on network independent of the types of users' devices is necessary. The proposed system is of a structure to administer mirroring on corporate network access traffic and categorizes users based on the connection IP. Context information is collected at the time of network access, use and termination separately. When user accesses corporate network using his or her personal mobile device, a captive portal linked to the company's authentication server is accessed. In this case, browser information and User_Agent in HTTP packet are analyzed, and thus the access context information is collected.

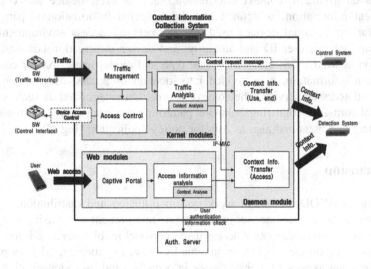

Fig. 2. Context information collection system configuration

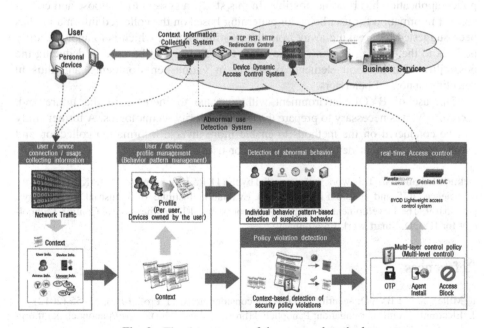

Fig. 3. The data process of the proposed method

Following the access, context information is collected using periodic network traffic that occurs during the course of using company's internal service. If network use is not detected for a set period of time, context information for termination is created (Fig. 2).

3.2 Detailed Elements of Context Information

In BYOD environment, context information, such as user, device and connection environment information, is defined and the collected information is patterned to identify various personal devices used and the network access environments. User information includes user ID and authority, and device information consists of such information as MAC, OS, browser, device type and model name. As for connection environment information, it is divided into location of access, access time, access network and accessed service. The context information categorized as such is used in deciding abnormality following behavior patterning for each user in terms of who, when, where and what and also as data for policy application (Fig. 3).

4 Conclusion

As a result of BYOD and smart work system diffusion and distribution, a flexible security method has become necessary in an environment for business operation through internal corporate system access using personal mobile devices. It has become possible to create different behavior patterns by collecting meaningful information in user environment as well as mobile device information and user identification values. Through this, the establishment of various security policies rather than uniformed policy application has become possible. In this study, a system to compose and collect context information for user behavior patterning based on the collected information has been suggested by breaking away from the existing system, which is to apply security policies to the existing network traffic only. This system can be used in deducing the possibility of behavioral elements occurring in various environments, and thus in detecting abnormal behaviors.

The use of BYOD environment will continue to increase in the future and, accordingly, it is necessary to prepare the related security technologies. A further study will be conducted on the methods to enable more diverse information collection and user behavior element definition necessary for user identification.

Acknowledgments. This work was supported by the IT R&D program of MSIP/KEIT (Ministry of Science, ICT and Future Planning/Korea Evaluation Institute of Industrial Technology). [10045109, The Development of Context-Awareness based Dynamic Access Control Technology for BYOD, Smart work Environment].

References

1. Miller, K.W.: BYOD: security and privacy considerations. IT Prof. **14**(5), 53–55 (2012)
2. Electronic Frontier Foundation: Panopticlick(browser fingerprint). https://panopticlick.eff.org/index.php?action=log&js=yes

3. Fyodor: Remote OS detection via TCP/IP stack fingerprinting, October 1998. http://www. insecure.org/nmap/nmap-fingerprinting-article.html
4. Smart, M.: Defeating TCP/IP stack fingerprinting. In: Proceedings of the 9th USENIX Security Symposium, August 2000
5. Virvilis N., Gritzalis D., Trusted computing vs. advanced persistent threats: can a defender win this game? In: Proceedings. of 10th IEEE International Conference on Autonomic and Trusted Computing, pp. 396–403, IEEE. Press, Italy (2013)
6. Singh, M., Patterh, M.S.: Formal specification of common criteria based access control policy model. Int. J. Netw. Secur. **10**(3), 232–241 (2010)
7. Singh, M., Patterh, M.S., Kim, T.H.: A formal policy oriented access control model for secure enterprise network environment. Int. J. Secur. Appl. **3**(2), 1–14 (2009)
8. Rhee, K., Jeon, W., Won, D.: Security requirements of a mobile device management system. Int. J. Secur. Appl. **6**(2), 353–358 (2012)

Iterative Design of a Sensor Network for the Evaluation of Pedestrian Facility Design Using Agent-Based Simulations

Wanling Chong, Chau Yuen$^{(\boxtimes)}$, Shisheng Huang, and Bige Tuncer

Singapore University of Technology and Design, Singapore 138682, Singapore
wanling_chong@mymail.sutd.edu.sg,
{yuenchau,shisheng_huang,bige_tuncer}@sutd.edu.sg

Abstract. This paper presents the iterative approach taken in the design of a sensor network for the purpose of evaluating pedestrian facility design. Specifically, sensors are to be used to measure pedestrian flows in a network of pedestrian walkways. Data collected by the sensors will be employed in agent-based pedestrian simulations for the visualisation and analysis of pedestrian flows. Using Fruin's (1971) Level-of-Service criteria, pedestrian flows will be evaluated to determine if they meet the requirements set out by the regulatory authorities for adequate pedestrian facility design.

Keywords: Iterative design approach · Agent-based simulations · Human-sensing · Sensor network · Pedestrian flows · pedestrian facility design · Pedestrian level-of-service criteria

1 Introduction

Singapore's public transportation network comprises the following modes: Mass Rapid Transit (MRT), Light Rapid Transit (LRT), bus and taxi. A seamlessly integrated network involves the design of adequate pedestrian infrastructure to connect the different transportation modes [3]. Pedestrian flow data is used to understand pedestrian movement patterns and peak periods/areas of usage, and to evaluate pedestrian facility design. Traditional data collection methods include the use of observations [5,6], interviews [7] and experiments [1]. We propose the alternative use of sensors, which are less labour-intensive and obtrusive than direct observational methods, and also allows information to be collected continuously over time.

In this paper, an iterative approach is adopted in sensor network design by employing pedestrian scenario simulations both before and after sensor installation. When employed before sensor installation, these simulations (1) clarify the

This research is supported by the MND Research Fund Sustainable Urban Living Grant.

© Institute for Computer Sciences, Social Informatics and Telecommunications Engineering 2015
R. Giaffreda et al. (Eds.): IoT360 2014, Part II, LNICST 151, pp. 110–117, 2015.
DOI: 10.1007/978-3-319-19743-2_17

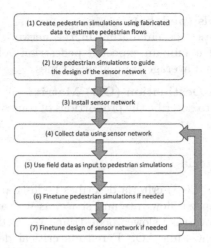

Fig. 1. Iterative approach to designing a sensor network

data required to create pedestrian simulations and to be collected by the sensors, and (2) identify potentially congested areas in the network, so that research resources can be directed to those areas. These findings can then be used to optimise the sensor network's efficiency in data collection. Simulations created after sensor installation will incorporate data collected by the sensors to refine the previously-created simulations. This allows initial assumptions made about pedestrian flows to be validated or refuted, estimates of pedestrian arrivals to be adjusted and pedestrian origin-destination matrices to be fine-tuned. Additionally, locations for the installation of more sensors (if needed) can be identified, or additional parameters to be measured determined.

2   Methodology

2.1   Iterative Design Approach

Figure 1 contains a visual representation of the iterative approach adopted in sensor network design. A test site in Singapore is adopted as a case study for the framework proposed in this paper.

2.2   Parameters of Study

To create the pedestrian simulations prior to sensor installation, the following parameters were assumed. Data collected by the sensors will subsequently be used to fine-tune these assumed parameters, as per Step 5 of the iterative design approach.

1. Pedestrian Speeds:
All pedestrians were assumed to walk at speeds following a normal distribution with a mean of 1.27 m/s and standard deviation of 0.14 m/s. These values were based on a study of pedestrian speeds in Singapore's MRT stations [8].

2. Pedestrian Arrivals (ped/hr):
A total of 10,000 pedestrians circulating in the network per hour was used, which is about 22 % of maximum expected pedestrian volumes at peak hours given train capacities and average train arrival times.

3. Pedestrian Origin-Destination (OD) Matrix:
OD matrices were used to describe the proportions of routes taken by pedestrians within the network.

2.3   Evaluation Criteria

Fruin's Level-of-Service (LOS) criteria describes pedestrian flows using coupled relationships between speed, flow rate and space, as well as qualitative factors, such as the ability to overtake slower pedestrians [2]. LOS A is the threshold of unhindered movement while LOS F reflects critical densities where movement is disrupted [2]. Singapore's Land Transport Authority (LTA) specifies that pedestrian flows/densities along corridors without commercial/transit facilities or information signages should not exceed LOS D [2], provided there are no cross-flows [4]. Additionally, LOS D should be an intermittent condition during peak hours [4]. The following set of evaluation criteria (Table 1) was thus formulated to determine the likelihood that pedestrian flows would satisfy LTA's requirements for adequate pedestrian facility design. These evaluation criteria were chosen arbitrarily, giving researchers the flexibility to alter them depending on their interpretation of the results or other requirements.

Due to the stochastic nature of the simulations, 100 iterations of each simulation were performed and results processed. For each iteration, pedestrian densities at three locations were obtained from the simulation every minute, and compared against pedestrian LOS criteria [2]. These locations (indicated in Fig. 2 as Points A, B and C) reflect critical congestion level zones in the pedestrian network.

3   Experimental Set-Up, Simulations and Results

3.1   Simulated Network Geometry

The simulated network (Fig. 2) contains eight entry/exit points, two of which are MRT station gantries. Another two entry/exit points are exits leading to/from the MRT station, while the remaining four lead to two shopping malls (labelled Malls A and B) adjacent to the MRT station.

3.2   Experimental Set-Up

AnyLogic 7 (trial version) was used to create pedestrian simulation models for this project. Due to functionality limitations of the trial version, some pedestrian routes were excluded from the simulations and are highlighted in blue/green in the following OD matrices.

Table 1. Summary of evaluation criteria

Evaluation Criteria				Satisfies LTA's
Not exceed LOS D	LOS D <5%	LOS E <1%	LOS F = 0%	requirements
✓	✓	✓	✓	Highly likely
✗	✓	✓	✓	Likely
✗	✗	✓	✓	Somewhat likely
✗	✗	✗	✓	Somewhat unlikely
✗	✗	✗	✗	Unlikely

Three experiments (Control (C), Experiment 1 (E1) and Experiment 2 (E2) were conducted. C was used both to estimate expected usage of the pedestrian network, as well as to establish a point of reference for comparison with E1 and E2.

Control Experiment (C). Pedestrian arrivals of 10,000 ped/hour were assumed, with a 70:20:10 ratio, representing the ratio of pedestrians entering the network via MRT, leaving the network via MRT, and remaining in the network (Fig. 3).

Pedestrian arrivals by MRT are likely to result in periodic discharge of a large number of pedestrians in a relatively short amount of time. This was modelled using the following arrival schedule for MRT Gantries 1 and 2 (Fig. 4), scaled to the magnitude of pedestrian arrivals. Pedestrian arrival rates at the remaining six entry/exit points were defined using Poisson distributions in ped/hour.

Experiment 1 (E1). Pedestrian flows were increased by 50 % from 10,000 ped/hour to 15,000 ped/hour. Arrivals per hour at each origin were increased proportionately. All other simulation parameters were kept constant compared to C (Fig. 5).

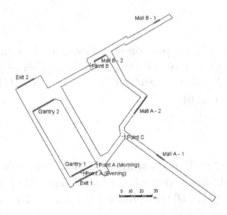

Fig. 2. Geometry of simulated pedestrian network

O/D	No of pp	Gantry 1	Gantry 2	Exit 1	Exit 2	Mall A 1	Mall A 2	Mall B 1	Mall B 2
Gantry 1	3425			0.88		0.05	0.05	0.02	0.02
Gantry 2	3550				0.85	0.02	0.02	0.055	0.055
Exit 1	425	1.00							
Exit 2	450		0.67			0.11	0.11	0.055	0.055
Mall A - 1	600	0.58		0.29	0.09			0.02	0.02
Mall A - 2	500	0.50		0.35	0.10			0.025	0.025
Mall B - 1	575		0.61	0.15	0.21	0.02			0.01
Mall B - 2	475		0.53	0.18	0.26		0.02	0.01	

Option not applicable
Omitted; assume pedestrian will choose exit closest to their destination
Omitted: limited options available in simulator

Fig. 3. Origin-destination matrix - control experiment

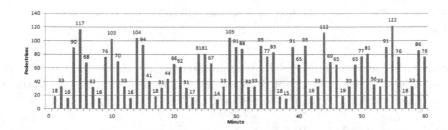

Fig. 4. Pedestrian arrival schedule (3500/hr)

O/D	No of pp	Gantry 1	Gantry 2	Exit 1	Exit 2	Mall A 1	Mall A 2	Mall B 1	Mall B 2
Gantry 1	5138			0.86		0.05	0.05	0.02	0.02
Gantry 2	5325				0.85	0.02	0.02	0.055	0.055
Exit 1	638	1.00							
Exit 2	675		0.67			0.11	0.11	0.055	0.055
Mall A - 1	900	0.58		0.29	0.09			0.02	0.02
Mall A - 2	750	0.50		0.35	0.10			0.025	0.025
Mall B - 1	863		0.61	0.15	0.21	0.02			0.01
Mall B - 2	713		0.53	0.18	0.26	0.02	0.01		

Option not applicable
Omitted; assume pedestrian will choose exit closest to their destination
Omitted: limited options available in simulator

Fig. 5. Origin-destination matrix - experiment 1

Experiment 2 (E2). The proportion of pedestrians heading to Malls A and B from Gantries 1 and 2 was increased (from 14–15 number of pedestrians heading to MRT Exits 1 and 2 (from 85–86 62–67 entering via MRT and remaining in the network constant (Fig. 6).

3.3   Results

Point A. Non-zero LOS F pedestrian densities were obtained in all experiments, with the highest observed in E1 (2.97 %). High LOS E pedestrian densities were also obtained (8.15 %, 16.60 % and 8.37 % for C, E1 and E2 respectively) (Table 2).

O/D	No of pp	Gantry 1	Gantry 2	Exit 1	Exit 2	Mall A 1	Mall A 2	Mall B 1	Mall B 2
Gantry 1	3475			0.67		0.17	0.12	0.02	0.02
Gantry 2	3450				0.62	0.02	0.02	0.17	0.17
Exit 1	475	1.00							
Exit 2	550		0.55			0.18	0.18	0.045	0.045
Mall A - 1	587.5	0.60		0.21	0.06			0.065	0.065
Mall A - 2	472.5	0.53		0.26	0.08			0.065	0.065
Mall B - 1	545		0.64	0.115	0.16	0.055			0.03
Mall B - 2	445		0.56	0.14	0.20	0.07	0.03		

Option not applicable
Omitted; assume pedestrian will choose exit closest to their destination
Omitted; limited options available in simulator

Fig. 6. Origin-destination matrix - experiment 2

Point B. Lower percentages of LOS A pedestrian densities were obtained in E1 and E2 (27.68 % and 28.55 % respectively) compared to C (56.98 %). Higher percentages of LOS E pedestrian densities were obtained for E2 (4.45 %) compared to E1 (1.02 %), while LOS F (0.02 %) pedestrian densities were obtained only for E2 and not for E1.

Point C. Lower percentages of LOS A pedestrian densities were obtained in E1 and E2 (51.08 % and 43.57 % respectively) compared to C (79.97 %). Higher percentages of LOS E pedestrian densities were obtained for E2 (1.07 %) compared to E1 (0.32 %). No LOS F pedestrian densities were obtained for all experiments (Table 3).

Summary. Most critical congestion levels were experienced in E2, followed by E1, then C. For Point A, pedestrian densities were unlikely to meet LTA's requirements for all experiments. This indicates that large numbers of pedestrians disembarking from the MRT, combined with the relatively small space between MRT Gantry 1 and Exit 1, are likely to result in high pedestrian densities at Point A. As for E2, more pedestrians were arriving from Malls A and B, instead of from the MRT Exits 1 and 2. This resulted in longer walking distances for pedestrians, and subsequently, longer durations spent in the pedestrian network, which caused increased congestion levels.

Table 2. Results - proportion of LOS at different points

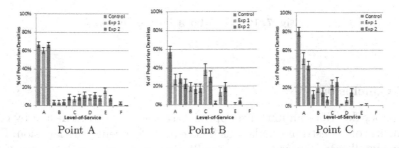

Point A   Point B   Point C

Table 3. Summary of results

Experiment	Point A	Point B	Point C
Control	Unlikely	Highly likely	Likely
Experiment 1	Unlikely	Somewhat unlikely	Somewhat likely
Experiment 2	Unlikely	Unlikely	Somewhat unlikely

4   Discussion and Conclusion

4.1   Design of Sensor Network

Based on the simulations' results, the following layout of sensors is proposed (Fig. 7). This includes a cluster of sensors at each entry/exit point to measure flows of pedestrians entering, exiting and heading towards and away from the entry/exit points. Additionally, sensors installed along the walkways can be used to measure pedestrian flows, which not only facilitates calibration of the pedestrian simulations, but also provides an immediate estimate of pedestrian LOS experienced along the walkways. From here, subsequent fine-tuning of the model and redesigning of sensor locations will allow relevant stakeholders to better evaluate the design of this pedestrian facility.

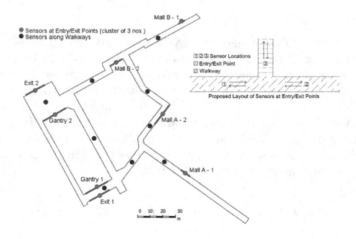

Fig. 7. Proposed Locations of Sensors

4.2   Conclusion

This paper describes an iterative approach to sensor network design by employing the use of pedestrian simulations before and after sensor installation. Prior to sensor installation, researchers can familiarise themselves with the creation and use of pedestrian simulations, and estimate the order of magnitude of expected pedestrian flows. The latter facilitates sensor network design as it informs sensor choice, and identifies critical locations for the placement of sensors to optimise data collection. Upon sensor installation, data obtained from the sensors can be used to refine and calibrate the pedestrian simulations. For example, assumptions made when creating the simulations can be validated/refuted, and estimates of pedestrian arrivals and their routes taken can be adjusted. The simulations also facilitate fine-tuning of sensor network design by identifying locations for the installation of more sensors, or determining additional parameters to be measured by the sensors.

References

1. Daamen, W., Hoogendoorn, S.P.: Experimental Research of Pedestrian Walking Behavior. Transportation Research Board Annual Meeting (2003)
2. Fruin, J.J.: Pedestrian planning and design, Metropolitan Association of Urban Designers and Environmental Planners (1971)
3. Lam, W.W.Y.: Building a Seamless Transport System through Walking. Paper presented at the International Transport Forum: Seamless Transport. Making Connections, Leipzig (2012)
4. Land Transport Authority. Architectural Design Criteria (Revision A3, May 2013). http://www.lta.gov.sg/content/ltaweb/en/industry-matters.html. Accessed 14 January 2013
5. Lee, J.Y.S., Lam, W.H.K., Wong, S.C.: Pedestrian simulation model for Hong Kong underground stations. In: Proceedings of Intelligent Transportation Systems, pp. 554–558 (2001)
6. New York City Department of City Planning Transportation: Division. New York City Pedestrian Level of Service Study. Technical report, New York (2006)
7. Thambiah, M., Adachi, T., Hagiwara, T., Kagaya, S., Uchida, K.: Evaluation of Pedestrian Level of Service on Sidewalks and Crosswalks Using Conjoint Analysis. Transportation Research Board Annual Meeting (2004)
8. Yeo, S.K., He, Y.: Commuter characteristics in mass rapid transit stations in Singapore. Fire Saf. J. 44(2), 183–191 (2009)

"I Expect Smart Services!" User Feedback on NFC Based Services Addressing Everyday Routines

Bente Evjemo[1(✉)], Sigmund Akselsen[1], Dag Slettemeås[2],
Arne Munch-Ellingsen[1], Anders Andersen[3], and Randi Karlsen[3]

[1] Telenor Research, Sykehusvn. 23, 9294 Tromsø, Norway
bente.evjemo@telenor.com
[2] National Institute for Consumer Research,
Sandakervn. 24c, 0405 Oslo, Norway
[3] UiT The Arctic University of Norway, 9037 Tromsø, Norway

Abstract. Smartphones are central to everyday activities. Paired with short distance radio technologies the range of smartphone application is extended and development of "smarter" services is enabled. A trial, including 60 pilot users, shows that the smartphone itself and its capability to emulate transaction and access cards are highly valued. In order to meet expectations adaptive and personalized features/services should be added, based on knowledge of the individual users' activities and communicated needs, as well as their curiosity for new adventures.

Keywords: Smartphone · NFC · Everyday routines · User study

1 Introduction

The mobile phone has changed from initially being a means for making individuals directly addressable to becoming a platform that provides innovative opportunities for smart services. A recent survey of mobile phone usage shows that in addition to making calls and sending messages people use the phone extensively for more than 30 different tasks on a daily basis, and they would even want to use it for more if the needed services were available [1]. These mobile services play an increasingly important role in transforming people's everyday lives and empowering societies to grow and progress.

Today about 90 % of handset sales worldwide are of so-called smartphones, with more advanced computing capability and connectivity than basic phones. A smartphone typically combines the features of a mobile phone with those of other popular consumer devices, such as a media player, a digital camera, or a GPS navigation unit. It also includes touchscreen computer features such as web browsing, Wi-Fi, and third-party apps.

Near Field Communication (NFC) technology has been part of this development since Sony and Philips agreed on a new specification based on RFID technology back in 2002. NFC consists of a set of close-range wireless communication standards that

© Institute for Computer Sciences, Social Informatics and Telecommunications Engineering 2015
R. Giaffreda et al. (Eds.): IoT360 2014, Part II, LNICST 151, pp. 118–124, 2015.
DOI: 10.1007/978-3-319-19743-2_18

enable devices to transfer small amounts of data to each other. It is considered a promising input to an innovative and sustainable mobile agenda.

The contactless feature of NFC enables the user to bypass several, often laborious, steps on the way to reaching the core service. Furthermore, a gentle tap on specific tag points can activate information services or transactional services and thus contribute to bridge the gap between digital and physical worlds [2].

This paper presents user feedback on a set of NFC services addressing everyday life routines, in a framework that recognizes mobile phone usage as highly individual [3]. The initiative referred to as the NFC City project has been run in the spirit of open innovation and included partners in the telecom, banking, transportation, physical access and information service sectors as well as academic institutions and governmental bodies [4].

2   The Multi-service Trial

Many trials have been conducted to explore user reactions to NFC services [5]. Most of them focus on single services and single routines and address the purchase/adoption phase of a technology usage cycle. These limitations were challenged in the NFC City project by conducting a trial where users were exposed to several services that they could naturally relate to. The trial lasted for 17 months and involved 60 students (mixed gender sample, 19-34 years, 25 % had no prior smartphone experience). They all received an NFC enabled smartphone (Samsung S3) when entering the trial.

The following services were implemented and launched stepwise during the trial period [6]: Prepaid coffee card; city bus travel card; housing access key; fitness poster at the gym; check-in tags at campus; information tags for canteen menus, evening events, timetables, and recent news from the student paper; and programmable tags for the students to develop their own personalized services.

The project applied an explorative approach to a set of research questions [7] and user feedback was collected throughout the trial (Fig. 1). This paper focuses on how attractive NFC services should be implemented.

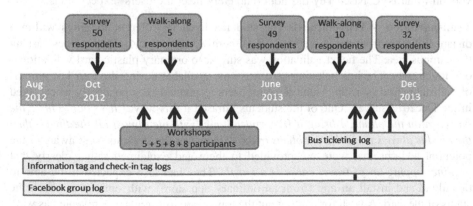

Fig. 1. User feedback was collected throughout the project period (Aug 2012 - Dec 2013)

3 Findings

Key findings are here presented relative to the students' daily routines. We will however first describe the role of the smartphone within the sample.

Smartphone Usage. The new phone was positively received by the pilot users. One of them put it this way (Dec2012 survey): *"For the first time I use mobile Internet. Web pages are easy to read – more easily than with my previous phones. Thus it is more interesting. I discover new stuff almost every day."* A check some months later (June2013 survey) showed that they used the new phone more often than the one they had before. The number of downloaded apps varied from just a few to more than 50, but most of them reported a number between 10 and 30 apps. They also claimed that the phone had become a more essential artefact to them, illustrated by this quotation: *"Often I use the phone as pastime, - for instance when I wait for the bus or during commercial breaks on TV. I can't remember how I coped with these pauses before – I would not like to return to an ordinary phone. I like the always on access to Internet. Whenever I need information I can check. I like the camera as well – I don't use my digital camera any more. I fancy the way my phone substitutes my diary, camera, mp3 player, and so on - and thereby relieves me from the hassle of dragging all these devices around."*

Leaving Home – Housing Key. Only 3 of the 60 participants got the opportunity to use the NFC based housing key solution. The whole sample was asked about their locking routines and where they kept their keys, etc. (most of them carried the key in their pocket of their jeans or jacket), and a digital key integrated into the mobile phone was regarded an attractive scenario.

We used an off-the-shelf hotel solution which included a snap lock feature, presumably a handy solution for hotel guests but not at all appreciated by the students. Locking guests into their house was also mentioned as a drawback while on the positive side the new solution ended numerous searches for keys. The possibility to distribute temporal keys over the air – for instance to a visiting friend – was requested but unfortunately not implemented in the trial solution. All in all, this rather simple version of an NFC based key did not completely meet the users' expectations.

Transportation – Travel Card. The students lived in different lodgings within a distance of 5 km from the university. All of them were pretty close to bus lines passing the campus area. The ticket validation was similar to ordinary plastic card validation – one touch only. The bus ticketing card was only available during the four last months of the trial period (see Fig. 1) but the pilot users responded very positively when asked in the Dec2013 survey. One of the students phrased it this way: *"It's cool to have the bus card on the phone. I bring it [the smartphone] with me almost all the time – then the card is always there. No problems in use."* However the students were aware of the potential add-ons that were not provided to them and exclaimed rather clearly that *"online topping-up of travel cards is a must!"* They had also expected to be able to download and install an app (from an ordinary app store) with options to check the status of the card. A wish for lending out the travel card to friends was revealed as well.

Organize the Day at Campus – Information Tags. Information tags were accessible at campus from the start of the trial period. The overall usage was still limited. One of the students explained it this way: *"This was a very simple way of accessing information. I would have used them [the information tags] even more if they better met my personal needs"*. The June 2013 survey showed that the users enjoyed the immediate and easily accessible information, emphasizing the daily menu tag and the bus schedule tags as particularly useful. These two information sources were both of the "quick check" kind that seemed to be a preference, and the bus schedule tag was contextualized as the content shown to the users was adjusted to the geographical position of each individual tag. We also found that the need of educating the users should not be underestimated, like for instance those who answer this way: *"I did not use the tags because I did not know how to use them and I was afraid of making a mess"*.

Visiting the Canteen – Prepaid Coffee Card. The emulated prepaid coffee card was accompanied by a status app showing the number of coffees left. The students got the coffee by touching a dedicated tag on the coffee bar counter with the smartphone. Disregarding some technical problems and the corresponding feedback related to that, the coffee card was welcomed as a convenient and cool way of paying. Some of the users pointed to cost as a reason to ignore the technical hassle: *"I did not buy a coffee card before it was offered at a reduced price. Until then the cost of problems and inconvenience was too high"*. Others emphasized efficiency aspects: *"The machine is very frequently out of order, which is disappointing, but when it works it is much cheaper and faster to buy with phone"*.

Training – Smart Poster Guide. A smart poster was placed nearby the training equipment in the campus gym, providing access to detailed information on muscle groups and how they best could be trained. The descriptions were accompanied by instructional videos and pictures. The feedback varied from one extreme to another: *"… this is rather useless"* / *"… this is a fantastic opportunity"*. Others were more concerned about potential problems: *"The phone is big, and without a cover, well, I think the phone can be damaged by staying close to warm and sweaty skin… when exercising I will focus on the activity – not paying attention to my phone."* However, they reflected eagerly on what a more attractive smart poster might look like: *"The content could be more relevant"*; *"The poster should have more instructional videos"*; *"I would like to check in at the gym with my mobile phone – that would make it possible to count the number of visits and then calculate the actual price per visit"*.

Back Home Again – Private Services. Carrying the mobile phone whenever and wherever at home was normal behavior among our pilot users. Thus it was interesting to see whether they welcomed the possibility to program tags for their private sphere. Some expressed joy and enthusiasm, like this one: *"Above the kitchen Table I have placed a tag that activates a calendar app. Below another table there is a tag activating YouTube on the PC – which again is connected to the TV-set. I have tags for managing burglar alarms, placed besides my bed. And more tags will come;-)"* Others were not fascinated at all. To encourage the tag production we invited them to join workshops. Here one of them explained: *"I did try to program a tag but I stopped because I became uncertain. You know, I have my entire life stored on this phone"*.

She was afraid that content on her phone could be lost or accidentally transferred to the NFC tag, or that unwanted data could be downloaded to her phone. The barrier was removed when the manner of operation was explained to her, guided by her questions and objections [8].

4 Discussion

The users were exposed to both pre-commercial services developed by professional actors as well as dedicated information services developed by students for the project. Furthermore, the everyday tasks that were addressed varied extensively. To select the most successful service is thus neither fair nor feasible. Still the travel card solution deserves particular attention as being by far the most used service.

Why did the travel card become the chosen one? One plausible explanation is that we had a biased sample that already used the bus on daily basis. Hence, the users could easily fit the service into existing routines of travelling. They experienced the smartphone as an easier means of validating tickets as it was always at hand (compared to travel cards found in wallets, pockets or purses). As such the *smartphone itself* and its *capability of emulating* a traditional plastic travel card provided the extra benefit. And further, when the first travel was done they had a prepaid card and an easy way ahead for the next travels.

Even though smartphones and NFC technologies add a new dimension to the existing services by way of tapping for immediate access to services, a simple substitution strategy seems too weak [9]. This is particularly the case for existing services that are experienced as efficient and successful. The travel card should, according to the pilot users, be improved with *"reading card status"* and *"online topping-up"* features. These functionalities can easily be offered by utilizing smartphone assets and resources (screen, security mechanisms, computational power, storage, etc.).

In addition to asking for extra features the pilot users also wanted more relevant services. These expectations can either be met by tailoring the features to individual preferences or by implementing contextual or personal content filters. A touch on today's menu tag would appear personalized and smart if the result on the mobile screen was presented according to individual taste, price and location preferences, written in the user's native language, and so on. By enabling users to tailor their own features and services an extra dimension to the quest for personalization could be added. This implies that service designers must not *"lock"* services into a particular mode, but allow for adaptive and situated services.

Making the smartphone a versatile tool for nearly every task in daily life may create paradoxical situations [10]. The more features added, and the more dependent the user becomes regarding his/her smartphone, the more anxiety may arise in terms of trust, security, privacy, etc. These concerns may reach a tipping point where the users become reluctant to use new services.

A key issue seems to be whether users foresee the smartphone as the ultimate device for "accessing the world", or whether they feel a need to diversify risks and pleasures by allowing other artifacts to address specific tasks. This implies that research must not only address the adoption or appropriation of *services* but also of the *specific devices* that allow for services to be accessed, and the *service environments* for device interaction.

5 Summary and Conclusion

In this paper we have presented findings from a longitudinal multi-service field trial involving NFC-services developed for smartphones. The services were highly different, addressing various aspects/tasks in everyday life. The house key was useful in the sense that the key was never lost (people take care of their smartphones), while easily accessible travel tickets were found most convenient by those taking the bus. The training poster as well as the other information services did not add much to existing habits but users believed them to have potential if more dynamic and tailored information was added. Technical problems seemed to overshadow expected benefits of keeping the coffee card on the mobile phone. The self-programming tags ended up being used sporadically by many, while others embraced them fully, finding a range of purposes they could address.

The services provided different benefits and evoked different emotions among the users, and the list of drivers and inhibitors is as long as the list of services. This means that transferability of adoption knowledge across services is not a simple task.

All in all, the *"contactless"* feature of NFC-services created an immediate wow-effect. At the same time expectations were high as to what these services could bring in terms of *"new adventures"* or in terms of *"consolidating existing tasks and routines"*. Consequently, marketing something as *"smart"* implies that users expect novel services with adaptive and personalized features and a sustainable wow-effect. Hence, the real task of smart innovation is not (only) understanding technology itself, but grasping both the *"adventurous"* and the *"mundane"* needs of consumers and how technology may address these.

References

1. GSMArena: Mobile phone usage report 2011: The things you do. Available from http://www.gsmarena.com/mobile_phone_usage_survey-review-592.php (2011)
2. Ishii, H., Ullmer, B.: Tangible Bits: Towards Seamless Interfaces between People, Bits and Atoms. In: Proceedings of CHI1997, pp. 234–241 (1997)
3. Barkhuus, L., Polichar, V.E.: Empowerment through seamfulness: Smart phones in everyday life. Pers. Ubiquit. Comput. **15**, 629–639 (2011)
4. NFC City project web site, http://www.nfccity.net
5. Coskun, V., Ozdenizci, B., Ok, K.: A Survey on Near Field Communication (NFC) Technology. Wireless Pers. Commun. **71**(3), 2259–2294 (2013)
6. Andersen, A., Karlsen, R., Munch-Ellingsen, A.: NFC providing user friendliness for technologically advanced services. HCI Int. 2013, LNCS, vol. 8017, pp. 337–346 (2013)
7. Slettemeås, D., Evjemo, B., Akselsen, S., Munch-Ellingsen, A., Wolf, S., Jørgensen, V.L.: NFC City: Co-locating NFC services in a multiservice trial approach. Proceedings IADIS Information Systems Conference, pp. 335–341 (2013)

8. Evjemo, B., Slettemeås D., Akselsen, S., Jørgensen, V.L., Wolf, S.: Simplicity – driving technology adoption or feeding uncertainty? Exploring consumer co-production of NFC services. IADIS Int. conf. ICT, Society and Human Beings 2013, pp. 129–132 (2013)
9. Hollan, J., Stornetta, S.: Beyond being there. CHI 1992, pp. 119–125 (1992)
10. Mick, D.E., Fournier, S.: Paradoxes of technology: consumer cognizance, emotions, and coping strategies. J. Consum. Res. **25**, 123–143 (1998)

Introducing Community Awareness
to Location-Based Social Networks

Pavlos Kosmides$^{(\boxtimes)}$, Chara Remoundou, Ioannis Loumiotis,
Evgenia Adamopoulou, and Konstantinos Demestichas

Institute of Communication and Computer Systems - ICCS, National Technical
University of Athens, Zografou, Athens, Greece
{pkosmidis, chremoundou, i_loumiotis,
eadam, cdemest}@cn.ntua.gr

Abstract. During the last years, Social Networks have been in the spotlight of
many researchers, trying to enhance them with pervasive features that will
simplify and facilitate users' experience. One of the most innovative additions to
social networks has been the introduction of communities in users' lifecycle.
However, there are still a lot of issues regarding the automation of this feature in
order to minimize user's effort to discover new communities and as a result, to
improve his experience. In this paper, we introduce the use of communities in
location-based social networks. We also present the proposed systems architecture including Processes and Services.

Keywords: Communities · Social networks · Location-Based · MVC

1 Introduction

The concept of "Virtual Communities" (VC) based on social networks is now widely
accepted by millions of users worldwide. Many networking platforms have been created, more or less differentiated from classical established networks, like Facebook [1]
and Twitter [2] attracting people with common interests and pursuits, thus building
virtual communities of users.

The MVC (Mobile Virtual Community) is the natural evolution of these communities, combining the features of a VC with the services offered by a smart mobile
device (smartphone) or tablet. As the usage of smartphones/tablets has increased and
the offered services have been improved, the MVC has ceased to be simply the mobile
version of VC. Instead, it has evolved and gained its own momentum.

There has been numerous works that deal with the existence of communities in social
networks and how we can take advantage of them. In [3], the authors view community
members relationships as cliques in a graph that represents the social network. They also
study members behaviour in communities and how their behaviour depends on the
communities that they belong to. Similarly, in [4] the authors identify communities in
social networks, based on interests and activities of users. Finally the authors in [5]
propose a model based on social theory, in order to find communities in dynamic social
networks. They present a social cost model and formulate an optimization problem in
order to find the community structure from the sequence of arbitrary graphs.

© Institute for Computer Sciences, Social Informatics and Telecommunications Engineering 2015
R. Giaffreda et al. (Eds.): IoT360 2014, Part II, LNICST 151, pp. 125–130, 2015.
DOI: 10.1007/978-3-319-19743-2_19

A survey has been conducted in [6] where the authors recognize the importance of communities as a feature of social networks. They also state the need for discovering communities in social networks and present some proposed approaches. They also introduce various types of social network and suggest a classification for community detection methods based on the type and nature of social networks.

In this paper, we combine the location-based social networks with the evolutionary concept of MVCs. Specifically we propose an innovative system architecture that takes advantage of the existence of MVCs, and adapts the popularity of nearby locations according to the communities that a user belongs. In addition, user preferences for specific locations, including the number of checkins as well as user's rating, are being processed in order to suggest MVCs to each user.

The following sections present in detail the designed architecture for the implementation of the abovementioned service, including foreseen components and the specified interactions among them. The architecture is designed using ArchiMate® [7] showing the application layer entities (application functions) and their relationship.

2 Popularity Options

The *Popularity options* service is responsible for collecting users' preferences, regarding the results that users expect to receive. Users can define the average age in order to display the results of popularity that relate to specific age groups. They may also choose to show results depending on the daytime period (morning, afternoon, evening) or choose a time window in which to limit the search results to the application. Finally, users are able to choose whether the results of the application will depend on a list of communities they have selected and they are registered to.

Figure 1 states the main application functions and components together with relevant interfaces and information flows for the *Popularity options* service. As shown, the following functions have been identified for the application layer:

- *Retrieve Avg Age:* this application function retrieves the average age that the user is interested in, in order to adapt the popularity list of the nearby locations.
- *Retrieve Time Criteria:* this application function retrieves the time criteria the user is interested in, in order to show the popularity list according to the daytime period (morning, evening, night).
- *Retrieve MVCs:* this application function retrieves the list of MVCs that the user is part of and desires to include them to the computation of the popularity statistics. In this way, the popularity list of the nearby locations will be adjusted according to other users' rates that belong in the same MVCs.
- *Retrieve Time Interval:* the time interval that the user wants to adjust the popularity statistics is retrieved with this function. For example, the user might be interested in producing a popularity list with ratings that took place during the last week or month.
- *Send to platform:* this function is responsible to communicate with the remote platform and to send users' preference in order to be elaborated.

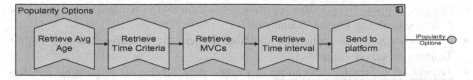

Fig. 1. Popularity options – main application components, functions and interfaces.

3 MVC Aware Machine-Learning Engine Training

The *MVC aware machine-learning engines training* service is responsible for the centralized training of machine-learning engines which will be used by the *MVC Suggestions* service (described in Sect. 4). The centralized training is made on the platform side.

Figure 2 summarizes the main application functions and components together with relevant interfaces, main data objects and information flows for the *MVC aware machine-learning engines training* service.

As can be seen from the diagram presented, the application functions can be divided into two categories. The following application functions have been identified for the first category:

- *Retrieve CheckIns per MVC:* this application function retrieves the checkIns that have been made to one location from members that belong to a specific MVC. This is made for all available MVCs and data are retrieved from the MVCDB (MVC Database).
- *Retrieve Rating per MVC:* this application function retrieves the ratings that have been made to one location from members that belong to a specific MVC. This is made for all available MVCs and data are retrieved from the MVCDB.
- *Generate MLE:* this application function is responsible for the creation of the Machine-Learning Engines that will be used for the training process.
- *Retrieve Relevant Training Datasets:* this application function retrieves the relevant dataset that will be used for the training process from the MLTDB (Machine Learning Training Database).
- *Select training options:* this application function selects and defines the training options for training the datasets.
- *Perform MLE Training:* MLE training is performed on this application function with regard to the retrieved training datasets and the options that were defined in the previous application functions.
- *Store MLE:* the resulting MLEs are stored in the MLEDB (Machine Learning Engine Database) through this application function.

The above mentioned application functions are implemented by the application component named *MLE Training Execution*.

The application functions of the second category are:

- *Periodic Triggering:* this application function periodically sends messages to trigger the Machine-Learning Engine Training.

- *Retrieve Manual Trigger:* this application function allows manual triggering of the Machine-Learning Engine Training.
- *Retrieve events:* this application function triggers the Machine-Learning Engine Training based on events.
- *Trigger MLE Training Execution:* this application function is responsible for triggering the MLE Training Execution component, after it receives the appropriate message from the above functions.

These application functions are implemented by the application component named *MLE Training Scheduler.* The main purpose of this component is to initiate the generation of new MLEs.

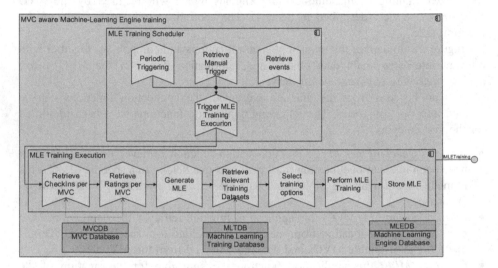

Fig. 2. MVC aware Machine-Learning Engine training – main application components, functions, interfaces and data objects.

4   MVC Suggestions

The *MVC Suggestions* service is responsible for performing estimation of the MVCs that a user may be interested in, according to his preferences.

Figure 3 states the main application functions and components together with relevant interfaces, main data objects and information flows for the *MVC Suggestions* service. The applications that can be identified from the diagram are the following:

- *Retrieve Popularity Options:* this function retrieves the popularity options that the user has defined from the *Popularity options* service.
- *Retrieve Related MLE:* the MLE that has been trained from the *MVC aware Machine-Learning Engine training* service is retrieved from MLEDB (Machine Learning Engine Database).

- *Use alternative means for MVC suggestions:* in case there is any problem retrieving data required for successfully estimating the suggestions list, such as no relevant MLE having been created yet, this function uses a fallback mechanism to provide estimations with alternative means.
- *Estimate MVCs for Suggestion:* This function finally provides the estimated list with suggested MVCs.

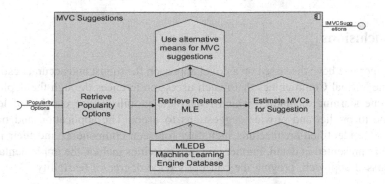

Fig. 3. MVC Suggestions – main application components, functions, interfaces and data objects.

5 Device Triggering

The *Device triggering* application component, which runs on the mobile device, is responsible for triggering the *MVC aware Machine-Learning Engine training* service after specific events that take place on user's mobile device (Fig. 4).

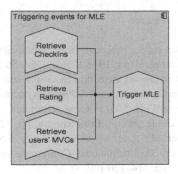

Fig. 4. Triggering events for MLE – main application components and functions.

For the *Triggering events for MLE* component, the application functions that have been identified are the following:

- *Retrieve CheckIns:* this application function retrieves user's checkIns that were made on a specific location.

- *Retrieve Rating:* this application function retrieves the ratings that the user has made for a specific location.
- *Retrieve users' MVCs:* this application function retrieves the MVCs that the user selects to include in his popularity options.
- *Trigger MLE:* this application function triggers the MLE training mechanism.

The main purpose of this component is to initiate the generation of new MLEs and its application functions are not mapped to any business layer processes.

6   Conclusions

In this paper, we have discussed on a novel approach for robust and accurate estimation of Mobile Virtual Communities that match users' preferences through the deployment of machine learning techniques which render the mobile device capable of learning over time to predict and provide suggestions to users. The application and business layers of the identified architecture, including foreseen components and their interactions, were presented in detail. Further research activities include the implementation of the discussed approach, proving the concept's wide degree of feasibility.

Acknowledgments. This work has been performed under the Greek National project WikiZen (11ΣΥN_10_1808), which has received research funding from the Operational Programme "Competitiveness & Entrepreneurship" of the National Strategic Reference Framework NSRF 2007–2013. This paper reflects only the authors' views, and the Operational Programme is not liable for any use that may be made of the information contained therein.

References

1. Facebook: https://www.facebook.com
2. Twitter: https://twitter.com
3. Modani, N., Dey, K., Mukherjea, S., Nanavati, A.A.: Discovery and analysis of tightly knit communities in telecom social networks. IBM J. Res. Dev. **56**(3), 618–630 (2010)
4. Moosavi, S.A., Jalali, M.: Community detection in online social networks using actions of users. In: 2014 IEEE Iranian Conference on Intelligent Systems (ICIS), pp. 1–7 (2014)
5. Tantipathananandh, C., Berger-Wolf, T.Y.: Finding communities in dynamic social networks. In: IEEE 11th International Conference on Data Mining, pp. 1236–1241 (2011)
6. Pourkazemi, M., Keyvanpour, M.: A survey on community detection methods based on the nature of social networks. In: 3rd International Conference on Computer and Knowledge Engineering, (ICCKE 2013), pp. 114–120 (2013)
7. ArchiMate® 2.1 Specification. http://pubs.opengroup.org/architecture/archimate2-doc/. Accessed May 2014

Motivating Citizens to Contribute to the Smart City: A Public Safety Case Study

Roxanne Piderit[1(✉)], Stephen Flowerday[1], and Sean McLean[2]

[1] Univeristy of Fort Hare, 50 Church St, East London, South Africa
{rpiderit, sflowerday}@ufh.ac.za
[2] IBM, 70 Rivonia Rd, Johannesburg, South Africa
seanm@za.ibm.com

Abstract. Smart Cities have received a significant amount of attention in recent years. The East London Smart City Public Safety Project aims to use citizens as an information source in order to report qualitative data in a natural language format. In order for this approach to be successful, an appropriate means of motivating citizens to contribute their observations voluntarily is necessary, and thus the aim of this paper. Motivational factors are identified through a survey administered to participants who have reported public safety matters. The survey is based on the constructs of the Theory of Planned Behaviour, namely: Attitude Toward Participation, Subjective Norm and Perceived Behavioural Control. From this study, it emerges that attitude toward reporting public safety matters and societal pressures are the most relevant factors determining a citizen's motivation to report public safety matters.

Keywords: Crowdsourcing · Motivation · Public safety · Smart city · Theory of Planned Behaviour

1 Introduction

The rapid growth of urban populations has given rise to concerns about the effective management of the city. Notable concerns arising from rapid urbanization include: waste management, human health concerns, traffic congestion, inappropriate infrastructure and similar public safety issues (Caragliu et al. 2011). Nam and Pardo (2011) estimates that half of the world's population lives in cities, and to avoid a resultant crisis, new ways of managing and operating the city are necessary. This has given rise to discussions of the smart city, especially as this trend is expected to continue for years.

Several working definitions of the smart city concept have been offered in literature. The key characteristics of a Smart City which can be derived from these definitions are: Infrastructure, Technology as an enabler and Coordination of city resources (Nam and Pardo 2011). These characteristics, in particular the coordination of city resources, are relevant to the Smart City Public Safety Project which provides a platform for the citizens of East London to report public safety matters they observe. For this purpose, an interactive voice recording (IVR) system was developed to record the contributions reported by the citizens. From these reports, information is extracted in order to identify

R. Giaffreda et al. (Eds.): IoT360 2014, Part II, LNICST 151, pp. 131–136, 2015.
DOI: 10.1007/978-3-319-19743-2_20

trends in the collected data. These trends can be used by the relevant authorities in order to ensure public safety matters are dealt with proactively rather than reactively by planning necessary interventions. However, in order for this approach to be effective sufficient data needs to be generated by the citizens (Cilliers and Flowerday 2013). For this reason, ensuring citizen's are motivated to contribute public safety reports is a necessary concern.

While the value of this project for East London citizens should be apparent, participation has been relatively low. Thus, the factors that affect motivation to participate in the Smart City Public Safety Project need to be investigated. As participation in this project is voluntary, these motivational factors differ to those of traditional systems. The Theory of Planned Behaviour provides the theoretical framework for this study. This theory was chosen as it has been used by numerous studies to understand people's motivations to perform certain tasks (Azjen 1991). In this study, the motivational factors impacting on a citizen's decision to report a public safety matter via the IVR are the focus.

A survey based on the constructs of the Theory of Planned Behaviour (TPB) was administered to those citizens who had participated in the Smart City Public Safety Project by reporting a public safety matter they had observed. The participants identified the importance of the motivational factors to further participation in the project. The results from the survey were analysed making use of descriptive statistical analysis. From the survey results, attitude toward reporting public safety matters and societal pressures are the most relevant factors determining a citizen's motivation to report public safety matters. This suggests the need to enhance the sense of value a citizen experiences from contributing to the Smart City Public Safety project.

2   The Context: The Smart City Model and Public Safety

As described previously, urbanization has placed city resources under severe strain and new means of providing effective service delivery are necessary. Rotiman et al. (2012) point out that citizen's reports about public safety matters may contain important information not usually obtained through traditional routes. Thus, crowdsourcing is proposed as an effective method to collect data from the citizens in order to overcome the challenges presented by continued urbanisation. This was the approach used in the Smart City Public Safety Project. The Smart City Public Safety Project was carried out in East London, South Africa, which falls within the Buffalo City Municipality. The current population is estimated at 440 000 (StatsSA 2012). In terms of public safety matters, the Directorate of Health and Public Safety provides for traffic and law enforcement, fire and rescue services, and disaster management (Cilliers and Flowerday 2013).

The Public Safety Crowdsourcing Project was initiated in order to propose and test a participatory crowdsourcing model for a developing country. An Interactive Voice Recognition (IVR) system was developed to provide a platform for citizens to report public safety matters. The IVR directed citizens through the process of reporting a matter via voice prompts (Cilliers and Flowerday 2013). Participants from the East London area were recruited through newspaper advertisements, distributed flyers and social media. In order to record public safety reports, participants were required to first register on the Project's website and accept the terms and conditions for participation. After registering, participants were expected to place calls to the IVR to report public safety matters. Thereafter, they completed the online survey to comment on the motivational factors impacting on their contribution.

Crowdsourcing is recognised as an innovative means of creating value from willing participants (Hammon and Hippner 2012). This involves the collection of information from a large group of people for a particular purpose, rather than relying on the individual contributions traditionally expected. For the Public Safety Crowdsourcing Project, the type of information required concerns public safety matters. By accessing the collective knowledge of the crowd about these public safety matters, the relevant authorities are able to obtain more accurate information on which to base planning for future interventions than would otherwise be possible (Hammon and Hippner 2012). In this way, the citizens are viewed as the sensors which provide relevant information.

In the public safety context, the salient benefit of crowdsourcing is the use of ordinary citizens to provide data on events they observe. However, this relies on the citizens motivation to participate (Satt 2011). The gathered data can be used to the benefit of the citizens in order anticipate future public safety matters and identify trends which indicate repetitive concerns (Bhana et al. 2013). This is consistent with the trend toward proactive approaches to handling public safety matters.

3 Theoretical Background: Theory of Planned Behaviour

The theory of planned behaviour has relevance to this study as it is centered around the user (in this case citizen) and their intention to perform a behaviour (in this case report public safety matters via the IVR). These intentions represent the motivational factors affect the behaviour desired (Azjen 1991). Azjen (1991) asserts that the stronger the intention, or motivation, the more likely the behaviour is to occur. Thus, in this study, the stronger the motivation, the more likely citizens are to report public safety matters. The theory of planned behaviour is depicted in Fig. 1 on the next page.

It is important to note that the motivational aspect is only relevant if the behaviour is under "volitional control" (Azjen 1991, p. 181). Thus, the citizen should be able to freely decide whether or not to report a public safety matter, regardless of other influencing factors. The other influencing factors relate resources and opportunities. These factors have previously been studied in this context (Piderit et al. 2013). This previous study acknowledged that cost is a relevant barrier for citizens placing calls to the IVR. In particular, telecommunications costs are an important barrier as these are relatively higher in South Africa. For this reason, the current phase of the project involves an incentivized approach to reduce the impact of these factors.

As this paper focuses on motivation to report public safety matters, it is assumed that the above approach would ensure that resource and opportunity needs are met. Citizens are therefore free to decide whether or not to place a call to the IVR. This decision is the focal point of this study. The theory is based on three factors which impact on intention (or motivation), namely:

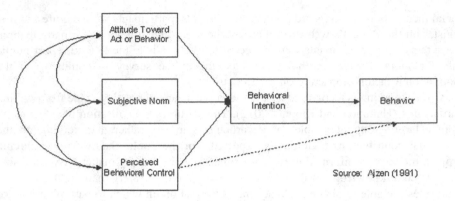

Fig. 1. The Theory of Planned Behaviour (Azjen 1991)

1. *Attitude Toward the Behaviour*: This refers to the positive or negative feeling a person has regarding performing the behaviour (Azjen 1991). In this study, this is the citizen's positive or negative feelings about reporting a public safety matter.
2. *Subjective Norm*: This refers to the social pressure to perform the behaviour (Azjen 1991). In this study, this refers to the extent to which citizen's feel that reporting a public safety matter is viewed favourably by their peers.
3. *Perceived Behavioural Control*: This refers to the ability to perform the behaviour (Azjen 1991). In this study, this is the level of difficulty the citizen perceives to be involved in the reporting of public safety matters.

Based on this theory, a questionnaire was developed to test the relevance of these elements. The method used for this study is described in the next section.

4 Method

The survey administered to participants was based on the constructs of the Theory of Planned Behaviour as follows:

1. *Attitude Toward Act or Behaviour:* Respondents were asked to comment on the extent to which they found it useful to report public safety matters.
2. *Subjective Norm*: Respondents were asked to comment on the extent to which they feel it shows empathy to people at risk to report public safety matters.
3. *Perceived Behavioural Control*: Respondents were asked to comment on the extent to which they feel better because they are doing something by reporting the public safety matter.

In total 400 people participated in the Public Safety project. Of these, 199 made complete, usable calls. 52 of these participants completed the survey. The Cronbach Alpha for the three constructs tested in the survey is 0.79 which is considered acceptable for studies leaning toward social sciences (UCLA 2013).

5 Identifying the Motivational Factors for Contribution to the Smart City Public Safety Project

The questions in the survey administered to the participants of the public safety project focused on the motivational factors relevant to making a contribution in the form of reporting a public safety matter. The results of these questions are reported in (Table 1).

Table 1. Survey results

Construct	Median	Mean	Agree	Disagree
Attitude Toward Participation	1 (Strongly Agree)	1.80 (Agree)	80.49 %	9.76 %
Subjective Norm	1 (Strongly Agree)	1.61 (Agree)	80.49 %	4.88 %
Perceived Behavioural Control	1 (Strongly Agree)	1.95 (Agree)	68.29 %	12.20 %

The results indicate that the participants found attitude toward participation and subjective norm (societal pressures) to be significantly more important as motivational factors than perceived behavioural control.

6 Recommendations: Motivating Citizens to Contribute

From the survey results, attitude toward reporting public safety matters and societal pressures are the most relevant factors determining a citizen's motivation to report public safety matters. Thus, the citizens feel that they are able to make an appropriate decision with regards to whether or not to report public safety matters. Both subjective norm and attitude toward participation indicate that citizens are motivated to participate by the prospect of a more efficiently run city. The improved functioning of the city will in turn benefit the citizens in terms of an improved standard of living. Currently, an airtime incentive is being offered in the second phase of the project, in order to overcome the key barriers to participation. Consideration is also being given to the role of feedback loops with city management and citizens as a motivational means.

7 Conclusion

This paper tested the three constructs of the Theory of Planned Behaviour in order to determine the key motivational factors for contribution to the Smart City Public Safety Project. From the findings of the survey, attitude toward reporting and societal pressures emerged as key motivational factors. This suggests the need to enhance the sense of value a citizen experiences from contributing to the Smart City Public Safety project.

References

Azjen, I.: The theory of planned behaviour. Organ. Behav. Hum. Decis. Process **50**, 179–211 (1991)

Bhana, B., Flowerday, S.V., Satt, A.: Using participatory crowdsourcing in South Aafrica to create a safer living environment. Int. J. Distrib. Sens. Netw. **2013**, 13 (2013). Article ID 907196

Caragliu, A., Del Bo, C., Nijkamp, P.: Smart cities in Europe. J. Urban Technol. **18**(2), 65–82 (2011)

Cilliers, L., Flowerday, S.: Trust in a crowd-sourcing system in order to improve public safety. In: 15th Annual Conference on World Wide Applications, Cape Town, S.A, September 2013

Hammon, L., Hippner, H.: Crowdsourcing. Bus. Inf. Syst. Eng. **4**(3), 163–166 (2012)

Nam, T., Pardo, T.A.: Smart city as urban innovation: focusing on management, policy, and context. In: ICEGOV 2011, Estonia, pp. 185–194, 26–28 September 2011

Piderit, R., Flowerday, S., Satt, A : Identifying barriers to citizen participation in public safety crowdsourcing in East London. In: iNEER Conference, Cape Town, S.A, December 2013

Roitman, H., Mamou, J., Mehta, S., Satt, A. Subramaniam, L.V.: Harnessing the crowds for smart city sensing. In: Crowdsens, Hawaii, pp. 17–18, 2 November 2012

Satt, A.: OCR proposal background participatory mobile crowdsourcing. Israel (2011)

Stats, S.A.: Census 2011: key results (2012)

UCLA SPSS FAQ: What does Cronbach's alpha mean? (2013). http://www.ats.ucla.edu/stat/spss/faq/alpha.html. Accessed 01 August 2013

What Makes People Change Their Preferences in Public Transportation – Opinions in Different User Groups

Martina Ziefle[✉] and Wiktoria Wilkowska

Human-Computer Interaction Center, RWTH Aachen University,
Campus Boulevard 57, 52074 Aachen, Germany
{ziefle,Wilkowska}@comm.rwth-aachen.de

Abstract. Mobility is a critical requirement for cities, but broadly accepted mobility concepts are difficult to realize. Environmental hazards, high costs, complex planning processes, affordability, accessibility and safety are crucial factors. Also, the demographic change in line with increasing individual transportation needs and mobility profiles aggravate a sustainable and topical planning of urban mobility. As the understanding of human needs is vital for the acceptance of novel mobility concepts, we explored pro- and contra-using motives for public transportation as well as aspects of conditional acceptance. Using an empirical approach, 580 persons answered a questionnaire in this regard. The results allow insights into opinions of age and gender related mobility needs in the public transport sector.

Keywords: Public transport · Mobility pattern · Acceptance · Pro-using arguments · Contra-using arguments · User diversity

1 Motivation and Related Work

Traffic situations in many cities worldwide have reached critical proportions. Not only do bumper-to-bumper traffic jams congest cities each day, especially at peak times. But environmental hazards such as the climate change and increasing CO_2-emissions urge communities and urban planners to sensibly develop novel public mobility concepts which might adapt to the critical mobility needs of modern cities. In addition, the demographic change has a considerable impact on mobility concepts: An increasing portion of older adults travelling around as well as the changed biographical roles and duties (children's ride to and from school or kindergarten, short distance city trips, tourist excursions or profession car poolers) require highly flexible transport systems at multiple scales (e.g., day-by-day or seasonally). Such transport systems should meet community needs such as accessibility, comfort, safety, sustainability, affordability, but also climate-related needs. In order to be context-adaptive, mobility options must be intermodal, flexible, and designed as "door-to-door" mobility chains [1]. Yet, in most of the European municipalities and communes, there is a predominantly technology-centered planning of infrastructural public mobility concepts. Even if technical and economic factors are key criteria for feasible and affordable mobility services, mobility

© Institute for Computer Sciences, Social Informatics and Telecommunications Engineering 2015
R. Giaffreda et al. (Eds.): IoT360 2014, Part II, LNICST 151, pp. 137–143, 2015.
DOI: 10.1007/978-3-319-19743-2_21

includes also a strong behavioral component [2] in relation to different mobility needs. Persons at different points in their life might have varying preferences with regard to specific means of transportation, be it as a matter of customization [3], family habits [4], or specific mobility needs, and one type of transportation might be perceived as more appropriate than others [5, 6]. Personal traits (standard of comfort, environmental morality), age and generation [7], but also gender do play a considerable role in transportation habits [8, 9]. As there is an urgent need in understanding people's attitudes towards the use of public transportation, this exploratory study aims at revealing user opinions regarding the use of means of public transportation, including all types (buses, trains, subways, etc.). Beyond pro-using arguments, on the one hand, and con-using arguments, on the other, possible circumstances are explored under which users would be willing to adopt public transport in the near future.

2 Method

To reach a large number of participants, the questionnaire method was chosen. Participants were asked via email to take part in the study. Completing the questionnaire took about 30 min. Items were taken from argumentation patterns of focus group studies [10, 11] which were carried out prior to this study. In total, 580 persons (17–86 years ($M = 31.3$ years; $SD = 11.6$); 47.6 % women took part. In age group 1, the mean age was 22.5 ($SD = 2$, $N = 200$); in age group 2, the mean age was 30.1 ($SD = 3.5$; $N = 292$), and in age group 3, the mean age 54.1 years ($SD = 9.9$; $N = 88$). As independent variables, gender and age were examined. Three age groups were formed: (1) <25 years of age, (2) 26–40 years (beginnings of the professional career), and (3) 41 + years (high professionals). Dependent variables were the levels of (dis)agreement to the *pro public transport* arguments and to the *contra public transport* arguments. Pro- and con-arguments were categorized within four dimensions (comfort, ecology, economy, and efficiency).

(1) PROs for using public transport

- *comfort-related arguments:* convenience, restfulness, possibility to take other persons/animals, sightseeing, time for other things (e.g., read, work, sleep)
- *ecology-related ('green') arguments:* eco-friendliness, to be outdoorsy
- *economy-related arguments:* low costs, affordability, price-performance balance
- *efficiency-related arguments:* punctuality, start points nearby, good availability, efficient destination reachability, flexibility, continuous mobility.

(2) CONs against using public transport

- *comfort-related arguments:* inflexibility, stressful, discomfort, disturbing travel passengers, too close contact with other passengers, overcrowded
- *ecology-related ('green') arguments:* ecological damage, weather dependency
- *economy-related arguments:* high costs, long waiting times
- *efficiency-related arguments:* lacking availability, slow locomotion, unpunctuality, lacking possibility to do other things (e.g., working), unreliability.

(3) Reasons for changes in mobility patterns: if changes occur in...

financial situation, health, movability, family situation, living situation, mobility needs, quality of public infrastructure.

3 Results

Data was analyzed by using M(ANOVA) procedures with repeated measurements. The significance level was set at 5 %.

3.1 Evaluation of PRO Arguments

The MANOVA yielded a significant omnibus effect of age ($F_{(2,586)} = 14.3$; $p < 0.000$). The age effect was most prominent in ecology ($F_{(2,586)} = 20.2$; $p < 0.000$) and economy related arguments ($F_{(2,586)} = 39.8$; $p < 0.000$), both being less important with increasing age (Fig. 1).

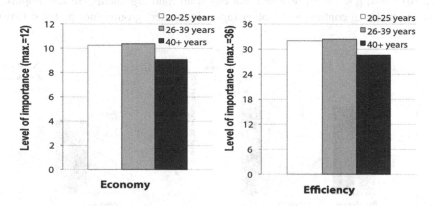

Fig. 1. Age effects on pro-using arguments.

Beyond the main effect of age, significant interacting effects of gender and age were revealed (Fig. 2) regarding ecological ($F_{(2,586)} = 14.4$; $p < 0.000$), economic ($F_{(2,586)} = 8.2$; $p < 0.000$), and efficiency related arguments ($F_{(2,586)} = 9.7$; $p < 0.000$).

3.2 Evaluation of CON Arguments

The next analysis is directed at the perceived barriers (Fig. 3). Again, a significant omnibus effect of age was found ($F_{(2,586)} = 5.6$; $p < 0.000$) that reached significance for ecological ($F_{(2,586)} = 3.8$; $p < 0.02$), economic ($F_{(2,586)} = 7.1$; $p < 0.001$), and efficiency related arguments ($F_{(2,586)} = 8.9$; $p < 0.000$). With increasing age, eco-friendliness is more while costs and efficiency are less important as decision criteria for

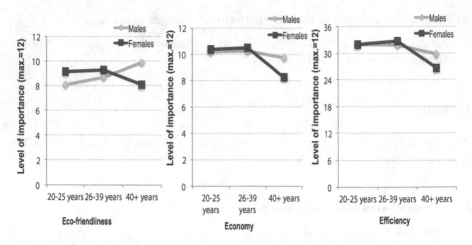

Fig. 2. Interacting effect of age and gender on arguments pro public transport

the use of public transportation. Also, the significant interaction of age and gender ($F(1,586) = 7.4$; $p < 0.000$) revealed that environmental arguments are less important for young males in contrast to all other (age and gender) groups (not pictured here).

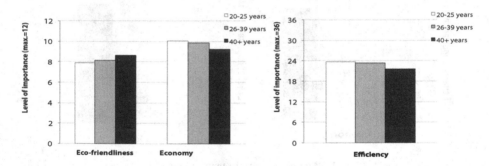

Fig. 3. Age effects on con-using arguments.

3.3   Conditional Acceptance Criteria

Finally, conditional circumstances were collected which could increase the acceptance to use public means of transportation (Fig. 4).

Considerable age effects were present regarding the evaluation of conditional acceptance towards using public means of transportation ($F(2,586) = 11.8$; $p < 0.000$). The oldest group seems to have quite different priorities in most of the lines of argumentation compared to the youngest group. The middle-aged group was partly in line with the oldest group (e.g., out of restricted mobility), partly with the youngest group (e.g., when the living situation, the family situation or the place of residence changes). Also, women reported to have a significantly higher conditional acceptance in contrast

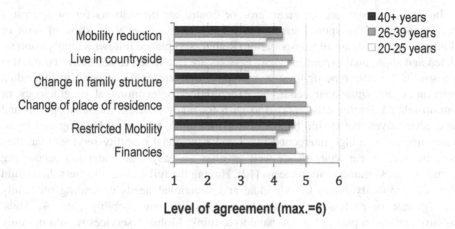

Fig. 4. Agreement to conditional acceptance criteria (1 = not at all, 6 = completely agree)

to men (F(1,178) = 2.4; p < 0.004) and they were more willing to change their mobility patterns depending on external reasons (e.g., change in family situations, living in country side) than men.

4   Discussion and Conclusion

Technological, infrastructural, or economic criteria are almost always the exclusive foci during the urban planning of mobility concepts and do not include the public. However, current developments show that ignorance towards human needs within the technical planning process of urban mobility might raise public protests and decision delays. The latter could be avoided if human mobility needs would be integrated early in the development process and if adequate and individually tailored public information and communication concepts would be launched. In order to understand human opinions with respect to using motives and barriers when using means of public transportation, an online survey was carried out and completed by 580 persons in Germany. Prior to the questionnaire, focus groups were run to find out which argumentation patterns and mental models about mobility needs prevail.

Overall, there was a higher positive motivation to use public means of transport than a negative motivation towards the usage of public transport (taken from the higher scores on confirmation of pro-using compared to contra-using arguments). Main pro-using motives were economy- and ecology-related reasons. Contra-using arguments were mostly the low comfort and the comparably low efficiency (unreliability, unpunctuality) of public transportation means.

User diversity is a critical factor for the usage of public means of transport. With increasing age, economy arguments were less and ecological arguments more important. Apparently, age corresponds to a higher awareness of responsibility for future generations as well as sustainability on a larger scale in terms of environmental morality. Environmentally friendly mobility concepts are also crucial for women, possibly due to their more family related perspective.

Insightfully, there are no static pro- or contra argumentations for or against a specific means of transportation. Mobility behaviors are not a question of faith or affinity to specific means of transportation. Rather, acceptance follows a highly context-related and situational dependent view. Persons are to a much lesser extent committed to a specific vehicle type or form or modality; they rather do respond to individual preferences and situational needs, be it ecological or economical or efficiency or comfort-related. Participants reported to wish for many different mobility options and travel alternatives that should be available all the time, have easy booking and registration interfaces, a high interconnectivity and intermodal mobility services (car, bus, tram, bicycle, or car sharing), as well as offer an easy and integrated accounting procedure across transportation means [12]. Having the full choice, dwellers then could adapt their mobility habits to individual and situational needs depending on family roles, private or professional needs, as well as life-long mobility patterns. Thus, mobility and urban planners might have to re-think. Mobility services should not only be designed according to technical and infrastructural or economic factors, but they should be designed along human-centered mobility and travel chains, with intermodal mobility services including different types of transportation means. These results may also have an impact on information and communication aspects for novel urban mobility concepts. The usage of public transport should not be praised as a patronizing top-down reasoning. Dwellers require mobility concepts that integrate their natural mobility needs and user diversity in the individual travel profiles, and also offer a timely and transparent public information and communication procedure.

Acknowledgements. This work was funded partly by the Excellence Initiative of the German State and Federal Government, partly by the German Ministry for Economic Affairs and Energy (Project Mobility Broker, reference number 01ME12136).

References

1. Ziefle, M., Schneider, C., Vallee, D., Schnettler, A., Krempels K.-H., Jarke, M.: Urban Future outline (UFO). A roadmap on research for livable cities, ERCIM News (N. 98) (2014). http://ercim-news.ercim.eu/en98/keynote-smart-cities
2. de Bruijn, G.J., Kremers, S.P., Singh, A., Van den Putte, B., Van Mechelen, W.: Adult active transportation: adding habit strength to the theory of planned behavior. Am. J. Prev. Med. **36**(3), 189–194 (2009)
3. Thøgersen, J., Møller, B.: Breaking car use habits: the effectiveness of a free one-month travelcard. Transportation **35**(3), 329–345 (2008)
4. Kunert, U.: Weekly mobility of life cycle groups. Transportation **21**(3), 271–288 (1994)
5. Ziefle, M., Beul-Leusmann, S., Kasugai, K., Schwalm, M.: Public perception and acceptance of electric vehicles: exploring users' perceived benefits and drawbacks. In: Marcus, A. (ed.) DUXU 2014, Part III. LNCS, vol. 8519, pp. 628–639. Springer, Heidelberg (2014)
6. Wilkowska, W., Farrokhikhiavi, R., Ziefle, M., Vallée, D.: Mobility requirements for the use of carpooling among different user groups. In: Ahram, T., et al. (eds.) 5th International Conference on Applied Human Factors and Ergonomics, pp. 401–413 (2014)
7. Turcotte, M.: Profile of seniors' transportation habits. Can. Soc. Trends **93**, 1–16 (2012)

8. Matthies, E., Kuhn, S., Klöckner, C.A.: Travel mode choice of women. Result of Limitation, ecological norm, or weak habit? Environ. Behav. **34**(2), 163–177 (2002)
9. Ziefle, M., Himmel, S., Holzinger, A.: How usage context shapes evaluation and adoption in different technologies. In: Rebelo, F., Soares, F. (eds.) 2nd International Conference on Human Factors and Ergonomics in Healthcare 2012, Advances in Usability Evaluation Part II, CRC Press, pp. 2812–2821 (2012)
10. Zaunbrecher, B., Ziefle, M.: Laypeople's perspectives on electromobility. A focus group study. In: Giaffreda, R., Caganova, D., Li, Y., Riggio, R., Voisard, A. (eds.) IoT 2014, LNICST, vol. 151, pp. 144–149. Springer, Heidelberg (2015)
11. Arning, K., Ziefle, M., Muehlhans, H.: Join the ride! user requirements and interface design guidelines for a commuter carpooling platform. In: Marcus, A. (ed.) DUXU/HCII 2013, Part III. LNCS, vol. 8014, pp. 10–19. Springer, Heidelberg (2013)
12. Himmel, S., Zaunbrecher, B.S., Wilkowska, W., Ziefle, M.: The youth of today designing the smart city of tomorrow. In: Kurosu, M. (ed.) Human-Computer Interaction, Part III, HCII 2014. LNCS, vol. 8512, pp. 389–400. Springer, Heidelberg (2014)

Laypeople's Perspectives on Electromobility: A Focus Group Study

Barbara S. Zaunbrecher[✉], Shirley Beul-Leusmann,
and Martina Ziefle

Human-Computer Interaction Center,
Campus-Boulevard 57, 52074 Aachen, Germany
{zaunbrecher,beul,ziefle}@comm.rwth-aachen.de

Abstract. Although many electric cars are readily available on the market and the charging infrastructure is expanded, the majority of people is still reluctant to buy and use an electric car. It is assumed that underlying motives and mental models play decisive roles for the acceptance. To gain insights into laypeople's concepts concerning electromobility, three focus group studies on perceived benefits and barriers with a total of 24 participants were conducted in which the participants discussed their perceived benefits and barriers of electric mobility. It was found that while participants' perceived benefits referred almost exclusively to environmental issues, the barriers concerned multiple thematic areas such as costs, infrastructure, security of the technology, and practicability. Overall, it has become obvious that many misconceptions and prejudices against electromobility and electric cars still exist which can only be overcome by adequate information and communication concepts.

Keywords: Electromobility · Technology acceptance · User-centered design · Urban systems · Focus group study

1 Introduction

More and more people will live in cities, bringing with them cars for individual motorized transport. This leads to increased traffic which, in turn, negatively affects the city climate. Already today, many cities regularly exceed the limits for fine particle concentration. Electric cars provide a solution to this problem without limiting the users in their access to individual motorized transport. Moreover, they are able to run on environmentally friendly, sustainable sources of energy instead of fossil fuels like traditional cars with combustion engines.

Despite these advantages over traditional cars, the market adoption of electric cars is slow: In Germany, only 6,000 of all cars newly registered in 2013 were electric cars, which equals a share of 0.2 % [1]. It is therefore essential to understand usage motives and barriers of potential users to be able to develop adequate communication and information strategies which ultimately can foster acceptance for electric cars.

Current acceptance research on electric mobility covers a wide range of methods and thematic areas. General acceptance studies include field studies on the relation between driven distance and attitude towards electric mobility [2], studies on the social

© Institute for Computer Sciences, Social Informatics and Telecommunications Engineering 2015
R. Giaffreda et al. (Eds.): IoT360 2014, Part II, LNICST 151, pp. 144–149, 2015.
DOI: 10.1007/978-3-319-19743-2_22

influence on perception and preference for electric vehicles [3], stereotypes on electric mobility [4], and studies on the influence of user factors on acceptance and preferences for electric cars [5, 6]. Other research focuses on special aspects of electromobility, investigating, e.g., psychological barriers of range [7].

While most of the studies used a quantitative approach, only few studies can be found that report the results of qualitative approaches although these are especially useful for new, not yet established technologies for which the acceptance-relevant parameters are not yet known. One of the few examples is Hoffmann et al. [8] who selected focus groups according to profiles of future users to discuss particular use cases of electromobility.

We applied a two-step research approach to gain a better understanding of user requirements and perceived barriers of electromobility. First, exploratory focus group studies were conducted which will be presented in this paper. Based on the results, a quantitative user study using an online survey was conducted [9, 10].

2 Focus Group Study

Three focus group studies were conducted in 2012. Participants were recruited among acquaintances and fellow students. The focus groups lasted around 2.5 h and were carried out on university campus. Two students who had received prior training moderated each focus group. Data were collected via audio-recording and note-taking by assistants who were not involved in the discussion.

2.1 Participants

The three focus groups were different with regard to the user characteristics of the participants. While group 1 contained mainly female students in their mid-twenties, groups 2 and 3 were more mixed regarding age, gender distribution, and job status.

2.2 Results

Although the groups were mixed in terms of participants, very similar concerns regarding electromobility were raised.

In the first group (7 participants), which consisted mainly of female students, different *areas of application* for electromobility were discussed. Although none of the participants could imagine buying an electric car themselves, they suggested that electric cars would be useful for courier services such as mail delivery. They also thought that taxis could be electric as well, as they are parked, often for longer periods of time, while waiting for customers, and they could use this time for recharging. This group had mixed opinions about using electromobility in public transport. On the one hand, they feared an increase of ticket prices as a result of the expensive e-busses ("It's clear who will have to pay the extra price"). On the other hand, one participant raised the idea that public transport could become cheaper by using electric busses, as they would not have to rely on expensive gasoline anymore. Overall, however, e-mobility in public transport was seen as more feasible than in private, individual transport.

General comments that were made about electric cars for private use concerned, e.g., the driving experience itself, which one participant expected to be like a normal car. Another participant was not sure if "they drive like normal cars," which expressed a general lack of knowledge about electromobility. Also, participants wished for bigger e-cars with more storage space and seats, probably because they had small 2-seaters like the Renault Twizy in mind when thinking about e-cars. Furthermore, they criticized that most e-cars they knew looked ugly, "like some cars out of the future," and wished for a more conventional design.

A lot of comments referred to *security issues* and it became clear that especially the battery of an e-car was a reason for concern. Participants feared, for example, leakages and the danger of explosion and thus concluded that accidents with electric cars would be more dangerous for the driver. They also had the impression that electric cars were less robust and would therefore "lose" in a crash with a traditional car. The missing engine noise was also discussed controversially as blind and old people with hearing disabilities could not rely on the sound anymore to recognize a car approaching them.

Much of the discussion also evolved around the topics of *range and charging*. Participants agreed that the range should be extended to at least 200 km and that flexibility would decrease if they had to "calculate how far (they) will be able to drive." They suggested using hybrid cars or range extenders so they would not "get stuck somewhere" once the battery was dead. One participant voiced that she would not be willing to drive more slowly just to go easy on the battery: "It's embarrassing and I would need twice as much time." Concerning the charging process, participants agreed that it took too long to recharge the e-car. They suggested that charging stations at home and at the workplace would be useful so that the car could recharge overnight and during working hours.

Environmental aspects were also discussed with regard to the source of electricity for the e-cars. The focus group members had the opinion that e-cars are not necessarily environmentally friendly as long as electricity is generated from fossil fuels or nuclear power plants.

In the second group (9 participants), which was mixed regarding age, gender, and job status, the arguments of the discussion were similar although more emphasis was placed on the general immaturity of electric mobility. For *fields of application*, participants, like those of group 1, also suggested that electric cars would be handy for companies with a lot of short-range deliveries such as pizza delivery, taxis, but also car sharing companies. In addition, they suggested that persons with prestige who drive a lot could function as role models, e.g., city majors. They did not dismiss the idea of an electric car for private, individual transport entirely but found that electric cars would be suitable as "second cars," in addition to a traditional car that could be used for long-distance trips. They were concerned that electric busses in public transport could not take as many people on board as a traditional bus, because of the lower power of the battery compared to a combustion engine.

General aspects discussed included, also like in group 1, the look of the electric cars. Participants agreed that most e-cars looked ugly and that they should not look different from traditional cars. When showing them pictures of e-cars resembling traditional cars, they commented that we had "selected good looking ones" which shows that the mental models of electric cars and actual e-cars diverged. Our group 2 participants stated that a requirement would be that the e-car is comfortable. The high costs of electric cars in comparison to traditional cars were also discussed.

Interestingly, the *security aspects* were also very similar to those discussed in group 1. In group 2, the danger when it comes to accidents such as leakage of battery acid, static charge, electric shocks, and short-circuits were mentioned. These thoughts were raised almost exclusively by a female participant, which mirrored the concerns of the all-female group 1. Additionally, danger from lightning was discussed although one expert dismissed this concern. Like in group 1, e-cars were associated with "plastic cars" and thus not considered as secure and robust as traditional cars. A further concern already raised in group 1 was that the reduced noise level could lead to e-cars being overlooked because people are used to listening for cars, but the participants of group 2 also recognized the benefit of reduced noise stress.

Arguments concerning the *range and the charging process* were also exchanged. Similar to group 1, participants of the second group found it "stressful" to plan the recharging. They had diverging opinions about which range was already possible today but mentioned a range extender to overcome the problem. Although they wished for an extended range, they were aware that the existing range is probably sufficient for most people, even if they commute to work each day. The laypeople in the group were also concerned about "memory-effects" of the battery, meaning that with more and more charging processes, the battery's maximum capacity would decrease. The expert in the round, however, denied this worry. Participants also discussed a trade-off between battery size and storage capacity of the car. They thought that with increased battery size, the range would also increase but at the same time, the storage space in the car would decrease. In contrast to this, a small battery would probably allow less range but also increase the storage capacity in the car, e.g., for passengers, bags, etc.

In general, participants of group 2 discussed many aspects related to the perceived *immaturity of the technology*. They had the impression, for example, that the grid is not ready yet to provide the extra amount of electricity to recharge e-cars. Also, it could be a problem that garages are not fit to deal with electric cars in case of problems. Participants also criticized the lack of charging infrastructure. Concerning the battery, they found that the weight-performance ratio was negative and thus research on lighter and more efficient batteries is needed.

Environmental aspects were discussed more controversially than in group 1. Not only was it mentioned, like in group 1, that the e-car is only as environmentally friendly as its source of electricity but the battery was also seen as a source for concern. After all, it has to be disposed of somewhere. In contrast to group 1, group 2 recognized the benefit of electric cars for the city climate and discussed the possible reduction of fine particles in the city. One participant seriously considered buying an e-car because of its environmental advantages that would give him a "clear conscience."

The third group (8 participants), like the second, was also mixed with regard to age, gender, and job status. Concerning the *fields of application*, electromobility was thought to function well in public transport. The participants elaborated on the idea of inductive charging, so that busses could recharge while waiting at bus stops. They were aware that research on this topic is already going on.

The group exchanged opinions on the *range and the charging process*, and it became clear that they were unsure how far an electric car was actually able to drive nowadays. They, like the other groups, criticized long recharging times. Innovative ideas for charging stations included supermarket parking spaces and street lights which function as charging stations.

They found, like group 2, that the battery is a potential *environmental* hazard because of its production and disposal processes.

Overall, they also criticized that information on electromobility was scarce.

3   Discussion and Outlook

The results show that electromobility still faces many prejudices and that several misconceptions exist about the functionality, security, and actual range. It has to be taken into account, however, that these data are highly culturally specific and that, especially in Germany which is a car-loving nation and has a long tradition of car industry, people hesitate to give up their beloved cars. From our results, it is reasonable to assume that user factors also play a role for acceptance, e.g., gender, as we found that especially the women were concerned about security issues. As we only had a very limited, not representative sample, future research should include a quantitative approach to statistically validate the influence of gender on security as a barrier.

Meanwhile, more "normal looking" electric cars are available for customers e.g. Tesla Model S, BMW i3, VW E-up!, so one major point of criticism of our participants was also recognized by the automobile industry. Interestingly, the visions of the participants that electric cars could be used for short-distance services has been put into practice by, e.g., the city council of Aachen (Germany) where some city cleaning teams use the e-car Renault Twizy as a means of transportation.

The possible range of electric cars was considered a major drawback. Although field studies have shown that the average range of an electric car would meet the mobility demands of a large amount of people ([7, 11, 12]), the wish for an extended range still persists. This topic thus seems to be a psychological one rather than one of technical feasibility as drivers have to be able to cope with limited range and uncertainty. Franke et al. [7] therefore propose better strategies and technological support to deal with the limited range rather than expanding the range itself.

Because of the qualitative nature of the study, quantitative follow-up studies have been conducted. As results have shown that perceived usefulness of electromobility is higher for public than for private mobility, it is necessary to investigate the acceptance of electromobility in public transport, e.g., busses, separately from the acceptance of electric cars for private use. In a second step, we therefore carried out a study on acceptance of electromobility in the context of private, individual transport [9] and, additionally, in public transport [10].

Acknowledgements. This work was funded partly by the Excellence Initiative of the German State and Federal Government (Project UFO), partly by the German Ministry for Economic Affairs and Energy (Project econnect Germany, ref. no. 01 ME 12052.

References

1. Kraftfahrtbundesamt (German Federal Motor Transport Authority): Fahrzeugzulassungen. Neuzulassungen von Kraftfahrzeugen nach Umwelt-Merkmalen. Jahr 2013. (New registrations of cars according to environmental features) (2013)
2. Buehler, F., Franke, T., Krems, J.F.: Usage patterns of electric vehicles as a reliable indicator for acceptance? Findings from a German Field Study. In: Presented at the Transportation Research Board 90th Annual Meeting (2011)
3. Axsen, J., Orlebar, C., Skippon, S.: Social influence and consumer preference formation for pro-environmental technology: the case of a U.K. workplace electric-vehicle study. Ecol. Econ. **95**, 96–107 (2013)
4. Burgess, M., King, N., Harris, M., Lewis, E.: Electric vehicle drivers' reported interactions with the public: driving stereotype change? Transp. Res. Part F Traffic Psychol. Behav. **17**, 33–44 (2013)
5. Egbue, O., Long, S.: Barriers to widespread adoption of electric vehicles: an analysis of consumer attitudes and perceptions. Energy Policy. **48**, 717–729 (2012)
6. Ziegler, A.: Individual characteristics and stated preferences for alternative energy sources and propulsion technologies in vehicles: a discrete choice analysis for Germany. Transp. Res. Part Policy Pract. **46**, 1372–1385 (2012)
7. Franke, T., Neumann, I., Bühler, F., Cocron, P., Krems, J.F.: Experiencing range in an electric vehicle: understanding psychological barriers. Appl. Psychol. **61**, 368–391 (2012)
8. Hoffmann, C., Hinkeldein, D., Graff, A., Kramer, S.: What do potential users think about electric mobility? In: Hülsmann, M., Fornahl, D. (eds.) Evolutionary Paths Towards the Mobility Patterns of the Future, pp. 85–99. Springer, Berlin Heidelberg (2014)
9. Ziefle, M., Beul-Leusmann, S., Kasugai, K., Schwalm, M.: Public perception and acceptance of electric vehicles: exploring users' perceived benefits and drawbacks. In: Marcus, A. (ed.) Design, User Experience, and Usability. User Experience Design for Everyday Life Applications and Services, pp. 628–639. Springer, Heidelberg (2014)
10. Ziefle, M., Beul-Leusmann, S., Zaunbrecher, B.S., Kasugai, K: Integrating the "E" in public transport. In: Giaffreda, R., Caganova, D., Li, Y., Riggio, R., Voisard, A. (eds.) IoT 2014, LNICST, vol. 151, pp. 150–156. Springer, Heidelberg (2015)
11. Greaves, S., Backman, H., Ellison, A.B.: An empirical assessment of the feasibility of battery electric vehicles for day-to-day driving. Transp. Res. Part Policy Pract. **66**, 226–237 (2014)
12. Pearre, N.S., Kempton, W., Guensler, R.L., Elango, V.V.: Electric vehicles: how much range is required for a day's driving? Transp. Res. Part C Emerg. Technol. **19**, 1171–1184 (2011)

Integrating the "E" in Public Transport

Information and Communication Needs for Electromobility

Martina Ziefle(⊠), Shirley Beul-Leusmann, Barbara S. Zaunbrecher,
and Kai Kasugai

Human-Computer Interaction Center, RWTH Aachen University,
Campus Boulevard 57, Aachen 52074, Germany
{ziefle,Beul-Leusmann,Zaunbrecher,
Kasugai}@comm. rwth-aachen. de

Abstract. In this research, we describe an empirical study, which aimed at exploring the acceptance for electromobility within public transport (e.g. electric buses). While electric cars are increasingly receiving public attention, electromobility in public transport is less known so far. Understanding individual arguments of adopting electromobility within public transport, the identification of possible pro-using motives as well as perceived drawbacks is essential in order to individually tailor a sensitive public communication. A questionnaire was carried out in which 208 lay people indicated the level of acceptance and the intention to use electromobility within public transport. In order to get a broad insight into argumentation lines and cognitive user models, perceived benefits and barriers were explored as well as potential circumstances (conditional acceptance factors), which might shape acceptance in the future.

Keywords: Electromobility · Public transport · Electric buses · Technology acceptance · User diversity · Adoption behavior of novel technologies

1 Motivation and Related Work

Today's cities and urban environments face a bundle of complex and, aggravating, interdependent challenges in the next decades. Increasing climate change and environmental threats by air pollution (e.g., CO_2 -emissions), decreasing shortcomings of fossil oil resources, urging societies to place emphasis on renewable energies. Also, the profile of dwellers and traveller has considerably changed over the last years. Due to demographic developments, diverse people with different biographical profiles and mobility needs require a novel, and context-adaptive mobility concepts [1].

Electromobility is one of the promising energy supply technologies, which could be a potent escape from the shortcomings in fossil energy, not only for automobiles but also for public transportation. The potential of electric mobility has been studied mostly for vehicles, from a technical [2], economic [3], logistic [4], environmental [5] point of view. Social science research showed hat there is considerable struggle for electric vehicles to create appropriate markets [6], at least in Germany. A high consumer acceptance for

© Institute for Computer Sciences, Social Informatics and Telecommunications Engineering 2015
R. Giaffreda et al. (Eds.): IoT360 2014, Part II, LNICST 151, pp. 150–156, 2015.
DOI: 10.1007/978-3-319-19743-2_23

alternative fuel vehicles is an important prerequisite to determine the practicality of a successful implementation [7]. Still, however, there is some reluctance to accept electric mobility for vehicles [8]. Yet, there is only few research connected to electromobility within public transport systems which is the main focus of the current study.

2 Questions Addressed and Logic of the Exploratory Approach

In this study we focus on user opinions regarding the use of electromobility in the context of public transportation, comparing perceived usage motives towards buses in contrast to E-Buses. Also, we explored the conditional acceptance by asking participants under which circumstances they would be willing to adopt electro-mobility within the public transport sector. In order to learn which using motives militate in favor of using alternative energy means in public transport and which kind of using barriers might be prevalent, we rely on a focus group study [9] prior to this study. The argumentation lines raised in the focus group discussions were taken up in the questionnaire study reported here.

3 Method

As independent variable the type of vehicle (bus vs. E-Bus), gender and age (young: 20–40 years, middle-aged: 41–60 years, older: 61–75 years) were examined. Dependent variable was the level of acceptance (benefits) and non-acceptance (barriers). Acceptance argumentations were categorized in different argumentation lines: environmental-, cost-, comfort-, trust- and technology-related argumentations for both, benefits and barriers. Also we asked for potential conditional circumstances, under which participants would accept electric buses.

The questionnaire items were based on previous empirical work [9]. The questionnaire was delivered online and focused on different acceptance items (Fig. 1).

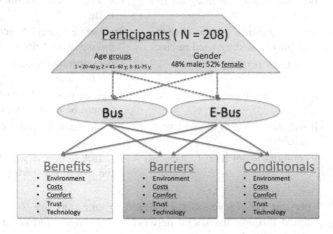

Fig. 1. Structure of the questionnaire

Benefits/Barriers of buses and E-Buses: The motives and barriers were conceptualized along five dimensions (identified on the base of user argumentations in the focus groups, which had been carried out prior to the questionnaire study [9]. Per dimension, we used three items and summarized the answers to an overall score. (Table 1). In addition, we asked for conditional circumstances, which would participants convince to make use of E-Buses. In general, 14 items were formed, taken again from the argumentations of previous focus groups [9].

"I would use E-Buses, if" (1) fuel costs further increase (2) tax reductions would be offered (3) families with many children would have free access (4) seating comfort would be higher (5) buses would take the most direct route (6) more luggage would be allowed (7) bus drivers would be checked for driving ability (8) security at bus stations would be assured, especially at nighttime (9) hooligans and rowdies would have no success (10) the German security standard would be guaranteed (11) buses would equal the most recent technological standard (12) the CO_2 emission in buses would be controlled for (13) there would be a quality seal for buses, and (14) if passenger could monitor emission status.

Table 1. Item examples for the evaluations of benefits and barriers of Buses and E-Buses. Items had to be answered on a Likert Scale (1 = I do not agree at all, 4 = I completely agree)

Bus	Benefits: reasons for using the bus	Barriers: reasons for not using the bus
Environment	It would help to protect the environment	Buses have a high energy consumption (heavy weight)
Costs	It saves costs on the long run	Bus tickets are expensive
Comfort	I do not need to look for parking spaces	Cleanliness and hygiene are low in public buses
Trust	Bus technology is reliable for me	Low trust in driving styles of bus drivers
Technology	Public transport has mature technology	Buses are not prepared for windstorms
E-Bus	Benefits: reasons for using the E-Bus	Barriers: reasons for not using the E-Bus
Environment	Its battery can be used to store the surplus created by wind turbines	To operate a fleet of such buses more power plants need to be built
Costs	It saves costs on the long run	Lower operational costs only benefit the operators
Comfort	It creates less traffic noise	To go easy on its battery the heater cannot be used in winter.
Trust	It will deliver me to my destiny reliably	I do not trust the technology
Technology	It conforms to novel safety standards	The lack of engine sounds increases the risk of accidents.

In total, 208 persons (18–75 years) volunteered to take part (49 % women). Participants were reached through the social networks of younger and older adults and reacted to advertisements in the local newspaper.

4   Results

Data was analyzed by using M(ANOVA) procedures with repeated measurements. The significance level was set at 5 %.

4.1   Perceived Benefits and Barriers

In a first step, the perceived benefits of buses and E-Buses are focused at. In Fig. 2 descriptive outcomes are shown for each of the argumentation categories (for which the single items were summed up). The MANOVA yielded significant effects of the bus type regarding environmental-related benefits ($F(1,197) = 54.4$; $p < 0.000$), also regarding cost-related benefits ($F(1,195) = 16.9$ $p < 0.00$), comfort-related benefits ($F(1,195) = 6.1$ $p < 0.02$), also for trust-related arguments ($F(1,198) = 73.2$ $p < 0.00$) and technology-related benefit perceptions ($F(1,198) = 148.4$ $p < 0.0$). As can be seen, only comfort arguments favor traditional buses over E-Buses - in all other categories the E-Bus is seen more beneficial. Neither age nor gender did significantly impact the perceived benefits in both bus types.

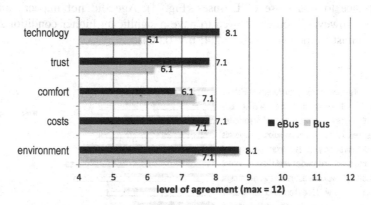

Fig. 2. Level of agreement (means) for the perceived benefits on different argumentation dimensions for buses and E-Buses (4 = not at all, 12 = completely agree)

A next analysis is directed to the perceived barriers (Fig. 3).

In Fig. 3, descriptive outcomes are depicted (along the five dimensions). As found, there were significant differences in the perceived barriers between buses and E-Buses in nearly all dimensions: environment ($F(1,193) = 4.7$; $p < 0.03$), costs ($F(1,194) = 43.3$ $p < 0.00$), comfort ($F(1,196) = 658.9$; $p < 0.000$) as well as trust-related barriers ($F(1,191) = 31.8$; $p < 0.00$). In contrast, perceptions with respect to technology-related barriers of buses and E-Buses are comparably high.

While gender did not impact perceived barriers, age was a significant source of barrier perception. With increasing age, costs for the E-Bus are seen less negative ($F(2,194) = 4.9$; $p < 0.008$), the trust in E-Buses is higher ($F(2,198) = 4.1$; $p < 0.002$) and technology-related barriers are seen as less negative ($F(2,187) = 3.9$; $p < 0.04$).

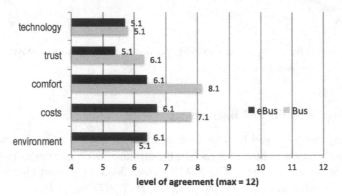

Fig. 3. Level of agreement (means) for the perceived barriers on different argumentation dimensions for buses and E-Buses (4 = not at all, 12 = completely agree)

4.2   Conditional Acceptance Criteria

Finally, participants had to indicate which conditional circumstances would increase the acceptance to make use of E-Buses (Fig. 4). Age did not impact conditional acceptance. However, women showed to have a significant higher conditional acceptance in contrast to men $(F(1,178) = 2.4; p < 0.004)$.

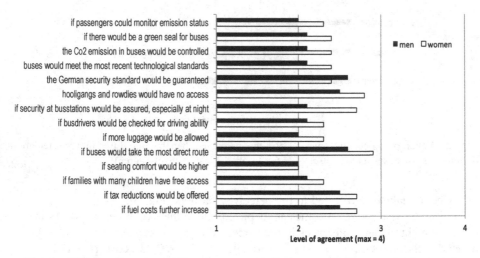

Fig. 4.   (Dis)agreement to conditional acceptance (1 = not at all, 4 = completely agree)

For men the only argument which militates in favor for using E-Buses in the near future is that the German security standard would be guaranteed in E-Buses $(F(1,178) = 4.6; p < 0.000)$.

5 Discussion and Future Research

In this study, perceived benefits and barriers of laypeople towards electric buses were assessed as well as the willingness to adopt electromobility in public transport respecting conditional acceptance arguments. Outcomes contribute to the understanding of major public opinion drivers for and against electric mobility in public transport. Overall, electric buses provide higher benefit perceptions than drawbacks – taken from the higher agreement to the benefits in contrast to the perceptions. Major positive arguments are the eco friendliness of the technology and the cost-savings on the long run. On the barriers' side, comfort, trust in the technology and high costs are seen as detrimental. Beyond the overall high uncertainty of the novelty of the technology, which drives the non-acceptance, it is interesting that the very same arguments are used for benefits and barriers. This is valid for the perceived trust in the technology (which is high for the novel E-Buses and at the same time low as the technology seems not to be mature enough) but also for the perceived costs (cost reduction on the long run is positive; high asset costs are negative). Gender and age were significant drivers of acceptance. Among conditional acceptance, women especially stress safety and security issues (at night, at bus stations, threat by other passengers). While these findings corroborate recent research in public transport [10], the raised concerns - though serious – are not specifically connected to electro-mobility but to public transportation in general.

Critically, one could argue that acceptance can only be assessed if persons rely on personal experience with using electric buses, which is still only scarcely available, at least in Germany. Acceptance might be thus formed by knowledge gaps and limited information. Consequently, individual beliefs, uncertainty as well as perceptions risks come into fore. In order to shape public acceptance, a diligent information policy and transparent communication rationale in this field is of high importance.

Acknowledgements. This work was funded by the German Ministry of Economics and Technology (01 ME 12052).

References

1. Ziefle, M., Schneider, C., Vallee, D., Schnettler, A., Krempels, K.-H., Jarke, M.: Urban Future outline (UFO). A roadmap on research for livable cities. ERCIM News (N. 98). http://ercim-news.ercim.eu/en98/keynote-smart-cities (2014)
2. Werther, B., Hoch, N.: E-mobility as a challenge for new ict solutions in the car industry. In: Bruni, R., Sassone, V. (eds.) TGC 2011. LNCS, vol. 7173, pp. 46–57. Springer, Heidelberg (2012)
3. Frischknecht, R., Flury, K.: Life cycle assessment of electric mobility: answers and challenges. Int. J. Life Cycle Assess. **16**, 691–695 (2011)
4. Ehrler, V., Hebes, P.: Electromobility for city logistics: the solution to urban transport collapse? Procedia-Soc. Behav. Sci. **48**, 786–795 (2012)
5. Held, M., Baumann, M.: Assessment of the environmental impacts of electric vehicle concepts. In: Finkbeiner, M. (ed.) Towards Life Cycle Sustainability Management, pp. 535–546. Springer, Netherlands (2011)

6. Yu, A.S., Silva, L.C., Chu, C.L., Nascimento, P.T., Camargo, A.S.: Electric vehicles: struggles in creating a market. In: Proceedings of PICMET, Technology Management in the Energy Smart World, pp. 1–13. IEEE (2011)
7. Egbue, O., Long, S.: Barriers to widespread adoption of electric vehicles: an analysis of consumer attitudes and perceptions. Energy Policy **48**, 717–729 (2012)
8. Ziefle, M., Beul-Leusmann, S., Kasugai, K., Schwalm, M.: Public perception and acceptance of electric vehicles: exploring users' perceived benefits and drawbacks. In: Marcus, A. (ed.) DUXU 2014, Part III. LNCS, vol. 8519, pp. 628–639. Springer, Heidelberg (2014)
9. Zaunbrecher, B., Ziefle, M.: Laypeople's perspectives on electromobility. A focus group study. In: Giaffreda, R., Caganova, D., Li, Y., Riggio, R., Voisard, A. (eds.) IoT 2014, LNICST, vol. 151, pp. 144–149. Springer, Heidelberg (2015)
10. Van Heck, J., Arning, K., Ziefle, M.: Safety and privacy perceptions in public spaces: an empirical study on user requirements for city mobility. In: Giaffreda, R., Caganova, D., Li, Y., Riggio, R., Voisard, A. (eds.) IoT 2014, LNICST, vol. 151, pp. xx–yy. Springer, Heidelberg (2015)

Application for a Personal Mobility Sharing System Using Two-Wheeled Self-balancing Vehicles

Naohisa Hashimoto(✉), Kohji Tomita, Akiya Kamimura,
Yusuke Takinami, and Osamu Matsumoto

Intelligent System Research Institute,
National Institute of Advanced Industrial Science and Technology (AIST),
1-1-1 Umezono, Tsukuba, Ibaraki 305-8568, Japan
{naohisa-hashimoto,k.tomita,kamimura.a,
matsumoto.o}@aist.go.jp

Abstract. To solve urban area traffic problems, one potential solution is to reduce traffic volumes. In order to do so, a modal shift from conventional passenger vehicles to public transportation and eco-vehicles, including personal vehicles, should be considered. We propose a personal mobility sharing system using the Segway. To evaluate this system, it is necessary to perform experiments under real conditions and gather experimental data for a social pilot study. This study introduces an application for a personal mobility sharing system using the Segway-type vehicle. The main feature of the proposed application is to gather and store experimental data on mobility sharing, and to assist a driver to use the Segway-type personal vehicle safely. Each vehicle is equipped with a tablet, on which the application is installed.

Keywords: Personal mobility · Mobility sharing system · Pilot study · Intelligent transportation system

1 Introduction

One potential solution to urban area traffic problems is reducing traffic volumes. To achieve this goal, a modal shift should be considered from conventional vehicles to public transportation and eco-vehicles, including personal vehicles. In this study, we focus on personal mobility and vehicle sharing to reduce traffic volume. Bicycle sharing projects have been initiated in the United States, France, and a few other countries. In the United States, several bicycle sharing projects are being widely used [1–6]. In Japan, a community cycle project organized by a local city government was initiated in a sightseeing area [7]. Such sharing systems are expected to be used for new and eco-transportation programs.

The rapid increase in the elderly population has caused several issues in Japan. Elderly people (above 65 years) in Japan have accounted for more road fatalities than any other age group, as shown in Fig. 1 [8]. The number of fatal accidents due to elderly drivers has increased nearly three-fold in the past 17 years, while the total number of fatal accidents has decreased by nearly 30 % during the same period [8].

© Institute for Computer Sciences, Social Informatics and Telecommunications Engineering 2015
R. Giaffreda et al. (Eds.): IoT360 2014, Part II, LNICST 151, pp. 157–162, 2015.
DOI: 10.1007/978-3-319-19743-2_24

Automobiles are the optimal transportation means for the elderly because they provide door-to-door transportation. However, a shift to public transportation from individual automobiles is required in order to solve current traffic problems. To resolve this problem, convenient and eco-friendly transportation must be provided for elderly people. Public transportation is convenient and eco-friendly, but the last-mile problem of getting each individual to their front door remains, especially for elderly people [9, 10]. To solve this last-mile problem, personal mobility is considered the only option.

To solve the two challenges of reducing traffic in urban areas and supporting elderly drivers, we propose mobility sharing with personal vehicles [15]. The main objective of this study is to evaluate the possibility of a mobility sharing system with two-wheeled self-balancing vehicles, and we have constructed an application for such vehicles in a personal mobility sharing system. The application is installed on a tablet equipped on each vehicle. The main feature of the application is to gather and store experimental data on mobility sharing, and to assist a driver to drive the vehicle safely in a real environment. The Tsukuba designated zone, sharing system, and the application for the system are described in this paper.

The Segway is trademarked by the Segway Inc. of New Hampshire, USA.

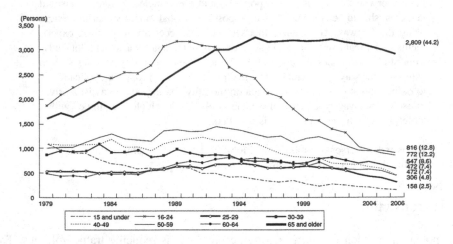

Fig. 1. Number of traffic accident fatalities in Japan by age group

2 Tsukuba Designated Zone for Experiments

As personal mobility is categorized as robotics in Japan, study experiments were performed in the Tsukuba designated zone [11], which was officially approved by the cabinet office in Japan on January 29, 2010. As of February 2012, Segway Japan, Hitachi Corporation, and the National Institute of Advanced Industrial Science and Technology (AIST) are all engaged in conducting personal mobility experiments.

Our experiments were conducted in the Tsukuba Center area, shown in Fig. 2. The terms, detailed roles of various operations in the experiment, and the definition of the

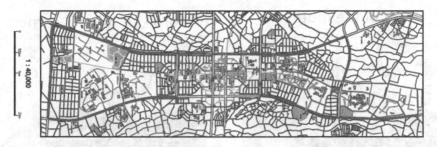

Fig. 2. Tsukuba Center area (zone bounded by the red line)

robot used in this experiment were established [11]. Existing regulations for conducting experiments in the Tsukuba designated zone [11] made it necessary to classify the personal vehicle experiments as a pilot study in order to control the regulations.

3 Application for Standing-Type Personal Mobility Vehicle

The purpose of our proposed personal mobility sharing system [15] is to facilitate transportation between the AIST building and the Tsukuba station, which is the nearest train station. The concept of the proposed system is similar to that of a bike- or car-sharing system [12–14], but personal mobility devices are used instead of other transportation options, and several types of data are tracked using sensors. We chose the Segway two-wheeled self-balancing vehicle [16] for our study, and introduced an application for our proposed sharing system. The application gathers experimental data including near-incident scenes and assists the driver to drive the personal mobility vehicle safely in real-world experiments. Because Segway-type vehicles have not yet spread in Japan, a large amount of experimental data will be necessary in order to evaluate the safety and the availability of these types of vehicles. In addition, Japanese drivers are inexperienced in driving Segway-type vehicles; thus, some assistance is required to ensure driver safety. Each vehicle is equipped with a tablet, in which the application is active. The tablet also has a GPS, acceleration sensors (X, Y, and Z), gyro sensors (yaw, pitch, and roll) and magnetic sensors, as shown in Figs. 3 and 4. The application shows the status information as follows:

1. Current map location. (Awareness of the current location is important for performing experiments in the designated zone, since experimental activity outside the designated zone is prohibited.)
2. Current time, departure place and time, and destination place and time.
3. Sensor information (acceleration, gyro, magnetic, and GPS).
4. Current driving status (estimated using the acceleration and gyro data) shown in Fig. 4. The application has four types of data sets and identifies the current status using the Block Sparse-Sparse Representation Classification method [17]. This algorithm can estimate a current status with more than 90 % accuracy.

160   N. Hashimoto et al.

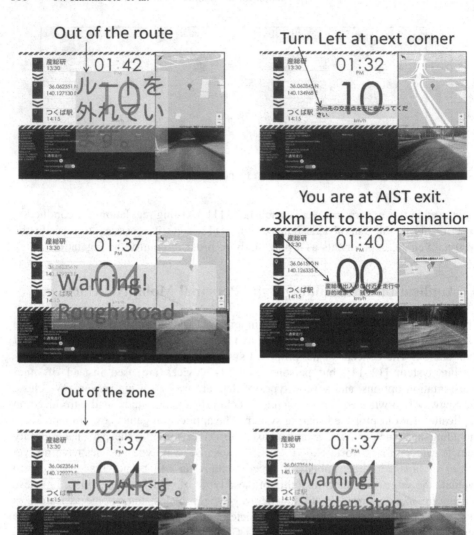

Fig. 3. Notifications estimated by the application (top-left: the application notices the driver is outside the planned route; top-right: the application shows a navigation route to a destination; middle-left: the application warns of a rough road; middle-right: the application notes the miles between the destination and the current location; bottom-left: the application notes that the driver is outside the zone; bottom-right: the application warns of dangerous driving)

5. Navigation information, as shown in Fig. 4.
6. Image captured from front camera.

In addition, the application stores all sensor data including the camera image.

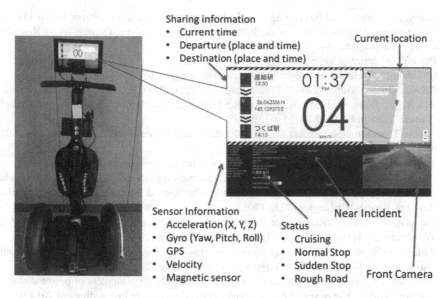

Fig. 4. Experimental vehicle and a screen capture of the application

4 Summary

We introduced an application for a personal mobility sharing system using a two-wheeled self-balancing vehicle. Experiments were conducted in real-world conditions to evaluate the system's potential. The application gathered experimental data and assisted the driver in driving the personal mobility vehicle safely. The functions of the proposed application included the awareness of the experimental area, the provision of warnings about dangerous driving situations, showing the current location and distance to destination, and obtaining and storing experimental data. We also plan to expand this personal mobility sharing system by increasing the number of personal mobility routes and stations for future experiments in different environments, and to perform future experiments with several types of subjects.

Acknowledgments. This study has been supported by the NEDO IT Yugo Project and the Tsukuba City Government.

References

1. Capital Bikeshare. http://www.capitalbikeshare.com/
2. Bike Sharing. http://www.pedbikeinfo.org/pdf/Programs_Promote_bikeshareintheus.pdf
3. Febbraro, A., Gattorna, E.: Optimizing dynamic ride-sharing systems. In: Proceedings of the 92th Annual Meeting of the Transportation Research Board, Washington, D.C. (2013)
4. Daito, N., Chen, Z.: Demand of bike sharing travels: evidence from Washington D.C. In: Proceedings of the 92th Annual Meeting of the Transportation Research Board, Washington, D.C. (2013)

5. Rixey, A.: Station-level forecasting of bike sharing ridership: station network effects in three U.S. systems. In: Proceedings of the 92th Annual Meeting of the Transportation Research Board, Washington, D.C. (2013)
6. Paris Velib. http://en.velib.paris.fr/
7. Community Cycle (in Japanese). http://kcc.docomo-cycle.jp/
8. Cabinet Office, White Paper on Traffic Safety in Japan 2006, p. 11 (in Japanese). (2006)
9. Balcik, B., Beamon, B.M., Smilowitz, K.: Last mile distribution in humanitarian relief. J. Intell. Transp. Syst. 12(2), 51–63 (2008)
10. Mineta Transportation Institute Report S-09–02, Using Bicycles for the First and Last Mile of a Commute, Report No. S-09-02 (2009)
11. Tsukuba Designated Zone Council (in Japanese). http://www.rt-tsukuba.jp/council/
12. Fan, W., Xu, Y.: Managing dynamic vehicle allocation for car sharing systems: a stochastic programming approach. In: Proceedings of the 92th Annual Meeting of the Transportation Research Board, Washington, D.C. (2013)
13. Lowyck, B.: CoCar, dynamic ride sharing service. In: Proceedings of the 19th Intelligent Transportation Systems World Congress, Vienna, Austria (2012)
14. Pihl, C.: Evaluation of german car sharing systems. In: Proceedings of the 19th Intelligent Transportation Systems World Congress, Vienna, Austria (2012)
15. Hashimoto, N., Tomita, K., Kamimura, A., Matsumoto, O.: Development of personal shared mobility system—use of segway as personal mobility device. In: Proceedings of 2014 World Congress on Intelligent Transportation Systems, Detroit, USA (2014, will be presented)
16. Segway. http://www.segway.com
17. Boyali, A., Hashimoto, N.: Block-sparse representation classification based gesture recognition approach for a robotic wheelchair. In: Proceedings of IEEE Intelligent Vehicles Symposium, pp. 1133–1138 (2014)

Multi-agent Simulator for Personal Mobility Vehicle Sharing

Kohji Tomita$^{(\boxtimes)}$, Naohisa Hashimoto, and Osamu Matsumoto

National Institute of Advanced Industrial Science and Technology (AIST),
Tsukuba, Japan
{k.tomita,naohisa-hashimoto,matsumoto.o}@aist.go.jp

Abstract. For future transportation, boarding type personal mobilities
are considered promising. On introducing such mobilities in community,
sharing is more prospective than owing. In this paper, we aim at considering expected change of human behavior, including modal shift, by
introducing such mobilities in society. In the hope of large scale demand
prediction and optimal planning of both location and capacity of the
personal mobility sharing stations, we have developed a prototype multi-
agent simulator. Parameters of simulation are determined by sharing
experiments in Mobility Robot Experimental Zone in Tsukuba using
Toyota Winglet long type and conjoint analysis based on questionnaires.
We obtained preliminary results for a realistic situation.

Keywords: Personal mobility · Sharing · Simulation · Mobility robot

1 Introduction

For future transportation, boarding type personal mobilities (simply called PMs
hereafter) are considered promising. They include Toyota Winglet [1], Segway [2],
and AIST micro mobility [3], and have many advantages as follows. They are
environmentally friendly. Their energy consumption is low compared to other
transportation means such as cars, buses, and trains. PMs do not emit carbon dioxide during operation. Furthermore, it is human friendly. Relatively slow
speed helps avoiding serious accidents, which are often fatal to elderly people.
PMs are well suited to the concept of compact cities [4,5], which is advocated
to solve various problems such as environmental, energy, and safety problems,
caused by urban mobility.

On introducing PMs in community, sharing is more prospective than owing.
Sharing usually costs much lower than purchasing. Users need not maintain or
repair. Moreover, necessary parking area is much smaller. It is especially effective
for connecting purposes from home or office to train stations or bus stops. If PMs
are introduced in town, human flow is changed and new behavior will emerge.
Sharing systems of PMs, however, have not yet studied enough.

As for sharing of mobility, bicycle sharing has been studied [6–8], and is
popular recently in big cities. Vélib in Paris, Barclays Cycle Hire in London,

© Institute for Computer Sciences, Social Informatics and Telecommunications Engineering 2015
R. Giaffreda et al. (Eds.): IoT360 2014, Part II, LNICST 151, pp. 163–168, 2015.
DOI: 10.1007/978-3-319-19743-2_25

and Capital Bikeshare in Washington, D.C. are examples of many successful systems. There, bicycles are rented at sharing stations and can be returned to any convenient station among many in the city.

In this paper, we aim at considering expected change of human behavior, including modal shift, by introducing PM sharing in society. In the hope of large scale demand prediction and optimal planning of both location and capacity of PM stations, we have developed a prototype multi-agent simulator. The behavior of mobility decision is modeled by the nested logit model [9]. One difficulty in such simulation is that the accuracy of simulation is not clear. To make the assumption closer to real situations, we use actual data obtained by experiments in Mobility Robot Experimental Zone in Tsukuba [10]. Parameters of the simulation were decided by the sharing experiments using four units of Winglet long type and conjoint analysis based on questionnaires. Supposed scenario for simulation here is traveling behavior of employees of our institute (AIST) for business trip between AIST and the nearest train station. We conduct simulations and evaluate the effect of introducing the sharing system of PMs.

2   Personal Mobility Sharing Simulator

2.1   PM Sharing

PM sharing seems prospective, but to evaluate the future demand of PMs, we need some evaluation method. Among various possible methods, micro simulation based on multi-agent model is suited for small to medium scale simulation because of its flexibility in configuration for individual agents with different characteristics in walking speed, riding speed and mobility preference attributed by age, gender, and so on. Also, various behaviors due to the limited number of PMs and capacity of PM stations on renting and returning are treated naturally.

Similarly to bicycle sharing, we need to consider the case where PM station is full upon return. In that case, the user cannot return the PM immediately to the station, and needs to wait or return it to another nearby station. Also, there is a problem that PMs may be accumulated at some station due to biased usage.

PM sharing is different from bicycle sharing in the following aspects.

– Charging time is required. When the mobility is returned to a station, some charging time, depending on the riding distance or time of the previous user, is necessary before it is rented to a new user.
– Seamless PM riding between indoor and outdoor is possible. Sometimes this helps much for visiting shopping malls, museums, etc.
– PMs can be carried easily in other transportation means such as trains and cars. This usage will expand PMs' range of operation.
– Because information processing capability is equipped, assistance by IT infrastructure will be easy.

2.2 Simulator Overview

We have developed a prototype simulator for PM sharing. A snapshot and a configuration diagram of the simulator are shown in Fig. 1. A schematic diagram of the whole framework, including behavior and decision models, is shown in Fig. 2.

We adopt a simple behavior model. Each agent is generated at some designated time in the simulator, who has start and the goal points, and then decides its behavior stochastically by a decision model. If the agent chooses, e.g., a bus, it walks to the nearest bus stop, waits and gets on a bus, gets off the bus at the bus stop close to its goal points, and walks to the goal. The free flow speed for waking and riding PMs are given but actual speeds decrease depending on the ratio decided by the attributes of the agent and the density of pedestrians on the same segment of the roads.

As a decision model, we adopt a nested logit model. The utility function of each mobility is assumed to be a weighted sum of factors such as distance, estimated required time, estimated delay time, and preference of main transportation means. Each agent can make decision of transportation means when

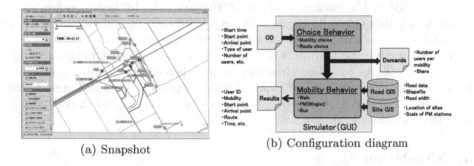

(a) Snapshot   (b) Configuration diagram

Fig. 1. Prototype simulator.

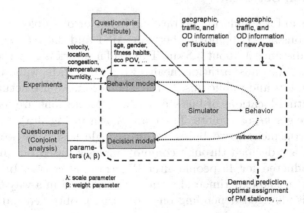

Fig. 2. Schematic diagram.

being generated, and, assug some digital aid, when receiving emptiness information on its heading PM station.

Parameters of the behavior model and the decision model for the simulator are decided by the experiments in Tsukuba and questionnaire. By feedback of such information, these models can be refined. Once a simulator with these models can be developed with geographic, traffic and OD information of Tsukuba, presumably, this can be applied to other places by providing such information of the areas, and simulation can be conducted for demand prediction or planning of optimal assignment of PM stations in both location and capacity.

2.3 Deciding Parameters

One difficulty in such simulation is that the accuracy is not clear. To make the assumption closer to real situations, we obtain actual data by small scale outdoor sharing experiments in Tsukuba Mobility Robot Experimental Zone using Toyota Winglet.

Tsukuba was approved in 2011 as Japan's first Mobility Robot Experimental Zone, which permits the boarding type robots to travel on public sidewalks with 3 m wide at the maximum speed of 10 km/h [10]. In Japan, riding such mobility on public sidewalks is generally prohibited and it is difficult to conduct experiments and obtain realistic data using PMs in other areas.

In the experiments, four units of Winglet were used. Winglet weighs 19.7 kg. It takes one hour for full charge from empty, and then one hour riding is possible for about 4 km. Fast charging in 15 min for 80 % is possible. It is in compact size compared to Segway, with ease of use, and can be much adapted in community especially in indoor environment.

3   Simulation

3.1 Simulation Settings

Supposed scenario for simulation is traveling behavior of employees of our institute (AIST) on business trip; moving between AIST and the nearest train station is focused. The distance is about 3.8 km. The road network is given to the simulator as a shapefile. As transportation means, we assume PMs, walk and two types of buses, shuttle bus and public bus. In the simulation, we use actual timetables of buses and actual locations of bus stops. Two PM stations are assumed to be located near the start/goal points. These are shown in Fig. 3(a).

In the decision model, two buses are in a single nest. The weights for the utility function are decided through conjoint analysis based on questionnaires, which were conducted for 45 people after PM training course. In terms of the behavior model, actual experimental results were utilized in a way that free flow speed of PMs is changed depending on the actually obtained data for several road segments.

Under the above settings, simulations were conducted from 9:00 to 17:00 by changing the number of generated agents and PMs. When there is no available

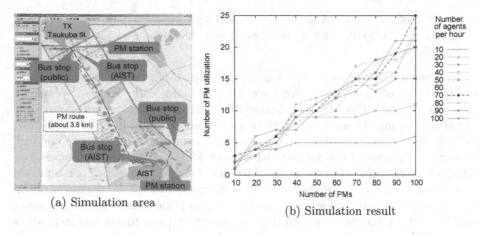

(a) Simulation area

(b) Simulation result

Fig. 3. Simulation.

PMs at a station, the users wait for a fixed amount of time, called maximum wait time. After the time, users give up using PMs and choose another means (walk, in this case). The wait time actually affects the utility of PMs, but it is difficult to estimate it in advance. Therefore, we conduct simulation 10 times with feedback of the simulated wait time of PMs.

Main parameters of the behavior model are as follows. Free flow speeds of PMs and walkers are 6 km/h and 4 km/h, respectively. Maximum wait time for PM at station is 500 s. Getting on/off the PMs takes no time. Moreover, we use a fixed time (15 min) for charging. Here, we consider only the case where PM stations are large enough to contain as many PMs so that PMs can be returned at any station any time.

3.2   Simulation Results

The snapshot of Fig..1(a) is from this simulation; the area shown is around Tsukuba Station. Lines indicate paths given by an input file and circles indicate moving agents. As an example of simulation results, the number of users using PMs is shown in Fig. 3(b). Each plot is the average of 5 simulation runs. Other parameters are: expected maximum delay time for buses is 20 min, route bus fare is 260 yen (as is), AIST bus is free, and emptiness notification ratio is 0. By changing these parameters, we can simulate various situations.

4   Conclusions

We have presented a prototype multi-agent simulator for personal mobility sharing. The simulator has the following features.

– The number of PMs are limited, and can be returned to any PM station within its limited capacity.

- Decision of users is modeled by the nested logit model.
- Various characteristic of the users, such as behavior and choice, can be configurable.

We conducted preliminary simulation and obtained results about share, the number of PM usage, and so on. We have lots of future work. We used plausible value for simulation parameters obtained from experiments and questionnaires, but still verifying the accuracy of simulation is not enough. In order to do this, calibration of the results should be considered. Also, we are planning to conduct sharing experiments in wider area with more PM stations and corresponding larger simulation. In that case we need to introduce other transportation means such as bicycles, trains, and private cars. Under the extensions, demands of the PMs can be evaluated under more realistic assumptions, and optimal planning of PM stations will be examined. Finally, different from just a transportation means, PMs are suitable for moving around for pleasure. Such activity should be incorporated as well.

Acknowledgment. This study was conducted in NEDO IT Fusion Project.

References

1. Winglet (in Japanese). http://www.toyota.co.jp/jpn/tech/personal_mobility/winglet.html
2. Segway. http://www.segway.com
3. Takei, T., Matsumoto, O., Komoriya, K.: Simultaneous estimation of slope angle and handling force when getting on and off a human-riding wheeled inverted pendulum vehicle. In: Proceedings of IEEE/RSJ International Conference on Intelligent Robots and Systems (IROS 2009), pp. 4553–4558 (2009)
4. Dantzig, G.B., Saaty, T.L.: Compact City: Plan for a Liveable Urban Environment. W.H Freeman, New York (1973)
5. Burton, E., Jenks, M., Williams, K. (eds.): The Compact City: A Sustainable Urban Form?. Routledge, London (2003)
6. DeMaio, P.: Bike-sharing: history, impacts, models of provision, and future. J. Public Transp. **12**(4), 41–56 (2009)
7. Midgley, P.: Bicycle-sharing Schemes: Enhancing Sustainable Mobility in Urban Aareas. United Nations, Department of Economic and Social Affairs (2011)
8. Lin, J.R., Yang, T.H.: Strategic design of public bicycle sharing systems with service level constraints. Transp. Res. Part E Logist. Transp. Rev. **47**(2), 284–294 (2011)
9. Train, K.E.: Discrete Choice Methods with Simulation, 2nd edn. Cambridge University Press, New York (2009)
10. Tsukuba Mobility Robot Council (in Japanese). http://www.rt-tsukuba.jp/council

The Added Value of a New, Innovative Travel Service: Insights from the UbiGo Field Operational Test in Gothenburg, Sweden

Jana Sochor[✉], Helena Strömberg, and I.C. MariAnne Karlsson

Division Design and Human Factors, Chalmers University of Technology,
SE-412 96 Gothenburg, Sweden
{jana.sochor,helena.stromberg,mak}@chalmers.se

Abstract. The aim of this chapter is to introduce the UbiGo transport broker service developed in Gothenburg, Sweden, and to discuss insights from the six-month field operational test regarding incentives for users adopting new travel services as well as perceived added value. Results are presented from participant questionnaires, interviews, and travel diaries. Findings suggest that potential early users are initially incentivized by curiosity, but that this must be transformed into practical incentives such as convenience and economic advantage if the users are to continue using the service. Customers also found added value in the "transportation smorgasbord" concept, 24-hour customer support, new types of subscriptions and tickets, and having everything in their smartphone, but wished for more personalized decision support and feedback. Concern for the environment functioned more as a bonus than as an incentive, meaning that the environmentally friendly choice must also be the practical choice in order to promote sustainability.

Keywords: Field operational test · Multimodal travel · Seamless travel · Travel service · Incentive · Added value

1 Introduction

On the one hand urban mobility is vital for the functioning of cities, on the other hand it causes problems in terms of e.g. emissions and noise. A large number of projects has been implemented to bring about changes regarding transportation of people. In addition to economic and legal measures, commuters have for instance been the targets of information and education campaigns to raise awareness and change attitudes towards mode choice, e.g. [1–4]. Other projects have tried to stimulate and motivate change through competitions or handing out free public transportation passes, e.g. [5–7]. Considerable efforts have also been made to increase the attractiveness of public transport, for instance by introducing vehicles with improved designs and traveler information, e.g. [8–11]. To alter people's travel habits is difficult, however, and the progress, albeit positive, is too limited to meet the challenges ahead; a more innovative solution is needed to bring about more radical changes.

© Institute for Computer Sciences, Social Informatics and Telecommunications Engineering 2015
R. Giaffreda et al. (Eds.): IoT360 2014, Part II, LNICST 151, pp. 169–175, 2015.
DOI: 10.1007/978-3-319-19743-2_26

In order to reduce traffic by maintaining or increasing the level of mobility for citizens (and goods), one challenge is how to use the current infrastructure more efficiently and to encourage multimodality. Technological approaches discussed are smartphone and web applications facilitating the processes of booking, ticketing, and organization of city logistics [12].

The Go:Smart project is an attempt to create better conditions for sustainable travel by demonstrating how new business models and partnerships can reduce the need for private car ownership in favor of seamlessness, multimodality, and use of information technology. The vision was an integrated mobility service for end consumers providing a seamless, multimodal journey experience including public transport interlinked with car and bike-sharing. The underlying assumptions behind the project were:

- Changes in travel behavior face deterring and incentivizing factors. Deterring factors include different efforts such as changing habits, a need for learning, economic investments, etc. Incentivizing factors are anticipated and perceived benefits, including economic gains, increased status, etc.;
- Incentives can be intrinsic as well as extrinsic [13] in terms of punishments or rewards. Providing feedback in terms of some kind of reward can have a positive effect on encouraging and maintaining a desired behavior, cf. [14];
- Current shifts in individuals' attitudes and values, cf. [14], in a more environmentally conscious direction, and the trends towards joint/shared ownership or no ownership at all (including car- and bikesharing) open up new possibilities for new types of travel offers.

Identified preconditions were that the desired changes cannot be brought about by the development of a single transport mode or by focusing solely on a shift from fossil-fuelled, private cars to public transportation, but by the integration of different transportation services, public and private, i.e. "collective transport"; and furthermore that the developments in Information and Communication Technology (ICT) as well as the dissemination of mobile ICT has made it increasingly possible to create and test new and smarter offers.

The Go:Smart project has involved the development and Field Operational Test (FOT) of an innovative transport broker service, named UbiGo, for sustainable transportation of people in urban environments. The service has attempted to bridge the gap between private and public transportation by taking on the role of a commercial actor, "a broker of everyday travel", offering customized transport services to fit the individual traveler's needs and requirements. More than 190 individuals became paying customers for six months (November 2013–April 2014).

This chapter presents early results from the FOT regarding which values – both added values to the individual customer and wider, social values – can be created or fostered by a new, innovative, ICT-based approach to mobility services. Questions posed were: What incentivizes people to become and remain customers? What added values – expected and unexpected – were created by the service concept?; by the ICT-based platform? What added values were expected but not realized?

2 The UbiGo Transport Broker Service

The UbiGo service offered its users one-stop access to a range of travel services through a web-interface adapted to smartphones (subsequently referred to as the app). It was built up as a monthly subscription service where a household (which may be comprised of multiple persons; adults and children) decided their desired combination of, and amount of credit for: public transportation, carsharing, car rentals, bikesharing, and taxi service. Credit could be topped up or rolled over. The subscription could also be modified on a monthly basis.

To access their travel services, the UbiGo traveler logged into the app via a Google- or Facebook-login, where they could activate tickets/trips, make/check bookings, and access already activated tickets (e.g. for validation purposes). The app allowed them to check their balance, bonus, and trip history, and get support (FAQ/customer service). Each participant received a smartcard, used e.g. to check out a bicycle or unlock a booked car, but also charged with extra credit for the public transportation system in case there was any problem using the UbiGo service. UbiGo included a customer service line open 24 h per day.

3 Method

The original participant group consisted of 83 customer subscriptions covering 195 persons: 173 adults and 22 children (<18 years). A total of 21 private vehicles were deliberately not used during the FOT (from November 1, 2013 to April 30, 2014).

To evaluate the participants' experiences and travel behaviors, data was collected via a mixed-methods approach including questionnaires, interviews, focus groups, and travel diaries, as well as workshops and logging of customer service issues. The "before", "during" and "after" questionnaires were sent out to all participants (optional for children) and completed by 164, 161 and 160 participants respectively (with 151 adults completing all three). Ex-post interviews were carried out with 14 individual participants and with three households. Three ex-post focus groups were also conducted. One-week travel diaries were completed by 40 ("before") and 36 ("during") participants, respectively.

Statistical analyses of the questionnaire data were performed with the software IBM SPSS. Recordings of all interviews and focus groups were transcribed in full for analysis. All trips in the "before" travel diaries were summarized and the participants' choices of travel mode were compared with the averages for Gothenburg.

4 Results

4.1 Socio-Demographics and Ex-ante Travel Behavior

From the "before" questionnaire (164 responses), the participant group had an average age of 38 years and consisted of approximately 50 % women. The majority was employed (80 %) and had a driver's license (88 %) although only 41 % stated that they have daily personal access to a car. The majority owned a bicycle (81 %) and had a public transportation card (88 %), but few were bikesharing members (19 %).

Most lived in apartments (80 %) and there was a mix of household types (mostly multiple adults with/without children) and income levels. Also, a slight majority did not own a car (52 %) and the majority was not a carsharing member (69 %).

A large majority of participants used the internet and apps on computers, tablets, and smartphones on a daily basis (88–91 % in all cases). (Note that one needs a smartphone in order to run the UbiGo app.)

An initial analysis of the "before" travel diaries (846 trips from 24 women and 16 men) revealed that the participants differed somewhat from the average Gothenburg resident [15]. In terms of car use, the participant group was most similar to the average person living in Central Gothenburg (27 % versus 24 %, respectively). However, their use of alternative modes differed somewhat in that more participants used public transportation (34 % versus 26 %, respectively) and fewer walked (24 % versus 39 %, respectively).

4.2   Incentives and Added Value

When asking participants about their *primary* reason for joining UbiGo ("before" questionnaire), *curiosity* was by far the strongest reason, with 63 % claiming this as their primary reason. In fact, all other reasons such as *convenience/flexibility, economy, environment, family member, gaining access to cars,* and/or *test living without a privately owned car* significantly lagged behind curiosity. According to the "during" questionnaire results, curiosity lost its dominant position (from 63 % to 25 %), while convenience/flexibility (22 %) and economy (14 %) increased as reasons to continue as a customer. Results from the "after" questionnaire revealed that convenience/flexibility became the dominant reason (30 %), followed by curiosity (21 %) and economy (14 %) (see Fig. 1).

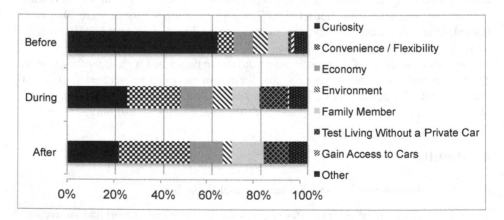

Fig. 1. Primary incentive of the participant group over time.

Besides the practical aspects of convenience/flexibility and economy, interview results revealed several other appreciated features:

- The "transportation smorgasbord" concept, with the majority of one's travel needs offered in one package. Here, environment comes into play, as participants were initially attracted to the concept of UbiGo and felt that it was an added bonus if it meant potentially more environmentally friendly travel as well.
- The type of subscription, where many people (not even living under the same roof) could be included in one subscription with one monthly invoice. Not only could customers get an overview of their monthly transportation expenditures, they could easily "support" other relatives (e.g. grown children or aging parents) as well.
- The daily public transportation ticket, reasonably priced, based on a more generous zone system, and activated once rather than using the tap-in/out system. It was also easy to upgrade to additional zones on a particular day.
- A smartphone-based system, illustrated by the participant comment: "I can forget my public transportation card, but I cannot forget my phone".
- 24-hour customer support with only one telephone number. Rather than different numbers for UbiGo and each subservice, all customer support was handled via one number, which could easily be found in the app.

Although not necessarily a feature that created added value (it was almost never utilized during the FOT), the "improved" travel guarantee, where UbiGo promised to deal with the expenditure and administration, is likely a feature that cannot be eliminated as it creates a sense of security. Surprisingly, the feature that could potentially be eliminated, or at least modified, is the bonus system for "eco-friendly" travel, where the UbiGo traveler accumulated points (based on reduced kg of CO_2 compared to making the same trip by private car) that could be exchanged for other goods and services. Most did not exploit the rewards offered by the bonus system, and those who did tended to do it at the very end of the FOT. Participants felt that if there was a bonus system, it should be tied to the service itself by giving internal, transportation-related rewards, rather than external rewards.

One feature that was lacking, but that customers wished for and that would likely create added value, is personalized decision support and feedback. Customers wanted the system to suggest alternatives based on various factors such as time, distance, cost, CO_2, etc., and they wanted the system to give them feedback about their travel behavior. Due to non-transparent pricing schemes, customers also wanted the system to help compare alternatives, e.g. the price of renting versus carsharing versus taxi.

5 Discussion and Conclusions

The UbiGo service was designed and implemented with the intention to contribute to a more sustainable transportation of people. The results demonstrate the potential and importance of ICT as a mediator in developing an innovative and attractive mobility solution such as UbiGo.

Although, as with any new service, there are still improvements to be made, the UbiGo broker service has been very well received and 79 % of the participants in the

FOT stated that they definitely wanted to continue using the service while 18 % stated probably (given certain preconditions). Indeed, in the "after" questionnaire, people stated that they used private car less and public transportation, walking, and cycling more often than before, and they also felt more negative towards private car and more positive towards public transportation, etc., than before. When asked how their travel behavior had changed, 35.6 % reported no change, while 42.5 % reported changes in mode choice, 34.4 % in pre-trip travel planning, 21.3 % in destinations, trip duration, and trip chaining, and 20.6 % in their amount of exercise. (Note that the type of change is not specified, e.g. more or less.) Of those who reported behavioral changes, only 2.9 % were dissatisfied with the changes and 17 % felt that the changes would not last, in particular if/when the service stops.

This initial analysis of the FOT shows that it is vital to generate interest and excitement about new transportation schemes. This is the primary reason that participants were attracted to the project or were willing to become customers in this FOT, with all that it entails. The results support also the notion that the innovation (here in terms of a practice) must offer some added value or relative advantage, cf. [16], to be adopted, i.e. the service must appeal to the users on a practical level and facilitate their daily travel. When it has not been curiosity motivating people, it has been convenience and economy, and it is these practicalities that will keep the users incentivized to continue using the service after the novelty and curiosity fade.

The results suggest furthermore that relative advantages cannot by replaced by rewards. In fact, the reward system appears to have played a minor role (if any) in the adoption of the new service. Moreover, although the environment is of concern for many, it has not proven to be a primary incentive (despite the participant group already having relatively more sustainable travel behavior based on the initial analysis of the "before" travel diaries). In this specific case, it is possible that informational feedback, cf. [17], on how "green" your travel patterns are could be just as, or even more, important to users. However, the eco-friendliness is not enough to attract a sufficient number of customers and a pro-environmental attitude will not suffice as an incentive for change, at least not for majority of travelers. If the environmental impact of transportation is to be reduced, then reductions must be achieved by making more sustainable travel behavior the *practical* choice, rather than the idealistic choice.

References

1. Batterbury, S.: Environmental activism and social networks: campaigning for bicycles and alternative transport in West London. Ann. Am. Acad. Polit. Soc. Sci. **590**, 150–169 (2003)
2. Brög, W., Erl, E., Mense, N.: Individualised marketing. Changing travel behavior for a better environment. In: OECD Workshop on Environmentally Sustainable Transport, Berlin (2002)
3. Henry, G.T., Gordon, C.S.: Driving less for better air: impacts for a public information campaign. J. Policy Anal. Manag. **22**(1), 45–63 (2002)
4. Midgley, P.: Bicycle-sharing schemes: enhancing sustainable mobility in urban areas. Background Paper, U.N. Department of Economic and Social Affairs, CDS 19/2011/BP8 (2011)

5. Fujii, S., Kitamura, R.: What does a one-month free bus ticket do to habitual drivers? An experimental analysis of habit and attitude change. Transportation **30**, 81–95 (2003)
6. Root, A.: Can travel vouchers encourage more sustainable travel? Transp. Policy **8**(2), 107–114 (2001)
7. Thørgersen, J., Møller, B.: Breaking car use habits: the effects of a free one-month travel card. Transportation **35**(3), 329–345 (2008)
8. Currie, G., Wallis, I.: Effective ways to grow urban bus markets – a synthesis of evidence. J Transp. Geogr. **16**(6), 419–429 (2008)
9. Dziekan, K., Kottenhoff, K.: Dynamic at-stop real-time information displays for public transport: effects on customers. Transp. Res. A-Pol. **41**(6), 489–501 (2007)
10. Monzon, A., Hernandez, S., Cascajo, R.: Quality of bus services performance: benefits of real-time information systems. Transp. Telecommun. **14**(2), 155–166 (2013)
11. Skoglund, T., Karlsson, M.: Appreciated–but with a fading grace of novelty. traveller's assessment of, usage of and behavioural change given access to a co-modal travel planner. Procedia-Soc. Behav. Sci. **48**, 932–940 (2012)
12. Smart Cities and Communities. http://eu-smartcities.eu/mobility_transport
13. Frey, B.S.: Motivation a limit to pricing. J. Econ. Psychol. **14**, 635–664 (1993)
14. Fishbein, M., Ajzen, I.: Belief, Attitude, Intention and Behavior: An Introduction to Theory and Research. Addison-Wesley, Reading (1975)
15. Swedish Transportation Administration: Resvaneundersökning 2011 Västsvenska Paketet. Technical report, Swedish Transportation Administration (2011)
16. Rogers, E.M.: Diffusion of Innovations, 5th edn. Simon and Schuster, New York (2003)
17. Dwyer, W.O., Leeming, F.C., Cobern, M.K., Porter, B.E., Jackson, J.M.: Critical review of behavioral interventions to preserve the environment: research since 1980. Environ. Behav. **25**, 275–321 (1993)

On the Design of a Cost-Effective
and Lightweight People Counting Sensor

Sanjana Kadaba Viswanath[1], Sai Ram Gubba[2], Balasundram Arunn[3],
Chandra Sekar Veerappan[1], and Chau Yuen[1]([✉])

[1] Singapore University of Technology and Design, Singapore, Singapore
yuenchau@sutd.edu.sg
[2] Indian Institute of Technology, Bhubaneswar, India
[3] University of Moratuwa, Moratuwa, Srilanka

Abstract. People counting finds applications in many scenarios where
the density of people present in an area is crucial. Although, there are
a lot of research on people counting using image processing and pattern
recognition, we focus on less complex, lightweight, cost effective, and low
energy people counters. In this paper, we have detailed methods and
algorithms for people counting using proximity sensors. We have also
shown the experimental results for various designs of people counters
and compared them with the actual results.

1 Introduction

People-sensing is gaining a lot of attention as ubiquitous computing and sensor
networks are increasingly focusing on human inhabited environments and their
behavior, especially, in applications, where activities of people are monitored and
analysed. People sensing plays an important role in applications such as crowd
monitoring, security management, and transportation systems.

In applications where traffic flow is important, crowd analysis needs to be
done to estimate the density of the crowd. Reference [1] details unsupervised
method to detect individuals in a crowded environment, thus counting the number of people accurately, even when they are moving in crowds. In military and
security applications, people sensing, or people counting plays a crucial role,
and [2] details vision based, real time people counting system at a security door.
In transportation systems, where the frequency of public transport plays an
important role in getting people around, deciding the frequency at which the
trains need to ply, [3] provides methods of counting people entering and leaving
a train and hence enabling decision on right train frequencies.

People counting algorithms, and methods vary largely with different mechanisms and sensors with different capabilities, ranging from cameras, CCTVs to
motion sensors, proximity sensors, and ultrasonic sensors. A lot of research on
people counting, has been done by using visual cameras for image processing and
pattern recognition to accurately count the number of people. For instance, [4]
shows a method for counting people entering or leaving a bus using video processing and [5] describes robust solution for people counting using image processing.

© Institute for Computer Sciences, Social Informatics and Telecommunications Engineering 2015
R. Giaffreda et al. (Eds.): IoT360 2014, Part II, LNICST 151, pp. 176–182, 2015.
DOI: 10.1007/978-3-319-19743-2_27

However, these techniques demand a high processing time, energy, and also are more expensive to install in scenarios, where power is limited. Therefore, to address cost-effectiveness, low-energy, and lightweight system to count the number of people in a given region while maintaining privacy, we have developed an efficient people counter with low error rates.

2   Overview

People sensing focuses on detecting the presence of a person, which can be used in applications such as automatically switching on/off a light; counting the number of people, so that we can estimate approximately how many people are present in a room; location of the person, so that we can know the exact location of the person; tracking a person, which gives temporal and spatial information of a person; and identity of the person, which specifies who the person is [6]. Such information can be fetched either by instrumented approach, where people carry instrument/device for sensing purposes, or uninstrumented approach, where people do not need to carry any device.

Instrumented approaches deal with devices communicating to other devices to notify their presence both temporally and spatially, which includes a GPS sensors, tracking application, etc., which are carried by people wherever they go. Uninstrumented approaches deal with sensors such as motion, proximity, pressure mats, cameras, microphones, etc., which are not meant to be carried by people. In an uninstrumented approach, single sensor gives accurate information only under certain circumstances and fails to provide information in others. In a few other scenarios, sensor fusion can provide useful information for people sensing by evening out the negative effects caused, when used individually. For instance, a fusion of microphone and camera can be used in applications such as conference rooms where the person speaking is focused by the camera [7].

Proximity sensor   Arc People Counter   Parallel people counter   Side people counter

Fig. 1. Different people counters

Although, a lot of research focusses on sensing and tracking people through image processing, we are focusing on algorithms to use cost-effective sensors for the implementation of people counting mechanisms. We mainly focus on using proximity sensors (ultrasonic sensors) in our research for people counting.

3   Three Designs of People Counter Using Proximity Sensors

Proximity sensor is used in our design for people counting. By varying the orientation and number of sensors used, we have developed three different people counters. In this section, we detail our people couters. Figure 1 shows different people counter set up.

3.1   Parallel People Counter

A parallel people counter, was built by placing 2 proximity sensors in parallel, at a distance of 80 cm. The sensors have a beamwidth angle of 55 degrees and range of 4 m. The number of sensors depend on the range of field that is to be covered for people counting. However, with this design, counting a person can be difficult in a place where the range of 2 sensors intersect and sometimes can result in double counting.

3.2   Arc People Counter

An arc people counter, was built by placing 3 proximity sensors in an arc shape, so that they can be deployed in a single place covering almost 3.5 m width for people counting. As compared to parallel people counter, for arc people counter, we do not need to worry about how many sensors to be installed and the distance between the sensors, but only need one arc people counter to cover the range.

3.3   Side People Counter

Side people counter was built by placing just 1 proximity sensor for people counting, with range of the sensor being 4 m, but, the optimal distance for accurate people counting is seen within the range of 2.9 m. As there may be some objects blocking in front of the sensor (especially, in corridors where usually there is an other pillar opposite to the pillar we have installed the sensor), our algorithm calculates the bouncing distance at the setup phase, by repeatedly looking for a bounce back obstacle. For instance, in a corridor, where there is an other pillar at 1.5 m, the bouncing distance will be assigned to 1.5 m. However, when there are no obstacles, default distance will be set to 2.9 m.

In all the three designs, it is challenging to accurately count the number of people when two or more people are passing by very closely.

4   Algorithms

We have developed two algorithms, one for parallel and arc people counter, and another one for side people counter. The following section details the algorithms. Each of the algorithms compute and ignore stationary objects around.

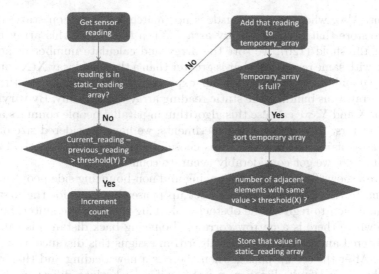

Fig. 2. Flow chart for arc and parallel people counter algorithm

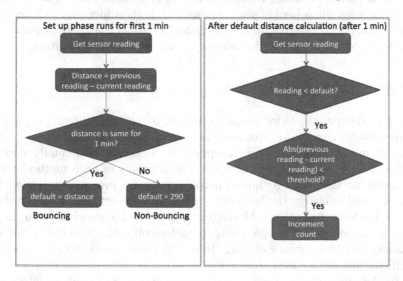

Fig. 3. Flow chart for bouncing and non-bouncing side people counter algorithm

Figure 2 shows a flow chart for arc and parallel people counter algorithm. In this algorithm, we fetch sensor readings periodically. When we receive a reading, we check if that reading matches any reading that is stored on static reading array, if it matches, we ignore that reading, else, we check the difference between the current reading and previous reading, and if that is more than a threshold, say Y, which was set to 80 for parallel and 100 for arc and can vary slightly according to the place, where the people counter is placed (so that if a person is carrying a bag, it should not be counted as another person), then we increment the count. Also, when the reading does not match any entry on static reading array, we store that in a temporary array. When the size of this array reaches a pre-set threshold (120), we sort the array and calculate number of adjacent elements with same reading, if that is greater than a threshold, say X(X can range from 20–40 and we set it to 30 for our experiments), we add that to the static reading array, thus building the static reading array dynamically. By varying the values for X and Y, we can use this algorithm in parallel people counters and arc people counters. All through our experiments, we have considered size of static reading array as 40 and this value was chosen by trial and error method and by setting it at 40, we got considerably accurate counts.

Figure 3 shows flow chart for bouncing and non-bouncing side people counter algorithm. In this method, there is a set up phase that runs for the first 1 min after installation to register the obstacles blocking the people counter, i.e., for a scenario where there is a narrow corridor, bouncing back distance is calculated and registered and people counting algorithm assigns this distance as a default distance. After the set up phase, when there is a new reading and that reading is less than the default distance, we check if the absolute difference between the previous and the current reading is less than a threshold (to avoid double counting in cases when people are carrying bags), then increment the counter. For non-bouncing, we set default distance to 290 cm as that is the optimal distance where proximity sensor give accurate values for people counting.

5   Experiments and Results

We conducted experiments for people counting, by placing all four people counters side-by-side, namely arc, parallel, side (with a bouncing object at 1.6 m), side (without any bouncing objects opposite), along with manually counting number of people passing by, to compare the accuracy of each method for 3 h. In our setup, we have used Arduino microcontroller for processing, and we have used solar panel to charge the batteries for people counters that can be installed outdoors. We have used 2000 mAh battery and 2 W solar panel for charging the battery, which makes the people counters self-sustainable. The cost estimation for building people counters can range from 122 USD for side people counter, to 200 USD for arc and parallel counters.

In Fig. 4 we present our observations for each of the four people counters. Over a period of one hour, there were total 132 people pass by, and side people counter with bouncing counted 120 (9.09 % error), side people counter with non-bouncing counted 125 (5.30 % error), arc people counter counted 113 (14.39 % error), and parallel people counter counted 104 (21.21 % error). By far, we observe that side people counter with bouncing, and non-bouncing are more accurate than the arc, and parallel people counters.

Our future work would focus on building algorithms to manage different traffic conditions and accurately counting people in passages and corridors in home/offices with different waking speeds, counting people in crowds, and determining the counting error in complex scenarios.

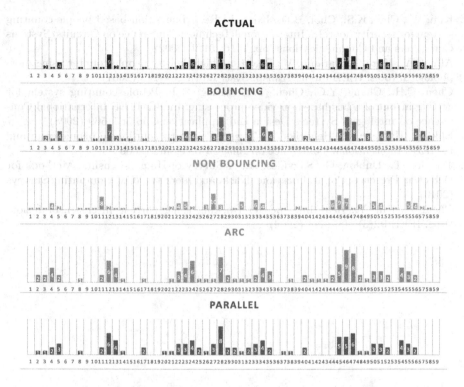

Fig. 4. People counting results with different methods

6 Conclusion

In this paper, we describe a cost-effective, lightweight, simple and low-energy people counting systems. We have worked on people counting algorithms using proximity sensors by varying their orientation and number of sensors used to cover a desired area. We show that side people counter design performs better than arc, and parallel people counter designs, with an error of 5.30 % for a period of one hour with 132 people passing by.

Acknowledgement. This research is supported by Singapore University of Technology and Design (grant no SUTD-ZJU/RES/02/2011) and MND Research Fund Sustainable Urban Living Grant.

References

1. Brostow, G.J., Cipolla, R.: Unsupervised bayesian detection of independent motion in crowds. In: IEEE Computer Society Conference on Computer Vision and Pattern Recognition, vol. 1, pp. 594–601 (2006)

2. Kim, W., Choi, K.S., Choi, B.D., Ko, S.J.: Real-time vision-based people counting system for security door. In: International Technical Conference on Circuits/Systems Computers and Communications, pp. 1416–1419 (2002)
3. Albiol, A., Mora, I., Naranjo, V.: Real-time high density people counter using morphological tools. IEEE Intell. Transp. Syst. 12(4), 204–218 (2001)
4. Chen, C.H., Chang, Y.C., Chen, T.Y., Wang, D.J.: People counting system for getting in/out of a bus based on video processing. In: 8th IEEE International Conference on Intelligent Systems Design and Applications, pp 565–569 (2008)
5. Elik, H., Hanjalic, A., Hendriks, E.: Towards a robust solution to people counting. In: IEEE International Conference on Image Processing (2006)
6. Teixeira, T., Dublon, G., Savvides, A.: A Survey of Human-Sensing: Methods for Detecting Presence, Count, Location, Track, and Identity. ACM Computing Surveys (2010)
7. Chen, Y., Rui, Y.: Real-time speaker tracking using particle filter sensor fusion. Proc. IEEE 92(3), 485–494 (2004)

Smart Tourist - Passive Mobility Tracking Through Mobile Application

Sanjana Kadaba Viswanath[1], Chau Yuen[1](✉), Xuefang Ku[2], and Xiang Liu[2]

[1] Singapore University of Technology and Design, Singapore, Singapore
yuenchau@sutd.edu.sg
[2] School of Software and Microelectronics, Peking University, Beijing, China

Abstract. Travel and tourism industry makes an evident impact on the world economy. Lack of real information on tourist sight-seeing places, is impacting trip planning for a major number of tourists. Growing smartphone users, increased sensing capabilities provided by smart phones, and the ability to share that data over the internet, presents an opportunity to build a mobile application that can provide an insight into mobility information through passive sensing. We have developed a mobile application to bridge the information gap by passively tracking tourist location and improvising tourist services using mobile crowd-sensing. Capabilities to cluster location data to form places of interest have been particularly focused in this paper. Finally, we present results for an initial experiment performed on a tourist to Australia.

1 Introduction

Tourism industry plays a big role in world economy. The Travel and Tourism industry contributes 2.2 trillion dollars to the world gross domestic product (9.5 %) and provides an impetus for creating 1 in 11 of the world's jobs, 4.4 % of total investment and 5.4 percent of total exports [1].

With the widespread adaptation of smartphones, with close to a billion being used by 2012 and expectation of 1.75 billion phones in 2014 [2], every major industry, including the tourism industry, is striving to adopt and expand on this platform to reach more customers and bridge the information gap. According to Trip Advisor's survey, 87 % percent of global travelers reported using a smartphone while on holiday [3]. The tourism industry has brought about sweeping changes to support this platform through review sites, booking websites, and information applications to improve experience for their customer.

Exponentially increasing smart phone users along with multiple sensing capabilities in-built in smart phones inspired us to build a mobile application to improvise tourism with simple yet powerful solution, providing a good opportunity through peer to peer sharing over passive tracking. Unlike the current solution that depends on the active review of the customer or paid reviews which

This research is supported and funded by Lee Li Ming Ageing Urbanism Programme, Lee Kuan Yew Centre for Innovative Cities, Singapore University of Technology and Design.

© Institute for Computer Sciences, Social Informatics and Telecommunications Engineering 2015
R. Giaffreda et al. (Eds.): IoT360 2014, Part II, LNICST 151, pp. 183–191, 2015.
DOI: 10.1007/978-3-319-19743-2_28

are sponsored by business owners, we focus on getting unbiased and passive feedbacks from real tourists.

Just like any Internet-of-Things (IoT) devices, smart phones provide computing, sensing and communicating capabilities and they fuel the evolution of mobility IoT as they feed sensor data to internet enabling either personal sensing or community sensing. To this end, mobile crowd sensing enables applications to continuously sense relevant sensor data for applications like intelligent transport systems [4], personal healthcare systems [5], etc. to process data to provide information. [6] demonstrates the effectiveness of mobile crowd-sensing to non-intrusively and passively collect mobile sensing data to detect wireless activity level in a large region.

In this paper, we propose a technology based on passive mobile tracking to provide an additional dimension to the review by using passive information about the trip for future travelers to fine-tune their trips and the tourism sector operators to get a better understanding of the places tourists spend their time in. We demonstrate a technology that bridges some of the trendiest developments in the current world's growth in tourism, widespread adaptation of smartphones, and use of mobile crowd-sensing to improve user experience. In this paper, we have detailed our current implementation by understanding the needs and requirements, the front end apps, the backend processing, and visualisation, and discussing results for an initial experiment on a tourist to Melbourne, Australia.

2   System Design Requirements

Tourists give a lot of importance for planning their trip and making sure the places they visit are worth the effort and time, so that they can make their holiday a memorable one. In a study for determining services for mobile tourist [7], results show that majority of tourists are interested in finding good accommodation, transport, food, and sight-seeing destinations. Although, there are many online review websites for hotel and food, we do not find any relevant information regarding sight-seeing destinations, especially those that provide us unbiased information on how much time other similar kind (eg., elderly-friendly, family-friendly, etc.) of tourists spare for a particular location. To this end, our objective was to provide recommendation for tourists by quantitative analysis on the places where other tourists visited during their trip, along with the time they spent in each place, and the route they took. This streamlines our system requirements as below:

- the place that they visited,
- how long they stay in each place,
- how people feel about the place,
- what that place is about (eg., food, hotel, sightseeing),
- if the place is family-friendly, elder-friendly, etc.,
- the activity the tourist is involved in, and
- how they access the place.

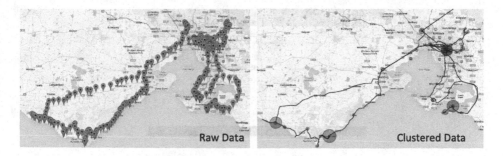

Fig. 1. Raw data(locations) vs clustered data(places)

In this paper, we describe a solution that passively tracks a tourist by fetching the locations that the tourist visited, and processing that as a place, and how long he stayed in each place. Figure 1, visualises data collected by smart tourist app. It compares raw data for the whole trip with processed/clustered data. It clearly shows clustered data shows useful information about the places visited by the tourist. Red circles are places of interest and blue circles are the places for accommodation. The path taken to go from one place to another is marked by black lines. The radius of the circles at each place denotes the amount of time the tourist has spent in that location. Our proposed solution not only provides recommendation to other tourists, but also provides a recorded memory of their trip through a personal diary on places they have visited without any effort.

Government agencies can benefit from our technology by planning their infrastructure to cater for the tourists needs, and improvise places that are less visited to invite more tourists. Our technology can aid businesses from getting a better knowledge of where tourists usually enjoy going, such that, they can have better business opportunities.

3   Mobile Application

In this section, we detail the design and implementation of various elements that have contributed to develop our mobile application. Location can be retrieved by GPS(Global Positioning System), Wifi Scan or Cellular network. We have used Android's Location API [8] to access the system location services to fetch location data.

3.1   Mobile Application Design

To encourage more tourists to learn from the feedback/experience from other tourists, we have developed an Android mobile application to fetch location data periodically from tourists' smart devices (eg., smartphones/tablets). The framework to fetch location data uses underlying Location API provided by Android SDK. After fetching location data, it is stored on local database on the device, which will later be uploaded periodically to cloud server.

Fig. 2. Screen shot of mobile app collecting multiple sensor data

Location data is requested periodically, once every 5 mins by the background service that runs continuously and non-intrusively. GPS provides the most accurate location fix with accuracies up to 5 m, however, it is challenging to get location when GPS satellites are not in range. In which case, we fetch location from network or wifi-scan.

Figure 2, shows information of various sensor data collected for an entire day by mobile application. The first row represents clusters, whereas the second row is activity track such as walking (denoted as 'F'), on vehicle (denoted as 'v'), and bicycle (denoted as 'b'), or is stationary(denoted as '_'). The third row represents if the person is talking (denoted by 'S') or others (denoted by '_'). Forth row shows surrounding noise level and fifth row shows battery percentage. Sixth row shows how the location data has been retrieved, such as GPS (denoted as 'G'), or network (denoted as '_'). Seventh row shows speed information provided by location object, and lastly, eighth row shows light sensor values.

We use MySQL, Apache webserver, PHP, and RESTful HTTP to store and manage data at the server. For secure communications, we support only https calls to the server. On the server, we have a database dedicated to store location information such as latitude, longitude, time, speed, accuracy, uploaded time and userId.

4   Backend Processing - Real-Time / Online Clustering Algorithm

Mobile application is designed to fetch location data and we have developed backed software to process the location data. In this section, we describe clustering algorithm, which considerably processes data to give useful information.

In particular, when the user is indoors and cannot get access to GPS, there is a huge number of location data that are distributed around the actual location, as in Fig. 3. Clustering algorithm plays an important role in grouping such points to plot on the map, so as to provide better understanding as to how user uses the space.

Clustering data has been focused in many applications including data mining, statistical data analysis, computation and vector quantisation [9], pattern

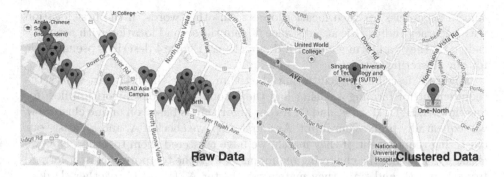

Fig. 3. Comparison of location data while indoor

Pseudocode

```
INPUT: locationDataArray          \\Data structure for storing location objects
Initialise temp to first element of locationDataArray,
for each location in locationDataArray, do:
            assign next to locationDataArray[location.next]
            assign distance to distance(temp, next)
            If distance <= sum of accuracies then:
                        equate temp to average (temp, next)
                        add next to tempArray
            else
                        add average(tempArray) to resultCluster
                        equate temp to next
end for
for each cluster in resultCluster do:
            If duration > threshold then:
                        add cluster to resultNode
end for
OUTPUT: resultNode
```

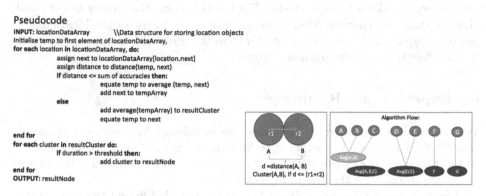

Fig. 4. Pseudocode   Fig. 5. Cluster algorithm flow

recognition [10] etc. K-means algorithm has had a lot of attention to combat data clustering problems from as early as 1965, when Forgy first published a standard k-means algorithm [11] to cluster data points by calculating distance between data points to predict the likelihood of data point belonging a cluster center. However, the major drawback of his approach was to predefine the value k, which is NP-Hard for arbitrary input [12]. On the basis of k-means algorithm, we have designed a clustering algorithm for non-specific number of cluster centers for arbitrary sequential input.

To enable real-time data visualisation of the places tourist visited, our algorithm is designed to have an online approach. Location object returned from android location API, contains a field for specifying accuracy of the location data returned, which states, accuracy for a location object as the radius of 68 percent confidence. In other words, if you draw a circle cantered at this location's latitude and longitude, and with a radius equal to the accuracy, then there is a 68 percent probability that the true location is inside the circle [8]. Carefully considering this, our clustering algorithm clusters location if the distance between the first location object from the second location object lies within the sum of accuracies for each location object. In other words, if the first location with accuracy radius r1 is at a distance d from the second location with accuracy radius r2, they can form a cluster if d <= r1+r2. Figure 4 describes pseudo code for our clustering algorithm.

Figure 5 describes the clustering algorithm, where the first part shows the requirement for forming a cluster and the second part shows algorithm flow for locations A, B, C, D, E, F, and G. As our algorithm is based on online clustering, we sequentially process our input. As a first step, we check if A, and B satisfy our clustering requirement, if they match, we have clustered them together. Now we check if C matches the clustering requirement with the temporary cluster formed from A and B, and since they match, we cluster A, B and C together. D does not match the clustering requirement with the cluster formed from A, B and C and hence, it will start a new cluster. E joins D to form the cluster but, F, and G, form their own clusters. After forming clusters, we highlight the location as a place for visiting if the duration is greater than the threshold. In our experiments, we vary our threshold from 5 min - 20 min.

5   Experimental Results

We conducted experiment by installing the mobile application on a Samsung Galaxy Note 10.1 tablet of a tourist to Melbourne. Smart Tourist system is able to locate all the places the tourist traveled to as well as demarcate the places according to the time they spent in each location.

Figure 6 shows a portion of Great Ocean Road with different threshold durations. We have the flexibility to adjust the threshold to be able to see different details, eg., if you set threshold to 5 mins you can see very fine details, but by

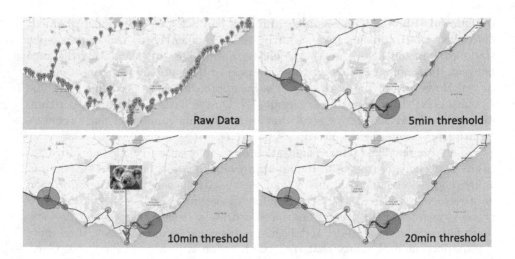

Fig. 6. Processed location data

Table 1. Places visited along great ocean road

Passive tracking		Survey	
Places	Duration (mins)	Activity	Recommendation (number of stars)
12 Rock Cafe	65	dinner	3
Lavers Hill	55	lunch	1
Twelve Apostles	40	sight-seeing	5
Lorne	40	lunch	2
Maits Rest	37	sight-seeing	4
Gibson Step	35	sight-seeing	5
Cape Otway Lighthouse	24	sight-seeing	3
Loch Ard Gorge	20	sight-seeing	5
Cape Otway	15	wild animals - koala	5
Cape Otway	15	wild animals - koala	5
Moonlight	15	sight-seeing	3
Twelve Apostles Visitor Center	10	gather information	2
Cape Otway Lighthouse Visitor Center	10	gather information	2
Bay of Island	10	sight-seeing	4
The Grotto	10	sight-seeing	4

setting it to 20 mins, you can only see those locations where tourist spent 20 mins or more.

Table 1, shows all the places visited and the time spent at each place by the tourist. First two columns are passively collected by our application, where as, third and forth are through survey, however, we can have the survey built in to the application in future.

Imagine that if over hundreds or thousands tourists install our application, we can get a very good statistics on how much other tourists have spent their time along great ocean road, the popular route they have taken, and how many nights people have stayed at that location. This information can greatly help the next tourist to plan his trip. Also, surveying the tourist that tested our application for Australia trip, he discovered that Colac is a nice town to stop by, however, as he was not aware of that and was rushing to his next spot, he missed seeing Colac. Hence, if he had the information provided by other tourists, he could have planned his trip so that he could allocate time for Colac. In addition, if the tourist provided feedback on the location, eg., marking down the location where he saw wild animals (as in Fig. 6), it would greatly help other tourists in locating wild animals.

6 Future Work and Conclusion

We have developed a software to capture and automate the information relating to tourists' experiences and time spent at each location. Going forward, we will develop a settings page so that, when a user goes on the trip, he can give information in terms of the kind of trip he is going on, whom is he traveling with, is it a family trip with young children, backpacking with friends, or together with elderly etc. By collecting information about the kind of trip, we allow tourist to plan his trip based on others who went on a similar setting.

With data coming from multiple tourists, we have to build statistics on the tourist reviews according to the information given by the tourist at the time of his trip about the kind of trip he is going on. Furthermore, we can build a survey, which tourists' might chose to fill at the end of the day, so as to make notes on their trip or voice their opinion about a tourist destination that can be shared with other tourists.

Since our algorithm currently is fetching location data at an interval of 5mins irrespective of where the tourist is, it would be preferable to design our data collection process such that we can focus on dynamic sampling rates with respect to activity recognition. For instance, when the tourist is resting at night, we can increase sampling time to 30mins to one hour, and when tourist is moving in a vehicle, we can reduce sampling to 1 min, so that we can get better knowledge of the path they travel in to go from one place to another. This approach may also be better energy efficient for mobile phones.

In this paper, we focus purely on location data for smart tourist and cluster them to give useful information, but in future we will work on using other sensor data as well. As shown in Fig. 2, we intend to do further study on the correlation of sensor data in mobility so as gain insights about tourist and their activities.

In this paper, we have specified a detailed study about our technology to improvise the experience of a tourist by learning from the experiences through passive tracking collected by peer tourists. We have developed a mobile application to collect various sensor data to passively get feedback from the tourists as well as providing them with a personal diary so that they can keep track of places they have visited. Furthermore, we have described our clustering algorithm to cater to spatial and temporal properties of our data to group raw location data into places of interest. Following the implementation, we have shown that our technology can be well suited to provide unbiased peer-to-peer reviews to tourists by passive data collection. With more mobility and location awareness, we are able to gain insights about users and their behaviours to engage them on a personal level. With connectivity like this, we are able to create new sources of value that companies, municipalities, individuals and more can leverage on.

References

1. Economic Impact of Travel and Tourism (2014). http://www.wttc.org/site_media/uploads/downloads/Economic_Impact_Summary_2014_2ppA4_FINAL.pdf

2. Smartphone Use by Tourism and Travel Consumers. http://www.targetingin novation.com/tlx/assets/documents/uploaded/general/Final%20Draft%20Report %20Layout%20v4.pdf
3. Trip Advisor Report. http://ir.tripadvisor.com/releasedetail.cfm?releaseid= 808058
4. Ali, K., Al-Yaseen, D., Ejaz, A., Javed, T., Hassanein, H.S.: CrowdITS: Crowd-sourcing in Intelligent Transportation Systems. In: IEEE Wireless Communications and Networking Conference (2012)
5. Nicholas Lane, D., Mohammod, M., Lin, M., Yang, X., Lu, H., Ali, S., Doryab, A., Berke, E., Choudhury, T., Campbell, T.A.: BeWell: a smartphone application to monitor, model and promote Wellbeing. In: ACM/Springer Journal of Personal and Ubiquitous Computing (PUC), Special Issue of Cross-Community Mining (2013)
6. Guo, W., Wang, S.: Mobile Crowd-Sensing Wireless Activity with Measured Inter-ference Power. IEEE Wirel. Commun. Lett. $2(5)$, 539–542 (2013)
7. Goha, H.D., Angb, P.R., Leea, C.S.: Determining services for the mobile tourist. J. Comput. Inf. Syst. $51(1)$, 31–40 (2010)
8. Android Location API. http://developer.android.com/reference/android/location/ LocationManager.html
9. Wagstaff, K., Cardie, C., Rogers, S., et al.: Constrained k-means clustering with background knowledge. In: International Conference on Machine Learning, pp. 577–584 (2001)
10. Jain, A.K.: Data clustering: 50 years beyond K-means. Pattern Recogn. Lett. $31(8)$, 651–666 (2010)
11. Forgy, E.W.: Cluster analysis of multivariate data: efficiency versus interoperability of classification. Biometrics 21, 768–769 (1965)
12. Drineas, P., Frieze, A., Kannan, R., Vempala, S., Vinay, V.: Clustering large graphs via the singular value decomposition. Mach. Learn. 56, 9–33 (2004)

Understanding the Impact of Data Sparsity and Duration for Location Prediction Applications

Alasdair Thomason[✉], Matthew Leeke, and Nathan Griffiths

University of Warwick, Coventry CV4 7AL, UK
{ali,matt,nathan}@dcs.warwick.ac.uk

Abstract. As mobile devices capable of sensing location have become pervasive, the collection and transmission of location data has become commonplace, enabling the creation of models of behaviour that support location prediction. With such devices often heavily resource-constrained, the nature of data used in location prediction must be understood in order to optimise storage and processing requirements. This paper specifically explores data sparsity and collection duration. The results presented provide insight which suggest: (i) a relationship of diminishing returns in predictive accuracy when collecting user location data at increased rates over a fixed period, and (ii) the duration over which a fixed size sample of location data is collected has a greater impact on predicative accuracy than data sparsity.

Keywords: Collection · Data · Duration · Location prediction · Sparsity

1 Introduction

Location-aware devices are routinely used by a significant proportion of the global population [8]. Data pertaining to a user's location can now be sensed, stored and shared in real-time through devices such as smartphones and tablet computers. Many applications might benefit from location prediction, including city planning, law enforcement, marketing, etc., however relatively little is understood regarding the necessary quality of data for forecasting. Much existing work assumes that location data can be stored indefinitely and at the highest rate afforded by a collection method [3,16]. These assumptions are inconsistent with the devices typically used to perform location analysis, which are generally battery-powered portable devices carried by an individual with limited storage and memory capability. As a result, data collectors must be able to justify the resolution and duration of collection mechanisms to users.

In this paper we consider two dimensions of data quality for location prediction. Specifically, we investigate data sparsity and collection duration, with a view to informing the design of data collection mechanisms and addressing user privacy concerns. Through the application of three established techniques in location prediction to data varying in sparsity and collection duration, it is

© Institute for Computer Sciences, Social Informatics and Telecommunications Engineering 2015
R. Giaffreda et al. (Eds.): IoT360 2014, Part II, LNICST 151, pp. 192–197, 2015.
DOI: 10.1007/978-3-319-19743-2_29

shown that: (i) there is a relationship of diminishing returns in predictive accuracy when collecting user location data at increased rates over a fixed period, and (ii) the duration over which a fixed size sample of location data is collected has a greater impact on predicative accuracy than data sparsity.

2 Related Work

Location prediction is widely recognised as being beneficial to providing location-aware services. Early work in this area considered the problem of predicting future locations within small, enclosed environments with a fixed number of discrete user locations, typically employing neural networks, Markov models or dynamic Bayesian networks [2,10,13]. Solutions to this problem have applications within offices, homes and public buildings but do not lend themselves to location prediction in large uncontrolled environments.

Motivated by applications such as cell tower handover — seamlessly passing a connection from one cell tower to another when a device is moving — research has considered location prediction in more open environments [7,17]. Ashbrook and Starner investigated the use of algorithms to extract a user's 'significant locations' from GPS data, and using these locations as the basis for the development of Markov models for location prediction [3]. Similar investigations have been conducted on GPS traces [14,15], online check-in data [9], and discrete real-world locations such as cell towers [4,6,16]. In contrast to the variety of location prediction approaches, existing work has generally considered near-continuous data collected over long time periods, an assumption explored in this paper.

3 Modelling the Location Prediction Problem

We characterise location data as a set of n-tuples, called *points*, containing location and time values, where a *location* is an identifier given to a distinct geographic area on the surface of the earth. The dataset, D_u, of a user, u, is therefore the set of all points associated with u, having inherent sparsity and duration.

$$D_u = \{x_{1,u}, x_{2,u}, ..., x_{n,u}\}$$

The mapping between a time range and set of visited locations for a user can be represented by unknown function, f_u, such that $f_u([start : end]) = S$, where S is a non-empty, potentially large, set of locations visited by the user during that period. It is the aim of location prediction to construct an approximation of the unknown function, $\hat{f}_u$, given a training set $TR_u \subseteq D_u$, such that $\forall y \in TR_u : time(y) \prec start$, which ensures that predictions are in the future.

3.1 Evaluation Model

The function $\hat{f}_u$ can then be used to produce a set of estimated locations, $\hat{S}$, for a specified time range, known as an evaluation window. This set can then be compared against the known set of visited locations for the same window, S. True Positives (TP), False Positives (FP) and False Negatives (FN) are intuitively defined as $S \cap \hat{S}$, $\hat{S} - S$ and $S - \hat{S}$ respectively. We define the set of True Negatives (TN) as $loc(TR_u) - (S \cup \hat{S})$, where $loc(TR_u)$ is the set of locations that exist within a user's training data. We can now define *accuracy* as:

$$ ACC = \frac{|TP| + |TN|}{|TP| + |FP| + |TN| + |FN|} $$

4   Experimental Setup

Data was collected by installing a bespoke smartphone application on mobile phones belonging to 5 members of the Department of Computer Science at the University of Warwick. Users ran the application for a period of several months, which recorded the time, latitude and longitude of the device every minute. We generated datasets of different sparsities and durations by selecting a random continuous subset of length n weeks from each collected dataset, and then sampling the truncated data according to a retention probability, r, where each point within the dataset had probability r of being included. Although our approach is limited to using data from only 5 users, this represents an improvement over existing work. The collection of such data is challenging, and existing approaches typically rely on data collected from a single individual [3,5], or on artificial simulated data [4,7,16,17].

Since location clustering remains an open problem, cell tower regions were used to discretise locations for prediction. There is no loss of generality with regard to the defined data model, since cell tower regions can be considered arbitrary geographical regions designed to maximise coverage.

4.1   Location Prediction Techniques

Formalising location prediction as a classification problem allows machine learning techniques to produce predictions for locations given a specific time. A training set of instances, in this case a set of points, is used to represent attributes of the user's current location. Each instance in the space, x_i, has a single classification, $f(x_i)$, where this classification is the location visited. A classifier is able to generate a prediction for a single instance of time, rather than for a time range. To obtain results for a time range, classifiers can be provided with test instances for every time step, in this case each minute, throughout the test range and the results merged to form a set spanning the evaluation window.

Several classification techniques have been shown to be effective for the problem of location prediction, including neural networks [10,13], decision trees [1,12] and support vector machines [11,12]. To ensure the results presented are representative, each of these techniques is used in this paper. Experiments were performed for each user using 4 different durations and 9 sparsities, with each repeated 50 times.

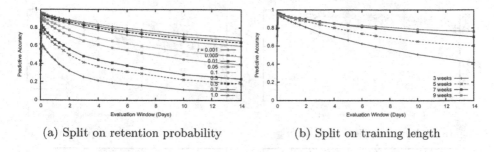

(a) Split on retention probability   (b) Split on training length

Fig. 1. Predictive accuracy against evaluation window averaged across classifiers

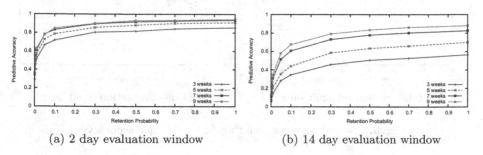

(a) 2 day evaluation window   (b) 14 day evaluation window

Fig. 2. Retention probability against predictive accuracy for different durations

5   Results

Each classifier performed similarly across all experiments, and so for brevity we present results averaged across classifiers. Figure 1 shows how predicative accuracy varies with evaluation window length. With an evaluation window of 0 days, the resulting predictions are for a single instance, meaning that $|\hat{S}| = |S| = 1$. As the evaluation window is increased to approximately 1 hour, prediction accuracy increases. This is because any error in a set of predictions made on an individual visiting a small number of locations, especially a single location, is likely to negatively skew predictive accuracy. As the set of visited locations increases, any single error has a reduced impact. Despite this, predictive accuracy declines as the evaluation window is increased further, likely due to the inherent complexity of human mobility. This finding can be used to inform the design of location-aware services, not least because the selection of an appropriate evaluation window can impact the utility of the service.

We now consider how sparsity and duration impact the performance of prediction techniques. Figure 2 shows how predicative accuracy changes with levels of sparsity for the different training durations. In particular, Figs. 2a and 2b show these results for evaluation windows of 2 and 14 days respectively. It can be seen that an increase in the proportion of location data, i.e., a reduction in sparsity, consistently yields increased predictive accuracy, although the increase is nonlinear. This change in growth rate is significant, since it demonstrates that the

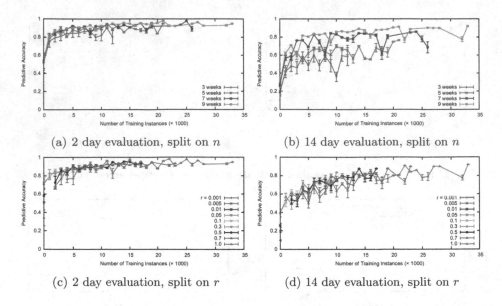

(a) 2 day evaluation, split on n (b) 14 day evaluation, split on n

(c) 2 day evaluation, split on r (d) 14 day evaluation, split on r

Fig. 3. Training instance count against predictive accuracy

increase in quality of service afforded is not necessarily linear with the amount of location data collected for prediction.

Figure 3 shows the relationship between number of training instances and predictive accuracy. The number of training instances is a function of both sparsity and duration — the same number of instances can be generated from a short duration with low sparsity or a longer duration at higher sparsity. In order to investigate the interplay between sparsity and duration, each graph shows the result of dividing the range of instance values $(0 - 35000)$ uniformly into groups of 1000, with data points falling into each grouping being averaged.

It can be observed from Figs. 3a and 3b that there is a marked difference in terms of predictive accuracy when drawing on training instances of longer duration (and therefore higher sparsity). With a fixed number of training instances, those drawn from a longer duration perform nearly uniformally better than those from a shorter duration. This finding is reinforced by Figs. 3c and 3d which show a less pronounced relationship between predictive accuracy and number of training instances when split on different retention probabilities. This substantiates the finding that the duration over which location data is collected is at least as, if not more, important to predictive accuracy than sparsity.

6   Conclusion

This paper has explored the impact of sparsity and duration on the accuracy of location prediction, with a view to informing the design of location data collection mechanisms. Our analysis is based on data collected from 5 individuals, which, although limited, improves on previous approaches that use a single individual's data [3,5], or on artificial simulated data [4,7,16,17].

In particular, we have demonstrated the performance of established location prediction techniques under general purpose models of data, prediction and evaluation. These results provide insight which suggests: (i) a relationship of diminishing returns in predictive accuracy when collecting user location data at increased rates over a fixed period, and (ii) the duration over which a fixed size sample of location data is collected has a greater impact on predicative accuracy than data sparsity.

References

1. Noulas, A., et al. Mining User Mobility Features for Next Place Prediction in Location-Based Services. In: ICDM, pp. 1038–1043 (2012)
2. Roy, A., et al. Location aware resource management in smart homes. In: PerCom, pp. 481–488 (2003)
3. Ashbrook, D., Starner, T.: Learning significant locations and predicting user movement with GPS. In: ISWC, pp. 101–108 (2002)
4. Lu, E., et al.: Mining cluster-based temporal mobile sequential patterns in location-based service environments. IEEE Trans. Knowl. data Eng. **23**(6), 914–927 (2011)
5. Fukano, J., et al.: A next location prediction method for smartphones using block-models, pp. 1–4. IEEE Virtual Reality (2013)
6. Akoush, S. et al.: Bayesian Learning of Neural Networks for Mobile User Position Prediction. Computer Communications and Networks, pp. 1234–1239 (2007)
7. Yava, G., et al.: A data mining approach for location prediction in mobile environments. Data Knowl. Eng. **54**(2), 121–146 (2005)
8. Google. Our Mobile Planet. http://think.withgoogle.com/mobileplanet/en/. Accessed July 2014
9. Cao, H., et al.: Mining frequent spatio-temporal sequential patterns. In: ICDM, pp. 82–89 (2005)
10. Petzold, J., Bagci, F., Trumler, W., Ungerer, T.: Comparison of different methods for next location prediction. In: Nagel, W.E., Walter, W.V., Lehner, W. (eds.) Euro-Par 2006. LNCS, vol. 4128, pp. 909–918. Springer, Heidelberg (2006)
11. Gomes, J.B., Phua, C., Krishnaswamy, S.: Where will you go? mobile data mining for next place prediction. In: Bellatreche, L., Mohania, M.K. (eds.) DaWaK 2013. LNCS, vol. 8057, pp. 146–158. Springer, Heidelberg (2013)
12. Nguyen, L., et al. PnLUM : System for prediction of next location for users. In: Mobile Data Challenge by Nokia Workshop at Pervasive (2012)
13. Vintan, L., et al. Person Movement Prediction Using Neural Networks. In: 1st Workshop on Modeling and Retrieval of Context (2004)
14. Gambs, S., et al. Next place prediction using mobility markov chains. In: 1st Workshop on Measurement, Privacy, and Mobility, pp. 1–6 (2012)
15. Scellato, S., Musolesi, M., Mascolo, C., Latora, V., Campbell, A.T.: NextPlace: a spatio-temporal prediction framework for pervasive systems. In: Lyons, K., Hightower, J., Huang, E.M. (eds.) Pervasive 2011. LNCS, vol. 6696, pp. 152–169. Springer, Heidelberg (2011)
16. Vukovic, M., Adaptive User Movement Prediction for Advanced Location-aware Services. In: SoftCOM, pp. 343–347 (2009)
17. Zhang, Y., et al. Location prediction model based on bayesian network theory. In: GLOBECOM, pp. 1–6 (2009)

SDWN 2014

Cognitive Internet of Things: A Unified Perspective (Invited Paper)

Syed Ali Raza Zaidi[1], Muhammad Zeeshan Shakir[2],
Muhammad Ali Imran[3]([✉]), Mounir Ghogho[1], Athanasios Vasilakos[4],
Khalid Qaraqe[2], and Des McLernon[1]

[1] University of Leeds, Leeds LS2 9JT, UK
{s.a.zaidi,m.ghogho,d.c.mclernon}@leeds.ac.uk
[2] Texas A&M University, Doha, Qatar
{muhammad.shakir,khalid.qaraqe}@qatar.tamu.edue
[3] University of Surrey, Guildford, UK
m.imran@surrey.ac.uk
[4] Kuwait University, Kuwait City, Kuwait
vasaliko@ath.forthnet.gr

Abstract. In this article, we present a unified perspective on the cognitive internet of things (CIoT). It is noted that the CIoT design is the convergence of energy harvesting, cognitive spectrum access and mobile cloud computing technologies. We unify these distinct technologies into a CIoT architecture which provides a flexible, dynamic, scalable and robust network design road-map for a large scale IoT deployment. A general statistical framework is developed and new metrices are introduced so that the design space of the CIoT can be quantitatively explored in the future. A brief overview of both the energy and spectral performances of the CIoT network is presented and its possible future extensions are highlighted.

Keywords: Internet-of-things · Cognitive radios · Cloud · Energy harvesting · Shared spectrum · Underlay · Interference

1 Introduction

The term 'internet-of-things' (IoT) was coined by Kevin Ashton in 1999. The central idea was to empower everyday objects with internet connectivity thus enabling pervasive and autonomous communication. The foundation of IoT is based on Weiser's [1] vision of profound software/hardware technologies that weave themselves into fabric of everyday life such that they become indistinguishable. The functionality and modalities of these technologies is distributed across a variety of interconnected objects. The inter-connectivity of these objects is pivotal as the collective intelligence of the IoT network emerges from simple object level interactions. In turn, such a collective intelligence can be credited with driving significant innovations in the context of various applications under the umbrella of smart homes and cities.

© Institute for Computer Sciences, Social Informatics and Telecommunications Engineering 2015
R. Giaffreda et al. (Eds.): IoT360 2014, Part II, LNICST 151, pp. 201–210, 2015.
DOI: 10.1007/978-3-319-19743-2_30

1.1 The IoT Grand Challenge

A recent survey from EiU [2] indicated that around 75 % of businesses are either actively considering or employing IoT enabled solutions. It is projected that around 500 billion [3] so-called 'smart things' will become part of our day-to-day activities by 2020. Consequently, the IoT faces the challenge of becoming heavy on 'things' while struggling on the connectivity frontier.

A quick glance at the frequency allocation charts provided by the regulatory bodies reveals that most of the prime spectrum is already assigned and the margin for accommodating the emerging wireless applications such as IoT is low. Consequently, it seems natural to think of the spectrum scarcity as a real challenge posed due to the high utilization of the Hertzian medium. However, a reality check on the usage patterns of the available spectral resources reveals that in a nutshell the spectrum scarcity is nothing but artificial. Spectrum occupancy measurements [4,5] have revealed that these licensed bands are highly under-utilized across space and time. From 13 % to 87 % of the radio spectrum remains unused across spatio-temporal domains. This sporadic utilization of scarce electromagnetic spectrum creates an artificial scarcity which in turn poses the inter-connectivity challenge for IoT. Regulatory bodies such as the FCC (in the USA) and Ofcom (in the UK) have already noticed that such under-utilization of the spectrum can be avoided by more flexible and dynamic spectrum access (DSA) mechanisms [6]. Radio spectrum is a multidimensional entity, i.e., frequency is not the only parameter/dimension which characterizes the spectral opportunity. Space, time, transmission power, polarization, medium access and interference all combinely shape the radio environment. The dynamic spectrum access (DSA) mechanism employs one or more of these parameters to break the shackles of rigidity imposed by the command and control mechanism. Cognitive radios (CRs) are envisioned to be the key enablers for provisioning DSA. CRs are based on opportunistic exploitation of radio spectrum across one or more dimensions. Nevertheless, while the CR platform renders itself as a promising solution for improving connectivity, its suitability in context of IoT is limited due to two main reasons:

1. High cost: CRs employ sophisticated hardware to derive operational environment awareness and so naturally the radio platforms costs are higher as compared to dumb radio terminals. For IoT solutions, the radio platforms will be embedded inside objects requiring both additional cost and form factors. Thus the radio platforms should be as simple as possible, ideally comprising of a single chip on which a radio transceiver is integrated with the micro-controller unit (MCU). Manufacturers such as Texas Instrument, Nordic Semi-conductor, Maxim, CSR ,etc., are already providing such simple solutions.
2. Energy consumption and life-time: CR terminals often pay the cost of opportunism in terms of their higher energy consumption. More specifically, the operational environment awareness is driven from the inference process which consumes more energy as compared to simple radio platforms. For the wireless access applications, energy consumption is not considered as a design

constraint due to supply of power from the grid. Nevertheless, for IoT based applications energy-consumption is of the utmost important. As discussed earlier, the radio platform is part of variety of objects, most of them having no/limited access to the power running on coin cells, etc. In this context, the cost of opportunism may be incurred in terms of the reduced operational life-time of these objects.

While object life-time is a critical aspect of design, the issue of so called 'green design' is further brought into play due to a predicted high volume of smart things. Specifically, as predicted in a recent report by Ericsson [3], the CO_2 emissions due to increased number of internet connected devices will increase from 800 Mtonnes to 1200 Mtonnes by 2020. In terms of net emissions, ICT will continue to maintain its 2 % contribution to the global carbon foot-print. Nevertheless, according to the Intergovernmental Panel on Climate Change (IPCC) current emission trends are far from sustainable, requiring exponential reduction to meet a 2°C rise in global temperature. In a recent survey by Cable News Network (CNN) it was estimated that a 2°C rise in global temperature will result in a 100 billion US dollar expense rise for addressing various challenges due to climate change. In summary, like all other sectors ICT should exponentially reduce energy consumption to operate in a eco-friendly manner. Thus in summary, for deployment of 500 billion IoT devices a clean slate design is necessary to address both energy and spectral efficiency issues.

1.2   Design Attributes and Proposed Architecture

The grand challenges posed in the context of the cognitive IoT (CIoT) can be easily translated into design attributes/constraints. To summarize, the radio platform employed in CIoT devices should be: (i) simple yet agile; (ii) spectrally efficient and (iii) low power with a minituarized form factor. To satisfy these design attributes, the definition of cognition in context of the IoT must be revisited. In particular, not only spectral agility is of a prime importance but power consumption awareness should also be embedded into the cognitive engine. We advocate that the cognitive engine must be equipped with a potential to harvest energy from ambient sources and in some cases from the objects themselves. For instance, consider smart door locks installed in modern houses. The radio transceivers on these locks can be powered using solar panels harvesting indoor ambient light from both natural and synthetic sources. Moreover, these locks can also harvest power from the mechanical motion of door itself. As smart objects have a very low-duty cycled traffic harvested energy provides a significant potential for designing self-sustainable so called 'zero-energy consumption' CIoT networks.

In this paper, we propose a cloud enabled CIoT platform as depicted in Fig. 1 to address the aforementioned challenges. From an object oriented programming approach it is well known that an object can be adequately described by its attributes and functionalites. These functionalites and attributes can be linked to external stimuli characterizing events. The behavior of the object in response to

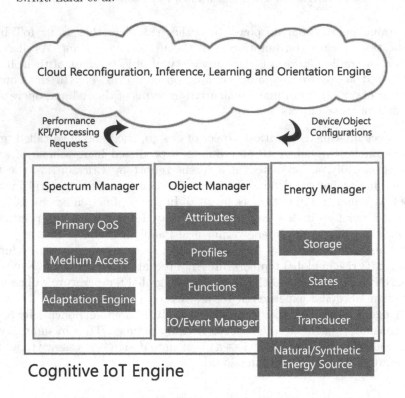

Fig. 1. Proposed architecture for cognitive IoT networks

an external stimulus is defined by the device profile. External and internal stim-ului may trigger interrupts which should be handled in accordance with device profile and current state. We propose that this object related functionality should be implemented in the so called 'object manager' which forms the central part of CIoT engine. The object engine coordinates with both the energy and spectrum managers to provide context awareness and indicate required quality-of-service or quality-of-information constraints. The object management life cycle can be simplified as most of the inference can be moved up to the centralized cloud processor. Thus objects can be made simpler by implementing basic look-up tables which map events, stimulus, attributes and functionality. Notice that the cloud based architecture provides flexibility of re-configuring the object manage-ment engine on the fly.

Spectrum and energy management engines are responsible for maximizing the spectral and energy efficiencies of a CIoT network. We advocate the use of a cognitive underlay based spectrum access which requires only transmit power/medium access probability adaptation at the CIoT platforms [7]. The intrinsic advantage of the proposed spectrum access is that its implementa-tion is simple and does not require additional sophisticated hardware. Based on the dynamics of the primary network, the cloud re-configuration engine can re-configure access probabilities and transmit power to guarantee that the QoS of the legacy network is not violated. Thus, implementing a robust co-existence framework between the primary users and the CIoT devices. The practical implementation of such a spectrum access would require a simple look up table at each device, i.e. CIoT platforms do not lose either their cost-effectiveness or the form factor through the implementation of the proposed cognitive access strategy. A general framework for performance characterization of these engines is introduced in a subsequent discussion.

2   Energy Outage Probability in Harvesting Empowered CIoT

In order to maintain generality, in this article, we do not restrict our analytical models to a particular scenario. We will present a general framework for performance characterization of the CIoT networks which can be employed to study various specific use-cases.

Harvesting energy from natural (solar, wind, vibration, etc.) and synthesized (microwave power transfer) sources is envisioned as a key enabler for realizing green wireless networks. In this context, the energy management engine plays a central role. Energy harvested from the ambient sources such as natural and man-made light, temperature gradients, vibrations and mechanical motions results in an energy field which possesses the following form

$$I_H(t, \boldsymbol{x}) = I_D(t, \boldsymbol{x}) + I_R(t, \boldsymbol{x}) \quad Watts/\text{m}^2, \tag{1}$$

where I_D is the deterministic power density and I_R captures random fluctuations in ambient power field due to the environment. In general, the power arrival process at a transducer has both spatial and temporal dynamics. For instance, the power arriving at a indoor solar panel is a function of its latitude, longitude, zenith angle, hour angle and the day number [8]. Transducers are not ideal in converting the ambient energy into output power. Generally, the input-output relationship of the transducer is non-linear. Thus the output load is often matched to provide a maximum energy transfer. In general, the power output of a transducer can be represented as

$$P_{out}(t, \boldsymbol{x}) = f_T(I_D(t, \boldsymbol{x}) + I_R(t, \boldsymbol{x})) \quad \text{Watts}. \tag{2}$$

where $f_T(.)$ is the non-linear transducer response. For instance, for the PV panel the output current can be expressed in terms of the ambient solar irradiance I_H (see eq. (1)) as follows [8]

$$I_{PV} = I_{sc}\left[1 - \kappa_3\left\{\exp\left(\frac{V_{PV}}{\kappa_4 V_{oc}}\right) - 1\right\}\right], \tag{3}$$

where $\kappa_3 = \left(1 - \frac{I_{MPP}}{I_{sc}}\right)\exp\left(\frac{V_{MPP}}{\kappa_4 V_{oc}}\right)$ and $\kappa_4 = \left(\frac{V_{MPP}}{V_{oc}} - 1\right)/\ln\left(1 - \frac{I_{MPP}}{I_{sc}}\right)$ which depends on the module parameters: (i) short circuit current I_{sc}; (ii) open circuit voltage V_{oc}; (iii) maximum power point voltage V_{MPP} and (iv) maximum power point current I_{MPP}. These parameters can be expressed as a function of the ambient temperature and global horizontal irradiance as

$$I_{sc} = I_{scs} \times \frac{I_H}{I_S} \times [1 + \varsigma_1(T - T_s)], \tag{4}$$

$$V_{oc} = V_{ocs} + \varsigma_2(T - T_s), \tag{5}$$

$$I_{MPP} = I_{MPPS} \times \frac{I_H}{I_S} \times [1 + \varsigma_1(T - T_s)], \tag{6}$$

$$V_{MPP} = V_{MPPS} + \varsigma_2(T - T_s), \tag{7}$$

where I_{scs}, V_{ocs}, I_{MPPS}, V_{MPPS} are defined at standard conditions, i.e., $I_S = 100\,\mathrm{mW/cm^2}$ for outdoor/$I_S = 100\,\mu\mathrm{W/cm^2}$ for indoor and $T_s = 25°C$ with ς_1 and ς_2 being the current and the voltage coefficients. These parameters are generally provided in the data sheet of a PV module. From Eq. (3), the output power of the PV panel can be computed as a function of the voltage as $P_{out} = I_{PV}V_{PV}$. Most of the modern day panels are equipped with maximum power point tracking algorithms[1]. The maximum output power can be extracted by adjusting the cell load resistance. The maximum extracted power is denoted by P_{out}^{max} and is computed by maximizing P_{PV} with respect to output voltage.

The short-fall of the energy for a certain desired power P_{req} can be measured in terms of the 'energy outage probability' as

$$\begin{aligned}\epsilon_{out}^{\{e\}}(t, \boldsymbol{x}) &= \mathbb{P}\{P_{out} < P_{req}\} = \mathbb{P}\left\{I_R < f_T^{-1}(P_{req}) - I_D\right\}, \\ &= \mathcal{F}_{I_R}\left(f_T^{-1}(P_{req}) - I_D(t, \boldsymbol{x})\right),\end{aligned} \tag{8}$$

where $\mathcal{F}_{I_R}(.)$ is the cumulative density function of I_R the random component of the ambient energy field for a certain time t and location $\boldsymbol{x}$. Generally, $f_T^{-1}(a)$ is a monotonically decreasing function with respect to a and thus ϵ_{out} is increasing function of P_{req}, i.e. with an increase in required power for a fixed time instance and a spatial location the energy outage probability also increases towards unity. The dynamics of the energy harvester and thus the management engine of a CIoT platform can be completely characterized in terms of energy outage probability.

3 Spectral Access Outage Probability in CIoT

Consider a large scale CIoT network co-existing with the primary network. The spatial distribution of both primary and CIoT nodes is captured by two independent *homogenous Poisson point processes* (HPPPs) $\Pi_p(\lambda_p)$ and $\Pi_c(\lambda_c)$ respectively[2]. Further assume that CIoT nodes employ a random access strategy similar to the slotted ALOHA MAC protocol to schedule their transmissions over

---

[1] Sometimes implemented at inverter level rather than panel level .

[2] The HPPP assumption is reasonable in the context of CIoT as the objects are deployed by the user and are spatially distributed across the entire city.

a shared medium. More specifically, at an arbitrary time instant both the primary and the secondary devices can be classified into two distinct groups, i.e., nodes which are granted with the medium access and those whose transmissions are deferred. If p_i denotes the medium access probability (MAP) for an arbitrary user $\boldsymbol{x} \in \Pi_i{}^3$, then the set of active users under slotted ALOHA MAC also forms a HPPP:

$$\Pi_i^{\{TX\}} = \{\, \boldsymbol{x} \in \Pi_i : \mathbb{1}(\boldsymbol{x}) = 1 \} \text{ with density } \lambda_i p_i, \tag{9}$$
$$\text{where } i \in \{c, p\}.$$

where $\mathbb{1}(\boldsymbol{x})$ denotes a Bernoulli random variable and is independent of Π_i. The received SIR of a typical primary user can be characterized as

$$\text{SIR} = \Gamma_p = \frac{h_p l(r_p)}{\sum_{i \in \Pi_p^{\{TX\}} \setminus \{\boldsymbol{x}\}} h_i l \left(\|\boldsymbol{x}_i\| \right) + \sum_{j \in \Pi_c^{\{TX\}}} \eta g_j l \left(\|\boldsymbol{x}_j\| \right)},$$
$$= \Gamma_p = \frac{h_p l(r_p)}{I_p + \eta I_c} = \frac{h_p l(r_p)}{I_{tot}}, \tag{10}$$

where $h_p, h_i, g_j \sim \mathcal{E}(1)$ random variables capturing the effect of Rayleigh fading, $l(r) = r^{-\alpha}$ is the path-loss function with $\alpha \geq 2$ being the environment dependent exponent, $\eta = \frac{P_c}{P_p}$ is the transmit power ratios of the CIoT and primary networks and r_p is the distance between primary transmitter and receiver.

The primary user's QoS constraint can be expressed in terms of the desired SIR threshold $\gamma_{th}^{\{p\}}$ and an outage probability threshold

$$\mathbb{P}_{out}^{\{p\}} (P_c, p_c) = \Pr \left\{ \Gamma_p \leq \gamma_{th}^{\{p\}} \right\} \leq \rho_{out}^{\{p\}}. \tag{11}$$

Notice that the primary user's outage probability is coupled with the aggregate interference generated by the CIoT network. Consequently, secondary access is limited subject to the constraint in Eq. (11). It can be easily shown that the maximum permissible MAP for the CIoT devices can be characterized as

$$p_c = \frac{f_{MAP} \left(\lambda_p, \lambda_c, \rho_{out}^{\{p\}}, \gamma_{th}^{\{p\}} \right)}{P_c^{2/\alpha}}, \tag{12}$$

where $f_{MAP}(.)$ depends on the primary networking parameters, the propagation characteristics of the co-located networks and the required QoS requirements. For an ad-hoc network $f_{MAP}(.)$ is characterized in [7] which can be easily extended to the cellular primary network. Generally, $f_{MAP}(.)$ decreases with an increase in the QoS requirement and/or the density of the primary transmitters. It decreases with an increase in a CIoT transmit power and increases with a decrease in the CIoT transmitter density. The spectral outage probability is the event that the

---

[3] With a slight abuse of notation, $\boldsymbol{x} \in \mathbb{R}^2$ is employed to refer to the node's location as well as the node itself.

CIoT transmitter is in a spectrum limited regime, i.e., it has had to defer its transmission for the current slot. Thus

$$\epsilon_{out}^{\{s\}} = 1 - \frac{f_{MAP}\left(\lambda_p, \lambda_c, \rho_{out}^{\{p\}}, \gamma_{th}^{\{p\}}\right)}{P_c^{2/\alpha}}. \tag{13}$$

Consequently, the relationship between spectral and energy outages can be characterized as follows

$$\epsilon_{out}^{\{e\}} = \mathcal{F}_{I_R}\left(f_T^{-1}\left(\left(\frac{f_{MAP}\left(\lambda_p, \lambda_c, \rho_{out}^{\{p\}}, \gamma_{th}^{\{p\}}\right)}{1 - \epsilon_{out}^{\{s\}}}\right)^{\frac{\alpha}{2}}\right) - I_D\left(t, \boldsymbol{x}\right)\right). \tag{14}$$

For the case of indoor solar energy harvesting, the formulation can be simplified using Eq. (3) as

$$\epsilon_{out}^{\{e\}} = \mathcal{F}_{I_R}\left(\Theta\left(\frac{1}{1 - \epsilon_{out}^{\{s\}}}\right)^{\frac{\alpha}{2}}\right), \tag{15}$$

where $f(x) = \Theta(g(x))$ implies that $c_1 g(x) \leq f(x) \leq c_2 g(x)$ following the Landua notation. From [9], we have that

$$\epsilon_{out}^{\{e\}} = \frac{1}{2}\left[1 + \text{erf}\left(\frac{\left(1 - \epsilon_{out}^{\{s\}}\right)^{-\alpha/2}}{2}\right)\right]. \tag{16}$$

This provides us with the spectral-energy outage operating curve (SE-OPC) for CIoT networks. The SE-OPC serves as a guideline to decide whether a CIoT network is operating in energy limited regime or the spectrum limited regime. The exact shape of the curve is coupled with the operating parameters of the harvester and the network. However, in this study we are only interested in the scaling behavior and thus do not consider the specific values.

4 Discussion and Future Directions

Figure 2 illustrates the SE-OPC for CIoT networks for the considered reference scenario of an indoor solar panel. It is clear that both the energy and spectral outage probability are positively coupled with each other. Specifically, both the spectral and the energy outages are increasing functions of the CIoT platform transmit power, i.e., a high transmit power for CIoT radio will result in:

1. vanishing transmission opportunities due to interference protection implemented by the cloud controller to guarantee the primary user's QoS requirement;
2. requiring an amount of energy for transmissions which cannot be fulfilled by the harvester.

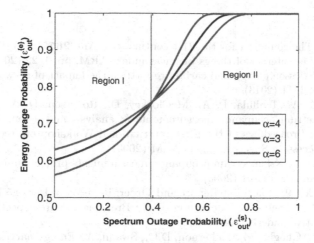

Fig. 2. SE-OPC for CIoT network for varying path-loss exponents (see Eq. (16)).

This leads to the conclusion that adopting a low transmit power will reduce both the energy and the spectrum outage probabilities. However, the low transmit power employed by a CIoT platform may not be able to guarantee the required QoS or QoI at each CIoT node. Consequently, the transmit power must be optimized by considering all three factors, i.e., energy and spectral outages and CIoTs throughput. Due to space limitations, the optimization of transmit power is deferred for the journal version of this article.

From the energy outage perspective, there exist two distinct regions. These regions mainly demonstrate the impact of an increase in the path-loss exponent. An increase in the path-loss exponent results in: (i) signal power reduction; (ii) rapid attenuation for co-channel interference. Thus intuitively these two regions demonstrate the power limited vs. interference limited operation.

5 Conclusion

In this article, we provided a unified architecture for the cognitive internet-of-things (CIoT) framework. We advocated that the definition of cognition must be extended to incorporate IoT specific design challenges. We solicited a cloud based cognitive underlay spectrum access for the IoT radio platforms. Furthermore, energy harvesting is proposed to attain so called self-sustainable network design. We introduce a novel statistical framework to characterize the energy and spectral outages in CIoT networks. The relationship between energy and spectral outages was explored for a reference scenario of indoor solar energy harvesting. It was shown that both outages are positively coupled as they are governed by the same underlying parameter, i.e., transmit power. It was shown that there exists tradeoff between minimizing the outages and maximizing the QoS and thus optimal transmit power must be adopted to maximize network level performance.

References

1. Weiser, M.: The computer for the 21st century. Sci. Am. **265**(3), 94–104 (1991)
2. E. I. Unit.: The internet of things business index. ARM, pp. 1–22 (2014)
3. E. I. Unit.: Ericsson energy and carbon report: on the impact of networked society. Ericsson, pp. 1–11 (2013)
4. McHenry, M. A., Tenhula, P. A., McCloskey, D., Roberson, D. A., Hood, C.S.: Chicago spectrum occupancy measurements & analysis and a long-term studies proposal. In: Proceedings of the First International Workshop on Technology and Policy for Accessing Spectrum, p. 1. ACM (2006)
5. McHenry, M. A.: Nsf spectrum occupancy measurements project summary. Shared spectrum company report (2005)
6. Fcc, E.: Docket 98–153. First Report and Order: Revision of Part **15** (2002)
7. Zaidi, S.A.R., Ghogho, M., McLernon, D.C.: Breaking the area spectral efficiency wall in cognitive underlay networks
8. Zaidi, S.A.R., Ghogho, M., McLernon, D.C., Swami, A.: Energy harvesting empowered cognitive metro-cells. IEEE Workshop on Cognitive Cellular Systems (2014)
9. Huishi, L., Jian, S., Sige, L.: Reliability evaluation of distribution system containing microgrid. In: 2010 China International Conference on Electricity Distribution (CICED),pp. 1–7. IEEE (2010)

Secure Communication over Software-Defined Networks

Stefan Rass[1]([✉]), Benjamin Rainer[1], Matthias Vavti[1], Johannes Göllner[2], Andreas Peer[2], and Stefan Schauer[3]

[1] Alpen-Adria-Universität Klagenfurt, Universitätsstrasse 65-67,
9020 Klagenfurt, Austria
{stefan.rass,benjamin.rainer}@aau.at, matthias.vavti@edu.aau.at
[2] National Defence Academy of the Austrian Federal Ministry of Defence and Sports,
Vienna, Austria
{johannes.goellner,andreas.peer}@bmlvs.gv.at
[3] AIT Austrian Institute of Technology GmbH, Lakeside B10A,
9020 Klagenfurt, Austria
stefan.schauer@ait.ac.at

Abstract. We report on work in progress towards a practical implementation of a software defined overlay network that provides data delivery services at a freely definable and provably optimized quality of service. Our example implementation establishes transparent secure transmission, where security is in terms of confidentiality, authenticity and availability. Using general techniques from game-theory, we show how to simultaneously optimize several performance indicators of a transmission service, taking care of interdependencies and using security as a showcase application.

Keywords: Communication · Security · Pareto-optimality · Game theory

1 Introduction

Software-defined networking (SDN) provides new means of managing computer networks. It eases the provisioning of forwarding strategies, and resource allocation, and provides means to monitor traffic by separating the control plane and data plane on network devices [8] (cf. Sect. 1.1). We pursue the goal of providing secure communication over networks. Security is here a "joint" property consisting of *confidentiality*, *authenticity* and *availability*[1].

We employ SDN for realising strategies (transmission paths) in the network that provides the highest quality of security ("QoS") for a specific communication between two entities (the sender and the receiver). Nodes in-between the

---

[1] We deviate from the standard setting in enterprise security, where *integrity* replaces *authenticity*. However, since authenticity usually implies integrity on a technical level, we can safely go with our modified "definition" here.

© Institute for Computer Sciences, Social Informatics and Telecommunications Engineering 2015
R. Giaffreda et al. (Eds.): IoT360 2014, Part II, LNICST 151, pp. 211–221, 2015.
DOI: 10.1007/978-3-319-19743-2_31

communication path may be subject to an attack. Each node has certain properties (e.g., software version, accessibility for external personnel). With the use of these properties, we derive the set of nodes that are likely to be attacked. For example, a certain software version may indicate that there exists an exploit that grants root access. The adversary may attack any node in the network, except the sender and receiver. The sender and receiver may use multipath transmissions (MPT) for communicating by employing an appropriate protocol (cf. Sect. 1.2). In order to find secure communication paths through the network, we employ game theory, where the adversary *plays* against the sender and receiver (each party trying to maximize its payoff). Our testbed allows to model a network, i.e., enterprise networks and it provides the possibility of implementing the security strategies in the network by means of an application layer protocol (cf. Sect. 1.3).

The paper is organized as follows. Section 2 provides the theoretical preliminaries on our game theoretic approach. Section 3 provides practical insights on the implementation of our approach using our testbed. Finally, Sect. 4 summarizes the paper and provides an outlook on future work.

1.1   Enterprise Communication

Secure communication in a perhaps widely distributed enterprise infrastructure is strongly dependent on the user's awareness and willingness to follow guidelines and best practices. Security breaches may indeed occur, due to users finding it difficult or cumbersome to apply proper encryption or digitally sign a message for authentication.

On the contrary, technology like virtual private networks (VPN) or transport layer security (TLS, formerly known as secure socket layer – SSL), enjoy wide acceptance and are examples of what is nowadays called "usable security" [4][2].

Pursuing this idea further, why not have a *software-defined virtual network* in a system that transparently delivers messages in a secure manner, without burdening its user with details of security?

The benefits of having a software defined network on top of a physical one (yet sharing its topology) is manifold, as (1) it minimizes risks of accidental misuse, as users are no longer directly responsible for or involved in technical matters of security, and (2) it presents a neat dual use of network redundancy for purposes beyond availability, by adding naturally to the enterprise risk management (details of which will briefly be explained in Sect. 1.2).

1.2   Multipath Transmission

Briefly speaking, multipath transmission (MPT) delivers a message over a network by utilizing multiple mutually disjoint paths (intersecting only at the sender and receiver's nodes). Using different encodings of the payload, we can use such techniques to increase throughput (split a message into parts and transmit them

---

[2] Here, we neglect issues of IT administration to properly set up and run the underlying system, which may be far from a trivial task.

in parallel), increase reliability (send several copies of a message in parallel) or increase security (use secret-sharing techniques to hide information from eavesdroppers on a limited subset of channels [5]).

A technical difficulty of setting up MPT in a real life network is the lack of respective support in layers below the application. Although the internet protocol – theoretically – could do source-routing along pre-defined paths (as it is necessary for MPT in wired networks with fixed topology), such features are mostly not supported by network devices or otherwise deactivated for security reasons (note the irony). The problem is less prevalent in wireless (ad hoc) networks, and suitable protocols are more developed and more intensively investigated [1]. Software-defined networks (on the application layer) let us elegantly overcome obstacles known from wired (or partially wireless) networks that would otherwise hinder the effective use of MPT.

MPT has seen fruitful applications in wireless and wired networks, towards goals of security [6,7,16], reliability [3,15] or media delivery [13]. However, common to most of that preliminary work is their focus on a *single particular* goal, leaving effects on other performance indicators of interest mostly aside. Exploiting the full potential of MPT in all its applications, is a matter of theoretical considerations on how to use MPT to get the most from it, and practical matters on how to properly run it over a network whose hardware would not play the game properly. These issues are both discussed in Sects. 2 and 3.

1.3 Our Testbed

To properly set up, test and verify the services of a software-defined network, it is useful to rebuild standard enterprise network topologies in the lab, so as to have a realistic testbed on which a software defined overlay network can be studied. To this end, let us construct our enterprise infrastructure as being a globally acting pharmacological corporation, with many subsidiaries all over the world (distribution sketched in Fig. 1) that are interconnected over an MPLS network. Intranets at each branch follow reference network topologies, such as sketched in Fig. 1 or simpler.

Now, suppose that we seek to establish a software-defined overlay network in this enterprise for a transparent, reliable and secure delivery of content within the company. The goal is thus to simultaneously optimize several performance indicators, including at least the following: (1) reliability, (2) confidentiality, (3) authenticity and (4) bandwidth/latency. The first three indicators are quantified in terms of probability (for a successful transmission), and the fourth indicator is a bandwidth estimate. Hence, we seek to establish a good quality of service (QoS), where the service level agreement is made up of several things that are potentially interdependent and require a "holistic" treatment. Section 2 sketches how this can be done in theory, and Sect. 3 reports on practical implementations thereof.

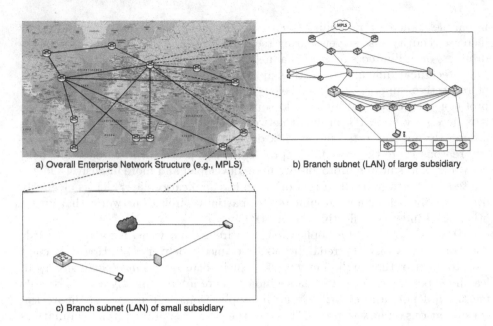

a) Overall Enterprise Network Structure (e.g., MPLS)   b) Branch subnet (LAN) of large subsidiary

c) Branch subnet (LAN) of small subsidiary

Fig. 1. Testbed

2   Theoretical Groundwork

A concept to assure optimal performance of multiple performance indicators has been discussed in [9]. While this work has been focused on security, the idea is not limited to this application. In brief, the idea of running a communication infrastructure in a way to optimize several of its performance indicators is based on certain degrees of freedom on how load is balanced in the network and how the routing is done (this is the point where a software-defined overlay network becomes most useful as it spares changes to running infrastructure).

The basic idea is bought from the concept of zero-sum games, where two players engage in a competition towards selfishly maximizing their own good at the cost of the other. Adopting the perspective of one of these players, the zero-sum strategy gives a minimum guaranteed performance, no matter what the opponent actually does (as long as his actions remain within known action sets) [2]. This can be extended towards multiple goals (latency, security, etc.), as was first done by [14] and revisited in [9]. In a nutshell, let $u_1, \ldots, u_n$ be performance indicators referring to all aspects of interest (can be probabilities, bandwidths, etc.). Given a finite set PS_1 of network provisioning strategies (i.e., different (transmission) configurations) and a finite set PS_2 of potential problem scenarios (e.g., node failures, security breaches, etc.), computing performance indicators under specific scenarios from $PS_1 \times PS_2$ is a trivial matter of *simulating* the protocols (say, in OmNet++ or any handcrafted script program). For example, MPT is straightforward to analyse, when the transmission configuration is the set of chosen paths, and the problem scenario is a set of outage nodes. Computing the effects on the security, bandwidth, etc. is easy by a plain protocol simulation. Computing the network performance in all scenarios from $PS_1 \times PS_2$ creates a set of matrices (each having dimension $|PS_1| \times |PS_2|$, where $|\cdot|$ denotes a set's cardinality), from which we can compute an optimal network provisioning strategy x^* (being a randomized choice rule on all valid configurations from PS_1), and performance level vector $v = (v_1, \ldots, v_n)$, with the following two properties [9]: given that the transmission parameters are (drawn from) x^*, we have

Assurance, meaning that $u_i \geq v_i$, i.e., v_i is the minimum guaranteed performance, regardless which problem scenarios from PS_2 arise with which frequency, and

Efficiency, meaning that any different transmission configuration $x \neq x^*$ deteriorates the performance in at least one of our indicators, i.e., there is an index i so that $u_i < v_i$.

In the background, computing x^* and v is a matter of solving an $(n+1)$-person game, in which the network provider (player 0) competes with n opponents, each of which seeks to minimize the network performance in a different regard (zero-sum regime on each indicator). This zero-sum construction yields assurance and efficiency exactly as it does in the scalar case of a single performance indicator. It is therefore occasionally referred to as a *(Pareto-optimal) security strategy* [14]. For example, in seeking minimal latency, we may define x^* as the rule to always choose the currently most reliable path(s). Likewise, towards best security, we may choose the paths with best protection (not necessarily being the most reliable ones). The framework of [9] shows how to simultaneously take care of all these goals. The numerical computation of x^* and v is possible by an iterative algorithm, adapted from [12] (showing how to solve "one-against all"-type games), which we implemented in our prototype. The tricky part is to have the infrastructure do the MPT according to the optimal (randomized) configurations x^*, which is where software-defined networks come in extremely handy.

3 Practical Implementation

Basically, our prototype implementation does randomized source-routing on the application layer (OSI layer 7). More precisely, given a topology with redundant connections (found in most reference network structures such as sketched in Fig. 1), x^* is a set of paths (or path bundles) that shall be selected with prescribed probabilities (i.e., x^* is actually a probability distribution supported on the transmission configuration set PS_1). The network itself is defined by a set of instances of the client software, running at different machines in the network. Each client can act as sender, receiver or (passive) relay on layer 7, where confidentiality is assured by cryptographically enhanced MPT[3]. Availability is determined by whether or not *all* packets reach their destination. Authenticity is achieved by a simple multipath authentication scheme detailed in [11].

The computation of x^* and its implied quality-of-service vector v are computed by an enhanced version of the system described in [10], implementing the method of [12] to compute x^* and v as defined in [9].

A Worked Example: To practically test and demonstrate the feasibility and security of our system, we implemented a Java demonstrator application that handles the routing and cryptographic operations necessary to deliver a message securely from a sender to a receiver. The example network that we treat here is simplified for plausibility without requiring the reader to do the math underneath the theoretical groundwork (as sketched in Sect. 2) to "verify" the correctness of the results and the example.

The network consists of five nodes that are interconnected as shown in Fig. 2. For authentication, the protocol in [11] adds message authentication codes (MACs) to the payload that are based on secrets shared with other nodes in the network (common secrets being indicated by dashed connections). To verify the authenticity of a received message, the receiver simply asks other nodes in the network to verify the MAC. In that sense, the system sort of resembles how handwritten signatures can be checked on printed documents without electronic or cryptographic help.

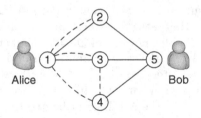

Fig. 2. Example network

The efficient assurance of optimal security in terms of authenticity, availability and confidentiality uses single-path transmission over a randomly chosen path $1 \to x \to 5$ where x is chosen uniformly from $\{2, 3, 4\}$. It is easy to see that an attacker gaining control over one or two nodes has only a one-out-of-three chance to learn the information, which yields a 66 % chance of the message being

---

[3] Actually, a rather simplified version of perfectly secure MPT, which splits a message m into a set of random strings so that their XOR recreates m. Despite there being much better practical protocols, in case of two-path transmissions, our scheme is isomorphic to a one-time pad and thus unbreakable. This security is, however, bought at a higher risk of communication failure in case that one or more packets get lost. Thus, the two goals "confidentiality" and "availability" are somewhat conflicting.

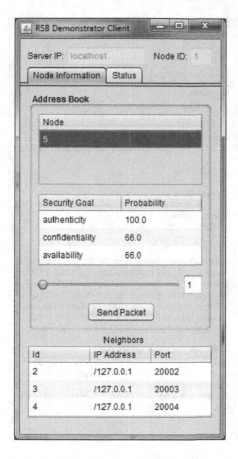

Fig. 3. Sender's (Alice's) view (demonstrator prototype)

delivered (availability) in privacy (confidentiality). If the receiver Bob asks all three nodes $\{2, 3, 4\}$ to verify the attached MACs, then there is even a 100 % guarantee of a forgery to be detected upon one rejected MAC verification. This security assurance is displayed in Alice's window (corresponding to node 1 and shown in Fig. 3). The address book shows to which receivers (in our case only node 5, which is Bob) she can deliver messages to. The lowest part of the window shows this node's direct neighbors in the network. This is important to demonstrate that a node needs only local information on the network topology, as it is concerned only with where to send the packet away, but it does not need to know the full network topology. The entire transmission works along several (in our case only one) intermediate node, any of which needs only local (and hence minimal) information about the full network.

The likelihoods of a confidential delivery can, at the cost of investing much additional transmission overhead, be raised arbitrarily close to 1 by repeating the process to deliver a set of random numbers $r_1, \ldots, r_{n-1}$ and encrypting

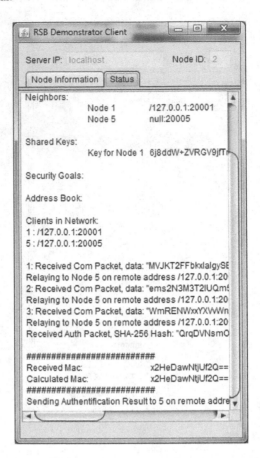

Fig. 4. View and data of intermediate node 2 (demonstrator prototype)

the payload m in the final blow as $r_n := m \oplus r_1 \oplus \cdots \oplus r_n$ (where $\oplus$ is the bitwise XOR), so that each $r_1, \ldots, r_{n-1}$ on its own would perfectly conceal the message m like a one-time pad. In turn, this requires all packets to be correctly delivered, thus lowering availability of the channel in much the same way. More sophisticated error-correcting transmission schemes (see e.g., [5]) can elegantly cover for this tradeoff, but are outside our scope here.

Our prototype can be configured to take any number of given rounds; in the example this would be $n = 5$ repetitions. Figure 5 shows a log print of all information that this node receives, displaying the recovered message ("Hello Bob!") in the middle of the window. As the log of the intermediate node 2 shows, see Fig. 4, this node receives some but not all (only three of the five) packets necessary to reconstruct the final message for Bob; the entirety of required messages being listed in the log of Fig. 5. So, a potentially hostile node 2 would – in an information-theoretic sense – be unable to learn anything from sniffing on the network traffic.

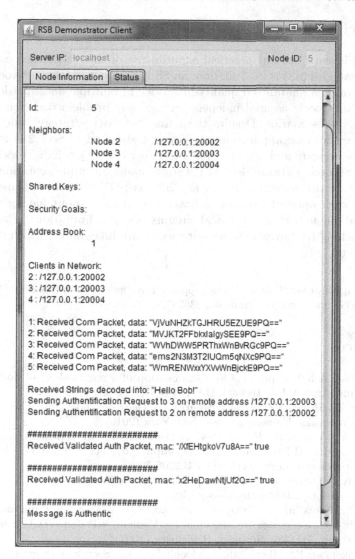

Fig. 5. Receiver's (Bob's) view (demonstrator prototype)

The other information displayed in the window(s) relates to network topology information and the (base64-encoded) authentication keys shared with the neighbors (in case of node 2, this would be only node 1, with which the dashed edge indicates the existence of a shared key for MAC verification. In turn, node 1 would use this shared key to have node 2 verify the MAC that Alice attached originally (the details of this authenticity verification conversation are as well displayed in the log files of the involved nodes; Figs. 4 and 5).

4   Conclusion

The lesson learnt from our practical experiments on the theoretical concept of security strategies (SS) is twofold: first, an SS is a way in which a network can be utilized towards a guaranteed quality-of-service in multiple and interdependent aspects. This QoS is assured independently of any problem occurrence within a known set of scenarios. Despite the name "security strategy" and security being a nice showcase application, the concept sketched in Sect. 2 is in *no way restricted to security* and can be applied to many other QoS indicators straight-forwardly. Second, software defined networks make an implementation of such security strategies most simple and feasible, as SDN give the full freedom to implement such optimal network utilization regimes without having to worry too much about underlying technical circumstances or limitations. Thus, applications reaching far beyond the security scope are imaginable, which this work may stipulate.

Acknowledgements. This work was supported by the Austrian Research Promotion Agency (FFG) under project grant no. 836287.

References

1. Abbas, A.: A hybrid protocol for identification of a maximal set of node disjoint paths. Int. Arab J. Inf. Technol. (IAJIT) **6**(4), 344–358 (2009)
2. Alpcan, T., Başar, T.: Network Security: A Decision and Game Theoretic Approach. Cambridge University Press, New York (2010)
3. Djukic, P., Valaee, S.: Reliable packet transmissions in multipath routed wireless networks. IEEE Trans. Mob. Comput. **5**, 548–559 (2006). http://doi.ieeecomputersociety.org/10.1109/TMC.2006.72
4. Finley, K.: Online security is a total pain, but that may soon change (2014). http://www.wired.com/2014/06/usable-security/
5. Fitzi, M., Franklin, M., Garay, J., Vardhan, S.H.: Towards optimal and efficient perfectly secure message transmission. In: Vadhan, S.P. (ed.) TCC 2007. LNCS, vol. 4392, pp. 311–322. Springer, Heidelberg (2007)
6. Kotzanikolaou, P., Mavropodi, R., Douligeris, C.: Secure multipath routing for mobile ad hoc networks. In: International Conference on Wireless on Demand Network Systems and Service, pp. 89–96. IEEE Computer Society, Los Alamitos (2005).doi:http://doi.ieeecomputersociety.org/10.1109/WONS.2005.31
7. Li, Z., Kwok, Y.K.: A new multipath routing approach to enhancing TCP security in ad hoc wireless networks. In: International Conference Workshops on Parallel Processing, pp. 372–379 (2005). doi:10.1109/ICPPW.2005.11
8. Nunes, B., Mendonca, M., Nguyen, X., Obraczka, K., Turletti, T.: A survey of software-defined networking: past, present, and future of programmable networks. In: Communications Surveys Tutorials, vol. (99), pp. 1–18. IEEE (2014). doi:10.1109/SURV.2014.012214.00180
9. Rass, S.: On game-theoretic network security provisioning. J. Netw. Syst. Manage. **21**(1), 47–64 (2013). http://www.springerlink.com/openurl.asp?genre=articleid=doi:10.1007/s10922-012-9229-1

10. Rass, S., Rainer, B., Vavti, M., Schauer, S.: A network modeling and analysis tool for perfectly secure communication. In: Proceedings of the 27th IEEE International Conference on Advanced Information Networking and Applications, pp. 267–275. IEEE Computer Society Press (2013, in press)
11. Rass, S., Schartner, P.: Multipath authentication without shared secrets andwith applications in quantum networks. In: Proceedings of the International Conference on Security and Management (SAM), vol. 1, pp. 111–115. CSREA Press (2010)
12. Sela, A.: Fictitious play in one-against-all multi-player games. Economic Theory 14, 635–651 (1999). doi:10.1007/s001990050345
13. Singh, V., Ahsan, S., Ott, J.: MPRTP: multipath considerations for real-time media. ACM Multimedia Systems Conference (2013)
14. Voorneveld, M.: Pareto-optimal security strategies as minimax strategies of a standard matrix game. J. Optim. Theory Appl. **102**(1), 203–210 (1999)
15. Wen, H., Lin, C., Yang, H., Ren, F., Yue, Y.: Modeling the reliability of packet group transmission in wireless network (2007). http://citeseerx.ist.psu.edu/view doc/summary?doi=10.1.1.132.483
16. Zhao, L., Delgado-Frias, J.: Multipath routing based secure data transmission in ad hoc networks. In: IEEE International Conference on Wireless and Mobile Computing, Networking and Communication, pp. 17–23 (2006). doi:http://doi. ieeecomputersociety.org/10.1109/WIMOB.2006.1696359

Integrating WMN Based Mobile Backhaul with SDN Control

Kari Seppänen$^{(\boxtimes)}$, Jorma Kilpi, and Tapio Suihko

VTT Technical Research Centre of Finland, Vuorimiehentie 3, Espoo, Finland
{kari.seppanen,jorma.kilpi,tapio.suihko}@vtt.fi

Abstract. Resilient high capacity and low delay millimeter wave wireless mesh networks (WMNs) can provide suitable backhaul connections for future broadband mobile networks. The WMN solution is best suited in cases where base stations are installed in locations without optical fiber connection to transport network, e.g., small-cell deployment to hot spots in dense urban areas. Recently software defined network (SDN) concept has become popular in many networking areas including mobile networks. One of the key promises is to provide an efficient way for network operators to extend and create new services. As the whole network is controlled by a single central entity that is based on software code, it would be easy to make large scale network upgrades without need to wait that updates are available for all network elements (NEs). There is, however, a clear conflict between SDN ideas and WMN operation. The performance and reliability of the latter one is heavily depended on fast local reactions to, e.g., link degradations. Centralized control would introduce longer delays in reactions. In this paper, we are proposing a concept which solves these problems and allows for combining the best features of both WMN and SDN.

Keywords: Wireless mesh · SDN · Mobile backhaul · Network abstraction · Network virtualization

1 Introduction

Increasing capacity demands in broadband mobile networks call for new solutions especially in dense urban areas. To meet these needs, the traditional macro-cell architecture has to be augmented with small cells that cover the hot-spot areas. One of the major problems in small-cell deployment is the lack of suitable fixed wireline backhaul connections in many potential installation sites. Furthermore, this development can easily lead to multiplication of the number of cells by a factor of 10. This means that the cost of small-cell installation must be brought down as low as possible with, e.g., zero-configuration [1].

Installing new fiber optic network connections for micro cells is very costly in dense urban areas and, in many cases, also very time consuming because of the required planning and official permits. Thus, the use of wireless backhaul connections is a natural choice for these kind of small-cell scenarios. However,

© Institute for Computer Sciences, Social Informatics and Telecommunications Engineering 2015
R. Giaffreda et al. (Eds.): IoT360 2014, Part II, LNICST 151, pp. 222–233, 2015.
DOI: 10.1007/978-3-319-19743-2_32

the capacity requirements for LTE-A and forthcoming 5G are such (≥ 1 Gbit/s per base station) that they are hard to meet with current wireless systems. Millimeter wave (mmW) RF systems (e.g., 60 GHz or 71–88 GHz) can provide ample capacity to meet the requirements.

Using mmW RF technology makes it necessary to apply narrow-beam directed point-to-point links between stations to provide sufficient link budgets for usable link spans. This is actually an advantage as it increases the total system capacity compared to omni-directional transmissions. However, narrow mmW beams are rather vulnerable to disturbances and thus the reliability of an end station with only one point-to-point link could be quite low. The solution for this problem is to have mesh connectivity between end stations (from now on WMN nodes) and gateways. Moreover, using WMN for backhaul connectivity allows for having reliable multihop paths between micro cells and WMN gateways and thus extending the area that can be covered with a single WMN.

Software-defined networking (SDN) consists of techniques that facilitate the provisioning of network services in a deterministic, dynamic, and scalable manner. SDN currently refers to approaches of networking in which the control plane is decoupled from the forwarding functions and assigned to a logically centralized controller. The SDN architecture, with its software programmability, provides agile and automated network configuration and traffic management that is vendor neutral and based on open standards. Network operators are able to dynamically adjust the network's traffic flows to meet the changing needs while optimizing the network resource usage. An OpenFlow-based SDN is formed by switches that forward data packets and communicate with one or more controllers using the OpenFlow protocol. An OpenFlow controller configures the forwarding behavior of the switches by setting packet processing rules in their flow tables. A rule is composed of match criteria and actions. The match criteria are multi-layer traffic classifiers that inspect packet headers and identify the set of packets to which the actions will be applied. The actions may involve modification of the packet and forwarding through a defined output port, for example.

In this paper, we are proposing a concept that will integrate an existing mmW WMN backhaul solution with SDN-based centralized transport network control. The main goals of our concept are to resolve the conflict between local and centralized control as well as to provide "plug-and-play" style incremental network extension. Furthermore, the capability of sharing the network resources among multiple mobile network operators (MNOs) is a very important target.

The structure of the paper is following: in Sect. 2 we provide background information about using WMN to provide backhaul connectivity and about related work in SDN; in the next Sect. 3 we present our solution for controlling a WMN-based backhaul with SDN; in Sect. 4 we discuss about the potential problems we have identified this far; and, finally, Sect. 5 ends this paper with some conclusions.

2   Background

First in this section, we explain some of the most critical requirements that are imposed on WMN by broadband mobile backhaul (MBH) and then we describe the main characteristics of our WMN backhaul concept. Then we will go through some related work about SDN and WMN as well as SDN and mobile networks. Finally, we discuss about the trade-offs between centralized versus local control.

2.1   WMN Based Small-Cell Backhaul

Small-cell backhaul should be seen as a part of the whole mobile network infrastructure and WMN portion as a last mile segment of the backhaul connection [1]. Thus, events in WMN, like failures, can affect the rest of the network by, e.g., triggering handovers between base stations and fixed network side protection switching. This means that, to get best advantages from alternative backup paths that WMN provides, the fault recovery mechanisms at that level should operate, in the most of the cases, faster than "normal" telecom grade protection (50 ms).

There are already some concepts that integrate mmW radio links in backhaul and SDN ideas, e.g., hybrid wireless optical MBH described in [2]. In our concept, we are utilizing a novel mmW WMN MBH system that has been developed in various earlier projects [3,4]. This WMN concept is not limited to repeater (or relay) configurations but it supports meshed multihop paths allowing better coverage and more alternative routes. As a single WMN can be fairly large, multiple gateways to fixed network are also supported.

Packet forwarding in the proposed WMN concept is done at flow level. Flows are identified by inspecting L2 and/or L3 headers, e.g., Ethernet MAC addresses together with VLAN Id and PCP (Priority Code Point), or IP addresses and DSCP (Differentiated Services Code Point) field. Each WMN flow can be assigned to a separate path and these assignments can change dynamically based on network state. In case of congestion or link failure, high priority traffic can get better service while the best effort traffic suffers most of the damage. It is also possible to split one traffic flow to multiple paths as long as the paths end at the same gateway. Due to related processing overheads, this is usually applied only for "fat" non-realtime traffic flows.

2.2   Related Work

The applicability of SDN in carrier networks has been analyzed in [5]. The identified key challenges are performance vs. flexibility, scalability, security, and interoperability (backward compatibility) with existing networking technologies. Our work aims at finding solutions for these challenges in a software-defined WMN-based mobile backhaul.

Especially, in WMNs that are formed of commodity devices, node isolation and network fragmentation may occur frequently, which makes the application of centralized control problematic. To exploit the benefits of SDN while mitigating the drawbacks, [6] proposes to use the combination of a distributed routing protocol (OLSR) and OpenFlow in a Wireless Mesh Software Defined Network (wmSDN). In this solution, OpenFlow is used for balancing traffic load among Internet gateways of the mesh. On the other hand, our WMN system applies autonomous routing, load balancing, fault recovery, and other traffic management functions. Still, the WMN requires coordinated topology management and resource allocation. To that aim, we present the WMN to the SDN controller through an aggregating network abstraction, provided by a "mediator" function that implements a Hardware Abstraction Layer (HAL). The mediator translates between the SDN and WMN's operation models.

In general, a HAL is required to "hybridize" mixed networks, which contain pure legacy and SDN devices, in order to hide the idiosyncrasies of legacy network equipment such that on the outside the equipment looks like one or more SDN switches. The HAL concept [7] proposed by EU FP7 ALIEN project encompasses three types of integration model for different use cases depending on the tightness of the coupling between HAL and the legacy equipment and the multiplicity of devices that the HLA covers. One of the HAL implementations is xDPd (eXtensible OpenFlow DataPath daemon) developed within the ALIEN project.

When the WMN is considered as a legacy network segment partition in a mixed SDN network, the WMN is abstracted as a virtual SDN switch, among the native SDN switches. This is in contrast to the technology migration approaches, like HybNET [8], in which a legacy network is abstracted as a virtual link between the SDN switches.

2.3 Local vs Centralized Control

As explained earlier in this section, current and future mobile backhaul requirements are such that it is of paramount importance to hide all WMN impairments as perfectly as possible. In the best case, the WMN portion of the backhaul connection would be seen as a reliable bit-pipe – with somewhat elastic capacity. To achieve this kind of performance, it is necessary that fault management mechanisms inside WMN react to failures and other events much faster than other fault management mechanisms in the network. In practice, this means just few 10 s of ms time scales. As the delays inside WMN could be something like 1 ms per hop, the only viable way to achieve the required reaction speeds is to use local protection and recovery mechanisms.

One of the common main ideas of SDN is the optimization of the whole network configuration as the network state is (in principle) known by a single centralized control entity. This would make the usage of network resources more efficient and, at the same time, make it possible to utilize simple and cheap network equipment.

The main problem with WMN based backhaul and centralized control is that WMN is potentially very dynamic environment. Moreover, optimizing its operation requires lots of quite specific information from each link as well as detailed system specific understanding. Thus, centralized control for WMN would require transferring a considerable amount of status information and configuration commands between WMN nodes and centralized control entity. Furthermore, the centralized controller would have to, in practice, replicate the WMN control plane to provide the necessary functionality.

All this would cause extra traffic in the network and additional delays to fault protection operations. As the same functions can be handled locally, this is hard to justify. However, centralized control is very attractive alternative for configuring and controlling end-to-end traffic flows and backhaul connections. Thus, it would be quite beneficial if the local and centralized control could be made to live together by utilizing the best features from both.

3 SDN Configurable WMN

Our solution to the problem of integrating WMN MBH with SDN control is to leave the most of the WMN functions as they are in our WMN concept and to use SDN only to configure end-to-end connections. However, SDN controller cannot be allowed to configure routing inside the WMN as that would mess up the fault recovery, load-balancing and other WMN operations — and, *vice versa*, any self-configuration action taken by WMN would confuse the SDN controller. Thus, a key part of the solution is to hide the WMN internal structure and operations from SDN layer.

The WMN backhaul solution proposed in this paper will be a part of larger backhaul system that includes also fixed legacy and SDN transport network portions and covers the whole backhaul connection from base stations to MNO's mobile core network (e.g., EPC). One of the main ideas in this backhaul system is to provide virtualized network slices to multiple operators. While the virtualization concept *per se* is out of scope of this paper, the support for virtualization is included in some of the WMN backhaul features. Most clearly this can be seen in network infrastructure extension procedures (see Sect. 3.2).

3.1 WMN Abstraction

Network (or topology) abstraction is a powerful tool that allows construction of hierarchies in SDN [9]. The main idea is the same as with abstractions in programming in general: to give the programmer an access to information he needs while hiding all the internals from accidental manipulations. This abstraction principle is exactly what we need in hiding WMN operations from SDN controller.

The key elements of our abstraction model are that the whole WMN domain is represented as a single virtual SDN switch and that each WMN node port connected to a micro cell is shown as a separate (virtual) port in that switch (see Fig. 1). This effectively hides all the WMN functionality from the upper layers while it, at the same time, offers full control to configure all traffic flows from and to the micro cell. This abstraction model can also be used to hide the

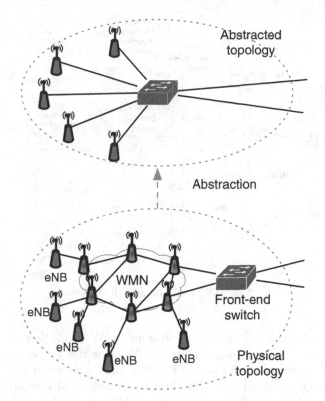

Fig. 1. Hiding physical WMN topology using network abstraction. The SDN controller layer sees only a single switch and base stations seem to be attached directly to it.

existence of multiple WMN gateways (GW) in a single domain and, which is quite useful, hide all such protection mechanisms inside WMN that could cause moving traffic flows from one gateway to another.

Hiding the existence of multiple GWs and traffic flow rerouting from one GW to another requires some extra functionality between WMN and fixed transport network. In our concept, we are using WMN Front-end Switch (WFS) to handle this functionality, i.e., switching the WMN traffic flows so that they appear to originate from a single virtual port. At the control plane, WMN Mediator Function (WMF) takes the responsibility of providing the SDN control interface and interpreting SDN commands given to WFS and translating them into WMN's control operations (see Fig. 2). In practice, the WMN abstraction is done by WMF.

In our WMN system, the traffic flows are, in practice, tunneled between WMN nodes and GWs, and the paths that these tunnels take are changing dynamically (down to ms scale). Even the target GW for a flow can change if necessary. In earlier configurations with legacy networks, the GWs terminated these tunnels and only customer payload was forwarded to fixed network. However, in this abstraction model, we have to hide some peculiarities of WMN from

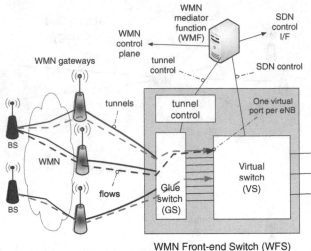

Fig. 2. WMN Front-end switch structure.

the SDN control plane, e.g., flows moved from a GW to another and flows from one base station passing through different GWs. For this purpose, we use additional tunneling between GWs and WFS. The main purpose of this tunneling is to carry information about flow identification (source WMN node) to WFS.

The changes in traffic flow routing over WMN can be detected in two ways: the WMN control plane sends a notification about path reselection to WMF or WFS detects that a traffic flow has moved from one GW-WFS tunnel to another. The latter case can be handled in OpenFlow (OF) like manner: WFS sends the "unknown" packet to WMF that makes the WFS reconfiguration after inspecting the packet header (in this case, tunnel specific header). In our WMN system, downstream and upstream traffic can have separate paths and even via separate GWs. However, in this case, we are forcing each flow to use the same GW in both directions. This allows that also downstream GW change can be triggered by WMN node. Thus, when the change of the GW for the upstream traffic is detected, WFS is reconfigured also to reroute downstream to the same GW. The GWs automatically adapt to this change and the paths for upstream and downstream traffic between GW and WMN node can still be different.

We will also support direct base station to base station connectivity (e.g., for LTE X2 traffic). The idea is, that when the mediator identifies a SDN command that tries to configure a connection between two WMN side ports in WFS, it asks WMN control plane to configure a direct connection inside WMN. Thus, the traffic can take the shortest route instead of being hauled over WFS. However, this causes also some problems with port statistics: it is not sufficient to just return the counters from WFS but we have to merge these values with intra-WMN traffic counters.

Our current design is based on two virtual switch instances inside WFS (as shown in Fig. 2). The Glue switch (GS) is taking care of routing WMN flows between GWs and WFS virtual ports. These virtual ports are, in fact, WMN side ports of the second switch instance, Virtual switch (VS). While it would be possible to create the same functionality using only one switch, this two-switch approach has some clear advantages. In practice, we can use some existing virtual switch as VS, e.g., Open virtual switch (OVS) or Indigo virtual switch (IVS). In such case, WMF can pass most of the OF commands directly to VS and VS has all the required functionality to provide (in this configuration) the abstracted network view for SDN controllers. Furthermore, all effects of the changes in traffic flows in WMN side are limited to GS.

3.2   Incremental Network Infrastructure Extension

In our network extension scenario, a new micro cell is installed to a hot-spot location and after power switch-on, the new micro cell should be brought into active state automatically. The new micro-cell base station can be connected to an existing WMN node or the WMN node can be installed at the same time (as a separate co-located unit or integrated to the cellular base station). In the latter case, WMN self-configuration procedures will first initialize the WMN node, which can then provide transport network connectivity for the micro-cell base station. In any case, the network infrastructure extension should not need any human interaction besides the actual physical installation procedure and powering up the new equipment.

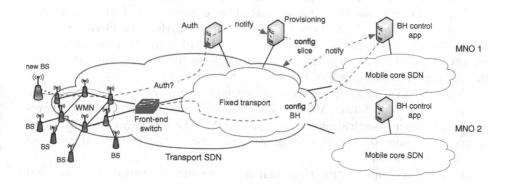

Fig. 3. Infrastructure extension use case.

During the WMN node configuration, the WFS is also configured to facilitate network extension. WMN control plane notifies WMF about the new WMN node and its configuration. Using this information, WMF adds new virtual ports to WFS virtual switch and configures each port so that all micro-cell authentication related messages are forwarded to authentication function ("Auth" in Fig. 3). All other traffic can be dropped by default until further configuration.

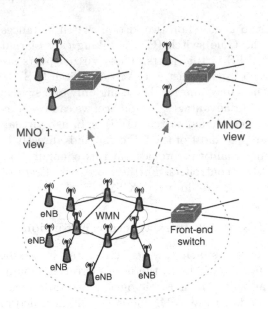

Fig. 4. Virtualized and abstracted network views for MNOs.

When the new micro-cell base station is installed and switched on, it should first try to authenticate itself and get some basic network configuration information. At first phase, authentication packets are received by Transport Network Operator's (TNO's) "Auth" service that identifies the owner of the new base station. If the identification and authorization is successful, TNO's provisioning element will reconfigure network virtualization so that the virtual port, to which the new base station is attached, will be added to the network view of correct MNO. As a result, each MNO should have its own virtualized view to the abstracted WMN (see Fig. 4).

When MNO's network controller is notified about the new port and thus about the new base station, MNO can continue with its own authentication procedures. When authentication has been passed, MNO can activate, e.g., backhaul control application that configures connections between the new base station and mobile core network.

In certain configurations, there can be a site switch owned by MNO and connected to WMN node port. If the site switch is fully transparent, there should be no specific new requirements for the network extension procedure — in MNO's network view, there can be just more than one base station attached to each port. However, if we want to make it possible for MNO to control the site switch as a SDN switch, things get a little bit more complicated. One possibility is that site switch can authenticate itself in the same manner as base stations. Yet this could be quite unrealistic scenario as it is likely that MNOs want to use low cost off-the-shelf equipment. An alternative approach is that one of base stations can detect and configure the site switch. In this case, the site switch should start its operation in transparent mode and change to SDN mode only after MNO's control applications have made the required configurations.

At the moment, we are planning to use FlowVisor (FV) for network virtualization. It should provide sufficient functionality for WMN virtualization but it is still unclear if it can meet the needs of the whole backhaul virtualization.

4 Discussion

There are some issues about reliability in the current WMN abstraction scheme. Only one WFS between WMN and fixed transport network is a clear single point of failure. It is true that failure rates at fixed network side hardware are much lower compared to, e.g., WMN link failures – especially if high-availability equipment is used. However, this situation is not satisfactory if, above all, WMN is used as a part of mobile backhaul network. This problem cannot be solved just by adding a second WFS in parallel as it would break down the WMN abstraction. One possibility is to mimic some kind of MC-LAG (Multi-Chassis Link Aggregation Group) functionality (similar constructions are already used in current network edge realizations) and hide that functionality inside WMN abstraction.

Network virtualization in SDN is quite commonly understood simply as just slicing physical resources (e.g., OpenFlow switches) to provide somewhat isolated network slices for multiple SDN controllers. In this simple virtualization model, all controllers can see the actual physical topology of their network slice. In our concept, the network abstraction hides the actual physical topology and, in this sense, it is not directly compatible with the current "controller should know everything" models. Our ideas of network virtualization are closer to, e.g., ITU-T Y.3011 model of Logically Independent Network Partitions (LINPs) and we are studying if we can steer the development of our backhaul concept more towards that direction [10].

When the WMN is shown as a virtual switch to the MNO, each switchable connection (which is actually a path or even a collection of paths) has some resiliency metric (path availability) due to mesh connectivity and some path E2E delay metric(s) due to predictable link scheduling. Given the routing and the scheduling of the WMN, these metrics have some computable optimal targets and measurable realizations.

One potential problem with our WMN abstraction model is that there is no clear capacity concept inside the WMN. The link throughputs are not the only varying factor as the dynamic path selection is also changing path allocations. Thus, the capacity one flow "sees" might fluctuate all the time. Furthermore, the flows traveling between base station and virtual port seen by SDN control can have separate paths and thus they do not share the same fate. The first problem is with SDN flow configuration: if the MNO wants do capacity reservations, then what capacity value should be given to each virtual port. The second problem is with capacity fluctuations: if MNO tries to optimize SDN flow routing by monitoring flows, it is necessary to quickly identify which impairments are due to WMN (can't do anything) and which ones caused by rest of the MBH.

When two or more MNOs have slice of the same WMN the capacity problem has another dimension: temporarily the capacity of the WMN can be lower than the sum of the slices sold to the MNOs. There should be some business oriented but fair approach to diminish the available capacity of all MNOs.

A possible solution is to define the marketable capacity of the WMN as a function of the (total) available capacity of the gateway(s') links. This means that capacity fluctuations of the gateway links only are taken into account. Capacity fluctuations of all other links are ignored. This information would be readily available at the gateway(s), without signalling delays. As far as the mesh topology assumption holds this approximative approach is actually quite justified, but in real life there will also be non-mesh topologies, e.g., tail sites and ignoring the capacity fluctuations of these unprotected tail links is less justified.

This WMN capacity and network abstraction problem is one thing that we have to study further in the later development phases. At the moment, it is quite difficult to advance with the analysis of these challenges without any hands on experimenting.

5   Conclusions

In this paper, we presented our solution to the problem of how to integrate WMN with SDN in mobile backhaul context. Instead of trying to figure out how to control WMN directly with a centralized SDN controller, we are proposing that network abstraction should be used to hide the whole WMN from the SDN layer. This abstraction means that the SDN controller sees the whole WMN as a single SDN switch that can be controlled normally as any other switch. A key component in our concept is the WMN Front-end switch that allows us to hide also the GW changes from the controller. Another important feature besides network abstraction is the support for incremental network infrastructure extension that is made possible by a combination WMN self-configuration and WMN node client authentication. This feature supports also network virtualization and thus the MBH infrastructure can be shared with multiple MNOs.

We are currently working to demonstrate these functions in our WMN testbed. Moreover, we are continuing to study the open items that are discussed about in the previous section. Therefore, we are looking forward to be able to present the real hands on results from the testbed as well as a more complete concept.

Acknowledgments. This work has been performed in the framework of the CELTIC-Plus project C2012/2-5 SIGMONA. The organisations on the source list would like to acknowledge the contributions of their colleagues to the project, although the views expressed in this contribution are those of the authors and do not necessarily represent the project.

References

1. NGMN Alliance: Small cell backhaul requirements (2012)
2. Bojic, D., Sasaki, E., Cvijetic, N., Wang, T., Kuno, J., Lessmann, J., Schmid, S., Ishii, H., Nakamura, S.: Advanced wireless and optical technologies for small-cell mobile backhaul with dynamic software-defined management. IEEE Commun. Mag. **51**(9), 86–93 (2013)
3. Taipale, T.: Feasibility of wireless mesh for LTE-advanced small cell access backhaul. Master's thesis, Aalto University School of Electrical Engineering (2012). http://lib.tkk.fi/Dipl/2012/urn100686.pdf
4. Wainio, P., Taipale, T.: Wireless mesh access backhaul for small cell base stations. In: Costa-Requena, J. (ed.) Innovative Solutions for Mobile Backhaul, CELTIC/CP7-011 MEVICO (2012). http://www.mevico.org/D32.pdf
5. Sezer, S., Scott-Hayward, S., Chouhan, P.K., Fraser, B., Lake, D., Finnegan, J., Viljoen, N., Miller, M., Rao, N.: Are we ready for SDN? Implementation challenges for software-defined networks. IEEE Commun. Mag. **51**(7), 36–43 (2013)
6. Detti, A., Pisa, C., Salsano, S., Blefari-Melazzi, N.: Wireless mesh software defined networks (wmSDN). In: 2013 IEEE 9th International Conference on Wireless and Mobile Computing, Networking and Communications (WiMob), pp. 89–95, October 2013
7. Report on hardware abstraction models, Deliverable D2.1, EU FP7 Project ALIEN, January 2013. http://www.fp7-alien.eu/files/deliverables/D2.1-ALIEN-updated.pdf
8. Lu, H., Arora, N., Zhang, H., Lumezanu, C., Rhee, J., Jiang, G.: Hybnet: network manager for a hybrid network infrastructure. In: Proceedings of the Industrial Track of the 13th ACM/IFIP/USENIX International Middleware Conference, Middleware Industry 2013, pp. 6:1–6:6. ACM, New York (2013)
9. Monsanto, C., Reich, J., Foster, N., Rexford, J., Walker, D.: Composing software-defined networks. In: Proceedings of NSDI 2013: 10th USENIX Symposium on Networked Systems Design and Implementation (2013)
10. Recommendation ITU-T Y.3011 Framework of network virtualization for future networks (2012)

Energy Impact of Heterogeneous Wireless Networks on Mobile Devices

Pavlos Kosmides[✉], Miltiades Anagnostou, Chara Remoundou, and Dimitris Pagkalos

School of Electrical and Computer Engineering, National Technical University of Athens, Heroon Polytechneiou Str. 9, 15773 Zografou, Athens, Greece
{pkosmidis,miltos,chremoundou,dimpaga}@cn.ntua.gr

Abstract. The last decades are characterized by a rapid development in the area of wireless communications, including both Radio Access Technologies (RATs) and mobile terminals. Mobile terminals are equipped with multiple interfaces, while there is a variety of heterogeneous wireless networks that users can be connected to. However, the continuous switching of interfaces or the adhesion to a single interface, can result in the depletion of a mobile phone's battery. In the current work, we study the problem of energy depletion in smartphones under various access technologies and applications. In particular, a testbed was implemented and real measurements were collected concerning the energy efficiency of different access technologies and different users' applications. The experimental results enlighten the impact of the access network and the mobile applications on the battery life of mobile devices.

Keywords: Heterogeneous wireless networks · Mobile devices · Energy efficiency

1 Introduction

Given the rapid growth of the wireless networks and the trend of mobile users to always seek the "best available connection" (Always Best Connected) [1] the need for provisioning more than one RAT at any single location has raised during the last decades. For example, in a large city like Athens, the population coverage for 3G and 4G is greater than 97 % and 46 % respectively [2], while there are hundreds of access points for connecting to Wi-Fi. On the other hand, recent studies suggest that after seven years since Apple launched the iPhone, creating a new market, the number of smartphones surpassed one billion worldwide and is estimated to double by 2015. More than 89 % of the smartphones that are sold in the market, are used in a daily bases. Smartphones are carrying on average more than 450 Mbytes per month either through cellular networks, such as HSPA, HSPA + , LTE and WiMAX networks or via WLAN.

It is widely known that the battery life of smartphones is one of the major concerns of the users. This is why there are many studies in the literature that concentrate on the optimization of the operation time of mobile phones [3–5]. This work, following the above trend, focuses on the battery life of mobile terminals, by measuring the power

© Institute for Computer Sciences, Social Informatics and Telecommunications Engineering 2015
R. Giaffreda et al. (Eds.): IoT360 2014, Part II, LNICST 151, pp. 234–240, 2015.
DOI: 10.1007/978-3-319-19743-2_33

consumed in a smartphone. Specifically a testbed was implemented and real measurements were collected concerning the power consumption of mobile devices, which were connected to different RATs, serving different user's applications. The mobile devices were equipped with Android OS, and they run an implemented application that measures the consumed power, based on the interface used for the connection.

The rest of this paper is organized as follows. In Sect. 2, we briefly outline the available tools and methods that are used for this study as well as the proposed systems' architecture. In Sect. 3 we present the test scenarios that were followed to retrieve measurements from mobile devices, while in Sect. 4 we present our results. The paper is concluded in Sect. 5.

2 Methods and Tools

As mentioned above, mobile phones market is rapidly developing, while modern smartphones are equipped with multiple interfaces, allowing the connection to different RATs. In addition, users have access to different kinds of technologies regarding wireless technologies, satisfying their need for voice, video and data applications. One of the predominant operating systems is the Android OS.

Androids' architecture is based on conventional versions of the Linux kernel, with many improvements to facilitate inter-process communication (IPS), memory and energy management (see Fig. 1) [6]. Lower layers, connected with the core (hardware), are written in C and C++ and include a large number of open-source libraries such as WebKit, libpng and libsqlite.

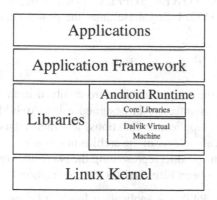

Fig. 1. Androids' architecture.

Android is an open source project and provides a flexible software development kit (SDK), allowing developers to make customizations. Most applications are implemented in Java, while through the provided SDK, developers can have access to core libraries and variables, such as the devices' battery level or the amount of power that is consumed.

As a Linux distribution, Android provides an event mechanism which relies on runtime events generated by the kernel, recording changes on the hardware of the system. These events are handled by the *uevent* daemon [7]. The data that are generated from the *uevent* daemon and are related to power measurements, can be accessed in the */sys/class/power_supply/battery* folder of the users' device. The available events may vary from device to device. A list with the most common available data that are produced from the uevent is presented in Table 1.

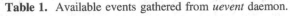

Table 1. Available events gathered from *uevent* daemon.

uevent variables
POWER_SUPPLY_PRESENT
POWER_SUPPLY_NAME
POWER_SUPPLY_STATUS
POWER_SUPPLY_CHARGE_TYPE
POWER_SUPPLY_HEALTH
POWER_SUPPLY_PRESENT
POWER_SYPPLY_ONLINE
POWER_SUPPLY_TECHNOLOGY
POWER_SUPPLY_VOLTAGE_NOW
POWER_SUPPLY_VOLTAGE_AVG
POWER_SUPPLY_CURRENT_NOW

In this paper, we are interested for the power that is consumed when the device is connected to one of the available RATs. From the above list, the events that can extract this information are the POWER_SUPPLY_VOLTAGE_AVG and the POWER_SUPPLY_CURRENT_AVG. Using these data, the power consumption can be computed as follows:

$$Power = Voltage * Current \tag{1}$$

A representation of the testbed architecture involved in the scope of this paper is depicted in Fig. 2. The architecture is designed using ArchiMate® [8] showing the application layer entities (application functions) and their relationship.

As shown, the application layer of the architecture consists of one product related to the mobile device and one product representing the platform. For the mobile device, the following functions have been identified for the application layer:

- *Connect to available RAT:* this application function connects the mobile device to one of the available heterogeneous RATs.
- *Gather information related to RAT:* this application function retrieves the available information regarding the RAT e.g. sim operator, cell id.
- *Gather information related to application:* this application function gathers the available information related to the application that the user is using each time, namely voice, video, data.

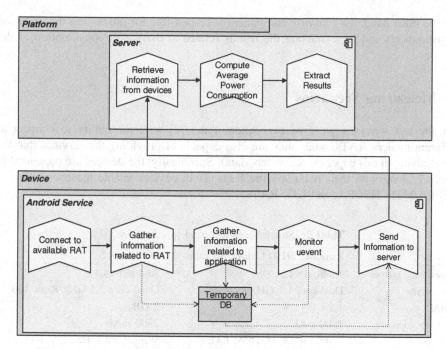

Fig. 2. Testbed's architecture.

- *Monitor uevent:* this application function monitors the uevent daemon and whenever the location of the user, or the cell id, or any variable related to power consumption is changed, it retrieves data for the voltage and the current of the device.
- *Send information to server:* this application function, once the measurements are over, it sends the gathered information to the platform server, in order to be processed.

Similarly, for the platform we recognize the following functions for the application layer:

- *Retrieve information from devices:* this application function retrieves the measurements from the mobile devices.
- *Compute Average Power Consumption:* this application function is responsible for computing the power that was consumed, using the retrieved data from the mobile devices.
- *Extract results:* this application function extracts the final results regarding a mobile device's power consumption, in order to be graphically represented.

The *Android Service* component is running on the background of the Android device, collecting necessary data for the estimation of the power consumption of the device, while it is connected to a RAT, serving one of the available applications (voice, video, data). Once the measurements are taken, they are uploaded to the platform server.

On the other hand, the *Platform* component is responsible for processing the collected measurements and for extracting the results related to the power consumption of the device.

3   Measuring Scenarios

For the test scenarios we used two different devices with the ability to connect to different modern RATs, while they are also capable of providing the services that we are studying in this paper (voice, video, data). Specifically, the devices are presented in Table 2 along with their main specifications. Both devices enable the connection to WiFi, UMTS, HSDPA, and LTE RATs.

Table 2. Smartphones technical specifications.

Device	Samsung I9190 Galaxy S4 mini	LG Nexus 5
Operating system	Android v4.3	Android v4.4
Processor	Dual-core 1.7 GHz Krait	Quad-core 2.3 GHz Krait 400
RAM	1.5 GB	2 GB
Battery capacity	1900 mAh	2300 mAh
Interfaces	WiFi, GPRS, HSDPA, LTE	WiFi, GPRS, HSDPA, LTE

For the RATs that needed outdoors measurements, the test scenarios were taken in a residential area, where the network coverage for all three RATs (UMTS, HSDPA, LTE) was satisfying (see Fig. 3). Test scenarios related to the WiFi technology, were made inside the university campus of the National Technical University of Athens.

Fig. 3. Residential area for test scenarios (GPRS, HSDPA, LTE).

The scenarios for each RAT can be categorized according to the three offered services namely voice, video and data, as described in Table 3. Each category represents a set of services that are provided to users through their mobile devices.

Table 3. Test scenarios.

	Voice	Video	Data
Services	voice call, VoIP	video call, video streaming	FTP, web browsing

4   Results

In this section we present the results obtained from the test scenarios as described above. Figure 4 demonstrates, for the voice scenario, the power that is consumed on a mobile device, when it is connected to one of the available RATs, compared to the RSS integrator (RSSI). Similarly, Figs. 5 and 6 show the results for the video and the data test scenarios respectively.

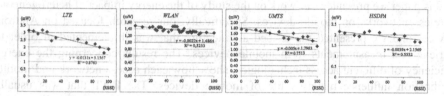

Fig. 4. Power consumption per RAT for voice application.

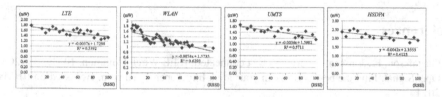

Fig. 5. Power consumption per RAT for video application.

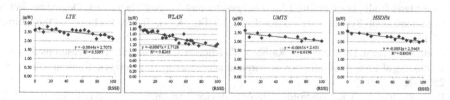

Fig. 6. Power consumption per RAT for data application.

In general, as the signal strength gets higher, the power that is consumed on the mobile device is getting lower. This can be justified because when the signal strength is strong, the mobile device doesn't need to increase the transmit power in order to communicate with the BS. On the other hand, when the signal strength is low, in order to achieve connectivity the mobile device consumes more battery power.

Studying the power consumption per RAT, as we can see for the voice scenario in Fig. 4, LTE consumes more power on the mobile device, while HSDPA, UMTS and WiFi (in descending order) consume less. A similar behaviour can be observed in Fig. 6 for the data scenario but to a lesser extent, where LTE again consumes more power than the other RATs. According to [9] this is well expected since LTE is much less power efficient, and the key contributor is the tail energy, controlled by Ttail.

On the contrary, for the video scenario (Fig. 5) HSDPA is the RAT that gives higher power consumption compared to the other studied RATs. Although LTE was expected to produce higher values, due to the high speed that it provides, data are buffered very quickly resulting to having periods with minimum data transactions.

5 Conclusions

In this paper we presented our work on the study of the energy impact of heterogeneous wireless networks on mobile devices. Specifically, our research focused on Android devices and we presented the testbed architecture that was implemented in order to retrieve real measurements from mobile devices. The results concerning the energy efficiency of different access technologies, show how each access network and mobile application influence battery's life of mobile devices. The RAT that was usually leading to higher power consumption was LTE. However, for services like video streaming, LTE was more power efficient since the required data for the video were buffered in a short time.

References

1. Gustafsson, E., Jonsson, A.: Always best connected. IEEE Wirel. Commun. **10**, 49–55 (2003)
2. OpenSignal, Find the best network in your area. http://opensignal.com. Accessed on 01 May 2014
3. Rasih Celenlioglu, M., Ali Mantar, H.: Location history based energy efficient vertical handover scheme. In: 1st International Symposium in Innovative Technologies in Engineering and Science, pp. 989–998. Akademik Platform, Turkey (2013)
4. José María Rodríguez Castillo, J.M.: Energy-Efficient Vertical Handovers. Degree project in Communication Systems Second level, 30.0 HEC. KTH, Royal Institute of Technology (2013)
5. Gomez, K., Boru, D., Riggio, R., Rasheed, T., Miorandi, D., Granelli, F.: Measurement-based modelling of power consumption at wireless access network gateways. Comput. Netw. **56**, 2506–2521 (2012)
6. Paul, K., Kundu, T.K.: Android on mobile devices: an energy perspective. In: 10th IEEE International Conference on Computer and Information Technology, pp. 2421–2426. IEEE Press, New York (2010)
7. Bandelier, T.: U.S. Patent No. 8,588,851. Washington, DC: U.S. Patent and Trademark Office (2013)
8. ArchiMate® 2.1 Specification. http://pubs.opengroup.org/architecture/archimate2-doc/
9. Huang, J., Qian, F., Gerber, A., Mao, Z.M., Sen, S., Spatscheck, O.: A close examination of performance and power characteristics of 4G LTE networks. In: 10th International Conference on Mobile Systems, Applications, and Services, pp. 225–238, ACM, New York (2012)

An Adaptive Channel Utilization Method with Traffic Balancing for Multi-hop Multi-channel Wireless Backbone Network

Yuzo Taenaka[1]($\boxtimes$) and Kazuya Tsukamoto[2]

[1] Information Technology Center, The University of Tokyo, Tokyo, Japan
taenaka@nc.u-tokyo.ac.jp
[2] Department of Computer Science and Electronics, Kyushu Institute of Technology,
Fukuoka, Japan
tsukamoto@cse.kyutech.ac.jp

Abstract. This chapter presents an effective channel utilization method for a multi-hop wireless backbone network (WBN) constructed with multiple channels. In the previous work, we proposed a novel OpenFlow based management framework for the WBN, which enables access points to handle the unlimited number of channels simultaneously. Since the framework also enables us to easily and programmably use channels for packet forwarding, the utilization of multiple channels can be potentially optimized, thereby maximizing the network capacity of the WBN. However, since the previous work focused on the framework, the effective use of multiple channels was not completely addressed. Therefore, in this chapter, we propose a channel utilization method that balances the amount of traffic among multiple channels to maximize the network capacity. Through the performance evaluation in a real testbed, the proposed method can effectively use all channels in a 3-hop WBN.

Keywords: Effective channel utilization · Multiple channels · Wireless backbone network · Multi-hop communication · OpenFlow · WLAN

1 Introduction

Wireless mesh network (WMN) consists of two sorts of APs: gateway AP (IGW: Internet gateway) providing the Internet reachability to other APs and other APs constructing multi-hop wireless backbone network (WBN) to reach the Internet. Since a WMN can extend its coverage because of the ease of WBN extension, WMNs have been already deployed in wide area (e.g., shopping mall).

The WMN again attracts much attention as the promising large-scale wireless access network for emerging applications such as smart-grid communication, machine-to-machine communication, and mobile data offloading. The amount of traffic in such kind of communication is going to grow drastically along with the penetration of the devices. It is expected that more than 50 billion wireless devices including sensors, smart meters, and smartphones will connect to the

© Institute for Computer Sciences, Social Informatics and Telecommunications Engineering 2015
R. Giaffreda et al. (Eds.): IoT360 2014, Part II, LNICST 151, pp. 241–247, 2015.
DOI: 10.1007/978-3-319-19743-2_34

Internet [1] and CISCO forecasts that the amount of mobile data traffic from such devices is increased by about 11 times between 2013 and 2018 [2]. However, existing WMN always suffers a limited network capacity due to the nature of multi-hop network. Therefore, the network capacity of WBN has to be increased especially on a single route toward the Internet (IGW).

Since the capacity of a single channel is physically limited, the effective use of multiple channels on WBN is absolutely necessary to expand the network capacity. To date, a routing protocol and channel assignment with multiple channels are mainly studied [3–6] but have the limitations on the number of channels APs simultaneously use and on the effective use of multiple channels. The previous work [7] proposed a new WBN, which handles the unlimited number of channels simultaneously. Also, a multi-channel management framework by exploiting OpenFlow was presented. However, since the previous work focused on the framework, the effective use of all available channels is not addressed.

In this chapter, we propose a channel utilization method that dynamically controls traffic on multi-channel WBN. Since our WBN has multiple wireless links with different channels between neighboring APs, the proposed method controls all traffic on WBN to balance traffic volume between all channels at each hop. Finally, the performance of the method is evaluated in a real testbed.

2   Related Work

The way to increase the network capacity is mainly studied by a multi-channel routing protocol with channel assignment [3–6]. Although the use of multiple channels is effective to increase the network capacity, many studies assume an AP with few interfaces (IFs) [6] due to hardware equipment, thereby limiting the increase of the network capacity. Since we actually observed that there are more than three vacant channels in 5 GHz band), the number of channels each AP simultaneously uses should be flexibly increased in accordance with the number of vacant channels.

The studies on the routing basically switch paths (with different channels) based on the routing table. However, these protocols cannot simultaneously use multiple links between two neighboring APs because the routing table contains only a single path (channel) to reach a destination IP address. To effectively utilize multiple channels, packets should be transmitted on different channels even if all packets have a same destination IP address. Thus, a traffic management framework that dynamically changes paths is essential.

IEEE standards of 802.11n/ac can increase the capacity by the channel bonding. The technology mandatory requires that consecutive channels (2, 4, or 8 channels) are vacant. In a real environment, it is difficult to monopolize the use of such channels because there are sometimes multiple but not consecutive vacant channels. Thus, the flexible way of integrating multiple channels is crucial.

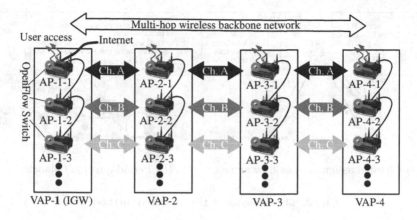

Fig. 1. VAP and WBN with multiple channels.

3   OpenFlow Based Management Framework

This section introduces our OpenFlow based management framework proposed in the previous work [7]. To handle the unlimited number of channels, we first employ a virtual AP (VAP) shown in Fig. 1. A set of APs (sub-APs), each of which uses a single but different channel for the WBN, is connected by Ethernet and then constructs a VAP handling multiple channels. From this architecture, the number of channels can be flexibly increased by adding sub-APs for VAP.

Since an existing technology cannot exhaustively utilize multiple channels, we next employ the OpenFlow technology to programmably control the channel utilization based on *flow* management. A flow is defined by various identifications between layer 1 and 4. In this study, we use 4-tuple (source/destination IP address and port number) as the flow identification.

OpenFlow consists of a controller (OFC) and switches (OFS). An OFC determines control rules of flows called *flow entries* (a pair of flow identification and action) and registers them to OFSs. An OFS controls each flow by following the registered rules. The registration is conducted when the OFS initially connects with an OFC and/or when the OFS receives unknown packets (i.e., the packet does not match any flow entries) and reports it to the OFC (called *packet_in*). We assume that an OFS is installed in all APs in this study. Also, an OFC is connected to all OFSs directly by Ethernet to avoid the effect on the control traffic. Note that, since our focus is to increase the network capacity on a single route to an IGW, we assume a WBN with a chain topology such as Fig. 1.

4   Adaptive Channel Utilization Method

Although the framework enables us to programmably guide packets through multiple channels, the way of maximizing the network capacity is still necessary. In the previous work [8], we implemented two channel utilization methods

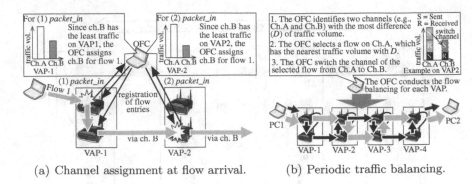

(a) Channel assignment at flow arrival.   (b) Periodic traffic balancing.

Fig. 2. The behavior of the proposed method.

that multiplex conventional WBNs. In both methods, the OFC allocates either channel in the arrival order of *packet_in*. The methods are different in multi-hop relay manners: each flow is transmitted on a persistent channel (BCA-PC), while being transmitted on a different channel for each hop (BCA-DC). However, the capacity of all channels cannot be fully consumed when a data rate of each flow is different. That is, because a channel is selected for each flow in the fixed order, a channel allocated for a flow with large data rate may be congested but will be allocated for a new flow even if the other channels are still underutilized.

To solve the problem, we propose a method that adaptably balances the traffic amount of all channels. Since the OFC guides each flows depending on its traffic volume from the aspect of traffic balancing on all channels, the whole capacity can be exhaustively consumed, thereby maximizing the network capacity. The procedures of our proposed method are described in following sections.

4.1 Arrival of a New Flow

All OFSs initially have no flow entries and thus must report *packet_in* at every arrival of new flow. Also, an OFC periodically collects the total amount of transmitted/received byte (traffic) for each channels of individual VAP based on a PortStats request/reply exchange at certain interval (*MonInt*). Since the Port-Stats indicates the cumulative traffic volume, we use the difference between two consecutive results of the PortStats transmitted for short interval (*StatsInt*).

When a new flow arrives at a VAP (Fig. 2(a)), the VAP sends *packet_in* to the OFC. The OFC determines the identification of the flow based on 4-tuple and selects a channel with the least amount of traffic. After the OFC registers the corresponding flow entries to the OFS(s) in the VAP, the VAP starts to forward packets of the flow through the selected channel. The next hop VAP also sends *packet_in* to the OFC when receiving a packet of the flow and then the OFC selects a channel in the same manner. In this way, the OFC guides packets of the flow through the channel with the least traffic volume at each hop. Note that, if the traffic volume on all channels is same (or there are no flows), the OFC selects a channel used by the first sub-AP.

Table 1. Throughput (Mbps).

	Maximum	Median	Minimum	Average
Conventional WBN (1ch)	9.54	9.48	9.40	9.48
BCA-PC (2ch)	11.47	11.35	11.28	11.36
BCA-DC (2ch)	15.82	15.76	15.65	15.74
Proposed method (2ch)	19.00	18.87	18.75	18.88

4.2 Periodic Traffic Balancing

To keep balancing the traffic volume on all channels, the OFC periodically checks the difference of traffic volume on all channels for each VAP (Fig. 2(b)). This check is periodically performed at the interval of *MonInt* as well as the periodic PortStats.

At the check for each VAP, the OFC identifies two channels (OFSs) whose difference of the traffic volume is the largest (this difference is referred as D). Then, the OFC collects the traffic volume of every flow on the OFS treating more traffic by exploiting a FlowStats request/reply exchange. Since the Flow-Stats provides the cumulative number, we use the difference of two consecutive results of the FlowStats transmitted for *MonInt* as a traffic volume of flow. The OFC next selects a flow that has the nearest traffic volume with $\frac{D}{2}$ and switches channels of the selected flow to the channel carrying the minimum traffic volume. In the same way, the OFC periodically balances traffic volume on multiple channels on all VAP, thereby utilizing the network capacity efficiently.

5 Performance Evaluation

5.1 Experimental Setup

We implement the proposed method on the OFC (Trema) and then conduct its performance evaluation. In the implementation, *MonInt* is configured to 1 s and *StatsInt* is 500 ms. We employ Buffalo WZR-HP-AG300H as a sub-AP and install OpenWrt firmware with Open vSwitch (version 2.1.0) to it. The OFC connects to OFSs by Ethernet. We also use the same topology (3-hop and 2 channels WBN) with Fig. 2(b) and place sub-APs to 0.7 m apart from each other. They operate IEEE802.11a with two channels of 40 and 48. Two PCs (PC1 and PC2) are connected to VAP1 and VAP4 directly by Ethernet.

5.2 Evaluation Result

In this experiment, PC1 transmits multiple flows to PC2 but their data rate is imbalanced each other. That is, PC1 transmits a flow of 1 Mbps UDP and a flow of 0.1 Mbps UDP at 5 s interval for 18 times (e.g., 1 Mbps, 0.1 Mbps, 1 Mbps,

0.1 Mbps ... totally, 19.8 Mbps), alternately. We then measure the network capacity by the total throughput received at PC2. The throughput is averaged for 30 s after 5 s since the transmission of all flows is started.

We here compare the proposed method with three comparative methods: a conventional WBN and our previous proposals (BCA-PC and BCA-DC) [8]. The conventional WBN uses a single channel but other methods use 2 channels simultaneously. The experiment is conducted for 9 times and the summary of the results is shown in Table 1. From Table 1, the conventional WBN can carry around 9.5 Mbps traffic, which is considered as the maximum capacity with 3-hop WBN with a single channel. Although BCA-PC/DC can use 2 channels simultaneously, the throughput is not double of the conventional WBN. Because both BCA-PC/DC allocate a channel in order of *packet_in* arrival, all 1-Mbps flows (totally, 18 Mbps) are concentrated on one specific channel so that the network capacity is inherently overloaded. As a result, the total throughput is saturated. BCA-DC switches channels at each hop to avoid the congestion but its improvement is limited. The proposed method brings almost the double of the conventional WBN. Therefore, the traffic balancing brought by our proposed scheme is effective to utilize the network capacity of all channels.

6   Conclusions

In this chapter, we proposed an OpenFlow based channel utilization method that adaptably allocates a channel for each flow to balance the amount of traffic transmitted on each channel. We implemented the method and evaluated its performance in a real testbed. Through the comparison with other methods, we can conclude that the proposed method can bring the largest network capacity even if the data rate of each flow is imbalance. For the next study, we will extend the method to control the dynamic traffic like TCP.

Acknowledgments. This work was partly supported by the Japan Society for the Promotion of Science, Grant-in-Aid for Scientific Research (C)(No. 24500075).

References

1. OECD. Machine-to-machine communications: connecting billions of devices. OECD Digital Economy Papers, No. 45, January 2012
2. Cisco Visual Networking Index. Global Mobile Data Traffic Forecast Update (2013–2018)
3. Pathak, P.H., Dutta, R.: A survey of network design problems and joint design approaches in wireless mesh networks. IEEE Commun. Surv. Tutor. **13**(3), 396–428 (2011)
4. Benyamina, D., et al.: Wireless mesh networks design - a survey. IEEE Commun. Surv. Tutor. **14**(2), 299–310 (2012)
5. Alotaibi, E., Mukherjee, B.: A survey on routing algorithms for wireless Ad-Hoc and mesh networks. Comput. Netw. **56**(2), 940–965 (2012)

6. Si, W., et al.: An overview of channel assignment methods for multi-radio multi-channel wireless mesh networks. J. Parallel Distrib. Comput. **70**(5), 505–524 (2010)
7. Taenaka, Y., Tsukamoto, K.: An efficient traffic management framework for multi-channel wireless backbone networks. IEICE Commun. Express **3**(3), 98–103 (2014)
8. Tagawa, M., et al.: Network capacity expansion methods based on efficient channel utilization for multi-channel wireless backbone network. In: Proceedings of the 2014 International Workshop on Smart Complex Engineered Networks (SCENE), August 2014

Toward Active Charging for Software Defined Wireless Networks

Brian Lee$^{(\boxtimes)}$, Yuansong Qiao, and Niall Murray

Athlone Institute of Technology, Athlone, Ireland
blee@ait.ie, {ysqiao,nmurray}@research.ait.ie

Abstract. A programmable networking approach to charging for services in software defined wireless networks (SDWN) could greatly facilitate the service innovation that is anticipated therein. It would allow service differentiation through customized charging and would support the provision of composite services across multiple providers. In this position paper we consider how earlier approaches to active charging can be combined with the 3GPP charging framework and recent SDN inspired cellular architectural innovations to provide an active charging infrastructure for SDN. Our analysis shows that active charging in SDN is technically feasible, commercially beneficial and incrementally deployable.

1 Introduction

Software defined networking (SDN) has been one of the principal trends in networking in recent years. SDN facilitates network programmability i.e. the ability to dynamically load software programs into network nodes in order to implement new features or modify existing capabilities. The combination of network programming and network virtualisation– including network function virtualisation (NFV)– promises of great service innovation. Service providers' will spin up virtual networks on demand to provide new end-to-end services. Network service providers also will have opportunities to quickly create new services through the convergence of network and cloud computing. Programmability will enhance collaboration between network providers and OTT service providers to provision loosely coupled composite services combining network and OTT services. Flexible service composition will require equally flexible charging support in the network service providers operation and business support systems (OSS/BSS) as e.g. in the recent the suggestion to allow content providers to cover usage charges for mobile subscribers, [1]. Service providers will seek to provide tailored billing perhaps even on a subscriber level.

It is our contention that programmable networking can greatly facilitate the provision of flexible charging schemes for both composite services and virtual network based value added services. Current charging systems are not however geared to meet these challenges, not least of which because they assume a very network operator centric view of the world. However the idea of a programmable/active networking charging infrastructure is not an unobtainable vision. Rather, the combination of recent SDN inspired cellular architecture proposals [1], active charging proposals, [16, 17]

© Institute for Computer Sciences, Social Informatics and Telecommunications Engineering 2015
R. Giaffreda et al. (Eds.): IoT360 2014, Part II, LNICST 151, pp. 248–253, 2015.
DOI: 10.1007/978-3-319-19743-2_35

and current charging systems, [6, 7], provides a firm base for development of such a charging infrastructure - how to do so is the subject of the remainder of the paper.

A novel proposal (SoftCell) to re-architect the cellular core network architecture based on use of SDN principles is outlined in [1]. The key thrust of this proposal is that *"The network should consist of a fabric of simple core switches, with most functionality moved to low-bandwidth access switches (at the base stations) and a distributed set of middleboxes that the carrier can expand as needed to meet the demands, A logically-centralized controller can then route traffic through the appropriate middle-boxes, via efficient network paths, to realize a high-level service policy"*. A "high level service policy" is based on subscriber and application attributes including network provider, device type, subscriber type etc. Another suggested extension is to provide 'local software agents' in the switches to perform simple actions such as polling counters and comparing against thresholds. This re-architecting will help provide for more fine-grained and real-time monitoring and accounting. The capability to provide flexible high-level policies will also allow for a more active and flexible approach to charge calculations. Another factor that motivates our approach is the potential to place policy agents on mobile devices for applications such as mobility control [3], or charging based on dynamic pricing [2].

The rest of this paper is structured as follows: Sect. 2 describes current network charging concepts– in particular those for 3GPP. It also outlines previous research efforts addressing charging for composite services. Section 3 describes prior research on active charging while Sect. 4 combines these different threads to show how an active charging infrastructure can be derived for SDN based wireless network. Finally Sect. 5 outlines our conclusions.

2 Charging Concepts

A definition of charging is given in the 3GPP standards, [8] as the *"function ....whereby information related to a chargeable event is collected, formatted, transferred and evaluated in order to make it possible to determine usage for which the charged party may be billed"*.

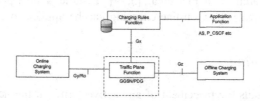

Fig. 1. 3GPP Charging Architecture

Figure 1 above (from [4]) depicts the (flow-based) 3GPP charging architecture (including the interface types of which specific details can be found in [7])

The Traffic Plane Function (TPF) monitors the usage of resources under its control and generates charging (or accounting) information when a chargeable event occurs.. Processing of the consequent charging event to yield a cost for resource usage may take-place in online or offline modes. In the online case charging takes places in real-time. The TPF must check with the Online Charging System (OCS) before allowing resource usage. The OCF is the central function and coordinates the overall charging process. Typically it assigns an initial quota for resource usage in the CTF and initiates re-authorisation to extend the session if needed.

Flow based charging is an extension of the charging system to enable service specific charging on the bearer i.e. flow level. It is realised by a combination of the TPF, the Charging Rules Function (CRF) and the Application Function (AF) [7]. The CRF decides which rules to apply based on resource information from the TPF and session and media information received from the AF. The TPF is configured based on policies called charging rules which are contained in the CRF. i.e. the CRF installs filters on the TPF to enable it to identify the service session flows. The AF provides the services for which flow based charging occurs.

The flow-based charging physical architecture has changed evolved over time. In the first evolution charging control and resource policy control (gating and QoS control) have been combined into the Policy and Charging Control (PCC) functions. The TPF has evolved to become a Policy and Charging Enforcement Function (PCEF) and the CRF has evolved to become the Policy and Charging Rules Function (PCRF). Since Release [11, 7], the Traffic Detection Function (TDF) has been introduced to apply policy and charging for "over the top" (OTT) services i.e. Internet services which are not provided by an AF e.g. Skype or Netflix. The TDF is essentially a deep packet inspection network element and may be implemented stand-alone or integrated with a PCEF.

In the *composite service* delivery model service components may be provided by different service providers and the (composite) end-user service is provided by a federation of different service providers with one provider acting as an overall service aggregator or broker. Charging for such services is complicated by the need to coordinate charging across different providers, to correlate charging identifiers and to consider context based charging i.e. the tariff to be applied for a component may depend on the components/service provider it is used with to provide the overall service.. Most researchers in this area, [5, 9], assume a post-paid charging while Van Le, [10] investigates how on-line charging can be applied to composite services.

3 Active Charging

Active charging entails the placement of an "active tariff" in the network to calculate the cost in real time. This contrast to the 3GPP case where policy based accounting is employed to monitor resource usage.

One approach to active charging based on "active tariffs" is described in [11], which proposed to push all accounting and charging onto end-user hosts, Charging is on a per packet basis and tariffs, which are Java objects, are disseminated to end-users via multicast, where each multicast group corresponds to a network service. The provider can access the users machines remotely and generate billing reports at a range of temporal frequencies. The system can be used for dynamic pricing where prices are matched to network state– see also [2].

In [12] the author describes a real-time charging approach based on a combination of active networking and policy management. The work describes (i) a charging functional reference model and (ii) a programming language (APPLE) for the definition of charging programs and policies and (iii) and an runtime execution environment (PEACH) to enable charging program execution. PEACH is focused on charging only i.e. it assumes accounting functions exist already. The APPLE language enables both the definition of (passive) charging schemes and tariffs via a *Rule* construct as well event-driven active rating logic via a *Module* construct. The reference model describes interaction between the traffic session agent and a related charging session agent function (CSA), which in turn is comprised of a number of sub-functions. The *charge analysis function* (CAF) is a policy server and contains the policies to determine how charging should be handled for a particular service. The *charge session coordinator* (CCP) is stateful and event driven and coordinates the charging for particular service session. The *charge execution point* (CEP) carries out the actual charging for a particular service i.e. executes an active tariff to calculate the charges for a session. The CEP periodically outputs the calculated charges towards a *charge accumulation point* (CAP).

PEACH in fact supports runtime mobility of modules between nodes which would enable a charging session to follow the end-user or enable migration of the session state to/from an end-user terminal. PEACH is intended to be a flexible framework to support arbitrary service models and hence may be deployed in many configurations e.g. for a particular service there could be a number of CEP or the CSA could be duplicated across multiple service providers. It can quite easily support the requirements for flexible, customizable charging schemes and loosely coupled composite OTT service charging as described in the opening chapter through allowing embedding of OTT service provider charging logic inside the service provider network– unlike the composite charging systems described in the previous chapter which all assume a tightly coupled composite charging tree rooted at a service broker/aggregator.

4   Application to SDN

The extensive use of policy based approaches in SDN, [8], taken together with the cellular architecture in [1] suggest a synergistic overlap of SDN and LTE to evolve current systems towards active charging.

In the first phase SDN can move toward a 'policy based accounting' architecture based on the functional changes suggested in [1]. New functions on the controller include the ability to specify flexible policies based on subscriber attributes -including e.g. network provider, subscriber type etc.– and a subscriber information base that stores and maintains subscriber information. The switches in turn also contains new functions such as a local 'software agent' that performs limited local computation - such as counter thresholding– deep packet inspection (DPI) and header compression.

It is possible to frame these proposals in a 3GPP charging architecture context. The new high level policy module may be seen as 'porting' the PCRF to an SDN controller. The associated subscriber information base corresponds, in part at least, to the 3GPP Subscriber Profile Repository (SPR). The proposed switch changes support the inclusion of the Traffic Plane Function (TPF) in the switches. The net effect of these changes is to introduce distributed policy based accounting to SDN. (Although described in the context of cellular i.e. LTE networks these innovations may have of course a broader application in other SDN domains also.) Exactly how these new controller charging modules would interact with each other and other controller modules is an open question as is exactly which functions would be controller based or external applications that interact with the controller over a north bound interface.

One can extrapolate this distributed accounting approach to envisage the placement of TPF functionality on the mobile device itself. By and large the technologies to do so are present today already – certainly the mobile devices contain the required computational and software capabilities.

A starting point in toward active charging is to consider the overlap of the PEACH active charging reference model on the proposed phase one accounting architecture just discussed. The PEACH charge analysis point (CAP) corresponds to the rating function of the OCS. The charge coordination (CCP) corresponds to the online charging function (OCF) OCS component. It is clearly a network level function and thus can be seen as an SDN controller module. The charge execution (CEP) on the other hand is intended to be distributed to the network elements in a manner as envisaged by the switch local agents - the inclusion of DPI in the switches providing extra support also. Following the argument above the CEP could also be migrated to mobile devices as well. However the CEP is foreseen to be an active charging element i.e. the CEP is a computer program and requires an execution environment. In the PEACH architecture the CEP effectively executes a rating rule and calculates a charge which it outputs towards a charge accumulation point (CAP). This is in contrast to the 3GPP approach which maps the rating into a resource usage threshold which is then monitored. From a programming model and distribution perspective PEACH and 3GPP policy and charging are towards opposite ends of the spectrum and SoftCell provides an important architectural bridging step on the road toward active charging. We can also anticipate that some programming model aspects of both approaches will appear in an evolved active charging environment e.g. PEACH may adopts the 3GPP resource limit approach rather than compute the charge on each event. There are of course many challenges and open questions to be answered to design and deploy such a system. These include (but are not limited to):

- *Detailed architecture design*: - Much more work is needed to understand charging requirements– both functional and non functional in order to decide the optimal design and placement of active charging logic.
- *Effects of NFV:* - NFV can certainly be considered as an enabler for active charging-exactly how remains to be investigated.
- *Programming models and execution environments*: Languages such as Frenetic and Pyretic, [8], support formulating policies in subscriber relevant terms rather than

lower level network. More work is required to understand the charging needs in order to see if current solutions suffice or if totally new approaches are needed.

5 Conclusion

We have described active charging approach for SDN which is based on a combination of a proposed SDN based cellular network core architecture, 3GPP online charging and a previous active charging proposal. We have shown how an active charging infrastructure can be incrementally deployed and have illustrated service scenarios which can benefit from active charging.

References

1. Jin, X., Li, L.E., Vanbever, L., Rexford, J.: Softcell: scalable and flexible cellular core network architecture. In: Proceedings of the ninth ACM Conference on Emerging Networking Experiments and Technologies (CoNEXT 2013) (2013)
2. Sangtae, H. et al.: TUBE: time-dependent pricing for mobile data. In: Proceedings of the ACM SIGCOMM 2012 Conference on Applications, Technologies, Architectures, and Protocols for Computer Communication (2012)
3. Singh, J., Bacon, J.:S BUS: a generic policy-enforcing middleware for open pervasive systems. Technical report UCAM-CL-TR-847, University of Cambridge, February 2014. http://128.232.0.20/techreports/UCAM-CL-TR-847.pdf
4. Kuhne, R., Huitema, G., Carle, G.: Charging and billing in modern communication networks – a comprehensive survey of the state of the art and future requirements. IEEE Commun. Surv. Tutors. **14**(1), 170–192 (2012). First Quarter
5. Grgic, T., Matijasevic, M.: An overview of online charging in 3GPP: new ways of utilizing user, network and service related information. Int. J. Net. Manage. **00**, 1–24 (2012)
6. 3GPPTS32.240: Telecommunication management; Charging management; Charging architecture and principles
7. 3GPP TS 23.203: Policy and charging control architecture (Release 11), Februay 2014
8. Monsato, C. et al.: Composing software-defined networks. In: USENIX NSDI (2013)
9. Jennings, B.,Malone, P.: Flexible charging for multi-provider composed services using a federated two-phase rating process. In: Network Operations and Management Symposium, NOMS (2006)
10. van Le, M., Huitema, G.B., Rumph, F.J., Nieuwenhuis, L.J.M., van Beijnum, B.J.F.: Design of an online charging system to support IMS-based inter-domain composite services. In: Pfeifer, T., Bellavista, P. (eds.) MMNS 2009. LNCS, vol. 5842, pp. 1–14. Springer, Heidelberg (2009)
11. Briscoe, B., et al.: Lightweight policing and charging for packet networks. In: Proceedings 3rd IEEE Conference on Open Architectures and Network Programming, OPENARCH 2000, Israel (2000)
12. Lee, B., O'Mahony, D.: Policy based charging in multimedia networks. In: Royo, J.D., Hasegawa, G. (eds.) 8th International Conference on Management of Multimedia Networks and Services. LNCS, vol. 3754, pp. 145–155. Springer, Heidelberg (2005)

Optimal Backhaul Resource Management in Wireless-Optical Converged Networks

Ioannis Loumiotis[✉], Evgenia Adamopoulou, Konstantinos Demestichas, and Michael Theologou

National Technical University of Athens, Athens, Greece
i_loumiotis@cn.ntua.gr

Abstract. The introduction of the new 4G technologies promises to satisfy the increasing demands of the end-users for bandwidth consuming applications. However, the high data rates provided by 4G networks at the air interface raise the need for more efficient management of the backhaul resources. In the current work, the authors study the problem of the efficient management of the backhaul resources at the side of the base station. Specifically, a novel scheme is proposed that, initially, predicts the forthcoming demand using artificial neural networks and, then, based on the prediction results, it proactively requests the commitment of the appropriate resources using linear optimisation techniques. The experimental results show that the proposed scheme can efficiently and cost-effectively manage the backhaul resources, outperforming the traditional flat commitment approaches.

Keywords: Resource management · Backhaul network · Artificial neural networks

1 Introduction

During the last few years there has been a tremendous growth of bandwidth consuming mobile applications [1], resulting in an increasing demand for higher data rates at the access network. The introduction of the new 4G technologies promises to address this demand by offering increased capacity and extremely high data rates to the end-users. Towards this direction, the integration of the wireless access network with a passive optical network (PON) at the backhaul has been proposed. The high capacity of the PON can satisfy the increasing demand at the access network and provide Quality of Service (QoS) to the end-users. However, there are open issues in the proposed convergence regarding the allocation of the backhaul resources to the base stations (BSs).

Traditionally, network planning has been performed statically and it has been based on empirical methods, which led to a fixed, flat commitment of the resources. Though this method yielded satisfactory results in the previous communication standards, it cannot be implemented within a converged optical-wireless network, especially if the PON belongs to a different operator. As a result, the necessary resources should be calculated and committed dynamically to each BS.

© Institute for Computer Sciences, Social Informatics and Telecommunications Engineering 2015
R. Giaffreda et al. (Eds.): IoT360 2014, Part II, LNICST 151, pp. 254–261, 2015.
DOI: 10.1007/978-3-319-19743-2_36

The problem of backhaul resource management has been widely studied in the literature. However, the majority of these works, e.g. [2], investigate on the backhaul resource allocation problem only at the air interface and they cannot be implemented within a converged network. There are only a few studies in the literature that consider the resource allocation problem in a converged network architecture. In [3], the authors propose a resource allocation mechanism for a converged network infrastructure that improves the QoS performance, based on the forecasting of near future packet arrivals.

In the current work, the authors propose a novel algorithm for the optimal management of the backhaul resources that can provide QoS to the subscribers, while minimising the operational expenditure (OpEx) of the mobile operator (MO). The proposed scheme can be used in conjunction with software defined solutions in order to provide the appropriate resources to a Software-Defined network controller as proposed in [4]. Specifically, the algorithm consists of two phases. In the first phase, the BS predicts the forthcoming demand based on the collected historical data, using artificial neural networks (ANNs), and in the second phase, it requests the commitment of the appropriate information rates (IRs) from the PON operator. Specifically, in the second phase, a linear programming problem is formulated, based on the prediction results, that allows the BS to minimise the leasing cost (OpEx), while guaranteeing the QoS provisioning to its customers. Finally, for the validation of the proposed scheme, the authors use real data collected by fully operational BSs.

2   Backhaul Resource Management

The deployment and the configuration of the backhaul network is an issue that concerns only the MO. However, the Next Generation Mobile Networks (NGMN) Alliance has defined a set of high-level backhaul requirements in order to support the requirements of 4G networks and beyond. According to the NGMN Alliance, the backhaul network should provide a peak information rate (PIR) and a committed (average) information rate (CIR) in a flexible and granular way. Specifically, it is recommended that the CIR and PIR should be configurable in increments of 2 Mbps between rates of 2–30 Mbps, 10 Mbps between rates of 30–100 Mbps and 100 Mbps for rates beyond 100 Mbps, offering a "pay as you grow" model [5].

On the other hand, the PON itself provides the necessary mechanism for dynamic bandwidth allocation (DBA). In the downstream direction, it is the responsibility of the optical line terminal (OLT) to provide QoS-aware traffic management based on the respective service specifications and the dynamic traffic conditions. On the other hand, for the upstream direction, each queue in the optical network unit (ONU) can be provided with three different information rates; a fixed information rate (FIR), an assured information rate (AIR) and a maximum information rate (MIR). The part of the bandwidth above the AIR may be either non-assured or best-effort with the latter experiencing the lowest priority. It is noted that according to the G.984.3 standard, the sum of the FIR and the AIR should be typically equal to the CIR, while the MIR should not be higher than the PIR of the BS [6].

Therefore, in the context of an optical-wireless converged infrastructure, the BS should request the commitment of the appropriate IRs by the PON operator. These IRs can be variable with respect to time based on the BS's needs, and should be defined in a formal agreement between the two parties, called service level agreement (SLA). In the rest of the paper, it is considered that the BS requests for a FIR, an AIR and a non-assured IR in order to satisfy its subscribers' demands.

3   Intelligent Base Station

The efficient management of the backhaul resources requires BSs with enhanced processing capabilities. In the current approach, the authors consider the deployment of appropriate agents that offer to the BSs the necessary intelligence, as it can be seen in Fig. 1. Specifically, these intelligent agents are located at the side of the BSs and should be enhanced with processing capabilities that allow them to monitor, store and process the traffic demand statistics. Based on the collected data, the intelligent agents should be able to learn the traffic pattern and predict the forthcoming demand. To this end, the agents employ ANN schemes that can accurately predict the network traffic. The accurate prediction will allow the intelligent agent to proactively request the appropriate resources from the PON operator, exploiting the DBA mechanism described above and ensuring the QoS provisioning to its customers in an efficient and cost-effective way.

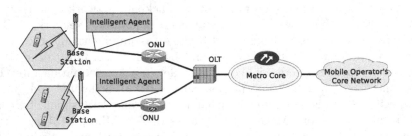

Fig. 1. Proposed network architecture.

4   Measurements and Traffic Characteristics

A key feature for the accurate prediction of network traffic is the identification of its inherent characteristics. There are many works in the literature which argue that network traffic has non-linear characteristics, and as a result, traditional methods of linear regression analysis cannot be efficiently implemented [7]. In order to identify the special characteristics of the traffic pattern, the authors use a set of 2464 data[1] collected by a fully operational BS located in the centre of Athens, capital of Greece. The collected data are hourly averaged measurements and refer to a period of 4 months. The BS provides High Speed Packet Access+ (HSPA+) connectivity and serves an area of 9 cells, providing 42 Mbps for the downlink case and 5.8 Mbps for the uplink case at each cell site. It is noted that a traditional resource allocation scheme would require the flat commitment of the resources by the MO, i.e. a bandwidth of 378 Mbps for the downlink case and 52.2 Mbps for the uplink case.

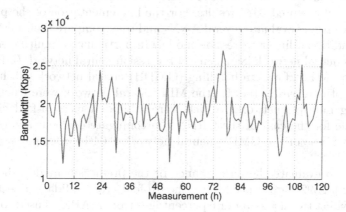

Fig. 2. Downlink traffic demand.

It is expected that the traffic pattern of the BS will experience certain periodicities due to the habitual behaviour of the users. As can be seen in Fig. 2, the traffic pattern experiences a peak during the rush hours in the morning and in the evening, while the demand is reduced during the night. As a result, the set of inputs for the ANN consists mainly of the day and time in which the measurements were collected and the output is the hourly-based averaged bandwidth demand. Assuming that $\mathbf{x}$ is a vector variable that denotes the input of the ANN and y is a scalar variable that denotes the output of the ANN, i.e. the estimated bandwidth, it holds that

$$\mathbf{x} = (day, month, date, hour, event) \tag{1}$$

where day is the specific day of the measurement (e.g. Monday), $month$ is the month of the collected measurement, $date$ is the sequence number of the day (e.g. 25), $hour$ is the hour of the day and $event$ is a binary variable that designates a holiday, which can potentially have an influence on the prediction process.

---

[1] The collected data are the aggregated demand experienced by the BS and correspond to a mixture of services requested by the subscribers.

5   Proposed Algorithm

The proposed algorithm consist of two phases. In the first phase the agent uses an ANN in order to predict the forthcoming demand and in the second phase, based on the prediction results, it calculates the appropriate IRs and requests their commitment from the PON operator.

5.1   Prediction Phase

It can be easily understood that the efficiency of the proposed scheme depends on the accuracy of the prediction results. For the implementation of the prediction process, the authors evaluate several ANNs and they compare their performance with the traditional linear regression model. In particular, a multilayer perceptron (MLP) neural network [8], a general regression neural network (GRNN) [9], and a group method for data handling (GMDH) neural network [10] have been used. The optimal parameters for the MLP neural network were calculated by constructing multiple networks, which were evaluated using 4-fold cross validation, while for the case of the GRNN the conjugate gradient algorithm was used. For the case of the GMDH neural network a 64th order polynomial was constructed.

In order to evaluate the performance of the prediction model, the authors used the first 2392 data. Specifically, the 10-fold cross validation technique is employed, whilst the mean absolute percentage error (MAPE) is used to compare the performance of the different models. The results are depicted in Table 1.

Table 1. Results of the validation process.

Prediction method	Downlink MAPE	Uplink MAPE
MLP	12.034	20.354
GMDH	11.561	18.786
GRNN	10.422	15.229
Linear regression	13.1068	20.793

It can be easily seen that the GRNN outperforms the other types of ANNs providing a MAPE of 10.42 % for the downlink case and 15.22 % for the uplink case. Based on these results, and the capability of GRNN networks to handle sparse data in real-time environments [9], it can be concluded that they constitute an ideal choice for the implementation of the prediction process.

Furthermore, it should be noted that the uplink traffic experiences a higher MAPE than the downlink traffic for all the above models. Hence, it becomes apparent that the uplink traffic is more difficult to be accurately predicted. This inefficiency lies in the fact that the subscribers of the BS contribute mainly to the downlink traffic, averaging the aggregated demand, and thus, the throughput experiences less variability [11]. On the other hand, only a few users have a notable contribution to the uplink traffic (the average uplink traffic is 1.5 Mbps), which experiences significant variations that constitute its prediction more challenging.

5.2   Resource Request Phase

In the resource request phase of the algorithm, the intelligent agent performs a prediction about the forthcoming demand using a GRNN and based on the derived results, it requests the appropriate resources that are consistent with the specifications of the NGMN Alliance [5].

For the validation of the second phase of the algorithm, the GRNN is trained using the first 2392 data, and then it predicts the demand for a period of three days (72 h) over new unseen data. The results of the prediction process are shown in Fig. 3.

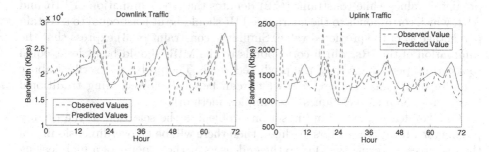

Fig. 3. Prediction of downlink and the uplink bandwidth.

Based on the prediction results, the BS should calculate the appropriate IRs and request their commitment from the PON operator. Undoubtedly, in order for the BS to guarantee the QoS provisioning to its subscribers, it should overdimension the estimated traffic demand by requesting a high percentage of the prediction results. Assume that I^F, $\mathbf{I}^A$, $\mathbf{I}^{NA}$ denote the FIR, AIR and non-assured IR that are requested by the BS. It is noted that according to the recommendation, the FIR is constant, and thus, I^F is a scalar variable, while $\mathbf{I}^A$ and $\mathbf{I}^{NA}$ are vector variables with 72 elements that correspond to every hour within the predicted period $\mathcal{T}$ (3 days). Furthermore, each IR requested by the BS has a different leasing cost for the MO. Let C_F, C_A and C_{NA} denote the leasing cost per capacity metric for the case of FIR, AIR and non-assured IR, respectively. It is expected that a FIR would be more expensive than the AIR, while the non assured IR should be the least expensive. Thus, it holds that $C_F > C_A > C_{NA}$.

As mentioned above, I^F, $\mathbf{I}^A$ and $\mathbf{I}^{NA}$ should be based on the prediction results of the first phase of the proposed algorithm. Specifically, certain percentages of the prediction results are considered essential in order for the BS to provide QoS to its subscribers. Let δ_1, δ_2 and δ_3 denote the QoS parameters that specify the threshold values of the necessary resources as a proportion of the prediction results. Thus, the intelligent agent should calculate the proper IRs in order to provide an enhanced QoS to the BS's subscribers in a cost efficient way.

The problem of the backhaul resources management is now formed as a linear optimisation problem:

$$\underset{I^F, I^A, I^{NA}}{\text{minimize}} \quad I^F C_F + \sum_{i \in \mathcal{T}} I_i^A C_A + \sum_{i \in \mathcal{T}} I_i^{NA} C_{NA}$$

subject to

(C.1) $\quad I^F \geq \delta_1 \min y$

(C.2) $\quad I^F + I_j^A \geq \delta_2 y_j, \ j \subset \mathcal{T}$

(C.3) $\quad I^F + I_j^A + I_j^{NA} \geq \delta_3 y_j, \ j \in \mathcal{T}$

where $y_i, \ i \in \mathcal{T}$, denotes the result of the prediction process. Constraint (C.1) implies that the requested FIR is at least equal to a percentage δ_1 of the minimum predicted value, while constraint (C.2) denotes that the summation of FIR and AIR, which corresponds to the guaranteed IR should be at least equal to a certain percentage δ_2 of the predicted value. Similarly, constraint (C.3) express that the summation of the IRs, which corresponds to the MIR, should be at least equal to a certain percentage δ_3 of the predicted value. The problem described above is a simple optimisation problem which can be easily solved using traditional linear programming techniques (i.e. simplex method).

One key feature in the optimisation problem is the selection of the quality parameters. If the parameters are high, then there will be an overdimensioning of the resources, ensuring the QoS to the end-users at the expense of a high leasing cost. Hence, there is a tradeoff between QoS provisioning and cost-efficiency.

It should be noted that there is not a single optimal choice for the quality parameters. Each BS should select the appropriate values of δ_1, δ_2 and δ_3 based on its own needs. For instance, an urban BS, which serves many subscribers with high demands, should prefer to overdimension the available resources in order to guarantee the QoS provisioning.

The results of the proposed scheme for a choice of $\delta_1 = 0.6$, $\delta_2 = 1$ and $\delta_3 = 1.4$ and leasing costs $C_F = 80$, $C_A = 70$ and $C_{NA} = 50$ are depicted in Fig. 4. From this figure, it becomes apparent that the proposed algorithm can satisfy the requested demand, providing an efficient and cost-effective way for the management of the backhaul resources.

According to the above results, the accurate prediction of the forthcoming demand improves the utilisation of the resources. In contrast to the proposed scheme, a traditional allocation method of the backhaul resources would require the flat commitment of 378 Mbps for the downlink case and 52.2 Mbps for the uplink case, so as to satisfy a worst case scenario, constituting, thus, the bandwidth allocation process in next generation mobile networks highly inefficient.

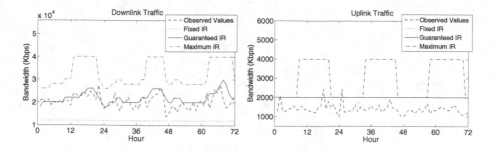

Fig. 4. Requested IRs by the BS.

6 Conclusion

In the current paper, the problem of backhaul resource management in a wireless-optical converged network is studied. The authors exploit the DBA mechanism offered by the PON and propose a scheme that allows the efficient and cost effective management of the backhaul resources. Specifically, intelligent agents at the side of the BSs are used to predict the forthcoming demand using the historical traffic data, and based on the prediction results, they request the commitment of the necessary IRs from the PON. The experimental results show the appropriateness of the GRNN for the prediction process and the efficiency of the proposed scheme.

References

1. Cisco: Cisco Visual Networking Index: Global Mobile Data Traffic Forecast Update, 2013–2018. White paper (2014)
2. Yi, S., Lei, M.: Backhaul resource allocation in LTE-Advanced relaying systems. In: Wireless Communications and Networking Conference, pp. 1207–1211 (2012)
3. Ranaweera, C., Wong, E., Lim, C., Nirmalathas, A., Jayasundara, C.: An efficient resource allocation mechanism for LTE-GEPON converged networks. J. Netw. Syst. Manage. **22**(3), 437–461 (2014)
4. Riggio, R., Gomez, K., Goratti, L., Fedrizzi, R., Rasheed, T.: V-Cell: going beyond the cell abstraction in 5G mobile networks. In: IEEE Network Operations and Management Symposium, pp. 1–5 (2014)
5. NGMN: Optimised Backhaul Requirements. White paper (2008)
6. ITU-T G.984.3: Gigabit-capable Passive Optical Networks (G-PON): Transmission convergence layer specification. Recommendation (2008)
7. Zhang, P.: Time series forecasting using a hybrid ARIMA and neural network model. Neurocomputing **50**, 159–175 (2003)
8. Mitchell, T.: Machine Learning. McGraw-Hill, Maidenhead (1997)
9. Specht, D.: A general regression neural network. IEEE Trans. Neural Netw. **2**(6), 568–576 (1991)
10. Farlow, S.: The GMDH algorithm of ivakhnenko. Am. Stat. **35**(4), 210–215 (1981)
11. NGMN: Guidelines for LTE Backhaul Traffic Estimation. White paper (2011)

SaSeIoT 2014

DOOR: A Data Model for Crowdsourcing with Application to Emergency Response

To Tu Cuong[1]($\boxtimes$), Paras Mehta[1], and Agnès Voisard[1,2]

[1] Department of Mathematics and Computer Science,
Freie Universität Berlin, Berlin, Germany
{to.cuong,paras.mehta,agnes.voisard}@fu-berlin.de
[2] Fraunhofer FOKUS, Berlin, Germany

Abstract. Crowdsourcing allows us to employ collective human intelligence and resources in completing tasks in a wide variety of domains, such as mapping, translation, emergency response, and even fund raising. It first involves identification of a problem that can be solved using crowdsourcing and then its decomposition into tasks that workers can finish in a timely manner. Worker engagement analysis and data quality analysis are done afterwards. Such analysis activities are not supported by current platforms and are done in an ad-hoc fashion leading to duplicate efforts. As a first step towards realizing such analysis mechanisms, we propose a *D*ata m*O*del for cr*O*wdsou*R*cing (DOOR), which is based on a fuzzy Entity-Relationship model in order to capture the uncertainty that is inherent in any crowdsourcing process. To illustrate its application, we have chosen the problem of collection of data about incidents for emergency response.

Keywords: Data model · Emergency response

1 Introduction

The collective power of the crowd is being utilized today in a wide variety of applications, ranging from digitizing text [18], through image tagging [17], to mapping the world [13]. A considerable amount of research has already been done to review and categorize existing crowdsourcing systems and technologies [5,8]. All these systems require significant upfront investment into designing tasks and dealing with technicalities related to tasks. In other words, the infrastructures that support crowdsourcing are limited [2]. As a consequence, although programming frameworks for crowdsourcing are coming up [1,10,14], developers often end up spending a great deal of effort in dealing with operational aspects, rather than in designing the crowdsourcing tasks. Currently, the common workflow for experimenters is that they design the experiment, run it, collect the results, and finally analyze them. As a result, experimenters develop a set of tools around a crowdsourcing platform, e.g. Amazon Mechanical Turk [3], to ensure that experiments are successful. While this is fine for "one time"

© Institute for Computer Sciences, Social Informatics and Telecommunications Engineering 2015
R. Giaffreda et al. (Eds.): IoT360 2014, Part II, LNICST 151, pp. 265–270, 2015.
DOI: 10.1007/978-3-319-19743-2_37

experiments, it is certainly not suitable for experiments that run on a continued basis. Moreover, experimenters may want to conduct analysis while crowdsourcing is being done. The reason for doing this is that if experimenters realize that the data quality is low, they can increase the payment or change the description of tasks. As a first step towards addressing the aforementioned challenges, we propose a *Data Model* for cr*Owdsou*R*cing (DOOR).*

The proposed model is generic enough to be applied to different real-world crowdsourcing tasks, particularly in the geospatial domain. One of these is response to the occurrence of incidents, such as fires, traffic accidents, and crimes in urban areas. Such incidents can happen suddenly, without much warning, and do not leave much time to prepare and act. Our aim is to mitigate the impact of such events by detecting them early and by informing the affected population on time with relevant, actionable information. Crowdsourcing can assist in different tasks, starting from collection of data about incidents, through delegating tasks to volunteers, to receiving feedback. As the number of people equipped with smartphones and wearable devices grow, citizens become increasingly capable of capturing snapshots of their surroundings through the host of sensors embedded in these devices. Thus, crowdsourcing assumes a progressively prominent role in emergency response. In this paper, we describe the use of *DOOR* for the collection of geotagged reports about incidents.

The remainder of this paper is organized as follows. Sections 2 and 3 describe the workflow and the entities involved in crowdsourcing, respectively. Section 4 presents a brief discussion and concludes the paper.

2   Crowdsourcing Process

In crowdsourcing, we have two main parties: *requesters* and *workers*. A requester has a problem and wants to solve it with the help of the crowd. An example could be the image tagging problem, where a requester would like to have tags for her images. These tags help build image search services. Due to the nature of crowdsourcing, a problem needs to be divided into subtasks that can be finished quickly, e.g., in less than a minute. Some problems (like image labeling) can be divided easily. For others, this can be tricky, e.g., composing a poem. There have been researches into automatically decomposing a problem using recursive crowdsourcing [9], i.e., crowdsourcing the decomposition of a problem itself. This line of research is orthogonal to our research. Here, we assume the problem decomposition is already provided.

Once the problem is divided into subproblems, these subproblems are assigned to multiple users to collect their contributions. These contributions are then aggregated into a "result" for the original problem. The mechanism to aggregate answers (contributions) from workers into the result is called a *rewarding model*. The most popular rewarding model is majority voting where answers that receive the majority of votes are deemed correct and its corresponding workers are rewarded financially or through other means.

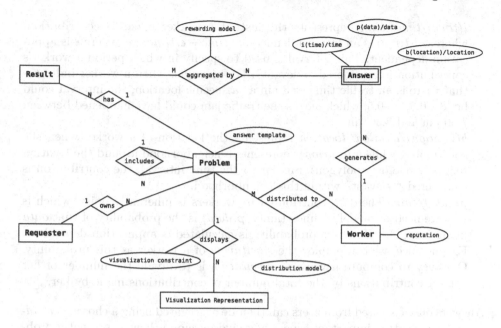

Fig. 1. The DOOR model

We also note that in crowdsourcing, it can be either requesters or workers who initiate the crowdsourcing process. In our previous example, i.e. image tagging, a requester is the active side. On the other hand, Volunteered Geographic Information (VGI) [6] or user generated geospatial content, such as geotagged tweets, is also a form of crowdsourced data which can be processed to produce useful information (e.g., epidemic predictions). In these cases, the workers (who tweet) are the active entities.

3   Crowdsourcing Data Model

In Fig. 1, we use an Entity-Relationship diagram to depict the *DOOR* model. In this model, we have 5 main entities, namely *Requester, Worker, Answer, Result,* and *Problem.* The *Requester* and *Worker* entities in the model represent the task provider and the task worker in the crowdsourcing process, respectively, while the *Problem* and the *Result* entities model the task and the end result, respectively. The recursive nature of problems (or tasks) are captured in our model as the relationship *Includes* between *Problems* themselves. They are distributed to *Workers* using *distribution model* which relies on statistics, such as workers *reputation* and problem type. When a problem is presented to a worker, she can choose an answer and possibly provide ancillary data, such as location, photo, or any input generated by her mobile's sensors. These contributions are captured by the weak entity *Answer.* Since it is an important entity, we describe its attributes in details as follows.

- *i(time)/time: time* represents the instant a worker makes a contribution, whereas $i(time)$ is an interval defined as $[time - \epsilon, time + \epsilon]$ where ϵ is application dependent. This interval is used to specify in which period a worker's contribution is considered "relevant". For example, when a worker indicates that there is an traffic time at 8 am at a specific location, the interval could be $[8 - 0.5, 8 + 0.5]$ which means the traffic jam could have happened between 7:30 am and 8:30 am.
- *b(location)/location: location* represents the location of a worker when she contributes, while $b(location)$ represents a neighborhood around the location (e.g., a circle or a polygon). Similar to the time interval, the contribution is considered "relevant" within this neighborhood.
- *p(data)/data:* The data contributed by workers is inherently noisy, which is why we need to model its uncertainty. $p(data)$ is the probability of that *data* being accepted. How this probability is calculated is application dependent. For instance, we can employ the *reputation* of a worker as this probability. One way to compute a worker's *reputation* is to divide the number of her correct contributions by the total number of contributions made by her.

Answers once collected from users can then be aggregated using a chosen *rewarding model*. Another important aspect in crowdsourcing is how to present a problem to a worker. This is modeled by the *answer template* attribute of the *Problem* entity and by the relationship *Displays* with the *Visualization Representation* entity. An answer template could be an HTML (HyperText Markup Language) file which is used to generate a user interface for workers. Since workers can take part in a crowdsourcing process using different devices, the answer template needs to be adapted based on the *visualization constraints*. For example, CSS (Cascading Style Sheets) can be used to display an HTML file properly on different devices.

In the scope of collection of data for emergency response, crowdsourced incident reporting can help in the early detection of the incident occurrence and in the reinforcement and validation of data collected through hardware infrastructures, like sensor networks. Moreover, updates from the field from citizens can assist in maintaining constant situational awareness. For example, in the event of a fire outbreak, people on the site can report on the extent of the fire perimeter with pictures, video footages, estimates of the damage, and the number of occupants in the affected area. This can improve the response time of the authorities, reduce or help prioritize their workload, and increase citizen participation and transparency in crisis response. It also allows the people themselves in staying updated by receiving regular information about the incident from other members of the community.

We now focus on a specific scenario of a fire in a building complex in an urban area which is detected by the fire department through smoke alarms and calls to the emergency services. The fire department sends out notifications to the people to inform and advise them, and to ask the people at the scene for updates. Our proposed model can be applied to this scenario where people respond back with information about the fire, as depicted in Fig. 2.

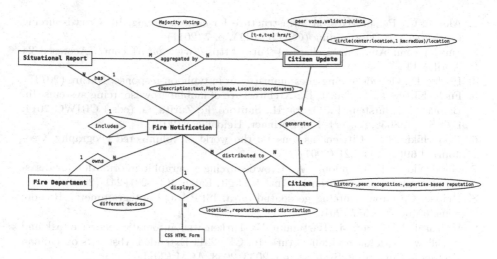

Fig. 2. The DOOR model in emergency response

4   Discussion and Conclusions

The potential of crowdsourcing in aiding emergency response efforts has been widely discussed [4,5,7,12,15]. For gathering field data and maintaining constant situational awareness, sharing data using smartphones can be employed [11, 19]. Platforms, such as Ushahidi [16], have proven useful time and again in situations of crises. All of these efforts share a common workflow. It first involves identification of a problem that can be solved using crowdsourcing and then its decomposition into tasks that workers can finish in a timely manner. Job distribution, worker engagement analysis, and data quality analysis are done afterwards. Such analysis activities are not supported by current platforms and are done in an ad-hoc fashion leading to duplicate efforts. As a first step towards realizing such analyses, in this paper, we proposed the DOOR data model. The model was designed to cope with data uncertainty with a bias towards spatial and temporal data. Moreover, in order to illustrate that DOOR is generic enough to be used in real-world applications, we instantiated it in a disaster management scenario. A software prototype is being developed at our group using DOOR.

Acknowledgements. This research is carried out in the framework of the GEOCROWD project funded by the European Commission.

References

1. Ahmad, S., Battle, A., Malkani, Z., Kamvar, S.: The jabberwocky programming environment for structured social computing. In: Proceedings of the 24th Annual ACM Symposium on User Interface Software and Technology, pp. 53–64. ACM (2011)

2. Alonso, O.: Perspectives on infrastructure for crowdsourcing. In: Crowdsourcing for Search and Data Mining (CSDM 2011), p. 7 (2011)
3. amazon.com: Amazon Mechanical Turk. https://www.mturk.com/. Accessed 24 April 2014
4. Butler, D.: Crowdsourcing goes mainstream in typhoon response. Nature (2013)
5. Fuchs-Kittowski, F., Faust, D.: Architecture of mobile crowdsourcing systems. In: Baloian, N., Burstein, F., Ogata, H., Santoro, F., Zurita, G. (eds.) CRIWG 2014. LNCS, vol. 8658, pp. 121–136. Springer, Heidelberg (2014)
6. Goodchild, M.F.: Citizens as sensors: the world of volunteered geography. Geo-Journal **69**(4), 211–221 (2007)
7. Goodchild, M.F., Glennon, J.A.: Crowdsourcing geographic information for disaster response: a research frontier. Int. J. Digit. Earth **3**(3), 231–241 (2010)
8. Heipke, C.: Crowdsourcing geospatial data. ISPRS J. Photogrammetry Remote Sens. **65**(6), 550–557 (2010)
9. Kulkarni, A.P., Can, M., Hartmann, B.: Turkomatic: automatic recursive task and workflow design for mechanical turk. In: CHI 2011 Extended Abstracts on Human Factors in Computing Systems, pp. 2053–2058. ACM (2011)
10. Little, G., Chilton, L.B., Goldman, M., Miller, R.C.: Turkit: human computation algorithms on mechanical turk. In: Proceedings of the 23nd Annual ACM Symposium on User Interface Software and Technology, pp. 57–66. ACM (2010)
11. Mehta, P., Müller, S., Voisard, A.: Movesafe: A framework for transportation mode-based targeted alerting in disaster response. In: Proceedings of the Second ACM SIGSPATIAL International Workshop on Crowdsourced and Volunteered Geographic Information, GEOCROWD 2013, pp. 15–22. ACM, New York (2013). http://doi.acm.org/10.1145/2534732.2534735
12. Munro, R.: Crowdsourced translation for emergency response in Haiti: the global collaboration of local knowledge. In: AMTA Workshop on Collaborative Crowdsourcing for Translation (2010)
13. OpenStreetMap Community: OpenStreetMap. http://www.openstreetmap.org/. Accessed 04 April 2014
14. pybossa.com: Pybossa. https://pybossa.com/. Accessed 01 June 2014
15. TechCrunch: Help Me Help uses crowdsourcing to make disaster response more efficient. http://techcrunch.com/2013/07/04/. Accessed 24 March 2014
16. Ushahidi Inc.: Ushahidi. http://ushahidi.com/. Accessed 04 April 2014
17. Von Ahn, L., Dabbish, L.: Labeling images with a computer game. In: Proceedings of the SIGCHI Conference on Human Factors In Computing Systems, pp. 319–326. ACM (2004)
18. Von Ahn, L., Maurer, B., McMillen, C., Abraham, D., Blum, M.: recaptcha: Human-based character recognition via web security measures. Science **321**(5895), 1465–1468 (2008)
19. Zheng, L., Shen, C., Tang, L., Li, T., Luis, S., Chen, S.C.: Applying data mining techniques to address disaster information management challenges on mobile devices. In: Proceedings of the 17th ACM SIGKDD International Conference on Knowledge Discovery and Data Mining, KDD 2011, pp. 283–291. ACM, New York (2011). http://doi.acm.org/10.1145/2020408.2020457

Security Perspectives for Collaborative Data Acquisition in the Internet of Things

Vangelis Gazis[1], Carlos Garcia Cordero[1,2], Emmanouil Vasilomanolakis[1,2],
Panayotis Kikiras[1], and Alex Wiesmaier[1] (✉)

[1] AGT Group (R&D), Darmstadt, Germany
{vgazis,cgarcia,evasilomanolakis,pkikiras,
awiesmaier}@agtinternational.com
[2] Technische Universität Darmstadt, Telecooperation Group, Darmstadt, Germany

Abstract. The Internet of Things (IoT) is an increasingly important topic, bringing together many different fields of computer science. Nevertheless, beside the advantages (IoT) has to offer, many challenges exist, not at least in terms of security and privacy. In addition, the large number of heterogeneous devices in (IoT) produces a vast amount of data, and therefore efficient mechanisms are required that are capable of handling the data, analyze them and produce meaningful results. In this paper, we discuss the challenges that have to be addressed, when data analytics are applied in the context of the (IoT). For this, we propose a data acquisition architecture, named *CoDA*, that focuses on bringing together heterogeneous *things* to create distributed global data models. For each layer of the proposed architecture we discuss the upcoming challenges from the security perspective.

Keywords: Internet of Things (IoT) · Security challenges · Data acquisition · Data analytics

1 Introduction

Over the last decade, the Internet of Things (IoT) has emerged as an umbrella concept for the disruptive application of advances in embedded sensors, low power wireless networking and distributed computing [26]. Its original definition envisioned a world where computers would relieve humans of the Sisyphean burden of data entry by automatically recording, storing and processing, in a proper manner, all information relevant to human activities [18]. With human involvement being the exception, Machine-to-Machine (M2M) communication is understood as a major component of the IoT portfolio of technologies. IoT represents the prime embodiment of the ongoing convergence between device-oriented sensor networks and data-oriented applications. Facilitated by the Internet portfolio of technologies, the latter utilizes data from the physical world captured by sensors to improve processes of modern life (e.g., in industrial manufacturing, health care, energy production, etc.). Not surprisingly, key industry players, as

© Institute for Computer Sciences, Social Informatics and Telecommunications Engineering 2015
R. Giaffreda et al. (Eds.): IoT360 2014, Part II, LNICST 151, pp. 271–282, 2015.
DOI: 10.1007/978-3-319-19743-2_38

well as prominent market analysts, have repeatedly acknowledged the importance of IoT and its economic impact [10,11,17,24].

Recently, multiple interpretations of what the (IoT) is about have been proposed [8,19,25]. The European Commission (EC) defines IoT as "things having identities and virtual personalities operating in smart spaces using intelligent interfaces to connect and communicate within social, environmental, and user contexts" [22]. The use of Web technologies in the IoT to support peer-to-peer interactions between things is referred to as the Web of Things [20]. The Telecommunication Standardization Sector of the International Telecommunication Union (i.e., ITU-T) defines IoT as a global (i.e., distributed) infrastructure for the information society, enabling advanced services by interconnecting a disparate gamut of (physical and virtual) things based on, existing and evolving, interoperable information and communication technologies [23]. Not surprisingly, security and privacy concerns are paramount in this emerging world where things may autonomously communicate and exchange information with each other in a way that is transparent to human beings.

Transparent M2M communication is the key aspect of the IoT, enabling collaboration between devices and, as a result of this collaboration, the creation of new data. Analyzing this new data becomes of crucial importance as many hidden variables can be data-mined. The endless possibilities of collaboration and the communication ubiquity between devices requires a new architectural model that would enable the processing of large amounts of data in the context of IoT. Data analytics has to be built, therefore, on top of a new architecture for accessing and gathering data, which we denominate herein as the (CoDA) architecture.

In the usual context of data-mining and analytics, CoDA becomes the bottom layers that represent the storage locations where data is gathered. In the IoT, centralized locations where all generated data is stored cannot be expected. With CoDA, it is possible to build typical data analytics tools that acquire all information through a common layer that encompasses all device communication capabilities in the IoT.

Herein, we highlight and elaborate upon the challenges associated to the application of data analytics (e.g., model learning, data fusion, etc.) in the IoT. We propose a data acquisition architecture, named *CoDA*, that enables heterogeneous *things* to be brought together and support the creation of distributed global data models useful for data-mining. Furthermore, for each layer of the proposed architecture we discuss major challenges from a security perspective.

The remainder of this paper is organized as follows. In Sect. 2 we discuss how a data analytics architecture has to be adapted for the IoT. Subsequently, in Sect. 3, we propose a sub-architecture, named CoDA, that addresses specific IoT challenges in the data acquisition layer, and discuss the respective security challenges. Finally, Sect. 5 concludes this paper and discusses future directions.

1.1 Related Work

Established in 2012, oneM2M is a partnership among major ICT standards development organizations around the world [28,29]. The founding SDOs include the

Association of Radio Industries and Businesses (ARIB), the Telecommunication Technology Committee (TTC) of Japan, the Alliance for Telecommunications Industry Solutions (ATIS), the Telecommunications Industry Association (TIA), the China Communications Standards Association (CCSA), the European Telecommunications Standards Institute (ETSI) and the Telecommunications Technology Association (TTA) of Korea. Currently numbering approximately 200 members, oneM2M is developing joint specifications and technical reports for the M2M service layer. oneM2M is also liaised with major industry alliances (e.g., Open Mobile Alliance, BroadBand Forum) and Internet standardization bodies (e.g., IETF, IEEE). Candidate Release 1 of the oneM2M specifications was recently published. These specifications define the functional architecture in terms of logical elements, their functional capacities and their interfaces. They also define the oneM2M core protocol and its technology bindings to the HTTP and CoAP protocols, as well as device management enablers that incorporate the respective standards from the BroadBand Forum (BBF) [16] and the Open Mobile Alliance (OMA) [27]. Collectively, these form a common services layer for a wide range IoT applications.

The Routing Over Low power and Lossy networks (ROLL) working group of IETF is developing a routing architectural framework for the IPv6 protocol tailored to resource-constrained devices (e.g., embedded devices). The IETF Constrained RESTful Environments (CORE) working group is developing a framework for resource-oriented applications intended to run over the IP protocol on resource-constrained networks (e.g., M2M networks based on the IEEE 802.15.4 standard [21]).

Regional Standards. The European Telecommunication Standards Institute (ETSI) published Release 1 of its M2M standard on November 2011. These introduce an M2M platform for M2M service providers where IoT applications are supported through platform agnostic interfaces [12–14]. They thus define a system architecture that enables integration of a diverse range of M2M devices (e.g., sensors, actuators, gateways, etc.) into an end-to-end platform. The latter offers to applications a standard interface for accessing data and services made available over these (typically last mile) devices.

Starting with Release 10, 3GPP has included support for (device terminated and device originated) Machine Type Communications (MTC). The objective is to ensure that 3GPP network installations will support M2M applications deployed on a very large scale [1]. 3GPP2 has assessed the traffic impact of M2M applications on the cdma2000 network infrastructure (e.g., huge population of communicating devices, low traffic volume per device, etc.) [2] and amended its specifications accordingly. M2M work in 3GPP2 is now aligned to the M2M work in 3GPP and the M2M architecture work done in ETSI as part of an access-agnostic architecture [2–4].

In the Telecommunications Industry Association (TIA), Engineering Committee TR-50 M2M on Smart Device Communications (SDC) has developed an M2M framework. The latter abstracts the technological details of underlying transport networks (wireless, wireline, etc.) and provides a convergence layer for M2M applications [31].

The ATIS M2M Focus Group (FG) has addressed the M2M, Smart Grid and Connected Vehicle markets, with M2M understood as an horizontal layer spanning across multiple vertical domains (e.g., Smart Grid, Connected Vehicle). The ATIS M2M work is currently integrated to the 3GPP MTC work program [7] and further advanced there. ATIS has addressed carrier portability issues (e.g., waiving the need for SIM card swapping, remote reconfiguration, etc.), management procedures (e.g., provisioning, billing, etc.), transport (e.g., peering) and security issues of IoT applications.

2   Data Analytics Architecture for the IoT

A generic framework of an IoT data analytics framework needs to deal with a high degree of heterogeneity, e.g., in terms of storage facilities of the underlying infrastructure, data types and representation formats, processing modes, and, analytic algorithms. These concerns are reflected in its stratification which includes four layers, i.e., *Scalable Analytics, Analytics Enabler, Scalable Processing* and *Data Acquisition*. Figure 1 shows an overview of a generic IoT data analytics architecture.

2.1   Scalable Analytics

The *Scalable Analytics* layer encompasses the range of use cases that employ data analytics in the context of IoT (i.e., the vertical domains of IoT data analytics). As seen in Fig. 1 these include (but are not limited to) critical infrastructure

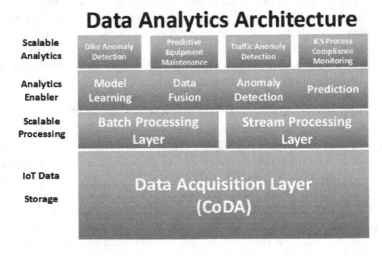

Fig. 1. High level view of a generic data analytics architecture for the IoT

monitoring (e.g., dike anomaly detection), industrial IoT (e.g., predictive equipment maintenance, ICS process compliance monitoring) and Smart City (e.g., traffic anomaly detection). However, in the rest of this paper we focus on the subsequent layers, i.e., the specific mechanisms that are required in order to provide the *Scalable Analytics* with the necessary capabilities and relevant data.

2.2   Analytics Enabler

The *Analytics Enabler* layer provides the hosting environment for the deployment and execution of analytic algorithms, along with their associated model data. It provides mechanisms to deploy/undeploy a packaged analytic algorithm in a particular hosting environment, e.g., an Amazon Machine Image, an OSGi container. To this end, it realizes capability negotiation mechanisms to match the requirements and constraints of a particular analytic algorithm to those of the available hosting environments. Provisioning a deployed analytic algorithm with the necessary model data is also supported by the capability negotiation mechanism as part of the post-deployment and pre-execution phases. Finally, it includes a workflow engine for scheduling the execution of compositions of analytic algorithms and the coordination of their input/output dependencies.

From the perspective of analytics function, the majority of IoT applications, including security and privacy ones, are based on a combination of the following capacities:

1. *Model Learning*, where a formal representation of (some aspects of) the real world is built from recorded measurements of relevant phenomena in the real world. For instance, IoT traffic management applications typically feature the building of a model of observed traffic patterns.
2. *Data Fusion*, where multiple pieces of data (which may be of different types and modalities) are combined to render data of better quality, e.g., in terms of accuracy in data values. For instance, observations from different sensors that are proximal to each other can be combined to provide a more accurate observation about a phenomenon in their particular location.
3. *Real-Time Anomaly Detection*, where (real-time or near real-time) measurements of particular phenomena in the real world are contrasted to values estimated from a model (e..g, one that has been developed through a model learning process for those particular phenomena, formulated analytically, or, a combination of both approaches) and any observed deviations are reported. This is particularly relevant and frequent for administrative levels tasked with real-time control of critical assets, e.g., Demand/Response control processes in a Smart Grid environment or traffic management processes in the context of Smart City.
4. *Prediction*, where (possibly real-time) measurements of particular phenomena in the real world are applied to a model (that has been developed through a model learning process for those particular phenomena) to generate a forecast (e.g., forecasted demand for electricity in a particular urban area).

There are additional analytics capacities involved in other IoT applications, however, these are either more of an elementary nature (e.g., data clustering), or, feature in a small niche of IoT applications (e.g., simulation) [6,15].

2.3 Scalable Processing

The *Scalable Processing* layer realizes the computational capabilities required by the *Analytics Enabler* layer. It provides computational resources, e.g., CPU cycles, thread pools, to support the execution of each particular analytic algorithm. Different computing modalities are supported, depending on the real-time profile of the data fed to the analytic algorithm.

- *Batch Processing* where input data is not subject to a real-time requirement, e.g., historical data at rest. Typically this is achieved through the Map/Reduce paradigm of computing supported by the popular Hadoop framework that achieves scalability under a bulk mode of computation.
- *Stream Processing* where input data is subject to a real-time requirement, e.g., streaming real-time data. Commonly, this regards the treatment of events (where an event describes the occurrence of a significant situation in terms of attribute-value pairs) in a so-called Complex Event Processing (CEP) framework founded on the Event-Condition-Action (ECA) paradigm. With different levels of significance attached to each event and with unpredictable times of occurrence for each event, this mode of processing fits the requirements of a process in control of assets of importance, e.g., operational procedures occurring within a Smart Grid context.

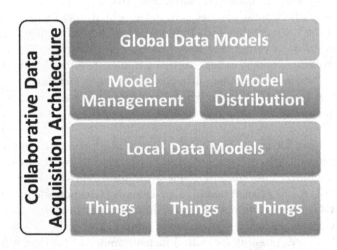

Fig. 2. Different layers of the envisioned Collaborative Data Acquisition architecture

2.4   Data Acquisition

The *Data Acquisition* layer describes all the processes that are required to produce meaningful data starting from the heterogeneous layer of *things* to the global data models. We argue that, in the context of IoT, this layer is of particular importance as it has to deal with the shortcomings of generating data from a large number of diverse and low-resourced devices. Therefore, we extensively discuss this layer and propose a distinction of four additional sub-layers in the upcoming Sect. 3.

3   CoDA: Collaborative Data Acquisition Architecture

In this section we describe our vision of a collaborative data acquisition architecture for the IoT, as well as the respective security challenges. Figure 2 provides an overview of the so-called CoDA architecture.

3.1   Data Acquisition Architecture

The IoT is composed of multiple objects, or *things*, that are capable of generating data constantly. Each such object analyzes and creates data according to its particular capabilities. That is to say, each different thing generates data that concerns only the phenomena it is capable of sensing, i.e., it is equipped with sensory instruments for. The result heterogeneity of the data complicates matters when different processes need to access a collection of all the data generated by things. To enable processes to access heterogeneous data, it is important to develop an architecture capable of conveying each thing with the ability of communicating data among itself and requesting processes in a common format.

Once mechanisms for acquiring and collecting data are in place, more advanced computations (by *things*) can be performed on top of the data easily. The IoT promises the availability and generation of vast amounts of data. If this data is easily accessible following security and user guidelines, services will be able to leverage *things* efficiently and produce valuable information. However, data acquisition is the fundamental and core aspect of any service that could be conceived and provided in the IoT.

Simple data collection services would already benefit from such a data acquisition architecture; however, services that embody an advanced analytic function, e.g., machine learning, would benefit the most. The standard flow of operations of such services (and machine learning algorithms in particular) requires, first and foremost, access to data.

This architecture proposes a four layer approach at making data available without requiring a central location to collect all data. The four layers are *things*; *local data models*; *model management and distribution*; and finally the *global data models*. The layer of *things* is concerned with the actual data generated by each individual set of *things*. The second layer of local data models is responsible for representing data from the lower layer (the *things* layer) so that it can be easily managed (i.e., it provides a convergence layer to enable management procedures). The third layer is a composition of two components, a component for managing the generated local data models and another component for distributing the models. The last layer, the global data layer, encompasses a collection of all data models that is easily accessible by users or service providers.

As previously stated, this architecture does not require a centralized unit to collect all data in one single location. Each thing is responsible for generating local data models that are shared among other *things* in their vicinity. Neighborhoods of *things* are created, e.g., by leveraging standard neighbour discovery protocols such as IPv6, where the same type of information is shared among themselves. An additional benefit of the local sharing of data is the facilitation of increased data availability and improved performance in accessing the data (i.e., as a distributed cache).

When a user queries, for instance, one particular data type, the user is able to issue such queries to any thing and this thing will be able to redirect the query to the right owner of the data.

In what follows we describe the components of the CoDA architecture as well as the security concerns that are entailed in the implementation of this architecture.

3.2 Introduction to the CoDA Architecture

We present an architecture that enables *things* to provide platform independent access to their data while also following security and user requirements. Figure 2 shows the different layers of CoDA.

Things. Each component in the IoT is essentially a *thing*. The bottom most layer of the architecture encompasses groups of *things*. Regardless of the *things* being exactly the same, this layer groups them by the data they produce. A group of things is a collection of *things* that produce the same data types.

Each group of *thing* is able to generate the same data conforming to specifications and the specific characteristics of the incorporated sensors. However, for the resulting communication to be effective, a common ground for the data generation process is required. This also requires standardized protocols for communication so that convenient data access is possible. These result in a multitude of *things* producing different data represented by the same common output format. In addition, each device in this layer requires a secure and unique identifier, e.g., a common secret, that enables interactions between owners and other *things* to be structured with the appropriate level of security [9, 30]. Simultaneously, every sensor needs to be able to support more than one consumer for the data it generates. Lastly, *things* are able to determine their owner, e.g., through a common secret. Determining ownership relationships allows *things* to choose the data to share.

Local Data Models. The second layer of the CoDA architecture is a data normalization component . The layer consists of models, standards and formats which specify the way and form of communication for all *things*. This is necessary due to the fact that by default the data produced by *things* would not necessarily conform to any particular standard. The normalization component effectively provides the required data convergence.

Data Management and Model Distribution. When each thing is able to produce meaningful output, the question that arises is how to distribute data efficiently. Due to the fact that in the IoT a vast amount of devices and sensors are interconnected, we envision distributed and P2P techniques being utilized in this level (in contrast to centralized approaches that would not scale). This can be realized by adopting mechanisms from the P2P and the wireless mesh networks areas [5], which allows *things* to create arbitrary communication links among each other.

Furthermore, in the basis of the existence of a basic communication overlay, a distribution layer in parallel is of high importance. At this point, the main challenge that needs to be addressed is determining which *things* should communicate with each other. A combination of the type of *things* as well as the knowledge of a common secret can provide an initial way to deal with this.

Global Data Models. The global data model layer is based on the fact that local models can be aggregated via the utilization of the aforementioned layers to form a mixed model. This has a twofold objective. First, it enables *things* to expand their capabilities through collaboration. For instance, a sensor can make use of data gathered from other sensors to perform complex tasks. Second, various services can query this layer to receive mixed information from the interaction of multiple *things*.

4   Security Challenges

Due to the unattended environment in which the *things* operate and the resource constrained nature of these devices in terms of computational capabilities, memory size, and available energy, it is not possible to just employ security schemes coming from regular computers or ad hoc wireless networks domain. Challenges in securing the IoT go beyond the standard C-I-A model. IoT security must and be lightweight to run in constrained devices, scalable to billions of devices, supporting heterogeneous devices, work in an unattended manner, and supporting decentralized solutions.

4.1   Data Acquisition

In order to implement the CoDA architecture in a secure way, many challenges need to be addressed [30]. The two main problems in the IoT is the absence of centralized points of service and the existence of numerous low-resource devices with power limitations. As a result, resource intensive mechanisms such as asymmetric cryptography or centralized architectures, like PKI infrastructures, are limited. Nevertheless, as not all *things* require strong security properties, more lightweight symmetric cryptographic techniques can be utilized. Moreover, sophisticated trust models need to be built to enable the deployment of access control limitations between owners and *things*.

It is necessary to distinguish in the layer of *things* who are the owners of a *thing* and manage the respective access control list of each. A common shared secret between the owners and a *thing* can be utilized along with unique identifiers. Moreover, the first two layers provide the necessary encryption services for guarantying the confidentiality and integrity of the generated data.

The model management and distribution layer need to be scalable, and resilient against attacks and failures. This means that the overlay has to function even when a number of sensors might not be working. Regardless of the utilized overlay, the architecture must provide sufficient capabilities to distinguish trusted *things* and foreign *things*. Finally, the global data models must ensure proper access control enforcement, and authentication for the *things* and owners.

A high level realization of the security challenges in our proposal can be envisioned by the utilization of a complex multi-layer symmetric-based encryption scheme. Multi-layer in this context refers to the various levels of trust that *things* must accommodate for a flexible and secure interaction among themselves and the owners. For instance, devices can have more than one owner, spanning up to an entire organization, and also different protocols might be used for their interaction.

4.2   Privacy and Trust

In general and especially in the IoT, privacy is more than just keeping personal information confidential. Examples for other privacy aspects that have to be considered are given in the following. *Identity privacy* refers to disclosing a user's identity if and only if needed and keep it secret otherwise. *Query privacy* refers to data retrieval without revealing to the sender (or any other party) which data was received. *Location privacy* means hiding a user's location to the reasonable extent whenever possible. *Footprint privacy* aims at minimizing a user's linkable (meta) data volume.

Similar to privacy, trust is in general, especially in the context of IoT, more than just relying on third parties. Four different areas of trust can be distinguished. *Device trust* refers to the user's confidence to interact with reliable sensors, as well as assessing the accuracy of the produced data. Sensors that are not handled according to specifications have the risk of producing inconsistent or wrong data. *Processing trust* reflects the need to deal with correct and meaningful data. *Connection trust* embodies the desire to exchange data only with the intended partners. *System trust* refers to the ability of using the interaction between *things* to confidently accomplish complex tasks.

4.3   Attacks

Just as any other network, an IoT network is subject to different types of attacks. Examples for attack categories that have to be considered are given in the following. *Physical attacks* on devices, e.g., destroying, analyzing, and/or reprogramming them. *Service disruption attacks* on routing, localization, etc. *Data attacks* such as traffic capture, spoofing, and similar. *Resource-consumption and denial-of-service (DoS) attacks* on (remote) resources and/or services.

5   Conclusion

The IoT is a prevalent concept that aims to permeate common things with the possibility of offering and consuming services. Each *thing* is capable of generating data through its sensors or by consuming services of other *things*. To handle the large amount of data that will be generated, a common architecture needs to be designed that will enable efficient and simplified communication between *things*.

We highlighted the challenges brought by the adoption of data analytic applications in the IoT and proposed the *CoDA* data acquisition architecture. *CoDA* enables heterogeneous *things* to be brought together efficiently in support of distributed global data models for data analytic applications. Our presentation of *CoDA* focused on security concerns, as these are paramount under a global data model. We foresee extensions of our work in the refinement of *CoDA* in the direction of privacy preserving approaches that are generically applicable to data analytics applications.

References

1. 3GPP. Ts 23.887; study on machine-type communications (mtc) and other mobile data applications communications enhancements (2013)
2. 3GPP2. S.r0141-0; study for machine-to-machine (m2m) communication for cdma2000 networks (2010)
3. 3GPP2. X.p0067-0; machine to machine (m2m) architecture and enhancements study for cdma2000 networks (2012)
4. 3GPP2. X.s0068-x; cdma2000 network enhancements for m2m (2012)
5. Alcaraz, C., Najera, P., Lopez, J., Roman, R.: Wireless sensor networks and the internet of things: Do we need a complete integration? In: 1st International Workshop on the Security of the Internet of Things (SecIoT 2010) (2010)
6. Future Internet Assembly: Internet of Things: an early reality of the Future Internet. Technical report, European Commission (2009)
7. ATIS. Assessments and Recommendations (2013)
8. Atzori, L., Iera, A., Morabito, G.: The internet of things: a survey. Comput. Netw. **54**(15), 2787–2805 (2010)
9. Atzori, L., Iera, A., Morabito, G., Nitti, M.: The Social Internet of Things (SIoT) when social networks meet the Internet of Things: concept, architecture and network characterization. Comput. Netw. **56**(16), 3594–3608 (2012)
10. Cisco. The Internet of Things (2013)
11. Ericsson. More than 50 billion connected devices (2013)

12. ETSI. Ts 102 689; machine-to-machine communications (m2m); m2m service requirements (2013)
13. ETSI. Ts 102 690; machine-to-machine communications (m2m); functional architecture (2013)
14. ETSI. Ts 102 921; machine-to-machine communications (m2m); mia, dia and mid interfaces (2013)
15. Future Media Internet Task Force: Future Media Internet Research Challenges and the Road Ahead. Technical report, European Commission (2010)
16. BroadBand Forum. Tr-069; cpe wan management protocol (2013)
17. Gartner. The Internet of Things (2013)
18. Gubbi, J., Buyya, R., Marusic, S., Palaniswami, M.: Internet of things (iot): a vision, architectural elements, and future directions. Future Gener. Comput. Syst. **29**(7), 1645–1660 (2013)
19. Gubbi, J., Buyya, R., Marusic, S., Palaniswami, M.: Internet of things (IoT): A vision, architectural elements, and future directions. Future Generation Computer Systems (2013)
20. Guinard, D., Trifa, V., Mattern, F., Wilde, E.: From the internet of things to the web of things: resource-oriented architecture and best practices. In: Uckelmann, D., Harrison, M., Michahelles, F. (eds.) Architecting the Internet of Things, pp. 97–129. Springer, Heidelberg (2011)
21. IEEE Standards Association. IEEE Standard for Local and metropolitan area networks Part 15.4: Low-Rate Wireless Personal Area Networks (LR-WPANs), September 2011
22. D G INFSO. Internet of Things in 2020: A Roadmap for the Future, INFSO D.4 Networked Enterprise & RFID and INFSO G.2 Micro & Nanosystems in co-operation with RFID Working Group of the European Technology Platform on Smart Systems Integration (EPOSS) (2008)
23. ITU-T. Recommendation itu-t y.2060, overview of the internet of things, June 2012
24. McKinsey. Disruptive Technologies (2013)
25. Miorandi, D., Sicari, S., De Pellegrini, F., Chlamtac, I.: Internet of things: Vision, applications and research challenges. Ad Hoc Netw. **10**(7), 1497–1516 (2012)
26. National Intelligence Council NIC. Disruptive Civil Technologies: Six Technologies with Potential Impacts on US Interests out to 2025, April 2008
27. OMA. Oma device management v1.2 (2013)
28. oneM2M Partners. oneM2M Partnership Agreement, July 2012. http://www.onem2m.org/docs/oneM2M_Partnership_Agreement.pdf (Accessed 10 February 2014)
29. oneM2M Partners. oneM2M Homepage, January 2014. http://www.onem2m.org/index.cfm (10 February 2014)
30. Roman, R., Najera, P., Lopez, J.: Securing the internet of things. Comput. **44**(9), 51–58 (2011)
31. TIA. Tia-4940.005: Smart device communications reference architecture (2012)

The Role of the Internet of Things in Network Resilience

Hauke Petersen[1], Emmanuel Baccelli[2], Matthias Wählisch[1(✉)],
Thomas C. Schmidt[3], and Jochen Schiller[1]

[1] Freie Universität Berlin, Berlin, Germany
{hauke.petersen,m.waehlisch,jochen.schiller}@fu-berlin.de
[2] INRIA, Valbonne, France
emmanuel.baccelli@inria.fr
[3] HAW Hamburg, Hamburg, Germany
t.schmidt@haw-hamburg.de

Abstract. Disasters lead to devastating structural damage not only to buildings and transport infrastructure, but also to other critical infrastructure, such as the power grid and communication backbones. Following such an event, the availability of minimal communication services is however crucial to allow efficient and coordinated disaster response, to enable timely public information, or to provide individuals in need with a default mechanism to post emergency messages. The Internet of Things consists in the massive deployment of heterogeneous devices, most of which battery-powered, and interconnected via wireless network interfaces. In this paper, we argue that the vast deployment of IoT-enabled devices could bring benefits in terms of data network resilience in face of disaster. Leveraging their spontaneous wireless networking capabilities, IoT devices could enable minimal communication services (e.g. emergency micro-message delivery) while the conventional communication infrastructure is out of service. We identify the main challenges that must be addressed in order to realize this potential in practice. These challenges concern various technical aspects, including physical connectivity requirements, network protocol stack enhancements, data traffic prioritization schemes, as well as social and political aspects.

Keywords: Design of resilient IoT infrastructures · IoT for crisis and emergency response

1 Introduction

Every year witnesses large-scale disasters around the world, affecting millions of people. A crucial aspect of crisis management is distribution of information, immediately after the disaster occurs. Usually, we rely on data communication networks to deliver information fast, reliably, anywhere, anytime. The Internet is today's communication backbone, used not only for transferring data but it is also utilized as back-end for voice communication [3]. Even though the Internet

© Institute for Computer Sciences, Social Informatics and Telecommunications Engineering 2015
R. Giaffreda et al. (Eds.): IoT360 2014, Part II, LNICST 151, pp. 283–296, 2015.
DOI: 10.1007/978-3-319-19743-2_39

is a highly interconnected system with several backup paths, it is vulnerable to the effects of large scale disasters, which can lead to local but also global communication outages and thus significant disruption of crisis management after such a disaster occurs.

In large scale disaster scenarios, typical approaches to (re)establish communication abilities yield manual installation of new hardware, which takes time. However, massive deployment of heterogeneous, Internet-enabled embedded devices is taking place, amounting to what is called the Internet of Things (IoT) [1]. A large part of these devices is battery powered and communicate wirelessly. Predictions show that their number will reach billions over the next decade [5,14], and will result in a very dense deployment which will significantly reshape the Internet's edge architecture, allowing for more decentralized and dynamic communication paradigms.

In this paper, we discuss to which extent the Internet of Things may increase network resilience in disaster scenarios. We argue that stakeholders—in particular the general public—would significantly benefit from leveraging the decentralized nature of the Internet of Things, that could enable minimal communication services in scenarios where the conventional communication infrastructure is inoperable. We analyze the main challenges that must be addressed in order to realize this potential. These challenges concern various technical aspects, including physical connectivity requirements, network protocol stack enhancements, data traffic prioritization schemes, as well as social and political aspects, that we detail in the following.

2   Current Communication in Disaster Scenarios

Communication in disaster scenarios is primarily driven by exchanging *important* instead of arbitrary information. Different groups of actors have different communication requirements, which finally lead to the deployment of the underlying technology.

2.1   Communication Requirements

A disaster may disconnect a complete country from the rest of the world or limit capacities to data with very low throughput. Ideally this remaining connectivity should be used by the most important services and actors, mainly for information-sharing and coordination. With passing time after a disaster happened these priorities are further subject to change. In the period of time following the initial impact the actual saving of human life is the most important action that needs to be coordinated. This is generally done between first responders such as fire-fighters, police, and technical response forces. For disaster with devastating impacts the prioritization of communication capabilities will shift after the initial time period towards governmental organizations and nongovernmental organizations that are concerned with providing foot and shelter and restoring the social systems.

During all phases there is further need of communication for the general public. The population in the affected areas has to be warned of threats and to be informed of retreat routes and similar information. People need further to communicate with relatives and other persons inside as well as outside the disaster area to check on their status [9].

The actors that operate in disaster areas and their used communication mechanisms can be categorized as follow.

First responders: Communication between teams using voice and text connections.

Governmental organizations: Communication between central situation centers using voice, text and further access to databases.

Non-governmental organizations: Coordination using voice and text communication, access to logistical databases.

The press: Sending texts out of the disaster area, audio and video broadcasts.

The general public: Emergency calls, status calls, receive news and situational updates, receive environmental/emergency warnings.

We compare the communication services in a three dimensional space with respect to basic communication parameters, needed throughput, the direction in which the data flows, and finally the requirements on timing constraints (cf., Fig. 1).

It is worth noting that the distinction between the actors is not exclusive. In particular, the general public covers multiple fields. With the advent of blogging, social networks, and micro messaging (e.g., Twitter) *citizen journalism* has been established to complement the press by public contributions. After the Tohoku earthquake in 2011, for example, $\approx 50\%$ of the photos related to the disaster in the Tokyo area have been uploaded to Flickr in less than 24 h. This information fulfills two purposes, it informs other people about the current state but also helps rescue teams to identify relevant areas. Previous disasters also shown that first responders are not only experts but also volunteers from the neighborhood, who help [9]. These observations have direct implications on the devices, which are used on-site, and thus on the deployed technology. Professionals such as press, NGOs, and first responders may own special hardware. The general public is equipped with mass market devices (e.g., smartphones) providing basic communication functionality. Building a more robust communication infrastructure should consider this and incorporate public devices.

The distance between two communication partners, which needs to be bridged, is diverse even within a group of stakeholders. Typical NGO scenarios illustrate this nicely. Field workers require short range communication between peers, as well as long range communication to request external data and to interact with external operation control center. Short range communication is limited to a smaller geographic area, in which long range communication bridges further distances. The latter is currently implemented in the Internet.

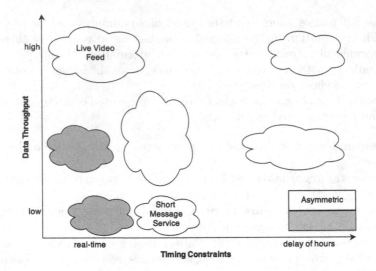

Fig. 1. Comparison of delay and throughput requirements of typical applications in disaster scenarios.

2.2   Dependency on Fixed Infrastructure

Today's communication is heavily based on the Internet. Originally, different infrastructures have been operated for voice and data traffic. This distinction continuously converges towards a unified backbone implemented by the Internet [3]. The Internet provides packet-based data delivery and allows for a wide range of communication services on top of the delivery infrastructure, making it more attractive compared to other backbones.

Successful communication in disaster scenarios is tied to the successful operation of the Internet. This relates to two perspectives, the outsider and the insider perspective. A disaster that affects Internet infrastructure components may also affect people living in areas which are geographically outside of the disaster region. During the localized 9/11 attack smaller Internet outages have been experienced in Japan, for example. Given that the Internet is the backbone of our daily communication this can lead to severe problems. People inside the disaster area rely on the Internet (or Internet technologies) to exchange information.

The proper operation of the basic Internet infrastructure depends on wired connections and fixed power supplies. Both components make the Internet vulnerable to breakdown caused by disasters. Large scale disasters by definition have in common that wide areas of land are affected by immense forces such as floods, storms, or earthquakes. These forces lead usually to an immense destruction of man-made infrastructure, which is also important for the Internet backbone. Buildings accommodating points of presence collapse (e.g., 9/11), oversea cables break (e.g., Japan earthquake 2011), or power supplies turn down (e.g., Italy blackout 2003), for example. Satellite Internet access replaces cables in specific regions but those equipment still represent rather fix component.

For Internet hardware, it can be distinguished between two basic classes of fault modes that leave the infrastructure in a non-working state: Systems can suffer recoverable fault or they can suffer permanent damage. For the first class typical fault modes are power outages and overload conditions. As soon as power is restored or overload conditions are resolved, the system can continue in normal operation and little intervention by the network operators is required. Typical types for the second class of fault modes are broken wires and physically damaged hardware. In both cases massive repair effort by technical personal is required, as hardware needs to be replaced or connections have to be rewired. In case of highly destructive disasters these fault modes are more common. During most disasters buildings and power grids collapse, and the repairs requires significant time. Both fault classes are in fact not independent of each other. The outage of a backbone router will lead to a redirection of traffic which can lead to an overload condition and subsequent failure of another router.

The 2003 Italy blackout demonstrated the consequences of long-range, cascading failures and the interplay between the Internet and the fix power grid. A storm caused cascading outage of several power stations, which caused a failure of the Internet infrastructure, finally leading to additional breakdowns of power stations.

A fast recovery of communication infrastructure is of utmost importance. The common approaches today are to set-up temporary connectivity using mobile 3G/GSM base stations, satellite up-links, and improvised wiring paired with mobile generators for power supply. All these techniques though have in common that considerable time is needed to set them up. Depending on the location of the disaster, the (heavy) equipment needs to be transported, deployed, and initialized. For the time this takes the connectivity in the disaster area is very limited with respect to reachability and capacity. Furthermore, in the meantime privately installed wireless infrastructure may conflict with regained communication networks. The Haiti earthquake 2010 strikingly illustrated this when local ISPs restored 90 % of the network using wireless technology but Non-Governmental Organizations (NGOs) accidentally broke network communication by taking over the wireless spectrum.

2.3 Towards a Disaster-Adaptive Communication Infrastructure

Without doubt the Internet is very fundamental to enable communication—before, during, and after a disaster happened. Even though the Internet is a highly connected infrastructure providing high redundancy, its resilience is currently limited due to very basic dependency on fixed infrastructure components. Evolving the Internet to a completely disaster agnostic infrastructure with full service capabilities is a rather unrealistic challenge even when applying future Internet technologies. However, narrowing the scope to *minimal communication* reduces complexity and complies with the principle needs in disaster scenarios.

To overcome the major dependency on fixed components, communication networks are complemented by wireless transmission and battery power. The Internet of Things (IoT) inherently implements this perspective. On the downside,

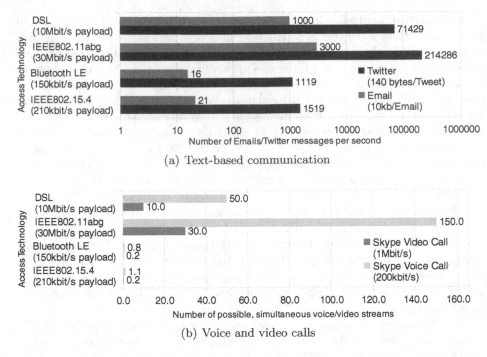

(a) Text-based communication

(b) Voice and video calls

Fig. 2. Usage of available throughput between two directly connected peers by typical applications for different access technologies.

wireless technology and low energy result in constrained throughput. For typical IoT access technologies Fig. 2 clearly indicates that still a reasonable amount of messages and calls can be exchanged between two parties. Building a disaster resilient communication network which provides these communication abilities in a stable deployment but with the flexibility of the Internet improves the current state of art.

3   Resilience Potential of the Internet of Things

The number of devices connected to the Internet has seen a steady growth since its creation. In the 90s, this growth was fueled by the advent of the hypertext transport protocol and the web. In the 2000s, this growth was driven by the new availability of wired broadband Internet access which enabled other popular applications such as multimedia streaming. Over the last decade, the growth has been driven by the emergence of wireless broadband Internet access via cellphones, laptops, tablets, and by novel, ultra-connected applications such as social networks. It is now projected that the growth will be fueled by the Internet of Things (IoT), i.e. the massive deployment of heterogeneous, communicating devices [5,14], ranging from wireless sensors to smart home appliances, which will blend in the global network, challenging the traditional notions of 'Internet host' and 'router'.

A significant part of the IoT thus consists in billions of battery powered devices that can communicate wirelessly, deployed in every location where humans shape their environment. In fact, most IoT devices use a communication architecture that is fundamentally richer that the conventional, infrastructure-based communication architecture employed to date. By leveraging a spontaneous wireless networking paradigm [4], such IoT devices are natively able to both (i) communicate via access points of the infrastructure if they are available, and (ii) communicate with one another autonomously, without the infrastructure as intermediary, if the latter is not available. Spontaneous wireless networking provides the necessary automatic mechanisms so that IoT devices can dynamically self-organize the relaying of data towards destination [12]. In that sense, each such IoT device is by default both host and router.

Thus, when one considers the IoT as a dense collection of battery-powered devices using a spontaneous wireless network paradigm, it becomes apparent that this architecture is naturally more resilient in face of disasters, and is less prone to the impacts described in Sect. 2.2. By running on battery power, nodes are not affected by power black-outs and damaged power cables. By using radio links the communication between devices does not suffer from broken wiring. Furthermore, by leveraging its dense deployment, and its ability to spontaneously self-organize wireless multi hop communication, the IoT brings a huge additional advantage: it comes with built-in redundancy. This means that even with a large loss of nodes, there is a good chance that the network will still consist in a giant component of physically connected nodes, which could be put to use immediately after the disaster happens.

Previous work on the connectivity of ad-hoc networks in disaster scenarios yields promising results [7, 11]. Approaches for disaster applications on top of this connectivity have also been proposed [13]. The communication systems considered in this work are homogenous in terms of the underlying hardware and routing protocols.

It is however projected that IoT devices will be very diverse with respect to characteristics including computation power, memory capacity and communication capabilities. While today's cell-phones are able to transmit and receive data using Wifi, Bluetooth, UMTS or LTE with throughputs ranging from a few Mbit/s to a few hundred Mbit/s, typical wireless sensor networks (WSNs) use radio standards that provide significantly lower throughput, in the range of a few hundred kbit/s [8]. In order to ensure connectivity over large areas, it is safe to assume that any IoT device that has survived the disaster in the area may be used as potential relay. Since the available throughput is smaller than the bottleneck on the path, it may thus be that a particularly constrained IoT device severely limits the available throughput towards a given destination. Furthermore, the routing mechanisms at work in large scale spontaneous wireless network may limit this throughput even more [6]. However, in any disaster scenario, a good rule of thumb is: limited connectivity is better than no connectivity at all. When looking at the communication requirements listed in Sect. 2, it becomes apparent that even a low throughput, text-based emergency service would help improving the coordination, speed and efficiency of disaster response, and that the availability of such a service may save lives as a direct consequence. Such mechanisms could enable diverse services including (i) emergency broadcast to all devices in an area to warn the general public, (ii) first-responder text-based situation reports communication to central coordination instances which can then make faster and more informed decisions, or (iii) individuals may emit emergency messages which allow response forces to detect and locate them in scenarios where some people are buried for instance.

It is furthermore noteworthy that a substantial part of the IoT is expected to consist in sensors that monitor various environmental parameters, thus providing quasi-ubiquitous sensing capabilities. Using these capabilities, coupled with the resilience of the IoT may provide crucial real-time data about disaster areas, which can help decision makers to better understand the impact of a disaster and react more appropriately. Available sensor data may range from temperature readings during bush fires, radiation readings after nuclear accidents or even destruction estimates based on the number and location of nodes that become unreachable.

4   Open Challenges

The IoT has considerable potential to contribute significantly to disaster resilience of communication networks as we discussed in Sect. 3. However, prior to succeeding in the 'grand challenges', the IoT is challenged by a variety of open questions and unsolved problems. Most challenges do not arise from the lack of existing technologies, but rather from a premature development of existing technologies and in particular from a lack of common standards and deployments that seamlessly interconnect. In the following section we will point out the areas where the most pressing issues arise.

4.1   Physical Connectivity and Hardware Limitations

Physical connectivity on a hardware level is the essential foundation to enable communication between devices. Sharing the same PHY and link layer is a requirement for data exchange between neighboring devices. For the IoT this means the use of common interface cards that use the same radio frequencies, modulations, link layer technology etc. Multiply connected gateways are required for transitioning network technologies.

A large heterogeneity of network access technologies, though, not only increases complexity of inter-networking, but may also lead to severe deployment problems in the wireless domain. Various radios that consume interfering frequencies of the limited spectrum by incompatible technologies may harm communication capacities at large without an ability to mutually coordinate.

Mobile phones broadly use 3GPP standards for data communication, such as UMTS, and increasingly LTE. In addition, modern phones and other hand-held devices (e.g., tablets) have further network interfaces such as IEEE 802.11 (Wifi) and IEEE 802.15.1 (Bluetooth). They are thus widespread candidates for bridging between radio technologies and serving as gateways. Similarly, millions of Wifi access points are deployed, each of which typically featuring a wireless and a wired network interface card for offering transit from small wireless 'cells' to the remaining Internet. Energy constraints typically restrict wireless sensors to a single wireless interface, either using a link layer based on IEEE 802.15.4 or Bluetooth Low Energy (BLE), which is not backward compatible. Other gateways like IEEE 802.15.4 border routers or Bluetooth 4.0 dual-mode devices need to be in place to integrate IoT devices.

In disaster scenarios, all available devices should form a single, largely connected network—as redundant as possible. Assuming the infrastructure is down (e.g., because of power blackout or cable damage), some battery-powered devices with multiple interfaces using different radio technologies such as smartphones, tablets, laptops will have to play the role of border routers to enable physical connectivity. However, it is noteworthy that these consumer devices typically neither have a IEEE 802.15.4 nor a BLE interface, which may lead to network partitioning because sensor networks using this link layer technology are unable to interconnect at the physical layer.

Moreover, since 30 years the industry has focused quasi exclusively on improving infrastructure-based wireless link layer technologies. It has largely ignored spontaneous wireless networking to the point that even today—15 years after the initial 802.11 standards were published—standard Wifi ad hoc mode is often not interoperable among vendors, if implemented at all. More generally, it remains to be seen how far new technologies can improve the performance of ad hoc, spontaneous wireless communication.

4.2 Logical Network Connectivity

The aim and outstanding success of today's Internet builds on its efficient and seamless way of interconnecting networks that use heterogeneous link layer technologies. This was achieved at large scale by using IP (the Internet Protocol) as the unique networking protocol and TCP/UDP at the transport layer. Wireless sensors and other constrained wireless devices are however too often based on proprietary network stacks (e.g., Zigbee or Nordic's Speedburst) that cannot interoperate across link layers or network borders. These confined networking solutions typically rely on specialized gateways to connect devices with the IP-based networks (i.e., the Internet).

Recently, the situation has improved, though, as the IETF has published relevant standards for the IoT. 6LoWPAN defines a lightweight network sublayer that enables constrained nodes (e.g., wireless sensors using IEEE 802.15.4) to interoperate natively with IPv6. 6LoWPAN thus enables a substantial fraction of IoT devices to connect directly to the Internet. It is projected that in the near future, proprietary network stacks will be phased out in favor of an IPv6 network stack using 6LoWPAN, as this brings not only benefits for vendors through standardization but also through faster time-to-market, cheaper development cycles leveraging well-known development practices and tools.

However, 6LoWPAN as a minimal standard of speaking IPv6 among devices is insufficient to orchestrate large scale spontaneous wireless networking, as required for disaster resilience described in Sect. 3. Improved disaster resilience relies on the ability of IoT devices to (i) dynamically reconfigure forwarding tables in order to route data over multiple wireless hops, towards destination, and (ii) dynamically adapt transport layer mechanisms to the particular versatility of multi-hop wireless communication. Both (i) and (ii) should be achieved automatically, without explicit configuration, without the need of intervention from users and network administrators, and without the help of infrastructure. Over the last decade, a significant amount of work has been accomplished in this field, which resulted in the publications of new routing protocol standards (e.g., RPL, OLSR) to cope with (i). More work is however needed to achieve better scalability of routing protocol overhead in practice—we are still far from the theoretical bounds. Furthermore, TCP modifications are desirable to efficiently accommodate multi-hop wireless communication to cope with (ii).

Additional auto configuration mechanisms are needed for IoT devices to be useful in case of disaster which results in unavailability of infrastructure-based networks. For instance, sensor networks and other IoT networks are mostly envisioned as stub networks which connect to the Internet through a given gateway. This gateway directly or indirectly determines the configuration of attached nodes, including parameters such as IP address, encryption details. Unless nodes reconfigure automatically these parameters upon detection of infrastructure unreachability, nodes that were in separate stub networks prior to the disaster may not be able to communicate with one another because the network layer will prohibit it—thus annihilating the chances of spontaneously interconnecting to form a single, large network spanning the disaster area. To efficiently enable this behavior, future work has to be carried out.

4.3   Prioritization of Data Traffic

Largely heterogeneous link transitions bear the problem of exhausting congestions that are likely to kill data flows. Assuming the connectivity gap is bridged at the MAC/PHY layer and at the network layer as described in Sects. 4.1 and 4.2, throughput may be very limited. The general idea is to use the available throughput for the most important services, as described in Sect. 2. A challenge that remains is thus the design of mechanisms that guarantees that only these services do use of the available throughput.

An idea could be to introduce a 'disaster mode' for IoT devices. Besides their normal mode of operation, IoT nodes could switch to an alternative mode of operation in which the goal becomes spontaneous maximization of connectivity in the sense described in Sect. 3. Furthermore, this special mode of operation could implement prioritization policies that would guarantee first responders or official organizations privileged access to the newly spawned communication network. This 'disaster mode' would be roughly comparable to the emergency call mode in today's mobile phones, where 911 calls are possible even if no registered SIM-card is activated.

In fact, such a mode of operation may be necessary anyway in case of disaster because, should massively deployed sensors and smart object resume their 'normal operation' automatically after the disaster, the limited throughput left available may be involuntarily clogged by 'unimportant' data traffic – a case that should be avoided. Note that this may also apply to other types of data traffic, e.g., system updates on smart-phones.

As promising as such an approach sounds, there are however important additional technical questions, as well as political questions, which have to be investigated. How/when exactly would such a 'disaster mode' be triggered? What kind of regulations are needed to force vendors to integrate this mode into their devices? How should such a 'disaster mode' be standardized?

4.4 Social Acceptance

As described in Sect. 3, leveraging IoT devices to mitigate the impact of a disaster on network connectivity implies that devices may be required to be operated outside their intended scope, and connect to external parties that normally do not have access to those devices. For example, if privately owned sensor networks were required to relay communication traffic on behalf of governmental agencies, or on behalf of other private individuals that must send/receive emergency information, the owners of such networks would need to allow a mode of operation that they do not fully control. Social acceptance of this category of usage should be studied, to prevent situations where owners of devices actively try to block any use outside their full control—preventing in effect the approach towards more resilience.

4.5 Network Security Aspects

The IoT in general presents a number of challenges in terms of application layer and network layer security. These security challenges naturally transfer to IoT use in case of disaster scenarios. In this context, one should avoid the usual reflex of initially leaving security aspects out of the picture because "every bit of the scarce throughput should be used for communication traffic". For example, there are a number of scenarios in which unprotected network traffic could be used by malicious third parties to intentionally interrupt or alter information that is exchanged between first responders or coming from emergency calls, e.g., large-scale terrorist attacks such as 9/11. As data is routed through the IoT, attackers could try to tamper with communications ways that cripple helper organization. Furthermore, the mechanisms that trigger devices to switch to 'disaster mode' operation should itself be secure in order to prevent attacks aiming to disrupt normal network operation. These challenges are directly related to lightweight, decentralized authentication schemes.

4.6   Towards Disaster Resilience

With the technology available today, the Internet of Things cannot yet be used to improve our communication networks resilience in face of large-scale disasters. Several challenges must be addressed beforehand. While from a technical perspective the open questions we have identified yield substantial issues to be solved there are no fundamental show-stopper to allow the IoT to mitigate the impact of a disaster on network connectivity. The main question is thus not whether the IoT can be leveraged to improve disaster resilience, but rather to which extent and how it should be adopted.

5   Conclusions

The Internet of Things is already here. Beyond traditional routers and Internet hosts such as PCs or smartphones/tablets, a new category of battery-powered, connected machines has emerged, and applications using these machines are announced and brought to the market on a daily basis. Projections indicate that massive deployment of such devices is dawning, and will soon revolutionize the edge architecture of the Internet, by leveraging not only infrastructure-based wireless networking but also spontaneous wireless networking. This enriched architecture can significantly improve the resilience of basic data communication services in face of disasters that damage conventional communication network infrastructure.

While the IoT is not able to provide the full range of communication services expected from pre-disaster Internet, one can nevertheless envision providing better-than-nothing services such as emergency micro-messaging, using IoT devices as relays and popular handheld devices (e.g. smartphones) as user terminals. This paper proposed an overview of this vision, and highlighted the major advantage such an approach could bring: the automatic reconfiguration of the network to interconnect surviving devices immediately after the disaster, even if the infrastructure is down and the power grid is out. Basic connectivity and simple text-based data communication could then remain available during the crucial gap between the time when the disaster occurs and the time when qualified manpower reach the area and set up dedicated hardware putting conventional communication infrastructure back in service.

There are however a number of challenges that need to be addressed before this vision can be realized. This paper provided an analysis of the different categories of issues that lie ahead. These concern on one hand technical aspects such as physical connectivity requirements, network protocol stack enhancements, or data traffic prioritization schemes, and on the other hand non-technical aspects such as social and political considerations. We argue that while the relevant technical issues are substantial, there are no identified show-stoppers. Concerning non-technical aspects, we argue that legislating on the matter would probably be necessary. We propose the definition of a mandatory 'disaster mode' of operation for IoT devices (similar to cellphone's 911 mode of operation), which could automatically kick in to reconfigure the surviving network elements in cases where infrastructure is out of service, enabling automatically basic connectivity and simple text-based data communication for emergency purposes. In future work, we will also analyse upcoming network paradigms such as information-centric networking, which shows potential in constrained environments and disaster scenarios [2,10].

Acknowledgements. This work was partially supported by ANR and BMBF within the SAFEST and Peeroskop projects, by the EU within the geocrowd project, and the DAAD within the guest lecture program.

References

1. Atzori, L., Iera, A., Morabito, G.: The internet of things: a survey. Comput. Netw. **54**(15), 2787–2805 (2010)
2. Baccelli, E., Mehlis, C., Hahm, O., Schmidt, T.C., Wählisch, M.: Information centric networking in the IoT: experiments with NDN in the wild. In: Proceedings of 1st ACM Conference on Information-Centric Networking (ICN 2014), pp. 77–86. ACM, New York, September 2014
3. Baldwin, J., Ewert, J., Yamen, S.: Evolution of the voice interconnect. Ericsson Review **88**, 10–15 (2010)
4. Cordero, J., Yi, J., Clausen, T., Baccelli, E.: Enabling multihop communication in spontaneous wireless networks. In: ACM SIGCOMM eBook on Recent Advances in Networking, ch. 9, vol. 1, pp. 413–457. ACM (2013)
5. Ericsson: More than 50 billion devices. Technical report, Ericsson White Paper (2011)
6. Gupta, P., Kumar, P.: The capacity of wireless networks. IEEE Trans. Inf. Theory **46**(2), 388–404 (2000)
7. Lien, Y.N., Jang, H.C., Tsai, T.C.: A manet based emergency communication and information system for catastrophic natural disasters. In: 29th IEEE International Conference on Distributed Computing Systems Workshops, ICDCS Workshops 2009, pp. 412–417. IEEE (2009)
8. Onwuka, E., Folaponmile, A., Ahmed, M.: Manet: a reliable network in disaster areas. J. Res. Nat. Dev. **9**(2), 105–113 (2013)
9. Palen, L., Liu, S.B.: Citizen communications in crisis: anticipating a future of ICT-supported public participation. In: Proceedings of ACM CHI, pp. 727–736. ACM, New York (2007)
10. Seedorf, J., Arumaithurai, M., Tagami, A., Ramakrishnan, K., Blefari-Melazzi, N.: Using ICN in disaster scenarios. Internet-Draft - work in progress 02, IETF, June 2014
11. Shimoda, K., Gyoda, K.: Analysis of ad hoc network performance for disaster communication models. In: 2011 10th International Symposium on Autonomous Decentralized Systems (ISADS), pp. 483–488. IEEE (2011)
12. Sundmaeker, H., Guillemin, P., Friess, P., Woelffle, S.: Vision and challenges for realising the internet of things. Cluster of European Research Projects on the Internet of Things, European Commision (2010)
13. Umedu, T., Urabe, H., Tsukamoto, J., Sato, K., Higashinoz, T.: A manet protocol for information gathering from disaster victims. In: Fourth Annual IEEE International Conference on Pervasive Computing and Communications Workshops, PerCom Workshops 2006, p. 5. IEEE (2006)

14. Vermesan, O., Friess, P., Guillemin, P., Gusmeroli, S., Sundmaeker, H., Bassi, A., Jubert, I.S., Mazura, M., Harrison, M., Eisenhauer, M., et al.: Internet of things strategic research roadmap. In: Vermesan, O., Friess, P., Guillemin, P., Gusmeroli, S., Sundmaeker, H., Bassi, A., et al. (eds.) Internet of Things: Global Technological and Societal Trends, vol. 1, pp. 9–52 (2011)

NFC Peer to Peer Secure Services for Smart Cities: LLCPS Concepts and Experiments with Smartphones

Pascal Urien[✉]

Telecom ParisTech, 23 Avenue d'italie, 75015 Paris, France
Pascal.Urien@Telecom-ParisTech.fr

Abstract. Proximity communication technologies, such as NFC (*Near Field Communication*) are today widely deployed in smart city environments. Contactless services based on NFC facilities are used for payment, transport or access control applications. There are supported by most of mobile operating systems. The NFC *Peer to Peer* mode is typically used for pushing small pieces of information in applications like Android Beams, or Personal Health Device Communication (PHDC), a family of devices comprising blood pressure meters, blood glucose meters, or body weight scales. Security (i.e. mutual authentication, data privacy and integrity) is a critical topic for P2P exchanges; however it is not specified by today standards. In order to solve these issues we introduced a security protocol (LLCPS) compatible with NFC standards and based on the well known TLS protocol. This Chapter describes an experimental platform built with commercial smartphones and presents some performances.

Keywords: NFC · P2P · Security · Iot · TLS · LLCP · LLCPS

1 Introduction

Proximity communication technologies, such as NFC (*Near Field Communication* [1]) are today widely deployed in smart city environments. Contactless services based on NFC facilities are used for payment, transport or access control applications. Major cities like Paris (*Navigo card*), London (*Oster card*), Venezia (*Imob card*), Seoul (*T Money Card*) use NFC tickets for their transport networks. NFC interfaces are more and more supported by EMV bank cards for contactless payments. Millions of electronic locks controlling hotels rooms, office doors, parking entrances are working with NFC key cards typically based on tags such as *Mifare Ultralight* [8].

Therefore smart cities already include multiple NFC kiosks connected to various information systems. During the last decade mobile devices powered by operating systems such as Android, RIM or Windows have been manufactured with NFC interfaces (according to [2] two in three phones to come with NFC in 2018). There is a trend to replace NFC card and tickets by application running in smartphones with internet connectivity. As an illustration, the EMVCO consortium is working on new payment technology called tokenization [9] compatible with NFC-enabled mobiles.

© Institute for Computer Sciences, Social Informatics and Telecommunications Engineering 2015
R. Giaffreda et al. (Eds.): IoT360 2014, Part II, LNICST 151, pp. 297–305, 2015.
DOI: 10.1007/978-3-319-19743-2_40

NFC has three working modes Reader/Writer, Card Emulation, and Peer to Peer (P2P). The two first are imported from legacy applications working with contactless devices powered by reader. The P2P mode [3] deals with two devices (the target and the initiator) managing their own power feeding (i.e. including batteries). It is used for pushing small pieces of information in applications like *Android Beams* working with the SNEP [5] protocol, or *Personal Health Device Communication* [7], a family of devices such as blood pressure meters, blood glucose meters, or body weight scales. Security (i.e. mutual authentication, data privacy and integrity) is a critical topic for P2P exchanges; however it is not specified by today standards. In order to solve these issues we introduced in [14, 16] a security protocol compatible with NFC standards and based on the well known TLS protocol. This chapter describes an experimental platform built with commercial smartphones and details some performances; a demonstration of this prototype was performed in [15].

This chapter is constructed according to the following outline. Section 2 recalls the main characteristics of the NFC P2P mode; it introduces the LLCP [4] protocol and the SNEP [5] service. Section 3 introduces LLCPS [14], a secure P2P protocol based on TLS. Section 4 presents the experimental platform; made with a smartphone and a NFC reader, and its software architecture. Section 5 summarizes experimental performances for operations secured by asymmetric procedures (RSA and X509 certificates, anonymous Diffie-Hellman over elliptic curves) and symmetric procedures (i.e. the TLS abbreviated mode). Finally Sect. 6 concludes this chapter.

2   About NFC Peer to Peer

The *Near Field Communication* (NFC) protocol is a proximity communication technology based on inductive coupling. According to the *Lenz* law a magnetic field of 5 A/m, pulsed at the 13,56 MHz frequency, induced a voltage of about 2 V on a loop with an area of 40 cm^2 (5 cm x 8 cm). Another interesting property of inductive coupling is the energy conservation; the energy delivered by the primary circuit (P_{PRI}) is consumed by the secondary (P_{SEC}) circuit according to the relation:

$$P_{PRI} = P_{SEC} = 2\pi f M I_{PRI} I_{SEC}$$

where f is the frequency, M the mutual inductance, I_{PRI} and I_{SEC} respectively the electric current in the primary and secondary circuit. The power feeding of the secondary circuit by the primary one is a physical assumption for devices proximity. NFC supports two functional modes:

- Reader/Writer and Card Emulation. A device named "Reader" feeds another device called "Card", thanks to a 13,56 MHz electromagnetic coupling. This mode is typically used with contactless smartcards or NFC tags.
- Peer to Peer (P2P). Two devices, the "Initiator" and the "Target" establish a communication link. In the "Active" mode these two nodes are managing their own energy resources. In the "Passive" mode the Initiator powers the Target via a 13,56 MHz electromagnetic field.

In this chapter we focus on the P2P mode which is more and more supported by smartphones running operating such as android, RIM and others.

2.1 About Logical Link Control Protocol (LLCP)

A P2P session occurs in four steps:

(1) *Initialization and Anti-collision.* The Initiator periodically generates a RF field and sends a request packet, acknowledged by a Target response packet. It manages anti-collision mechanisms in order to detect several Target devices.
(2) *Protocol Activation and Parameters Selection.* The Initiator begins a session with a detected Target by forwarding an *Attribute-Request* message, confirmed by a Target *Attribute-Response* message. These messages setup the functional parameters to be used by P2P exchanges.
(3) *Data Exchange.* Frames are exchanged via the *Data Exchange Protocol* (DEP [3]) that provides error detection and recovery. It works with small packets (from 64 to 256 bytes). The Initiator transmits *DEP-Request* acknowledged by *DEP-Response*. These frames typically transport LLCP [4] messages, which are detailed below.
(4) *De-Activation.* The Initiator releases the P2P session with the Target.

The *Logical Link Control Protocol* (LLCP) manages information exchanges during P2P sessions.

It may work according to connection oriented or connectionless paradigms. However all legacy P2P services used a connected paradigm, and this chapter only deals with this mode. The main advantage of connection oriented service is to manage potential traffic congestions, due to operating system overloads, via dedicated packets called RNR (*Receiver Not Ready*); we observed such packets with the RIM (BB10) operating system.

A LLCP packet is transported by a DEP frame. It comprises three mandatory fields, the *Destination Service Access Point*, (DSAP 6 bits), the *Source Service Access Point* (SSAP 6 bits), and *Protocol Type* (PTYPE 4 bits). An optional sequence field (8 bits) contains two (4 bits) numbers N(S) and N(R) respectively giving the number of the information packet to be sent and the number of the next information packet to be received. In the connected mode a service is identified by a name, or an integer (a well-known *Service Access Point*, SAP). A connection is performed via two dedicated LLCP packets, CONNECT and CONNECTION CONFIRM (CC). A CONNECT request to the well-known SAP number 1 (the *Service Discovery Protocol*) is a way to get an ephemeral SAP associated to a service name, and therefore to start a session with this named service. A NFC P2P server processes the CONNECT packet issued by a NFC P2P client. Figure 1 illustrates a connection to a named service, performed between an initiator acting as a NFC client, and a target hosting a NFC server.

2.2 The SNEP Service

The Simple NDEF Exchange Protocol (SNEP, [5]) is a simple service widely used to push data over LLCP. It comprises two main messages SNEP-PUT and SNEP-Success whose name are self-explanatory. A SNEP service is identified either by the well-known SAP number 4, or by the name *urn:nfc:sn:snep*. The information shuttled by SNEP-PUT message is encoded according the NFC Data Exchange Format (NDEF, [7]); this last-mentioned supports multiple formats such as text or URLs. NDEF contents are also hosted by NFC tags (such as the NXP *Mifare Ultralight* [8]), used as transportation tickets or key cards. In a typical SNEP dialog, the initiator detects a target; a P2P session is established, and thanks to LLCP the SNEP client sends a CONNECT request (either to the DSAP 4 or the DSAP 1) to the SNEP server confirmed by a CC packet. Thereafter the SNEP client pushes NDEF content thanks to the SNEP-PUT message, acknowledged in turn by a SNEP-Success. In a smart cities context, SNEP could be used by numerous services such as transportation or access control.

3 About LLCPS

One issue for NFC P2P exchanges is the lack of native security and privacy. Data are exchanged in clear form over the air. There is no data encryption and no pairing (i.e. mutual authentication) between the initiator and the target. The main target of LLCPS (LLCP secure, [14]) is to reuse the TLS protocol over LLCP in order to address these critical issues. TLS (*Transport Layer Security*) is a well-known IETF protocol, which is widely used for the internet security. According to the NFC standards a P2P name is associated to a service; in our context the *urn:nfc:sn:tls:service* string identifies a service such as SNEP whose privacy is enforced by the TLS protocol.

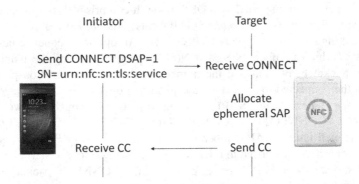

Fig. 1. P2P connection between a client (initiator side) and a server (target side)

TLS has two working modes, the full mode in which the client and the server may be authenticated by X509 certificates and associated private keys, and the abbreviated mode that reuses a previously opened full session, and which only deals with symmetric cryptography. A full session with strong mutual authentication may be interpreted as a pairing between initiator and target. A shared secret (the *master secret*) is created between these two entities, which is thereafter available for resume sessions, dealing with lighter symmetric cryptographic exchanges. The booting of a full session works with a four ways handshake, while a resume session only requires a three ways handshake. The EAP-TLS protocol [13] demonstrates how TLS messages may be gathered in blocks exchanged according to a half-duplex mechanism. LLCPS builds such TLS blocks, which are segmented in small LLCP packets (typically *128 bytes*) exchanged between initiator and targets devices. TLS supports various cryptographic algorithms such as RSA or Elliptic Curves (ECC). We developed an experimental platform and performed tests with two types of algorithms, RSA with X509 certificates, and anonymous Diffie-Hellman over elliptic curves (ECCDH anonymous).

4   The Experimental Platform

The experimental platform (see Fig. 2) is made of two parts, a smartphone (BB10, [12]) equipped with a NFC interface, and NFC reader (the ACS122, [10, 11]) delivering P2P facilities. The use case is an access control application (ticketing, electronic key) using SNEP, and running over the *urn:nfc:sn:tls:snep* service.

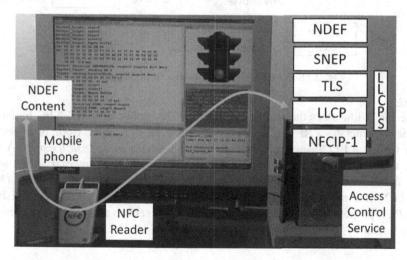

Fig. 2. The experimental LLCPS platform, controlling an electronic lock

4.1   The BB10 Smartphone

The smartphone phone is a BB10 model [12], powered by a POSIX operating system. The mobile application is written in the C language. The mobile embeds classical UNIX software libraries such as SOCKET for the TCP/IP connectivity, OPENSSL for

TLS facilities and LIBNFC for the NFC management. The NFC framework is managed by the following proprietary procedures:

- *nfc-connect()* and *nfc-disconnect()* starts and stops the NFC framework.
- *nfc-llcp-register-connection-listener()* registers the application for a particular NFC service identified by a name such as "urn:nfc:sn:tls:snep" in this use case.
- *nfc-llcp-read()* and *nfc-llcp-write()* handle NFC packets reception and transmission over the NFC radio. The maximum packet length is about 128 bytes. TLS messages are segmented and reassembled according to this size.
- The programming model is event driven; main procedures are associated to events such as *LLCP-CONNECTION*, *LLCP-WRITE-COMPLETE*, *LLCP-READ-COMPLETE*.

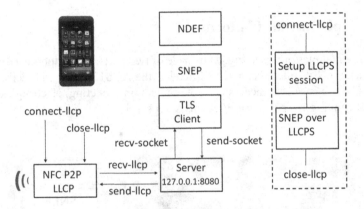

Fig. 3. Software architecture of the mobile application

The Fig. 3 illustrates the mobile application. The mobile acts as a NFC initiator; it periodically generates a RF field, and polls the presence of a target. Upon detection of a remote device, a LLCP session is started with the service *urn:nfc:sn:tls:snep*. A *TLS-Client*, working the OPENSSL library, exchanges data with an internal socket server (using the *127.0.0.1:8080* address) acting as a proxy with a software module (*NFC-P2P-LLCP*) that manages the LLCP session. When the TLS session is established a *SNEP-PUT* packet, transporting a NDEF payload is sent to the target and thereafter acknowledged by a *SNEP-Success* packet.

4.2   The NFC Kiosk System

The NFC kiosk system (see Fig. 4) is assembled around a NFC reader [11] delivering P2P services. Upon detection of a remote initiator, it waits for an incoming CONNECT packet including a supporting service name (such as *urn:nfc:sn:tls:snep*). This event is handled by the *accept-llcp()* procedure. A client software entity is internally connected to a TLS server (running at the *127.0.0.1:443* address) based on the OPENSSL library, and works as a proxy with the NFC LLCP software entity. When the TLS session is

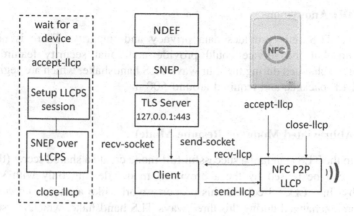

Fig. 4. Software architecture of the NFC kiosk.

established, a SNEP server, whose goal is to securely collect NDEF content, processes and produces secured SNEP messages.

5 Tests

According to the experimental platform previously introduced, a NFC SNEP client running on the Initiator mobile opens a TLS secure session with a NFC server running on the Target device, which performs an access control service. Both systems are using the OPENSSL library, and therefore support multiple cryptographic procedures. Among them we selected three security schemes:

- Key exchange with authentication dealing with RSA 1024 bits keys and X509 certificates.
- Anonymous key exchange using ECCDH, with a 163 bits elliptic curve (Sect. 163r1).
- Key exchange in the abbreviated mode; the mode use symmetric cryptography and required a previous successful full mode, either RSA or ECCDH anonymous.

In all these use cases the SNEP messages are ciphered by the RC4 algorithm and data integrity is provided by the HMAC procedure. We observe, on the target side, that for 128 bytes DEP packets, the reception requires about 85 ms, and the transmission about 65 ms; these experimental timings are higher than the expected values with a physical data rate of about 100 KBits/s.

5.1 RSA with Certificates

Both the Target and the Initiator hold X509 certificates and RSA 1024 bits private keys. Mutual authentication could be mandatory for services without native security; for example when a key value is pushed in a clear form. About 3100 bytes are exchanged during the four ways TLS handshake, which are segmented in 128 bytes DEP packets, and required around 2000 ms.

5.2   ECCDH Anonymous

In this mode TLS only provides data privacy and integrity. There is no mutual authentication, but the service could provide additional security features. About 440 bytes are exchanged during the four ways TLS handshake, which are segmented in 128 bytes DEP packets, and required around 500 ms.

5.3   The Abbreviated Mode (or Resume Mode)

According to the TLS standard a successful full mode create a shared secret (the *master secret*) that can be reused by the abbreviated mode, dealing only with symmetric cryptography. In a LLCPS context this property works like a pairing process. About 340 bytes are exchanged during this three ways TLS handshake, which are segmented in 128 bytes DEP packets, and required around 410 ms.

5.4   Secure SNEP Protocol

For all uses cases, once the TLS secure channel has been opened two protected packets (transported by the TLS record layer) are exchanged SNEP-PUT and SNEP-Success. On the Target side, about 46 TLS bytes are received in 188 ms and 26 bytes are transmitted in 32 ms.

6   Conclusion

In this chapter we presented a P2P platform secure by TLS built with commercial devices. It clearly demonstrates that a high level of security can be achieved for smart cities proximity services. However we observed performances issues with the emerging NFC technology.

References

1. Technical Specifications. http://www.nfc-forum.org/specs/
2. http://press.ihs.com/press-release/design-supply-chain/nfc-enabled-cellphone-shipments-soar-fourfold-next-five-years
3. ISO/IEC 18092, Near Field Communication - Interface and Protocol (NFCIP-1), April 2004
4. Logical Link Control Protocol, Technical Specification, NFC Forum™, LLCP 1.1, June 2011
5. Simple NDEF Exchange Protocol, Technical Specification, NFC Forum™, SNEP 1.0, August 2011
6. NFC Data Exchange Format (NDEF), Technical Specification NFC Forum™, NDEF 1.0, July 2006
7. Personal Health Device Communication, Technical Specification NFC Forum™, PHDC 1.0, February 2013

8. MF0ICU1, MIFARE Ultralight contactless single-ticket IC Rev. 3.9, NXP Semiconductors, 23 July 2014
9. EMV Payment Tokenisation Specification, Technical Framework, Version 1.0, March 2014, EMVCO
10. Lotito, A.; Mazzocchi, D.: OPEN-NPP: An Open Source Library to Enable P2P over NFC. In: 4th International Workshop on Near Field Communication (NFC) (2012)
11. PN532, User manual, Document Identifier UM0701-02, 2007, NXP Semiconductors
12. http://developer.blackberry.com/native/
13. RFC 5216, The EAP-TLS Authentication Protocol, March 2008
14. LLCPS, draft-urien-tls-llcp-00.txt, IETF Draft (2012-2014)
15. Urien, P.: A Secure Cloud of Electronic Keys for NFC Locks Securely Controlled by NFC Smartphones. In: IEEE CCNC, Las Vegas, USA (2014)
16. Urien, P.: LLCPS: A New Secure Model For Internet of Things Services Based On The NFC P2P Model. In: IEEE ISSNIP, Singapore (2014)

A Secure Self-Identification Mechanism for Enabling IoT Devices to Join Cloud Computing

Massimo Villari[✉], Antonio Celesti, Maria Fazio, and Antonio Puliafito

University of Messina, DICIEAMA,
Contrada Di Dio (S. Agata), 98166 Messina, Italy
{mvillari,acelesti,mfazio,apuliafito}@unime.it
http://mdslab.unime.it

Abstract. Nowadays, one of the major problems in Internet of Things (IoT) is the initial setup and boot up of new embedded devices that have to be connected over the Internet. On the other hand, another problem is the interaction of such devices with a Cloud computing environment. This paper deals with the possibility to automatically configure IoT devices in a secure way, so as to provide new added-value services. In particular, after a discussion of a Cloud scenario for IoT, we discuss how to perform a self-identification process in order to achieve a secure auto-configuration of IoT devices joining the Cloud. The paper deals with the design of secure IoT infrastructures.

Keywords: Cloud computing · IoT · Identification · Configuration · Security

1 Introduction

Nowadays, the increasingly penetration of sensing devices and the emerging concept Internet of Things (IoT) offer new possibilities for sharing data and services over the Internet. As highlighted in the *Digital Agenda for Europe* [1], one of the key challenges for the European Commission is to have a globally competitive Cloud infrastructure for the "Internet of Services" interconnected with "Things" distributed over remote areas. IoT is currently applied in many applications fields, such as in buildings construction, car traffic monitoring, environment analysis, health-care, weather forecast, video surveillances, etc. Definitely, there is not limit to the possible scenarios that can be accomplished combining IoT and Cloud computing. In our opinion, IoT can appear as a natural extension of Cloud computing, in which the Cloud allows us to access IoT based resources and capabilities, to manage intelligent pervasive environments. In addition Cloud computing can support the delivery of IoT services. Thus an IoT service can be considered as an on-demand Cloud-based Sensing and Actuation as a Service (SAaaS). One of the main problems in deploying IoT devices is the secure self-configuration of such devices that is necessary to interconnect them over the Cloud. In this paper, we analyze the existing issues regarding to the self-configuration of IoT devices that have to be connected over the Internet to join

© Institute for Computer Sciences, Social Informatics and Telecommunications Engineering 2015
R. Giaffreda et al. (Eds.): IoT360 2014, Part II, LNICST 151, pp. 306–311, 2015.
DOI: 10.1007/978-3-319-19743-2_41

a Cloud environment. In our opinion, an IoT device should be able to configure itself, interacting with the Cloud in a secure way, and downloading its customized features directly from remote providers. The paper we present hereby is strongly related to the design of secure IoT infrastructures. According to our vision, each user should be able to turn on his/her IoT device, connecting it via WiFi, and waiting for its self-configuration in order to interact with the Cloud. In order to self-configure IoT devices in a secure way and allowing them to interact over the Cloud, they should be equipped with capabilities including security keys, cryptographic algorithms, hidden IDs, etc. The rest of the paper is organized as follows. Section 2 discusses related works. Section 3 presents a possible scenario integrating IoT and Cloud computing. In Sect. 4, we highlight the main factors involved for a secure self-identification of IoT devices. In Sect. 5, we discuss how IoT devices joining a Cloud system can self-register themselves to perform a self-configuration process. Section 6 concludes the paper.

2   Related Work

In the near future, the heavy penetration of sensing devices into Internet applications will cause the explosion of the amount of data to be stored and processed, as very well described in [10]. Often Sensor Networks are considered as virtual devices [7]. Physical sensors can be mapped into virtual sensors clouds, hence Cloud Computing and Sensors Networks can be managed in the same way. Sensor Network and IoTs also reside a lot of problem in security context as described in [5,11] and [12]. The new concept of Mobile Cloud computing appeared in 2012. The concept consists in providing new services for Cloud users taking into account their movements and preferences. In [4], the authors investigated the delivery of mobile cloud services. They stated that services suffering from poor performance due to the mobile network fluctuations. Moreover, under the Smart Cities umbrella many works are dealing with sensors and Clouds, as well as in [9] and [8]. In [9], the authors have investigated the possibility to unify Resilient Cloud Computing and Secure IoT in smart cities scenarios. Security and resilience seen to look at the same perspective. In the same direction respect to our work is the work described in [6]. Here, the authors present an exhaustive analysis of sensor Cloud architectures benefiting of Arduino devices. Very similar is the study presented in [3] in which the service provisioning for sensors is assessed leveraging Clouds.

3   A Cloud Scenario for IoT

In this Section, we present a scenario in which several IoT devices interact with a Cloud system. Figure 1(a) shows different users holding several IoT devices connected to a domestic WiFi network. Each device is able to automatically configure it-self downloading its configuration from a given Cloud provider. Several datacenters belonging to a Cloud operator are spread over the world. For example, datacenter A is placed in USA, datacenter B is located in Europe, and

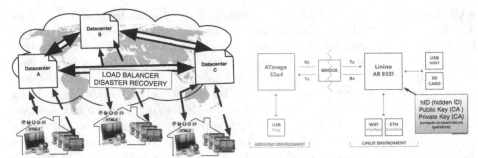

(a) Single Cloud Scenario with one oper-   (b) Arduino Yun extended with security
ator distributed among datacenters that   capabilities.
interact with IoT devices and Customers.

Fig. 1. The Cloud Scenario under investigation and the modified version of Arduino
Yun.

datacenter C is placed in Asia. Each datacenter collects data coming from IoT
devices connected in geographical area that it serves.

An indispensable requirement of the proposed scenario is that when an IoT
device moves from a datacenter to another, it should be able to self-configure
itself in a secure way.

4   Towards Secure Self-Identification of IoT Devices

This Section, we discuss how existing IoT embedded devices might be extended
and used to achieve the scenario previously described. According to the approach
discussed in this paper, these IoT devices should be onboarded with Security
Keys, Cryptographic Algorithms and Hidden IDs (hIDs).

4.1   Arduino Yun

In order simplify the discussion on how an IoT device can be extended with hardware security capabilities we consider Arduino Yun as reference. The Arduino
open hardware framework is a consolidated architecture able to fulfill the IoT
requirements especially for its cheapness and simplicity of utilization. Many versions, shields, and extensions exist over the market for the Arduino platform. One
of these versions is the new framework able to provide the Arduino capabilities
along with the Linux Embedded features that is referred as Yun device. Specifically, the Yun is distinguished from other Arduino boards by the fact that it can
communicate with the Linux distribution onboard, offering a powerful networked
computer with the easiness of Arduino. The Atheros AR9331 processor supports
a Linux distribution based on OpenWRT named Linino. Figure 1(b) shows how
Yun works. The left side of the picture depicts the Arduino part, whereas in the
right side there is the Linino part. Yun has a built-in WiFi/Ethernet boards that
enrich the Arduino part. The Linux embedded part can be used for accomplish-
ing the interactions with the Cloud.

4.2 Security Keys, Cryptographic Algorithms and Hidden IDs

In order to achieve the scenarios discussed in Sect. 3, an IoT device such as Arduino Yun should be equipped with a component mounted on the board during the manufacturing and offering several security capabilities as depicted in the right part of Fig. 1(b). In particular, these security capabilities should include: Security Keys (e.g., a couple of public/private keys X509v3 based (K_{pub}, K_{priv})), Cryptographic Algorithms, a hidden ID (hId). The hID is a numeric serial-number used by manufacturer for recognizing each board. It is hidden because no one must read it. Here, we introduced the concept of Obfuscated ID (obH) derived from the MD5 hashing function. The major property of an hashing function is its incontrovertibly, in fact it is also defined an one-way function (i.e., from the output of an hashing function it is not possible to deduct the input). Hence, looking at Eq. 1 the obH is useful for tracking the board without knowing its public MAC address and the board owner if the MAC-User association exists in the Cloud provider.

$$obH = hash(hID, MAC) \tag{1}$$

The obH is computed by Eq. 3, and it represents a board index that can be stored in whichever public database. According to Eq. 2, in any communication between the device and the Cloud operator a Message (M) can be included in the body of all communications concatenating obH, MAC, and a public key K_{pub}.

$$M = concat(obH, MAC, K_{pub}) \tag{2}$$

A signature strongly guarantees the trustiness of the sender. The public key K_{pub} is signed at production level during its manufacturing, using for example the Certification Authority (CA) of the manufacturer of the IoT device. Instead, the private key K_{priv} is not accessible externally from its chip endorsed in the device, but it can be used by the internal security algorithms.

$$SM = signature(K_{priv}, M) \tag{3}$$

4.3 Adding Secure Hardware Capabilities

Trusted Computing (TC), defined by the Trusted Computing Group (TCG) [2], combines hardware and software security mechanisms to enhance the security level of computing environments. TC implies the adoption of an hardware chip called Trusted Platform Module (TPM), that is able to provide Roots of Trusts (RoTs) and to extend its trust to other parts of the device by building a chain of trust. It offers facilities for the secure generation of cryptographic keys by means of a unique RSA key burnt into as it is produced (i.e., the Endorsement Key (EK)). The TPM includes capabilities such as machine authentication, hardware encryption, signing, secure key storage and attestation. Born for securing traditional Personal Computers, the TCG is currently looking at both embedded and mobile devices whose reference architecture specification drafts were released respectively in April and June 2014. The specifications provide guidelines on how to onboard the TPM in a device even though there have not been so many implementations yet on real hardware devices. TC and embedded systems are at the early stage, however, in our opinion, TC is a valid solution to develop hardware security capabilities in IoT devices interacting with the Cloud.

5   Registration Strategies of IoT Devices Joing the Cloud

The IoT device, e.g., the Arduino Yun extended with security capabilities, can follow two different registration methods:

- case A, Unsupervised: auto registration of MAC address and obH;
- case B, Supervised: end-user web registration of MAC address and obH.

In both the cases, the end-user needs to enable the IoT device to maintaing the WiFi network association using the wps button on his wireless AP. Hence, the IoT device can access the Internet performing the authentication as describe in Sect. 4. In the case B, the IoT device board flashes an orange LED, and after its partial registration it shows an orange fixed-on LED. The full registration is achieved when the end-user associates the IoT device board with his/her web profile. The users adopts a web site to register the board, in particular typing the MAC address shown in the external part of the box provided by the manufacturer. If the MAC in M match the MAC typed in the website, the board flashes a green LED, and the user can confirm the operation, otherwise (obtaining no flashing LED) he/she should repeat the procedure. After that, the full registration has been accomplished, the board shows a green fixed-on LED. Now the Cloud has the full control of the board, hence it can deploy firmware, managing configuration, install software and so on. The user only pushed a button (wps) and typed a code in the web site of the Cloud operator.

6   Conclusion and Future Work

In this paper, we discussed an approach to integrate the IoT with Cloud computing. In particular a system is presented analyzing the different elements involved and how they interact each other. Using the Arduino Yun as example, we discussed how IoT devices can be extended to support the interaction with the Cloud. In particular, we focused on a secure self-identification mechanism that allows a Cloud provider to deploy the firmware and configure the device. The paper deals with the design of secure IoT infrastructures. Currently, IoT devices are at the early stage and how argued in this paper, they are not ready yet to support complex Cloud scenarios, even though the roadmap toward innovative Cloud IoT services begins to be tracked. In future works, we plan to study the integration of the Trusted Computing in Arduino Yun for an advanced self-identification when the device joins a Cloud environment.

References

1. Unleashing potential of Future Internet and Cloud computing, November 2013. http://ec.europa.eu/digital-agenda/en/news/unleashing-potential-future-internet-and-cloud-computing
2. Trusted Computing Group (TCG). http://www.trustedcomputinggroup.org
3. Aslam, M., Rea, S., Pesch, D.: Service provisioning for the wsn cloud. In: 2012 IEEE 5th International Conference on Cloud Computing (CLOUD), pp. 962–969 (2012). doi:10.1109/CLOUD.2012.132
4. Ayadi, I., Noemie, S.: Adaptive provisioning of connectivity-as-a-service for mobile cloud computing. In: 2014 2nd IEEE International Conference on Mobile Cloud Computing, Services, and Engineering (MobileCloud), pp. 169–175 (2014). doi:10.1109/MobileCloud.2014.33
5. Celesti, A., Fazio, M., Villari, M.: Se clever: A secure message oriented middleware for cloud federation. In: IEEE Symposium on Computers and Communications (ISCC), pp. 35–40 (2013)
6. Chandra, A., Lee, Y., Kim, B.M., Maeng, S.Y., Park, S.H., Lee, S.R.: Review on sensor cloud and its integration with arduino based sensor network. In: 2013 International Conference on IT Convergence and Security (ICITCS), pp. 1–4 (2013). doi:10.1109/ICITCS.2013.6717876
7. Deshwal, A., Kohli, S., Chethan, K.: Information as a service based architectural solution for wsn. In: 2012 1st IEEE International Conference on Communications in China (ICCC), pp. 68–73 (2012). doi:10.1109/ICCChina.2012.6356972
8. Fazio, M., Paone, M., Puliafito, A., Villari, M.: Huge amount of heterogeneous sensed data needs the cloud. In: 2012 9th International Multi-Conference on Systems, Signals and Devices (SSD), pp. 1–6. IEEE (2012)
9. Suciu, G., Vulpe, A., Halunga, S., Fratu, O., Todoran, G., Suciu, V.: Smart cities built on resilient cloud computing and secure internet of things. In: 2013 19th International Conference on Control Systems and Computer Science (CSCS), pp. 513–518 (2013). doi:10.1109/CSCS.2013.58
10. Tu'n, A.L., Quoc, H., Serrano, M., Hauswirth, M., Soldatos, J., Papaioannou, T., Aberer, K.: Global sensor modeling and constrained application methods enabling cloud-based open space smart services. In: Ubiquitous Intelligence Computing, International Conference on Autonomic Trusted Computing (UIC/ATC), pp. 196–203 (2012)
11. Wang, Y., Lin, W., Zhang, T., Ma, Y.: Research on application and security protection of internet of things in smart grid. In: IET International Conference on Information Science and Control Engineering 2012 (ICISCE 2012), pp. 1–5 (2012). doi:10.1049/cp.2012.2311
12. Yao, X., Han, X., Du, X., Zhou, X.: A lightweight multicast authentication mechanism for small scale iot applications. IEEE Sens. J. **13**(10), 3693–3701 (2013). doi:10.1109/JSEN.2013.2266116

Making Effective Home Security Available to Everyone - Towards Smart Home Security Communities

Marcus Koehler$^{(\boxtimes)}$ and Felix Wortmann

University of St. Gallen, 9000, St. Gallen, Switzerland
{marcus.koehler,felix.wortmann}@unisg.ch

Abstract. The Internet of Things significantly reduces the prices of home security systems, thereby making home security available to everyone. Prior research provides the technical foundation for Smart Home security. However, frequent false alarms still remain a severe challenge. While current work in this domain mainly focuses on the improvement of sensors and algorithms, this study proposes a semi-automatic approach to tackle the false positives. It combines the concept of neighborhood watch communities with IoT technology in order to develop a Smart Home security community. Therefore, (1) this paper shows a positive influence of community features in the case of non-intrusive devices. Furthermore, (2) it points out the influence of personal relationships on perceived security. In consequence, there is a clear opportunity to strengthen security systems by establishing neighborhood watch communities.

Keywords: Internet of Things · Smart Home · Security · Intrusion detection · Semi-automatic · Neighborhood watch

1 Introduction

Smart Home security communities build upon two fundamental concepts: neighborhood watch communities and Smart Home security devices.

During the late 1960s, the neighborhood watch movement has emerged in the USA. It comprises of three different crime prevention and detection activities: engraving property, community organization, and block watch [1]. Engraving property is the announcement of a neighborhood community in order to deter possible criminals. The community organization increases the local social capital and thereby fosters a shared response to critical situations. Finally, block watch involves citizens in surveillance plans, which for instance comprise of patrols.

The impacts of neighborhood watch programs are promising. 40 % of the US citizens [2] and 29 % of the UK citizens [3] live in areas protected by neighborhood watch initiatives. A recent meta-analysis [2] shows that 15 of 18 studies prove the crime-reducing effect of neighborhood watch.

Current Smart Home security systems purely rely on a purely technical approach. In an attempt to create an overview of the current market, we clustered

© Institute for Computer Sciences, Social Informatics and Telecommunications Engineering 2015
R. Giaffreda et al. (Eds.): IoT360 2014, Part II, LNICST 151, pp. 312–317, 2015.
DOI: 10.1007/978-3-319-19743-2_42

Table 1. Overview of Smart Home security solutions

Security functionality	Obtrusiveness	
	low	high
Preventive	(1) Philips Hue	n.a
Detective	(2) Lockitron, Skybell, Scout	(3) Canary, Piper
Reactive		

existing solutions. We thereby assure mass market compatibility by setting a price limit of 500 USD. Clustering criteria were functionality and obtrusiveness. The functionality can be split into preventive, detective and reactive properties. Obtrusiveness can be classified depending on the use of video cameras in indoor environments and implied privacy concerns [4]. Three clusters can be identified (see Table 1): (1) Purely preventive solutions, (2) non-obtrusive alarm systems, and (3) obtrusive alarm systems.

How reliable can a security system perform its task? The base-rate fallacy [5] describes the difficulty of designing effective intrusion detection systems. Effectiveness is the ratio of relevant alarms to false alarms of the system. The absolute number of relevant alarms is low for security systems due to the low frequency of intrusions. In contrary, a high number of false alarms is likely even by reliable systems due to the commonness of the regular status.

Smart Home security communities try to leverage the crime-reducing effect of neighborhood watch approaches by using technology. First studies following this combination exist. Zeki et al. [6] present a technical approach which enables the sharing of video streams in order to evaluate the severity of an unusual event. The impact of such a solution is analyzed by a qualitative study of Microsoft research [7]. This study evaluates the use of shared outdoor cameras in order to detect suspicious activities. It shows the potential of such a solution, however also pointing out privacy concerns.

In conclusion, the positive influence of neighborhood watch communities has been shown by various researchers [2]. The idea to complement these communities with Internet of Things based technologies is not new. However, due to privacy concerns, research efforts have been restricted to communities which use street cameras [7]. In contrast to existing approaches, our research focuses on the liaison of indoor security and communities.

The structure of this paper follows. First, this section introduced the field of Smart Home security communities and presented related work. Second, the following chapter evaluates users' intention to participate in a Smart Home security community and thereby especially focuses on privacy aspects. Third, we study the potential composition of a Smart Home security community. Finally, we discuss the gained results and further research directions.

2   Smart Home Security Communities - Evaluating the Idea

As a first step, we want to understand the value of Smart Home security communities for our security device. Thus, we address the following research questions. (1) Do community features, i.e. the technical capability to include others into home protection, increase potential users intention to use a Smart Home security system? (2) Do powerful, yet privacy-intrusive security features such as video surveillance, increase or decrease potential users intention to use a Smart Home security system? (3) Do community and powerful, yet privacy-intrusive security features, have an interaction effect on users intention to use a Smart Home security system?

2.1   Study Design

We acquired 160 participants via Amazon Mechanical Turk [10] in exchange for a small monetary compensation. The participants were randomly assigned to one of four treatment combinations.

Corresponding to the related research, we built upon two device settings. (1) Less intrusive: This setting is based on our "Security Light" system and its motion detection technology. (2) More intrusive: The description of the Canary system[1] is taken as an example for a video based security system.

In respect to communities, we leveraged two fundamental settings. (1) Community: Community functionality was highlighted, i.e. the possibility was described to give other people access the security system information. Their potential ability to act in case of an intrusion was pointed out. (2) No community: No community functionality was mentioned.

On the basis of the described settings we deployed four treatment groups (2×2 factorial design). A subsequent item-based questionnaire measured the effects of our experiment. The metric assessing the intention to use was adapted from Davis [8]. To better understand the influence of privacy as a key constraint of intention to use [4], we measured privacy concerns based on Dinev and Hart [9].

2.2   Study Result

To assess the impact of community-based and privacy intrusive security features on the intention to use, we conducted a two-way Anova. There was a significant main effect of privacy intrusive security features on intention to use, $F(1,160) = 7.35$, p <.01. Specifically, intention to use was significantly higher in case of no video? settings. Furthermore, there was no significant main effect of community features on intention to use, $F(1,160) =.37$, p >.05. However, there was a weak interaction effect of privacy intrusive security and community features, $F(1,160) = 2.14$, p <.10. Community features increased intention to use in the "no video" condition, whereas they decreased intention to use in the "video" condition.

---

[1] http://canary.is/.

To better understand the role of privacy as a key driver of intention to use, we additionally conducted a two-way Anova on perceived privacy concerns. There was a weak main effect of privacy intrusive security features on privacy concerns, $F(1,160) = 2.96$, p <.10. Specifically, privacy concerns were higher in case of video settings. Furthermore, there was no significant main effect of community features on security concerns, $F(1,160) =.00$, p >.96. However, there was a significant interaction effect of privacy intrusive security and community features, $F(1,160) = 4.42$, p <.05. Community features increased privacy concerns in the "video" condition, whereas they decreased privacy concerns in the "no video" condition.

Applying these results, the study shows the value of a security community for our security solution. Due to privacy concerns, the study furthermore suggests a negative impact of a community on obtrusive security solutions.

3   Smart Home Security Communities - Understanding the Composition

As a second step, we want to study the composition of a Smart Home security community. We especially want to focus on the impact of private participants compared to institutions or companies.

3.1   Study Design

We acquired 50 participants via Amazon Mechanical Turk [10] in exchange for a small monetary compensation. Each participant had to evaluate eight person groups according to three criteria.

Person groups included private contacts and professionals. Private contacts were family, friends, neighbors, connections from a social network, and other users of a fictive security community named Beta. Professionals comprised the local police, security companies, and insurance companies. Person groups were shuffled during the study to avoid order effects.

Evaluation criteria comprised of three items: The ability of a person to act ("This person/institution could act appropriate in case of an intrusion."), perceived privacy ("I feel comfortable giving this person/institution access to the private data captured by the Beta security system") based on Dinev and Hart [9], and the intention to use ("I would ask this person/institution to support me in protecting my home and give him/her full access to the Beta app.") according to Davis [8].

3.2   Study Result

Figure 1 illustrates the results of our study. Three main findings follow: (1) The perceived ability to act is higher for family members and friends then for professional institutions while raising less privacy issues. (2) Users prefer sharing

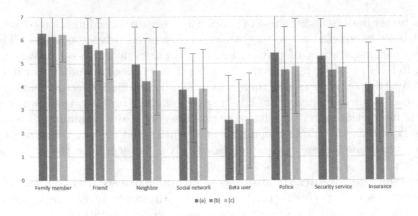

Fig. 1. Means and standard deviation of (a) ability to act, (b) perceived privacy during data sharing and (c) intention to invite in community depending on person characteristics.

data with family members and friends compared to their neighbors. (3) Anonymous members of social networks or security communities are the least preferable partners.

In consequence, security communities should leverage existing relationships to family members or friends. They can include neighbors or professionals. Furthermore, our study suggests not to rely on pure on-line relationships within the security community.

4   Discussion and Conclusion

Reflecting on the results, we see evidence for a general negative relationship between privacy-intrusive technology and the intention to participate in a security community. We expected that both non-intrusive and intrusive devices would benefit from a community. Therefore, we are surprised about the interaction effect between communities and privacy-intrusive technology. Our research suggests, that a positive community effect can only be achieved with non-privacy intrusive functionality.

We are furthermore surprised about the high perceived ability of family members and friends to act in case of an intrusion. Even though their means to intervene are limited, their perceived ability to act is the base for trustworthy Smart Home security solutions.

In line with [7], we encourage further research to explore the potentials of IoT-enabled security communities. We also see the potential to generalize the topic of Smart Home security communities and to apply to other research fields, e.g. ambient assisted living (AAL). AAL ensures the health, safety, and well-being of elderly people by the supervision of daily activities [11]. The reduction of false classifications, especially the elimination of false positives, is a relevant research question [12]. Here, the local community of Smart Home security communities can be used for the manual verification of alarms.

Acknowledgment. The present work is supported by the Bosch IoT Lab at the University of St.Gallen, Switzerland. The authors are grateful to the reviewers for thoughtful comments and helpful suggestions.

References

1. Rosenbaum, D.P.: The theory and research behind neighborhood watch: is it a sound fear and crime reduction strategy? Crime delinquency **33**(1), 103–134 (1987)
2. Bennett, T., Holloway, K., Farrington, D.P.: Does neighborhood watch reduce crime? a systematic review and meta-analysis. J. Exp. Criminol. **2**(4), 437–458 (2006)
3. Sims, L., Britain, G.: Neighbourhood watch: findings from the 2000 British Crime Survey (2001)
4. Nguyen, D.H., Bedford, A., Bretana, A.G., Hayes, G.R.: Situating the concern for information privacy through an empirical study of responses to video recording. In: Proceedings of the 2011 Annual Conference on Human Factors in Computing Systems - CHI 2011, p. 3207 (2011)
5. Axelsson, S.: The base-rate fallacy and the difficulty of intrusion detection. ACM Trans. Inf. Syst. Secur. (TISSEC) **3**(3), 186–205 (2000)
6. Zeki, A.M., Elnour, E.E., Ibrahim, A.A., Haruna, C., Abdulkareem, S.: Automatic interactive security monitoring system. In: International Conference on Research and Innovation in Information Systems (ICRIIS), pp. 215–220. Ieee, November 2013
7. Brush, A.J.B., Jung, J., Mahajan, R., Martinez, F.: Digital neighborhood watch: investigating the sharing of camera data amongst neighbors. In: ACM Conference on Computer Supported Cooperative Work, pp. 693–700 (2013)
8. Davis, Jr., Fred, D.: A technology acceptance model for empirically testing new end-user information systems: Theory and results. Ph.D thesis (1985)
9. Dinev, T., Hart, P.: An extended privacy calculus model for e-commerce transactions. Inf. Syst. Res. **17**, 61–80 (2006)
10. Buhrmester, M., Kwang, T., Gosling, S.D.: Amazon's mechanical turk a new source of inexpensive, yet high-quality, data? Perspect. Psychol. Sci. **6**(1), 3–5 (2011)
11. Hoque, E., Stankovic, J.: AALO: activity recognition in smart homes using active learning in the presence of overlapped activities. In: 6th International Conference on Pervasive Computing Technologies for Healthcare, pp. 139–146 (2012)
12. Botia, J.A., Villa, A., Palma, J.: Ambient assisted living system for in-home monitoring of healthy independent elders. Expert Syst. Appl. **39**(9), 8136–8148 (2012)

Earthquake Emergencies Management by Means of Semantic-Based Internet of Things

Gilberto Taccari[1]([✉]), Gabriele Bernardini[1], Luca Spalazzi[1], Marco D'Orazio[1], and Waleed Smari[2]

[1] Università Politecnica Delle Marche, Ancona, Italy
{g.taccari,g.bernardini,l.spalazzi,m.dorazio}@univpm.it
[2] Ball Aerospace and Technologies Corporation, Ohio, USA
smari@arys.org

Abstract. Semantic technologies can play a key role in representing, storing, interconnecting, searching, and organizing information generated/consumed by things. In order to evaluate its feasibility, this paper presents a set of reasoning mechanisms based on an IoT ontology to be applied in an emergency management scenario. The scenario presented in this paper consists in the earthquake emergency management.

Keywords: Semantic Web · Semantic reasoning · Internet of Things · Earthquake Emergency Management

1 Introduction

In the recent years, Internet of Things (IoT) attracted more and more researchers for its pervasiveness, the variety of involved technologies, and the several areas where it can be applied. On the other hand, the research on IoT must face several challenges, among them are *scalability*, w.r.t devices, data, and users interaction; *interoperability*, due to the heterogeneity of devices and platforms; *efficiency*, w.r.t. device energy consumption and bandwidth; *ubiquity*. This complexity produced at least three different visions of IoT: the *internet-oriented* vision, the *thing-oriented* vision, and the *semantic-oriented* vision [2]. Whereas the first two visions are quite obvious, the third one is one of the consequences of scalability and interoperability that pose issues related to how to represent, store, interconnect, search, and organize information generated/consumed by a plethora of physical and virtual (immaterial) things. According to several authors [2,4,8,19], such issues can benefit from semantic technologies.

Therefore, this work focuses on the semantic-oriented vision of IoT and applies semantic technologies to a specific scenario, in order to evaluate their potentialities: the *earthquake emergency management*. This work is part of the Italian project SHELL[1] — Research Objective OR4 "Safety & Security Manager".

---

[1] MIUR (the Italian Ministry of Education, Univesity, and Research) — Project SHELL (CTN01_00128_111357) part of the national cluster TAV (CTN01_00128).

© Institute for Computer Sciences, Social Informatics and Telecommunications Engineering 2015
R. Giaffreda et al. (Eds.): IoT360 2014, Part II, LNICST 151, pp. 318–327, 2015.
DOI: 10.1007/978-3-319-19743-2_43

Regarding the semantic-oriented vision, it should be considered that in spite of the great number of works in literature, the formal modeling of things by means of semantics is still an emerging area and there does not exist a de facto standard to do that. This obstructs the collaboration among Things themselves and between things and IT systems [4]. The only exception is represented by the Semantic Sensor Network (SSN) ontology, an outcome of the W3C Semantic Sensor Network Incubator Group [4]. Unfortunately, this ontology deals only with sensors, their sensing capabilities, the observations that they may produce, and their physical characteristics. No standard exists for actuators and a more general notion of things. On the other hand, other works deal only with specific application domains [19].

Regarding the emergency domain, previous works and recent disasters underline the importance of tools for earthquake disaster management [9] in order to assist people and rescuers during the event and so increasing the level of community resilience [5,18], especially in historic preservation areas and at urban scale. Up-to-now, a similar approach has been adopted for indoor fire management [11,14]: data involving the spread of fire and the position of people are acquired by sensors and processed by a central server; actions in response to the fire and to facilitate evacuating people are consequently performed through a series of actuators. In other words, this means that an IoT approach could be useful also for earthquake emergency management. Indeed, following the "smart city" network vision [1], IoT tools must involve real-time monitoring and include the information communication to both evacuating pedestrians and rescuers. This aspect is widely stressed in the aforementioned project SHELL-OR4.

This work provides the first step for an emergency management system based on the semantic-oriented vision of IoT. This is accomplished by means of a set of basic semantic reasoning techniques that can be combined to form the so-called Perception/Action Cycle. In order to do that, it exploits a general IoT ontology that extends the SSN ontology [15].

The paper is structured as follows: Sect. 2 briefly introduces the earthquake scenario and the related ontology is described in Sect. 3. Section 4 deals with the Perception/Action cycle, whereas some concluding remarks are reported in Sect. 5.

2   The Earthquake Scenario

Previous works [6] define the actors involved in the earthquake scenario (*Environment* and *Pedestrians*) and the related features that have to be monitored by different sensors in order to eventually activate a set of actuators, both at a single building or at urban scale. About the Environment, an immaterial sensor composed by a CAD or GIS database should describe the characteristics of the pre-event scenario, including urban plan, usable paths and safe areas [6]; moreover, each building should be related to its own seismic vulnerability [7], by using GIS techniques [17]. Physical sensors monitor the event and the scenario changes. A seismometers network could define fundamental earthquake data, such as duration, Richter magnitude and epicentre position [10]. Accelerometers would define the presence of site amplification [16] or the building response to the earthquake. Devices for crack or story drift (displacement) monitoring could assess the structural building health or the presence of local damage mechanisms or collapses [12]. Data from these building sensors could be merged with the ones from seismometers and losses estimation models, for the evaluation of scenario modifications (e.g.: ruins influence on evacuation routes [13]). The Pedestrians characteristics and positions [6], including people with disability and rescuers, should be monitored during the whole process. The IoT system would collect data from these sensors, and address particular actions to the actuators [14]. Pedestrians would be assisted during their evacuation by means of information regarding the correct behavior, the evacuation path to select, and how to gain the safe areas in the safest and fastest way. Notification messages (e.g.: SMSs) would be sent to them in order to interact with them. Moreover, fixed building elements (e.g.: escape lights in both outdoor and indoor conditions), or personal device (e.g.: smartphones) applications would be activated in order to indicate the evacuation path. Finally, rescuers have to be informed about crisis areas, damages on buildings, infrastructural fails, and Pedestrians in emergency conditions (e.g.: in ruined buildings or in not accessible areas).

3   The Earthquake Emergency Management Ontology

In order to formally describe entities and features that characterize the earthquake scenario, we take advantage of the IoT and Earthquake Emergency Management (EEM) ontologies proposed by Spalazzi *et al.* [15][2]. The IoT ontology extends the Semantic Sensor Network (SSN) ontology [4] and, beside the *Stimulus-Sensor-Observation pattern* [4] used to model sensors and observations, proposes the *Actuator-Stimulus-Operation pattern* that models actuators and operations. The above patterns allow the ontology to deal with sensor and actuator properties (denoted by the two equivalent concepts ssn:MeasurementCapability and san:ChangeCapability depicted in Fig. 1) in terms of accuracy (ssn:Accuracy), resolution (ssn:Resolution), precision (ssn:Precision), and other similar characteristics. These are related to particular conditions (denoted by the concept ssn:Condition), consequently several capabilities (one for each condition) can be associated to a given sensor or actuator. Furthermore, even each observation or operation (denoted by concepts ssn:Observation and san:Operation depicted in Fig. 1) can be associated with its properties (e.g. an observation with its accuracy). The EEM ontology is built upon the IoT ontology and deals with the modeling of specific sensors and actuators to be used in the earthquake scenario. We have concepts to describe sensing devices such as seismometers (eem:Seismometer), accelerometers (eem:Accelerometer), lasers to measure story drift displacements (eem:Laser), and the GPSes (eem:GPS), as well as to describe actuating devices such as signaling escape lights (eem:Signaling-EscapeLight), and alarm message notifiers (eem:AlarmMessageNotifier). Beside the

---

[2] Available at https://code.google.com/p/federated-cot-owl/source/browse/.

descriptions of things, the EEM ontology models also the features of interest
and their related properties that may be sensed and/or modified by the devices.
In this work we extend such ontology in order to provide all the knowledge to
implement the Perception/Action Cycle described in the next section. A fragment of this ontology is depicted in Fig. 1. Four subclasses of ssn:Observation
(eem:MagnitudoGreaterThan4, eem:AccelerationGreaterThan0.2g, eem:DiplacementGrea-
terThan0.003h, eem:VulnerabilityGreaterThan0.17) are created in order to represents
specific cases of observations that sensors may produce. These new classes
of observations are linked to three instances of eem:Intensity (eem:LowIntensity,
eem:MediumIntensity, and eem:HighIntensity) in order to specify which kind of intensity (i.e. damages) we have depending on the observed earthquake parameters.
Such instances are linked to operations too; in this manner we specify which operations have to be accomplished in relation with the intensity of the earthquake.
Finally, we add to the EEM ontology the concept that represents a person to
evacuate eem:PersonToEvacuate. We add to this concept the property dul:asLocation
that links a person to her/his geographical position represented by an istance of
the concept geo:Point taken by the GeoSPARQL ontology[3] that models spatial
concepts and their relations.

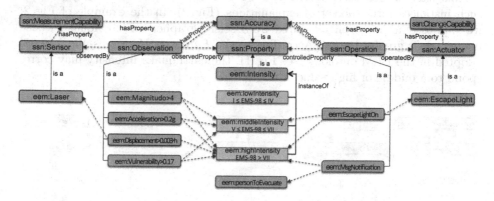

Fig. 1. An fragment of the EEM ontology.

4   EEM: Perception/Action Cycle

The Perception/Action Cycle extends the Perception Cycle proposed by Henson
et al. [8] taking into account the intention of acting as a consequence of what has
been perceived. In this respect, this model is rooted in the Belief-Desire-Intention
model proposed by Bratman [3] that has been widely used for developing intelligent agents. The Perception/Action Cycle consists of four basic activities:
explanation, discrimination, decision, and *justification.*

---

[3] http://schemas.opengis.net/geosparql/1.0/geosparql_vocab_all.rdf (Accessed: 2014-
06-26).

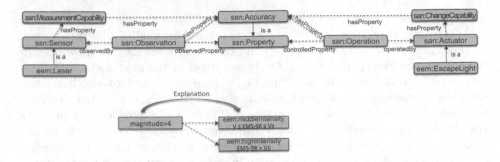

Fig. 2. An example of the Perception/Action Cycle: explanation.

Explanation. It deals with deriving a set of elements (that Henson *et al.* called *explanations*) that can explain what has been perceived. In the approach proposed in this work, one or more sensors produce a set of observations, such observations are semantically represented as RDF triples that are instances of ontology concepts as ssn:Observation and ssn:ObservationValue. As each instance of eem:MagnitudoGreaterThan4 is linked to a set of instances of eem:Intesity (Fig. 1), such instances form the set of explanations (Fig. 2). In the example of Fig. 2, we supposed it has been measured by a seismographer an earthquake whose magnitude is greater than 4. According to the *European Macroseismic Scale* [7] adopted in the EEM ontology (see Fig. 1), the earthquake intensity may correspond to a middle or high value.

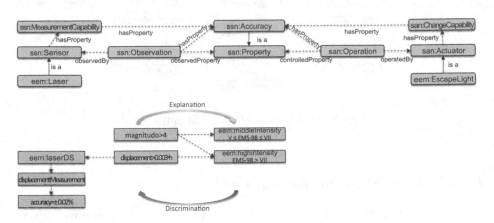

Fig. 3. An example of the Perception/Action Cycle: discrimination.

Discrimination. It should be noticed that the previous step can produce multiple explanations from the same set of observations. This set can be reduced by further observations. As the set of observations grows, the set of explanations shrinks. Once again, semantic reasoning can help us in establishing what are such further observations. Indeed, the ssn:observedProperty relation can be used to discriminate which kind of observations allow us to shrink the explanations (Fig. 3). As each subconcept of ssn:Observation is linked to a specific ssn:Sensor that has a set of capabilities (as accuracy, precision, and so on), thanks to *discrimination* we are able to obtain a list of sensors that can be used in order to produce the further observations we need and are able to guarantee the required capabilities. In the example of Fig. 3, we have to discriminate what is the earthquake intensity, therefore we need further observations. According to Fig. 1, we need to measure the horizontal displacement of a given building using a sensor with a given accuracy.

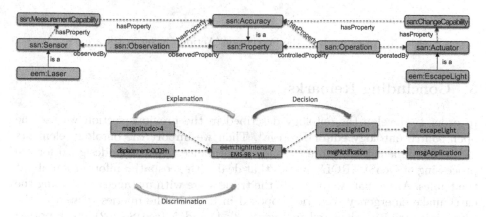

Fig. 4. An example of the Perception/Action Cycle: decision.

Decision. It is similar to *discrimination*. Indeed, it aims at looking for subconcepts of san:Operation that are linked to the explanations, i.e. they are linked to instances of ssn:Property (Fig. 4). As each subconcept of san:Operation is linked to a specific san:Actuator that has a set of capabilities, thanks to *decision* we are able to obtain a list of actuators that can be used in order to react to what has been perceived and, again, are able to guarantee the required capabilities. In the example of Fig. 4, we have to select the actuators to use. According to EEM ontology (Fig. 1), we need to turn on the escape lights and to send a message to rescuers. In this specific example, capabilities as accuracy and precision can not be applied to such a kind of sensors.

Justification. It is similar to *explanation*. Indeed, it aims at looking for all the instances of ssn:Property that justify the selected operation (Fig. 5). In the example of Fig. 5, we need to send to rescuers a message with the position of possible victims.

The activities above represent the building blocks to be used in order to define any kind of emergency management policy based on using (physical and virtual) things. It should be noticed how such basic reasoning services can be composed in any order.

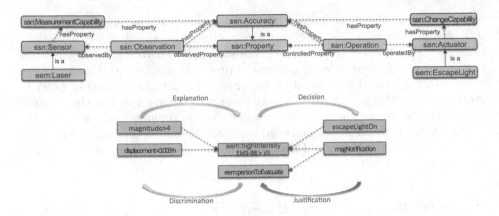

Fig. 5. An example of the Perception/Action Cycle: justification.

5 Concluding Remarks

In order to develop the ontology described in the previous section we use the open source ontology editor Protege[4]. Then we import the ontology elements in the Parliament triple store[5], a high-performance triple store designed for the processing of GeoSPARQL[6] queries that deal with geospatial information about the triples. After that, we populate the triple store with instances describing the earthquake emergency scenario proposed in Sect. 2. The queries related to the reasoning activities depicted in Figs. 2, 3, 4, and 5 (see Sect. 2) are reported in Figs. 6, 7, 8, and 9, respectively. It should be noticed as query 7 allows us to select sensors having a given accuracy. Furthermore, it should be noticed as query 9 allows us to select the localization of victims from all the data gathered by sensors. As a consequence, victim localizations can be sent to rescuers.

```
# Explanation query
SELECT DISTINCT ?intensity
WHERE {
    eem:MagnitudoGreaterThan4 ssn:observedProperty ?intensity.
}
```

Fig. 6. GeoSPARQL query implementing explanation.

The examples reported above show how very simple semantic reasoning techniques can provide a support to an emergency manager in refining its knowledge according to a first set of observations and, thus, finding which actuators should

---

[4] http://protege.stanford.edu/ (Accessed: 2014-06-26).
[5] http://parliament.semwebcentral.org/ (Accessed: 2014-06-26).
[6] http://www.opengeospatial.org/standards/geosparql (Accessed: 2014-06-26).

```
# Discrimination query
SELECT DISTINCT ?sensor
WHERE {
%   ?sensor a ssn:Sensor .
    ?sensor a ?sensorType .
    ?sensorType a owl:Class .
    ?sensorType rdfs:subClassOf ssn:Sensor .
    ?observation a eem:DisplacementGreaterThan0.003h .
    ?observation ssn:observedBy ?sensorType .
    ?sensor ssn:hasProperty ?capability? .
    ?capability a ssn:MeasurementCapability .
    ?capability ssn:hasProperty ?accuracy .
    ?accuracy a ssn:Accuracy .
    ?accuracy eem:hasValue ?a
    FILTER(?a <= 0.05)
}
```

Fig. 7. GeoSPARQL query implementing discrimination.

```
# Decision query
SELECT DISTINCT ?actuator
WHERE {
%   ?actuator a san:Actuator .
    ?actuator a ?actuatorType .
    ?actuatorType a owl:Class .
    ?actuatorType rdfs:subClassOf san:Actuator .
    ?operation a ?operationType .
    ?operationType a owl:Class .
    ?operationType rdfs:subClassOf san:Operation .
    ?operationType san:controlledProperty eem:highIntensity .
    ?operation san:operatedBy ?actuator .
}
```

Fig. 8. GeoSPARQL query implementing decision.

```
# Justification query
SELECT ?victim
WHERE {
    ?victim a eem:PersonToEvacuate:
            geo:hasLocation ?localization .
    ?localization geo:asWKT ?lWkt .
    FILTER(geof:sfWithin(?lWkt,
    "POLYGON((<coordinates>))"^^sf:wktLiteral))
}
```

Fig. 9. GeoSPARQL query implementing justification.

be activated adapting pre-defined emergency management policies to the current scenario. These preliminary experiments seem to confirm the feasibility of the proposed approach. Its application in a real scale scenario is the next step in our work. In order to do that, we are setting up an Emergency Management System (EMS) based on a knowledge base defined according to the above ontology. This application uses the basic reasoning activities presented in this paper. The knowledge base is populated in real-time with earthquake data coming from the Twitter service offered by the Italian Geophysical and Volcanology Institute (INGV)[7]. The story drift displacement is computed by means of a laser displacement sensor (produced by our own laboratories) connected to a Cubieboard2 (based on a ARM Cortex A7 dual core processor). An Android application plays both the role of sensor, sending geolocalization data, and the role of actuator, receiving notifications from the EMS. The experiments are still on going and the related results will be reported in a follow-up paper.

References

1. Asimakopoulou E., Bessis, N.: Buildings and Crowds: Forming Smart Cities for More Effective Disaster Management. In: 2011 Fifth International Conference on Innovative Mobile and Internet Services in Ubiquitous Computing (2011)
2. Atzori, L., Iera, A., Morabito, G.: The internet of things: a survey. Comput. Netw. **54**, 2787–2805 (2010)
3. Bratman, M.E., Israel, D.J., Pollack, M.E.: Toward an Architecture for Resource-bounded Agents. Technical report CSLI-87-104, CSLI, Stanford University (1987)
4. Compton, M., Barnaghi, P., Bermudez, L., Garca-Castro, R., Corcho, O., Cox, S., Graybeal, J., Hauswirth, M., Henson, C., Herzog, A., Huang, V., Janowicz, K., Kelsey, W.D., Le Phuoc, D., Lefort, L., Leggieri, M., Neuhaus, H., Nikolov, A., Page, K., Passant, A., Sheth, A., Taylor, K.: The SSN ontology of the W3C semantic sensor network incubator group. Web Semant.: Sci. Serv. Agents World Wide Web **17**, 25–32 (2012)
5. Cutter, S.L., Barnes, L., Berry, M., Burton, C., Evans, E., Tate, E., Webb, J.: A place-based model for understanding community resilience to natural disasters. Global Environ. Change **18**, 598–606 (2008)
6. D'Orazio, M., Spalazzi, L., Quagliarini, E., Bernardini, G.: Agent-based model for earthquake pedestrians' evacuation in urban outdoor scenarios: behavioural patterns definition and evacuation paths choice. Saf. Sci. **62**, 450–465 (2014)
7. Grünthal, G., (ed.): European Macroseismic Scale 1998 (EMS 1998). Cahiers du Centre Européen de Géodynamique et de Séismologie, vol. 15, Imprimerie Joseph Beffort, Helfent-Bertrange, Luxembourg (1998). ISBN No 2-87977-008-4
8. Henson, C., Thirunarayan, K., Sheth, A.: An ontological approach to focusing attention and enhancing machine perception on the web. Appl. Ontology **6**(4), 345–376 (2011)
9. Iwanaga, I.S.M., Nguyen, T., Kawamura, T., Nakagawa, H., Tahara, Y., Ohsuga, A.: Building an earthquake evacuation ontology from twitter. In: 2011 IEEE International Conference on Granular Computing (2011)
10. Klügel, J.: Seismic hazard analysis quo vadis? Earth-Sci. Rev. **88**, 1–32 (2008)

---

[7] Available at https://twitter.com/INGVterremoti.

11. Lin, C.J., Tseng, Y., Yi. C.: PEAR: Personal Evacuation And Rescue system. In: Proceedings of the 6th ACM workshop on Wireless multimedia networking and computing (2011)
12. Mita. A.: 8 - Sensing solutions for assessing and monitoring seismically-excited buildings. In: Sensor Technologies for Civil Infrastructures. Woodhead Publishing (2014)
13. Onorati, T., Malizia, A., Diaz, P., Aedo, I.: Modeling an ontology on accessible evacuation routes for emergencies. Expert Syst. Appl. **41**, 7124–7134 (2014)
14. Pu, S., Zlatanova, S.: Geo-information for disaster management. In: van Oosterom, P., Zlatanova, S., Fendel, E.M. (eds.) Evacuation Route Calculation of Inner Buildings, pp. 1143–1161. Springer, Heidelberg (2005)
15. Spalazzi, L., Taccari, G., Bernardini, A.: An iot ontology for earthquake emergency evaluation and response. In: 2014 International Symposium on Collaborative Technologies and Systems (CTS). IEEE (2014)
16. Strollo, A., Richwalski, S.M., Parolai, S., Gallipoli, M.R., Mucciarelli, M., Caputo, R.: Site effects of the 2002 molise earthquake, Italy: analysis of strong motion, ambient noise, and synthetic data from 2D modelling in san giuliano di puglia. Bull. Earthquake Eng. **5**(3), 347–362 (2007)
17. Tang, A., Wen, A.: An intelligent simulation system for earthquake disaster assessment. Computers & Geosciences **35**(5), 871–879 (2009)
18. Tveiten, C.K., Albrechtsen, E., Wærø, I., Wahl, A.M.: Building resilience into emergency management. Saf. Sci. **50**, 1960–1966 (2012)
19. Wang, W., De, S., Toenjes, R., Reetz, E., Moessner, K.: A comprehensive ontology for knowledge representation in the internet of things. In: 2012 IEEE 11th International Conference on Trust, Security and Privacy in Computing and Communications (TrustCom) (2012)

Author Index

Printed in the United States
By Bookmasters